Stephen P. Kershaw wrote h̶...................................̶, arguably the leading scholar on Greek myths in the world. He has taught Classics in numerous establishments, including Oxford University Department for Continuing Education and Warwick University. He runs the European Studies Classical Tour for Rhodes College and the University of the South.

A BRIEF GUIDE TO THE

GREEK MYTHS

STEPHEN P. KERSHAW

ROBINSON
London

Constable & Robinson Ltd
3 The Lanchesters
162 Fulham Palace Road
London W6 9ER
www.constablerobinson.com

First published in the UK by Robinson,
an imprint of Constable & Robinson Ltd, 2007

A copy of the British Library Cataloguing in
Publication data is available from the British Library

ISBN: 978-1-84529-512-7

Printed and bound in the EU

3 5 7 9 10 8 6 4 2

To my three Graces: Lal of the beautiful tresses,
lovely-ankled Dorothy, and keen-scenting Hebe

CONTENTS

LIST OF MAPS

ACKNOWLEDGEMENTS

Many people are deserving of my warmest gratitude: Phil and Dorothy Kershaw, Cyril Kershaw, Alan Guy, Philip Highley, Frank Haigh, John Betts, Richard Buxton, Andy Thompson, Rob Butler and Alyn Shipton. Thanks also to Swan Hellenic Cruises; my numerous colleagues at Oxford University Department for Continuing Education, Warwick University, European Studies and TCU; and Sukie Christiansen. None of the people mentioned here are in any way responsible for the shortcomings of this volume. Any omissions are my responsibility.

Particular thanks are due to Becky Hardie, Leo Hollis, Claudia Dyer and Morag Lyall at Constable and Robinson, without whose help and expertise I would never have been able to bring this project to fruition. Libations are due to *Tykhe, Kairos* and *Nemesis*. Underpinning everything has been the loyal late-night companionship of my spaniel Hebe, and the invaluable support and understanding of my wife Lal.

INTRODUCTION

Greece: a land of mythical dimensions. Where the spirit of hospitality welcomes you as a modern god. And the siren song draws you into its deep, blue waters. Where a gentle breeze through ancient ruins seems to whisper your name. And a dance till dawn can take on Dionysian proportions. In Greece, the myths are still very much alive. And in amongst them sits your own . . . patiently waiting for you to live. **Live your myth in Greece.** Ask your travel agent.[1]

Living in the twenty-first century we are constantly surrounded by the resonances of Greek mythology, and, though we seldom pause to reflect on it, we talk the language of myth all the time. We inhabit a chaotic world (Khaos was the primal void) where Trojan horses threaten our computers and Ajax is a cleaning product and a Dutch football team. Politicians dismiss their opponents' opinions as 'myths' (i.e. lies), while at the same time television archaeologists try to unearth 'the truth behind the myth' of Atlantis. Centaurs grace the pages of C.S. Lewis' *Narnia* books and J.K. Rowling's *Harry Potter* series; football managers say their star strikers have the Midas touch; a man can be an Adonis, a woman a siren or a harpy; and we all have our Achilles heel. Others are nymphomaniacs, use aphrodisiacs and read erotic literature – all activities with Greek mythological semantic roots. Meanwhile we undertake Herculean tasks, wrestle with our Oedipus complexes, make personal odysseys, and should certainly beware of Greeks bearing gifts.

There is nothing new in our fascination with the myths: no self-respecting Renaissance palazzo was complete without an array of mythological paintings, perhaps with underlying meanings referring to the politics of the day; opera has constantly drawn on the corpus of Greek myths, from Monteverdi's *Orfeo* through to Stravinsky's *Oedipus Rex* and beyond; dance has done the same, be it classical ballet or more contemporary pieces such as Martha Graham's *Andromache's Lament*. Film thrives on a Greek background, drawing directly on such myths as Jason (*Jason and the Argonauts*, directed by Don Chaffey, 1963) and the Trojan War (*Troy*, Wolfgang Petersen, 2004, where the abduction of Helen becomes an excuse for an attack on an eastern state by a 'Greek superpower' and has been seen as analogous to the recent American-led invasion of Iraq, which some commentators think has opened a Pandora's box in the Middle East), or operating more allusively as in Woody Allen's *Mighty Aphrodite* (1995), which deals with the power of love and parodies Greek tragedy at the same time. Rock, jazz and other contemporary music styles draw on the myths too, from Led Zeppelin's sublime 'Achilles' Last Stand' to Virgin Steele's ridiculous 'symphonic metal' *The House of Atreus*, from Ivo Papasov and his Bulgarian Wedding Band's *Orpheus Ascending* to the tumbling chords of the Anglo-Scandinavian jazz trio Stekpanna's 'Ikaros'. Ian Hamilton Finlay created a stunning garden at Little Sparta, Joe Tilson produced a series of Nine Muses at the most recent Royal Academy Summer Exhibition. There is no escape from Greek mythology.

This book provides an overview of a large amount of the raw material of Greek mythology, and makes constant reference to the original source material, as the myths speak most effectively when they speak directly. Very often there are several versions of the same basic story, told for different reasons by different authors at different times and places, and many of these variants will be highlighted. The book will also attempt to explore some of the resonance and relevance of the tales of Greece, from ancient Greek times to the twenty-first century.

A Brief Guide to the Greek Myths falls into three key areas:

1. In the first section, an exploration of myth and mythology: is it possible to define what Greek myths are? Can they be distinguished from other types of traditional tales, and is there a useful working definition?

2. In the second section we will make a journey through some of the main tales of Greek mythology. There is no pretence that this is a comprehensive survey of all the myths and their variants in all media. That would be a titanic task, but what the book tries to do is to lead the reader through many of these vibrant stories, on a loosely 'chronological' basis wherever this is possible or meaningful, from the origins of the gods through to the homecomings of the Trojan heroes. Familiar narratives such as those of Jason and the Argonauts, the Trojan War, and Odysseus will all be encountered, along with quite a few less familiar characters and motifs. In addition, the book often tries to explain interesting issues arising from the narratives, and discusses the myths and their wider relevance. Did the Trojan War really happen? What about Atlantis? How has mythical material been used or abused in more modern times? Are we just another part of the Greek tradition?

3. In the third section, a brief analysis of various scholarly (and less scholarly) interpretations of Greek myth from antiquity to the present. Scholars have agonized about the origins and meanings of myths for millennia, so the book presents a survey of some of the main intellectual approaches to myth from Euhemeros to Freud and beyond.

A Note on Names, Spellings and Dates

The question of how Greek names are transliterated into English is always a difficult problem, and has to be a personal decision. Until quite recently the convention was to Latinize Greek names and to Anglicize them on that basis. The Greek language does not have the letter 'c' and Latin does not have the letter 'k', although the letter 'c' is pronounced hard like 'k'. For instance, Kekrops is Latinized to Cecrops. The basic masculine form in Greek often ends in '–os' (Latin '–us'), the feminine in '–e' (Latin '–a') and the neuter in '–on' (Latin '–um'). For example, Menelaos becomes Menelaus. Below are some of the most important differences:

Greek	Latin	Greek	Latin
AI	AE	K	C
EI	I	KH	CH
OI	OE	OS	US
OU	U	E	A
EU	EV	ON	UM

Sometimes there is greater divergence: Klytaimnestra becomes Clytemnestra and Euandros becomes Evander, but often names are changed into their Roman (not always exact) equivalents, so that Odysseus becomes Ulysses, Hera becomes Juno, and Zeus becomes Jupiter. As this is a guide to *Greek* mythology, the approach favoured is to make straightforward transliterations in almost all cases, but to indicate where the Greek differs appreciably from what might be more familiar. So we will meet Akhilleus, Oidipous and Priamos rather than Achilles, Oedipus and Priam, but the 'Key Characters' lists will indicate the important variants.

All dates are BCE unless it is obvious or otherwise specified.

SECTION I

MYTHS AND MYTHOLOGY

A Greek living in the fifth century would not have needed a book like this. Their mythology was like the air they breathed, and it is only relatively late that we find handbooks of Greek mythology. The most important collection, which dates from the first century CE, is *The Library* by Apollodoros. This is an extensive work, and although the end is missing, we do have an abridged *Epitome*, which gives us a complete overview. What Apollodoros chose to include or omit has been extremely important in defining what we now think of as Greek mythology. He takes us from the creation of the gods down to the Odyssey and its sequels, and within those parameters the Trojan War is really the central event. Much of the mythical material heads towards it, with the climax occurring in Homer's *Iliad*, before the heroes make their way home. Most of the major texts are readily available in good English translations:

- Homer (eighth century): purported author of the *Iliad* (an episode during the Trojan War) and the *Odyssey* (Odysseus' homecoming after it), although the poems were the products of a long oral tradition before they were committed to writing.
- Hesiod (*c*.700): wrote the *Theogony*, dealing with the origins of the gods, the *Works and Days* and the fragmentary *Catalogue of Women*, which also contain important mythical material.
- The Homeric Hymns (seventh/sixth centuries): epic-style

poems honouring some of the major Greek deities which
include major stories from their mythologies.

- Pindar (518–438): a lyric poet whose work is replete with
  mythological allusions.
- Herodotos (mid-fifth century): the 'Father of History'. A
  widely travelled man who recorded a great many mythological tales despite his occasional scepticism.
- Aiskhylos (Aeschylus, 525–456), Sophokles (Sophocles,
  496–406) and Euripides (485–406): the 'Big Three'
  Athenian tragic dramatists, who drew heavily on the
  mythical tradition, and often reworked it.
- Aristophanes (c.445–385): an Athenian comic playwright who
  often parodied or subverted mythological stories in his plays.
- Plato (c.427–347): an Athenian philosopher who used 'myths'
  to illustrate his ideas, and who gave us the Atlantis story.
- Kallimakhos (third century): a learned scholar-poet
  working out of Alexandria in Egypt, who composed highly
  polished poems crammed with abstruse mythological
  allusions, including six Hymns to major deities.
- Apollonios Rhodios (third century): the librarian at
  Alexandria, whose *Argonautika* forms the definitive
  version of the Jason and the Golden Fleece story.
- Theokritos (third century): a Hellenistic poet whose work
  includes important poems on themes from the *Argonautika*
  and the life of Herakles (Hercules).
- Virgil (70–19): a Roman epic poet whose *Aeneid* tells the
  tale of the Trojan hero Aineias (Aeneas) and his journey
  from Troy to Italy.
- Ovid (43 BCE–17 CE): a Roman poet whose *Metamorphoses*
  covers a vast swathe of the Greek tradition. His tales of
  supernatural transformation became extremely popular in
  the Renaissance. He is arguably the most influential author
  about myth in Western literature.

- Plutarch (50–120 CE): a Greek biographer who wrote a series of 'Parallel Lives' of famous Greeks and Romans, including the Athenian hero Theseus.
- Pausanias (mid-second century CE): a Greek travel writer who recorded a large amount of mythical material garnered from the temples and sites that he visited.

In addition to these authors is a vast number of less well-known ones, some of whose work is fragmentary or lost, as well as scholars who wrote commentaries and notes (*scholia*) on the major works, which frequently give variant versions of the tales and preserve interesting snippets of information, often from works that no longer survive. Inscriptions and papyrus fragments also form an important part of the jigsaw.

Art has its place in the tradition too. Vase painting provides an enormous resource of images of stories that might otherwise remain unknown, or depicts alternative versions of those that do survive; sculpture often illustrates mythical scenes, either in an architectural context or in free-standing pieces; and we have descriptions of famous paintings that no longer exist, but which once provided vivid renderings of many mythological scenes.

The ancient Greeks were surrounded by their mythical heritage all the time. These tales were a vital part of how they defined who they were.

Myths and Traditional Tales
These days the words 'myth' and 'mythology' are used with a widespread range of meanings that vary according to context. The *Oxford English Dictionary,* for instance, defines myth as 'a purely fictitious narrative'.

'Myth' is regularly used to denote a widely held misconception, such as the idea that lemmings all jump off cliffs into the sea; it is a 'myth' that they do this, and Disney created it. 'Wikipedia Theory', referring to Wikipedia the online encyclopedia that can be edited by its users, states that myths are born when one 'Wikipedian' creates a lie/article, another adds more untruth to it, others still repeat the process, and the original lie/article becomes a self-replicating entity that breaks out of Wikipedia into the world at large.

But Greek myth is about far more than falsehood. The stories may be false, factually suspect, or not 100 per cent true in the form they are told, but this does not diminish their power, richness and relevance. They can have enormous social significance, and be used to embody the values of entire societies: as one scholar has argued, 'myth is "true" for those who use it',[1] and as far as most ancient Greeks were concerned, myths were far more than silly children's stories, even though some philosophers thought that was all they were. Xenophanes observed that man creates gods in his own image, as do donkeys:

> Yet mortal men imagine gods are born
> and dress like them, are shaped like them, and
> have their speech.[2]

To modern people the word 'myth' can be somewhat ambivalent: when politicians denounce an opinion as 'myth' they are usually rejecting it as wrong, possibly dangerous; but 'myth' can also have a nostalgic overtone of important realities concealed in the recesses of the past. Myth is frequently defined in terms of what is not myth: it is not reality (it is fiction); and it is not rational (it is absurd).

In essence Greek myths are traditional tales relevant to society, they are 'good to think with', and they embody a great deal of the way in which the Greeks understood their world. They were not regarded as revealed scriptures, let alone the truth about the gods, but they did help to define human beings' relationship with the gods. And one vital concept here is anthropomorphism: Greek gods took the form of men and women. This means that they often behave in a way that we associate more with humans than with gods: they fight, argue, sulk, get drunk and commit adultery, which means, of course, that it is easy to tell stories about them, and the personalities of the gods and heroes of Greek mythology are one of the features that make the tales so engaging.

The English word 'myth' goes back to the Greek word *mythos* – a tale, or something you say. It has a broad frame of reference ranging from a statement, to a story, the plot of a play, a conversation, and such like. Its meaning has also shifted over the centuries. For instance, at the time of Homer in the eighth century a *mythos* was not necessarily something untrue. In the *Iliad*, Hektor (Hector) asks a servant where his wife Andromakhe (Andromache) is:

> Then in turn the hard-working housekeeper gave him an answer [*mythos*]:
> 'Hektor, since you have urged me to tell you [*mytheisthai*] the truth . . .'[3]

The woman gives Hektor good information, and her answer is her *mythos*. Similarly when Akhilleus (Achilles) rejects a request to return to the fighting at Troy, the reaction of the envoys is illuminating:

> So he spoke, and all of them stayed stricken to silence
> in amazement at his words [*mythos*].[4]

Homer's heroes are expected to be adept with words, as well as formidable on the battlefield.

A slightly different nuance of *mythos* appears in the fifth-century historian Thukydides, who admits that his work might not appeal to what he calls *to mythodes* ('the *mythos*-quality'), but defends it as a serious historical narrative, not just a story or a tale. This was a major shift, and since that time the word has always been applicable to the corpus of Greek myths, although they are still told and enjoyed in spite of the fact that they are 'neither true nor probable', as one anonymous Latin writer put it.

The word 'mythology' in English can also muddy the waters: it can mean either the study of myths, or their content, or a particular set of myths. Furthermore, this material can be presented as texts, be transmitted orally, dramatized, represented in art, and constantly reinterpreted. One fact that can make Greek mythology somewhat confusing is that it comprises all the representations of myths ever produced. The following chapters will attempt to illustrate the richness and variety of this tradition.

We can perhaps gain a firmer understanding of the issue if we can ascertain who told myths, when, where, why and to whom, and luckily Greek literature has lots of references to the use of myths. They were often transmitted orally, frequently by women working at the loom:

> Is it the man
> Whose adventures we are told at weaving-time,
> The brave fighter Iolaos
> Who went with Herakles to his labours,
> And stayed with him to the bitter end?
> [. . .]
> Many a song and story I have heard
> Of sons that mortal women bore to gods,
> And not one tells of happiness.[5]

In Plato's *Republic* Sokrates speaks of the influence of myths told by mothers and wet nurses:

'These [stories] are of two kinds, true stories and fiction.[6] Our education must use both and start with fiction.'

'I don't know what you mean.'

'But you know that we begin by telling children stories. These are, in general, fiction, though they contain some truth. And we tell children stories before we start them on physical training.'[. . .]

'Shall we therefore readily allow our children to listen to any stories made up by anyone, and to form opinions that are for the most part the opposite of those we think they should have when they grow up?'

'We certainly shall not.'

'Then it seems that our first business is to supervise the production of stories, and choose only those we think suitable, and reject the rest. We shall persuade mothers and nurses to tell our chosen stories to their children, and by means of them to mould their minds and characters which are more important than their bodies. The greater part of the stories current today we shall have to reject.'

'Which are you thinking of?'

'We can take some of the major legends as typical. For all, whether major or minor, should be cast in the same mould, and have the same effect. Do you agree?'

'Yes: but I'm not sure which you refer to as major.'

'The stories in Homer and Hesiod and the poets. For it is the poets who have always made up fictions and stories to tell to men.'[7]

The most recent scholarly analyses emphasize that myths are traditional tales; and one definition that is widely approved of is that of Walter Burkert who suggests that 'Myth is a traditional tale with secondary, partial reference to something of collective importance.'[8] However, the traditional nature of Greek myths is by no means a straightforward issue, since a great many tales were recorded relatively late, which makes it difficult to pinpoint their dates of origin. And answering the question, 'Where do myths come from?' is fraught with difficulty. Homer, for instance, refers to the Theban stories, the Argonauts, and the Labours of Herakles, which must, therefore, pre-date the eighth century, but we can go further back than this. The approach known as 'comparative mythology'[9] suggests that Greek and ancient Hindu poetry not only shared similar formulaic phrases, but also had tales with closely corresponding motifs: Vedic Indra's fight against the demon Visvarupa, who had hidden his cows in a cave, invites comparison with Herakles' encounter with Kakos,[10] who had done the same to his cows and bulls. Some mythical themes seem to go back to time immemorial.

On the other hand, myth can be untraditional. In the *Odyssey* Penelope's suitors want to hear the newest song, and in fact many *mythoi* are not very old: for instance, the stories of the *nostoi* (homecomings) of the heroes from Troy[11] must date from after the Greek colonization of southern Italy in the eighth century. The originality of these *mythoi* must have been recognized at their premiere performances, even if they subsequently became an established part of the traditional body of myths. And of course, people can literally become 'legends in their own lifetime'. Much mythology is improvised: it is free-flowing, adaptable and adept at responding to new times and new experiences, and so myths can be contemporary inventions as well as ancient tales.

These days the Greek myths are normally read, but in Homer's day the *mythoi* were recited in front of an audience by the *aoidos* ('bard'), who, as a public performer, had to take his audience's tastes into account. Telling an unpopular new myth, or producing an unacceptable version of an old one, could result in offence and/or rejection, as happened in the case with Apollonios Rhodios' first version of the Argonauts tale.[12] However, as time went by the acceptance of myth changed, and so did the status of the poets, who grew much more aware of their own creativity: the Roman Virgil deliberately asserts his own originality when he starts his *Aeneid* with the words 'I sing of arms and the man';[13] Homer had appealed to the Muses for his inspiration: 'Sing, goddess, the anger of Peleus' son Akhilleus . . .'[14]

The development of literacy also changed the mythical environment, since intellectuals could now fix and analyse the myths, and philosophers and historians could attack them. When Pausanias recorded mythical stories at the places he visited in the second century CE, many of them were no longer relevant to the community, and yet their popularity lasted well into the Roman Empire: Ovid's *Metamorphoses* are one of the main sources of transmission for a great many Greek myths. It appears that myth, therefore, meant different things to the Greeks at different stages of their history.

It is often debated whether we can distinguish Greek myth from other types of popular tales, such as legends or fairy-tales. This particular distinction seems to go back to Jakob and Wilhelm Grimm in the early nineteenth century, since no European language had really differentiated them previously. Sometimes it is easier to separate the two as Terry Wogan discovered while commentating on the 1991 Eurovision Song Contest: 'It says here: "Peppino is a myth in the world of Italian song." He looks real enough to me. Perhaps they meant a "legend".' At other times, however, the choice is not so clear-cut, although many cultures have the separate words 'myth', 'legend' and 'folk-tale'.

Folk-tales are generally told in private and in prose. They can also be set in any time and any place. Fairy-tales often commence 'once upon a time' – they never specify where or when – and they often end 'and they lived happily ever after', a clear indication that the story is fiction. In addition, they often fail to give specific names to their characters, preferring generic or typical names like Jack, the Giant, or Little Red Riding Hood. Fairies, ogres and deities may appear, but the tales usually describe the adventures of animals or humans. The Greek myths are very different: the characters, especially the hero, are highly specific, and their genealogies are painstakingly outlined; they are attached to a particular region (which may vary according to where the myth is being told); and they are connected with families, tribes, cities, places, rituals, festivals, gods and heroes. As Burkert observes,[15] the story about Helen being carried off and brought back again is just a general type of story – there are many like it the world over – but because it contains Agamemnon of Mycenae, Menelaos of Sparta and Greeks fighting Trojans at Ilion, it becomes a myth through which fifth-century Greeks asserted their identity in relation to the Barbarians. Delete the reference and the myth turns into a folk-tale. Folk-tales seem to exist in isolation, while the Greek myths dovetail with other stories involving the same heroes. Moreover, although they frequently have moralistic overtones, fairy-tales are told to entertain, not to explain the world.

The English word 'legend' comes from the Latin *legenda*, 'things to be read'; 'myth' comes from the Greek *mythos*, 'something spoken'. Legends are more often secular than sacred, and their principal characters are human. They tell of migrations, wars, victories, deeds of great heroes, the succession in ruling dynasties, and they also include local tales of buried treasure, ghosts, fairies and saints. Yet, although they claim to be true, these legends do not normally claim to be divinely inspired; and unlike at Rome, where the foundation story of Romulus and Remus was apparently handed down in prose, for centuries Greek myths were the territory of the poets. So legends can again be distinguished from myths to some extent.

There are other types of story that the Greeks classified as *mythoi*. Aristophanes' *Wasps* is about the conflict between an old man, Prokleon, and his trendy son Antikleon, and it contains a scene in which Antikleon dresses his father up in fashionable clothes and tries to educate him in the etiquette of a sophisticated dinner party. He then asks Prokleon if he knows how to tell elevated stories in the company of learned and clever men, and his father says of course he can:

ANTIKLEON: What will you tell them?
PROKLEON: Oh, I know lots. There's the one about that Vampire that farted when she got caught; or I could tell them what Kardopion did to his mother –
ANTIKLEON: No, not that mythical stuff [*mythoi*]: something from real life – the kind of thing people usually talk about. Give it a domestic touch.
PROKLEON: Domestic, eh? Well, how about this? Once upon a time there was a cat and it met a mouse, and –
ANTIKLEON: My dear fellow, where were you brought up?[16]

Prokleon's examples humorously show how he has completely failed to grasp what Antikleon meant. The Vampire and Kardopion really belong to the category of folklore, which can come in various guises. One type of folk-tale is what the Greeks called the *ainos* or 'moral fable'. A collection of these fables was made in the early Hellenistic period by Demetrios of Phaleron and attributed to Aisopos (Aesop, sixth century) – 'Aesop's Fables'. One interesting aspect of the fables is that they can probably be dated as early/late by the wording of the morals that follow them. In the period prior to Alexander the Great a fable tended to be called a *logos*, but from the Hellenistic period onwards the word *mythos* was used instead: 'This *mythos* shows that . . .'[17]

The Ugly Slave Girl and Aphrodite

A master was in love with an ugly and ill-natured slave girl. With the money that he gave her, she adorned herself with sparkling ornaments and rivalled her own mistress. She made continual sacrifices to Aphrodite, goddess of love, and beseeched her to make her beautiful. But Aphrodite appeared to the slave in a dream and said to her:

'I don't want to make you beautiful, because I am angry with this man for thinking that you already are.'

Thus, one must not become blinded by pride when one is enriched by shameful means, especially when one is of low birth and without beauty.[18]

Another kind of folk-tale is represented by the stories told to each other by the semi-choruses in Aristophanes' *Lysistrata*. These are essentially stories that draw a moral connected with the immediate situation. So the chorus of old men sing a *mythos* about a young man who spurned women and marriage and spent his time hunting on the mountains:

> Yes, he was truly wise, this lad,
>> Loathed women through and through,
> And following his example we
>> Detest the creatures too.

The women then reply in kind:

> I'll tell a little tale [*mythos*] myself
>> (I like this little game)
> About a man who had no home
>> And Timon was his name.
> He lived among the thorns and briars,
>> And never served on juries;
> Some said his mother really was
>> A sister of the Furies.
> This Timon went away and lived
>> So far from mortal ken
> Not out of hate of women but
>> Because of hate of men.
> He loathed them for their wickedness
>> Their company he abhorred
> And cursed them long and loud and deep
>> But women he adored.[19]

Another type of folk-tale is the anecdote, which generally relates to a famous historical person and ends with a clever remark. Typical of these is the story of Xerxes' response to hearing that the bridges he had constructed across the Hellespont had been destroyed in a storm:

> Xerxes was very angry [. . .] and gave orders that the Helle-spont should receive three hundred lashes and have a pair of fetters thrown into it. I have heard before now that he also

sent people to brand it with hot irons. He certainly instructed the men with the whips to utter, as they wielded them, the barbarous and presumptuous words: 'You salt and bitter stream, your master lays this punishment upon you for injuring him, who never injured you. But Xerxes the King will cross you, with or without your permission. No man sacrifices to you, and you deserve the neglect by your acid and muddy waters.'[20]

This bears an interesting similarity to the story of King Canute commanding the incoming tide to halt: according to Henry of Huntingdon the king staged the scene to demonstrate to his fawning courtiers that he was powerless before the forces of nature and their creator, but later generations have made him an example of regal hybris like Xerxes.

Another kind of story is the joke. Over 250 ancient Greek jokes survive in a collection known as *Philogelos* (the Friend of Laughter). The butts of these jokes are generic types, usually Sicilians or people from Abdera, who for some reason were considered to be stupid, or someone labelled *skholiastikos*, a kind of idiot academic:

Someone met a skholiastikos and said, 'That slave you sold me has just died.' The skholiastikos replied, 'Funny, he never did anything like that when he was with me!'[21]

A Sidonian rhetorician was talking with his friends. One of them said it wasn't right to slaughter sheep, because they gave us milk and wool; and the other remarked that it wasn't right to kill cows either, because they gave us milk and ploughed the fields. At this the rhetorician replied that it wasn't right to slaughter pigs, as they gave us liver, and sow's udder, and kidney.[22]

Towards a Definition

So tales, *mythoi*, are told for a number of reasons: to entertain, to instruct, to persuade, to provide examples and so on. Myths are seldom told without a motive, and although the Greek word *mythos* seems to encompass what we might categorize as myth, legend and folk-tale, we can certainly make some general points:

- A Greek myth is a set of variants of the same story which exist either as texts, and/or in an oral form, and/or in art, or independently;
- The story concerns the divine or the supernatural, or the heroic, or animals or paradigmatic humans;
- The time-frame is usually indefinable by human chronology;
- Each re-telling or application produces a new variant;
- The tale is traditional;
- Myths are relevant to society.

'Myth' is mercurial, but a very useful working definition is this:

A myth is a socially powerful traditional story.[23]

In that sense it could be said that Greek mythology is fundamentally about human beings: what makes Greek myth mythical is not the participation of gods, talking animals or magic (although they can be present); it is the involvement of men and women who lived in the very remote past. But they were extraordinary men and women, as Aristotle wrote: 'In the old days, only the leaders were heroes, but the rest of the folk [. . .] were only men.'[24]

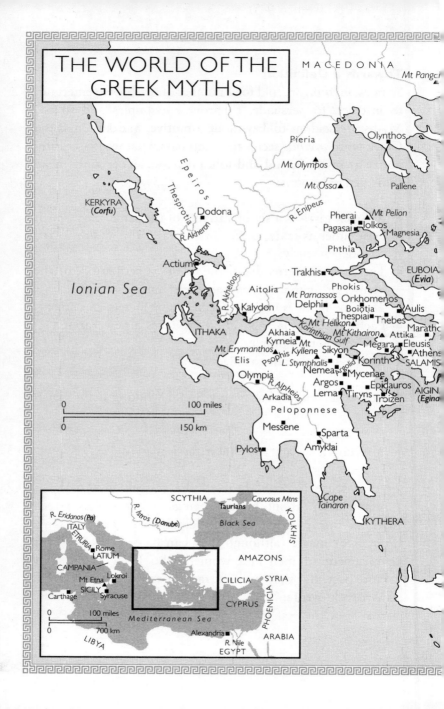

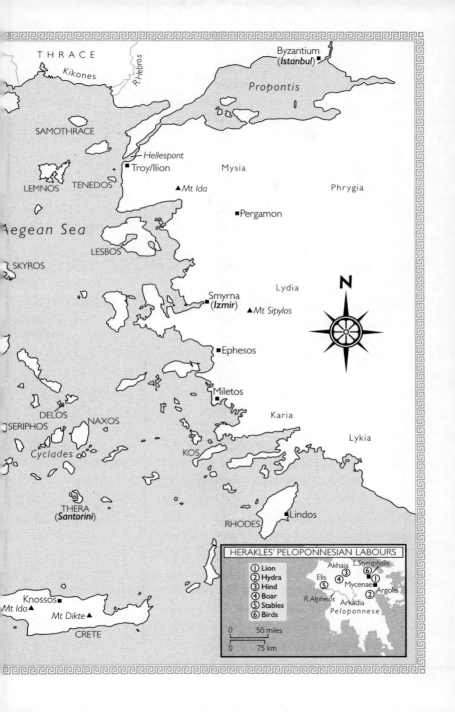

SECTION 2

FROM THE PRIMAL VOID TO A LOST CONTINENT: THE MAIN GREEK MYTHS

I

FROM CHAOS AND CASTRATION TO ORDER: THE BIRTH OF THE GODS

Key Characters

Khaos (Chaos)	The primordial void
Ouranos (Uranus)	The Sky, husband of Gaia (Earth); castrated by Kronos
Gaia (Gaea, or Ge)	The Earth; great mother goddess of earth and fertility; wife of Ouranos
Eros (Cupid or Amor)	Love
Kronos (Cronus)	Son of Ouranos and Gaia; overthrown by Zeus
Rheia/Rhea	Wife of Kronos
Zeus (Jupiter)	The supreme Olympian god; son of Kronos and Rheia
The Giants	Opponents of the Olympian gods
Typhoeus (Typhon/Typhaon)	Awesome hybrid monster, opponent of Zeus
The Titans	Mighty opponents of the Olympian gods
Hera (Juno)	Wife of Zeus
Aphrodite (Venus)	Goddess of sexual love

Creation myths, which tell of the origin of the world and the gods, are essential features of the mythologies of many cultures, and the Greek tradition is definitively expounded in the writings of Hesiod (*c*.700), whose crucial work is an epic poem called the *Theogony* ('The Origin [and Descent] of the Gods'). After a very genuine invocation to the Muses (by no means a flippant, Byronic 'Hail, Muse, et cetera!'), Hesiod not only introduces three divine generations that go back to the creation of the world, those of Ouranos and Gaia, Kronos and Rheia, and Zeus and Hera, but also provides an interpretation of the universal order over which Zeus comes to preside.

The First Generation: Ouranos (Sky) and Gaia (Earth) and their Titanic and Monstrous Offspring

According to Hesiod, Khaos (Latinized to Chaos) came into being first of all, and did so by an unspecified, asexual process. Clearly the Greek gods were not mighty enough to create the world by themselves. The Greek word Khaos has connotations of 'gaping' or 'yawning', and seems to be some kind of gaping void or primordial abyss. After Khaos came 'broad-bosomed' Gaia (Earth), along with 'misty' Tartaros, a gloomy place located the same distance underneath the earth as the earth is from the sky – a bronze anvil would take nine days and nights to fall from heaven to earth, and nine days and nights to fall from earth to Tartaros. At this point we also see the emergence of Eros (Love), described as the 'most beautiful of all the deathless gods', an awesome elemental power rather than a pretty Renaissance-style putto:

He makes men weak
He overpowers the clever mind, and tames
The spirit in the breasts of men and gods.[1]

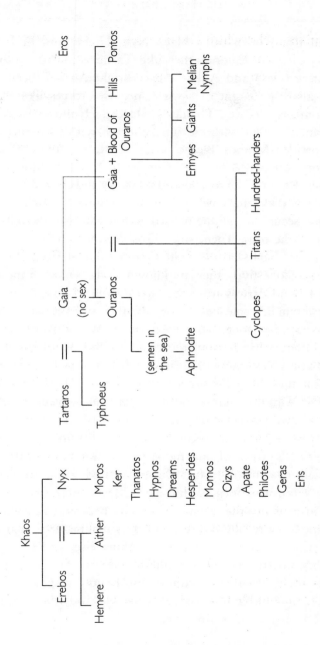

From Khaos also came black Nyx (Night) and Erebos (a dark, infernal region rather like Tartaros), who produced Hemere (Day) and Aither (Space/Bright Air – Ether). Nyx was also the parent of sinister, negative forces like Moros (Doom), Ker (Fate), Thanatos (Death), Hypnos (Sleep) and Dreams, and, without intercourse with anyone, the Hesperides, Momos (Blame), Oizys (Distress), Apate (Deceit), Philotes (Sexual Affection), Geras (Age) and Eris (Strife).

Like Khaos, Gaia reproduced asexually and created her equal Ouranos (Sky), to 'cover her all over, and be a resting-place, always secure, for all the blessed gods',[2] and then the hills and Pontos (the Sea). Then, since Eros was now fully operative, Gaia was able to have sex with Ouranos, and various offspring ensued. Collectively they are known as the Titans, a moniker that Hesiod derives from the Greek *teino* ('I strain') because they 'strain in insolence',[3] along with their siblings the Cyclopes (who each have one round eye in the middle of their forehead, but differ radically from the creatures that Odysseus meets, who reject the norms of society and do not respect the gods, in that they fight for order and justice on Zeus' side in his conflict with the Titans) and the mighty and violent Hundred-handers, who each had fifty heads and a hundred arms. Together they form a group of enigmatic and potent primeval monsters.

Clearly, powerful and monstrous children like this were difficult to control. In fact Ouranos hated them. As soon as each Titan was born, he hid it in a secret place in Gaia (or in Tartaros in other traditions). Gaia became stretched and strained as a result, and responded by making grey adamant, a mythical metal harder than anything else, and forming a mighty saw-toothed sickle. She asked her sons to help her repay their father's wickedness, and Kronos responded positively. Gaia hid him, gave him the sickle, and when Ouranos came to her longing for love,

> The hidden boy
> Stretched forth his left hand; in his right he took
> The great long jagged sickle; eagerly
> He harvested his father's genitals
> And threw them off behind.[4]

The blood from the castration fell on to Gaia and inevitably impregnated her, resulting in the birth of the Erinyes (the Furies, called Alekto, Tisiphone and Megaira), the Giants and the Melian (Ash-tree) Nymphs;[5] the consequence of the semen oozing from the severed member as it fell into the sea was the birth of Aphrodite.

Aphrodite's name was believed to be derived from the Greek *aphros* ('foam'), in which Hesiod says she grew. It touched on the island of Kythera (giving her the name Kythereia) and on Cyprus, where the goddess was born (which is why she is called Kyprogenea, 'Cyprus-born'). She is accompanied by Eros (indeed in other traditions Eros is her son), and together they form an irresistible procreative power. As the Roman poet Lucretius puts it his work *On the Nature of the Universe*:

> Into the breasts of one and all you instil alluring love, so that with passionate longing the [animals] reproduce their several breeds.[6]

In a beautiful yet ominous ode in his tragedy *Hippolytos*, Euripides tells how dangerous she can be:

> How terrible is the advent of Aphrodite.
> When thunder and flame fell upon Semele
> And she gave birth to Bakkhos, son of Zeus,
> Aphrodite laid her to bed,
> A bride in the embrace of Death.

The breath of her terror is felt in every land,
And as a bee's flight is the path of her power.[7]

Yet interestingly, especially in the midst of the violence of much of his poem, Hesiod elects to focus on the more favourable aspects of Aphrodite's power:

Eros is her companion; fair Desire[8]
Followed her from the first, both at birth
And when she joined the company of the gods.
From the beginning, both among gods and men,
She had this honour and received this power:
Fond murmuring of girls, and smiles, and tricks,
And sweet delight, and friendliness, and charm.[9]

Once the fabric of the Earth, Sky, Sea and Mountains is firmly established, Ouranos fades from Hesiod's narrative somewhat, but not before warning Kronos that he will be overcome by one of his own sons. Duly alerted, Kronos chooses his sister Rheia (or Rhea) to be his wife, and becomes king.

The Second Generation: Kronos and Rheia

The generation of Kronos and Rheia seems to be a transitional period: the Sun, Moon, Stars, Rivers and Winds all come into existence, as do personifications such as Themis (Divine Justice), Mnemosyne (Memory), Metis (Cunning Intelligence), Zelos (Glory), Nike (Victory), Kratos (Strength) and Bie (Violence).

Because of the prophecy that he would be dethroned by his own son, Kronos chose not to incarcerate his children in their mother's body as his father had done, but to shut them up in his own. Accordingly Hestia, Demeter, Hera, Hades and sometimes Poseidon were all duly swallowed at birth.

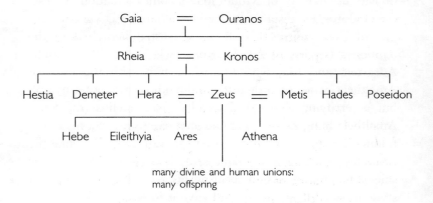

many divine and human unions:
many offspring

But when Rheia fell pregnant with Zeus, who is often known by the epithet Kronion or Kronides ('Son of Kronos'), she begged her parents, Gaia and Ouranos, to find a way of hiding the birth of her son and bringing the Erinys (Fury) down on Kronos. They advised her to go to Crete and give birth to Zeus there, and it has been suggested that this aspect of Zeus' mythology could go back to the Minoan civilization in the second millennium or even earlier, since he looks more like a primitive Mediterranean deity who embodies the processes of fertility within the earth, than the Indo-European sky god who rejuvenates them with life-bringing rain. If this is so, Hesiod seems to combine both aspects, since it is undoubtedly the sky god who defeats Kronos.

The place where Zeus was born and raised varies in different traditions – Hesiod calls it Lyktos, but sometimes it is a cave on Mount Dikte, or on Mount Ida, or some conflation of these: Apollodoros, for instance, names the mountain Dikte and calls one of Zeus' nurses Ida. Rheia entrusted her child to the *daimones* (spirits) called the Kouretes[10] and to the nymphs Adrasteia and Ida, who nourished him with the milk of Amaltheia, who, according to Kallimakhos, was not a nymph but a terrifying she-goat descended from Helios (the Sun). Amaltheia hung Zeus in a cradle on a tree to prevent his father finding him in heaven, or on earth or in the sea,[11] while the Kouretes performed noisy dances, clashing their spears on their shields to prevent Kronos hearing his cries. Rheia wrapped a stone in swaddling clothes and gave it to Kronos to swallow, which he did, thinking it was his newborn child.

So Zeus reached manhood, and as Kronos had overthrown his father Ouranos, so Zeus took over from Kronos. It is remarkable how these myths recycle their own motifs: both Zeus and Kronos violently depose their fathers, using a paternal atrocity as their grounds for doing so.

Ultimately Gaia forced Kronos to vomit up Zeus' brothers and sisters in reverse order, stone first. Technically this made Zeus the eldest child, since they had now all been born after him. Apollodoros tells us that Kronos was overpowered when Metis give him a drug, and an Orphic source claims that, on Nyx's suggestion, Kronos was drugged with honey, tied up, and castrated with the same sickle that he had used on Ouranos. According to Plutarch, Kronos sleeps for ever on a remote holy island near Britain;[12] the stone that Kronos vomited up became a cult object at Delphi.

With Kronos successfully vanquished, Zeus had to confront a new challenge in the form of a ten-year war against Kronos' siblings the Titans – the so-called 'Titanomachy'. Gaia

prophesied that Zeus could not win this war without recruit-
ing those who had been hurled down to Tartaros, so he slew
their female jailer Kampe and released them, unleashing a
literally titanic conflict:

> The boundless sea roared terribly around,
> The great earth rumbled, and broad heaven groaned,
> shaken; and tall Olympos was disturbed
> down to its roots, when the immortals charged.
> The heavy quaking from their footsteps reached
> Down to dark Tartaros, and piercing sounds
> Of awful battle, and their mighty shafts.
> They hurled their wounding missiles, and the voice
> Of both sides, shouting, reached the starry sky,
> And when they met, their ALALE![13] was great.[14]

The Cyclopes furnished Zeus with a thunderbolt,[15] to which
Hades added a helmet and Poseidon a trident, and Zeus won
the day, imprisoned the Titans in Tartaros, and installed the
Hundred-handers as their guards.

Vanquished though they were, the Titans left a considerable
legacy in terms of their offspring, which included: major
rivers; personifications such as Persuasion, Chance, Cunning,
Intelligence, Victory, Power and Force; thousands of nymphs
with shapely ankles; the Dawn, the Sun and the Moon; Atlas
and Prometheus; the Centaur Kheiron (Chiron); the winds
and the stars; Nereus, the Old Man of the Sea; Iris, the divine
messenger and goddess of the rainbow, and the Harpies; the
Gorgons and the semi beautiful-girl, semi raw-flesh-eating
snake Ekhinda; and the Nereids.

The victory over the Titans heralded the establishment of
the true world order. Zeus married Metis (Cunning Intelligence) and became King of the Gods, and various spheres

of influence were allocated by drawing lots: Zeus received the sky, Poseidon the sea, and Hades became overlord of the Underworld. As Poseidon eloquently puts it in Homer's *Iliad*:

> All was divided among us three ways, each given his domain.
> I when the lots were shaken drew the grey sea to live in
> forever; Hades drew the lot of the mists and the darkness,
> and Zeus was allotted the wide sky, in the cloud and the bright air.
> But earth and high Olympos are common to all three.[16]

The Greek Zeus is, in origin, the Indo-European sky god Dyaus. He has interesting connections. The Vedic sky god Dyaus derives his name from the Sanskrit root *diut*, 'to beam', and *diu*, 'sky' and 'day'; *Zeus pater*, 'father Zeus', comes from the same Indo-European root; the Nordic sky god Tiw, who gives his name to Tuesday, has the same derivation; and so does the Latin Jupiter, who has an older form Diespiter – the same root gives the Latin words *deus*, 'god' and *dies*, 'day'. But Zeus is more than just a sky god: he is the head of the gods who live on Mount Olympos (the 'Olympian Gods'), and his powers are nicely detailed in a fragment of Aiskhylos (Aeschylus):

> Zeus is the air, Zeus earth, and Zeus the sky,
> Zeus everything, and all that's more than these.[17]

Zeus was also the protector of the household, and could strike men down or raise them up at will:

> Through Zeus each man is famous or unknown,
> Talked-of or left obscure, through his great will.
> With ease he strengthens any man; with ease
> He makes the strong man humble and with ease

He levels mountains and exalts the plain,
Withers the proud and makes the crooked straight
With ease, the Thunderer whose home is high.[18]

The focus of Hesiod's *Theogony* is the gods. It has nothing
to say about the origin of humanity, but according to his
Works and Days the first human beings were created by the
Titans and lived during the reign of Kronos.

The Third Generation: Zeus and the Olympians

Zeus now had permanent control of the universe, but his
authority did not remain unchallenged.

Apollodoros tells us that despite their marriage Metis
turned into many shapes to avoid Zeus' advances. Zeus got
her pregnant with Athena even so, but it was prophesied that
after giving birth to her, Metis would then bear a son who
would supplant Zeus as King of Heaven. To forestall this
disastrous outcome Zeus swallowed Metis, so that she could
'counsel him in both good and evil plans'. He regularly carried
the epithet Metieta, 'the Counsellor', and by ingesting his
spouse he assumed the responsibility for giving birth to
Athena, the highly intelligent grey-eyed goddess. When the
gestation period was complete, in an incident that was very
popular with vase painters and which adorned the east pediment of the Parthenon at Athens, Hephaistos[19] split Zeus'
head open with an axe and Athena sprang forth fully armed.
His head-born daughter posed no menace to Zeus, and the
son who might have superseded him was never conceived.

Zeus still needed to overcome further threats, though, principally from Gaia and her progeny. She incited her children,
the Giants, into a conflict against the Olympians known as
the Gigantomachy. The conflict was another literary
favourite, and a very common subject for vase paintings and

temple sculptures ranging from the sixth-century Siphnian Treasury at Delphi to the Hellenistic Great Altar of Zeus at Pergamon. Some sources have the Giants born in Phlegrai, others in Pallene,[20] and the venue for the conflict also varies, but all agree on their matchless bulk and invincible might. They had long hair cascading from their heads and chins, and the scales of dragons for feet, and they assaulted the sky by hurling rocks and blazing oaks at it. The gods had an oracle that they could only vanquish the Giants with the aid of a mortal, so they recruited Herakles.

The Gigantomachy was a conflict that reflected its name. Herakles drew first blood by shooting Alkyoneus with an arrow, but as the giant was immortal in the land of his birth, and recovered when he fell to the ground, Herakles had to drag him out of Pallene to kill him; Porphyrion, the King of the Giants, attempted to rape Hera, so Zeus blasted him with a thunderbolt and Herakles (or Apollo) shot him dead; Apollo and Herakles teamed up to shoot Ephialtes in each eye; Dionysos accounted for Eurytos with his *thyrsos*; Hekate slew Klytios with her torches; Hephaistos slaughtered Mimas with missiles of red-hot metal;[21] Athena despatched Enkelados by hurling the island of Sicily on to him, and she flayed Pallas and used his skin as body armour; Poseidon chased Polybotes through the sea to Kos, where he broke off a piece of the island and threw it on him; Hermes donned the helmet of Hades, thereby rendering himself invisible, and slew Hippolytos; Artemis saw off Gration; the Fates wielded brazen clubs and battered Agrios and Thoas to death; Zeus destroyed the rest with thunderbolts and Herakles gave them the *coup de grâce* with arrows as they lay dying.

Gaia's quest for revenge did not stop with the Gigantomachy. She had a child named Typhoeus (or Typhon or Typhaon, according to tradition), whose paternity is given as Tartaros or Kronos, and whose tale is told, with variants, by a number of ancient sources. He was born in Cilicia (the southern coast of modern Turkey), and was the ultimate monstrosity, a ghastly man/beast hybrid, human from the thighs up, but so massive that he towered over the mountains and his head often scraped the stars. One of his hands could touch the west while the other touched the east:

> On his shoulders grew
> A hundred snaky heads, strange dragon heads
> With black tongues darting out. His eyes flashed fire
> Beneath the brows upon those heads, and fire
> Blazed out from every head when he looked round.
> Astounding voices came from those weird heads,
> all kinds of voices.[22]

From the thighs down he had huge coils of vipers, which hissed grotesquely; his body was winged or feathered; and dishevelled hair streamed on the wind from his head and cheeks.

Hissing, shouting and spouting a great jet of fire from his mouth, Typhoeus assaulted heaven with flaming rocks. In the *Theogony* Zeus has a relatively easy time of it: the shock and awe of his thunderbolts are sufficient to hurl Typhoeus down to Tartaros, where he becomes responsible for fierce rain-blowing winds. However, the conflict is more intense and difficult in other versions, where the Olympian gods metamorphose themselves into animals and flee to Egypt. Zeus stands his ground, though, and using thunderbolts and an adamant sickle he forces Typhoeus to flee, and gives chase as far as Mount Casius, near the mouth of the River Orontes in Syria. There the two engage in hand-to-hand combat. Typhoeus grips Zeus in his snaky coils, wrenches the sickle from his grasp, and severs the sinews of his hands and feet.

He then carries the helpless god through the sea to Cilicia, dumps him in the Corycian cave, hides the sinews in a bearskin, and assigns the semi-bestial she-dragon Delphyne to guard them.

However, Hermes and Aigipan ('Goat Pan') are able to steal the sinews and secretly reinstall them into Zeus.[23] Duly revived, he takes the offensive and showers Typhoeus with thunderbolts from a chariot of winged horses. Typhoeus flees to Mount Nysa, where the Fates trick him into tasting the ephemeral fruits by saying that they will strengthen him, and further pursuit sees the protagonists arrive at Mount Haimos in Thrace, where Typhoeus hurls mountains which Zeus blasts back with thunderbolts. A stream of blood gushes from Mount Haimos, 'the Bloody Mountain', (Greek *haima*, 'blood'), and when Typhoeus finally tries to escape via the Sicilian sea, Zeus heaves Mount Etna on top of him.[24] Various ancient authors allude to the idea that Etna's volcanic activity is caused by the thunderbolts thrown in this tussle, and J.G. Frazer goes so far as to suggest that volcanic phenomena and large fossil bones were the principal sources of these tales. Michael Grant says that Typhoeus' fate may be interpreted as a Greek suppression of the weird gods worshipped by the Hittites and Semites, and notes that Zeus is the forerunner of many dragon-slayers, including St George of Cappadocia.

With these conflicts finally at an end, and with his authority over the universe now on a firm footing, Zeus married his long-term partner Hera and sired Hebe, Eileithyia and Ares,[25] but that did not prevent him having intercourse with many other women, both mortal and immortal. Here again the traditions vary, but influential offspring included: Athena (born from Zeus' head after he swallowed Metis), the Seasons, the Fates, the Graces, Persephone, the Nine Muses (Kalliope, Klio, Melpomene, Euterpe, Erato, Terpsikhore, Ourania, Thalia and Polymnia), Artemis and Apollo, Pan, Herakles,

Perseus, Minos and Sarpedon, Helen, Kastor and Polydeukes (Pollux), and Dionysos.

Zeus' behaviour not only caused untold marital disharmony, but it really offended the early Christians, whose response is typified by Arnobius of Sicca's 'Was Juno [i.e. Hera] not enough for him?' Well, obviously not. Zeus' love life was nothing if not complex, although he usually seems to be well on top of the situation and not always too secretive about it. Indeed, just prior to making love with Hera in the *Iliad*, he tells her how much he wants her, and then proceeds to list many of his previous conquests:

> Now let us go to bed and turn to love-making.
> For never before has love for any goddess or woman
> so melted about the heart inside me, broken it to submission,
> as now: not that time when I loved the wife of Ixion
> who bore me Peirithoos, equal of the gods in counsel,
> nor when I loved Akrisios' daughter, sweet-stepping Danae,
> who bore Perseus to me, pre-eminent among all men,
> nor when I loved the daughter of far-renowned Phoinix, Europa
> who bore Minos to me, and Rhadamanthys the godlike;
> not when I loved Semele, or Alkmene in Thebe,
> when Alkmene bore me a son, Herakles the strong-hearted,
> while Semele's son was Dionysos, the pleasure of mortals;
> not when I loved the queen Demeter of the lovely tresses,
> not when it was glorious Leto, nor yourself, so much
> as now I love you, and the sweet passion has taken hold of me.[26]

On this occasion Hera has ulterior motives, and acquiesces, but she was not always so compliant: Hesiod tells how she gave birth to Hephaistos without intercourse in retaliation for Zeus giving birth to Athena.[27]

Zeus stands at the head of the Olympian gods, who have

strongly individualized powers and attributes. (See the table opposite.)

Echoes of Other Mythologies

The grisly yet compelling tales of the mutilation of fathers by sons have caused shock and offence since antiquity. Plato is all for banning the 'foul story about Ouranos' from his Ideal State:

> The story of what Kronos did, and what he suffered at the hands of his son, is not fit . . . to be lightly repeated to the young and foolish, even if it were true; it would be best to say nothing about it, or if it must be told, tell it to a select few under oath of secrecy . . .
>
> These certainly are difficult stories [says Adeimantos]
>
> And they shall not be repeated in our state, Adeimantos.[28]

Yet many scholars and artists have not rejected them as Plato did. The tales lend themselves to feminist interpretation, since Gaia is so fundamental and the feminine is aggressively assertive in them. However, it is encroached upon by masculine concepts of the divine, as patriarchy establishes supremacy (though not always total) over matriarchy. Structuralist analysts also have plenty to work with, as the tales are full of interesting binary oppositions: chaos/order; male/female; young/old; beautiful/ugly and so on. Freudians can make much of this too, particularly the castration motifs, and the repeated victories of ambitious sons over ruthless fathers. The Jungian archetype of the holy marriage appears three times (Ouranos and Gaia; Kronos and Rheia; Zeus and Hera), and the characters themselves can be seen as archetypes: earth mother and queen; sky father and king; both vying for control. The tales are also beautiful aetiologies – explanations of the origin of the Universe.

Deity	Sphere Of Activity	Attributes
Zeus (Jupiter)	'The father of gods and men'; sky; the weather; hospitality; supplication; oaths	Thunderbolt; eagle; sceptre
Hera (Juno)	Wife of Zeus (angry and jealous at his constant extramarital affairs); the integrity of marriage	Sceptre; crown; peacock
Poseidon (Neptune)	The sea; earthquakes; horses and bulls	Trident, often surrounded by sea-creatures
Athena (Minerva)	Domestic arts; warfare	Helmet, spear and shield; the snake-fringed *aegis* with the Gorgon's head; the owl; virginity
Apollo	Music; divination and prophecy; purification and healing; the Sun	Bow and arrows; the lyre; laurel
Artemis (Diana)	Hunting; wild animals; childbirth	Bow and arrows; hunting outfits; virginity
Aphrodite (Venus)	Sex; love	Girdle; doves; sparrows
Demeter (Ceres)	Corn and fertility of the land; the Eleusinian Mysteries	Torch; corn
Ares (Mars)	War	Helmet, spear and shield
Hephaistos (Vulcan)	Brilliant artisan; fire; metallurgy	Lameness; axe; anvil; blacksmith's tools
Hermes (Mercury)	Messenger of the gods; guide of the souls to the Underworld; fertility of flocks; thieves	Herald's staff; winged boots or sandals; traveller's broad-brimmed hat
Dionysos (Bacchus)	Intoxicated ecstasy; wine; drama	Ivy; vines; panthers; the *thyrsos*

It is, though, the comparatists who have perhaps made the most of these tales, since they regard them as not unique to Greece, but part of a worldwide set of myths that explain the separation of Earth and Sky. Certainly parallels present themselves: the ancient Egyptians believed in a marriage between Keb (Earth) and Nut (Heaven), although here the gender roles are reversed; the Kumana of South Africa call Earth their mother and Sky their father; the Ewe people of Togo think that the Earth is the wife of the Sky, and that they consummate their marriage in the rainy season, when the rain fertilizes Mother Earth and makes the seeds grow into Earth's children; and likewise myths from the Indian Archipelago personify Sky and Earth as husband and wife and hold that the consummation of their marriage is manifested in the rain, which fertilizes Earth, who gives birth to all manner of agricultural produce.

There are also some fascinating parallel myths to be found close to the Greek world, and the coincidences between Hesiod's *Theogony* and three Hittite poems, *The Myth of the Kingdom of Heaven*, *The Song of Ullikummi* and *The Myth of Illuyanka*, are especially striking. It is interesting that the Greek myth of Typhoeus usually locates his birthplace in Cilicia, which was on the very eastern limit of Greek settlement in the archaic period, and that key elements of the story happen at Mount Casius, which was way outside Greek territory. The Hittites were extremely powerful around 1460–1200, and at one time controlled an area that included Cilicia and Mount Casius. Cuneiform tablets written in the Hittite language suggest that elements of this myth were generated in the Near East.

The text of *The Myth of the Kingdom of Heaven* is fragmentary, but it is clear that Alalu, the first King of Heaven, is overthrown by his son Anu (Sky/Heaven), who in turn is overthrown by Kumarbi. Anu flees upward like a bird, but

Kumarbi bites off his penis and spits out his sperm, which hits the earth and produces various mountains, rivers and gods. However, he cannot spit out the seed of the storm god Teshub, who seems destined to overthrow Kumarbi's power and avenge his father Anu. When the god Kazal comes out of what might be Kumarbi's head, Kumarbi threatens to eat him. The text suggests that Kumarbi eats something hard – possibly a stone in place of the son that he intended to devour – and it hurts his mouth. He spits it out and it is placed somewhere to serve as a cult object.

Teshub manages to emerge from Kumarbi, perhaps via his penis (the 'good place'), and other tales say that Teshub deposes Kumarbi and banishes him to the Underworld. Kumarbi then wants vengeance, and according to the *Song of Ullikummi*, he becomes aroused by a huge and rather erotic rock, which he impregnates, creating Ullikummi, a diorite stone monster which is carried on the shoulders of Upelluri, the giant who supports heaven and earth, rather like Atlas. Ullikummi grows alarmingly: on his fifteenth day he is so big that the sea only comes up to his waist, and by the time Teshub looks down from Mount Casius and decides to attack him, he is 9,000 leagues in both height and width, and his head is higher than the gates of the city of the gods. However, the gods get the ancient copper knife with which they once severed heaven from earth, and use it to hack through Ullikummi's feet. This destroys his power and enables Teshub to defeat him.

This is not the end of Teshub's troubles, though. In the *Myth of Illuyanka* he is overpowered by Illuyanka ('Snake'), a dragon who takes away his heart and eyes. Teshub goes away, marries a poor man's daughter, and fathers a son who later marries Illuyanka's daughter. Then Teshub gets his son to ask his father-in-law for his heart and eyes back, and the request is freely granted. With the storm god back in action, the goddess Inara helps to defeat Illuyanka, by inviting him to a feast where he overindulges so grossly that he is unable to return to his lair. He is then killed by Teshub, and when Teshub's son intercedes on Illuyanka's behalf, the storm god slays him too.

Some of the key parallels between the Greek and Hittite succession myths could be tabulated as in the table opposite,[29] though not all the motifs occur in the same sequence.

From all this it appears that there is more than just a random connection between the Hittite and Greek succession myths. We might point to:

- a succession of similar-looking divine kings;
- monstrous challengers;
- recurrent motifs such as preventing the birth of children, castrating gods, male pregnancy caused by swallowing sperm, and the creation of other gods by spitting or splitting.

But once the myths are examined more closely, it appears that corresponding motifs often relate to different characters, and some motifs that occur only once or twice in the Hittite myths appear (with variations) for many characters or episodes in the Greek myths. For instance, the male pregnancy motif from the Kumarbi episode appears in the matching Kronos episode, but it also recurs in the myth of the birth of Athena, and possibly in the tale of the birth of Dionysos from Zeus' thigh;[30] the castration motif in the battle between Anu and Kumarbi appears not just in the castration of Kronos but of Ouranos as well; and the removal of Zeus' sinews by Typhoeus, using the same sickle that castrated Ouranos, seems to reverse the Hittite motif where Teshub uses the copper knife to attack the feet of Ullikummi.

Greek	Hittite
Triadic succession of gods: Ouranos (Sky), Kronos, Zeus (storm god).	Triadic succession of gods: Anu (Sky), Kumarbi (corn god), Teshub (storm god)
Ouranos is castrated by Kronos from within Earth's womb. Warns the Titans.	Anu is castrated by Kumarbi as he flees up to the sky. Warns Kumarbi.
Kronos swallows his children as they are born from Rheia; has children locked in his belly.	Kumarbi swallows Anu's genitals, is made pregnant, and has embryos in his belly.
Ouranos' blood and sperm impregnate Earth, who bears various gods.	Kumarbi spites out Anu's seed and impregnates Earth, who bears various gods.
Parent (Rheia) gives infant god (Zeus) to remote deities to be raised concealed in cave.	Parent (Kumarbi) gives infant god (Ullikummi) to remote deities to be raised concealed in earth.
Kronos swallows a stone instead of Zeus. The stone is set up in Delphi.	Kumarbi wants to devour his son (?) but eats something hard (a stone?). Sets it up as a cult.
Kronos vomits up children through his mouth.	Teshub is born from the 'good place'. Another god is possibly born from Kumarbi's head.
Zeus rules. Kronos goes to Tartaros.	Teshub rules. Kumarbi is displaced.
Kronos (or Tartaros) mates with Earth to beget Typhoeus, who rebels against Zeus.	Kumarbi mates with rock to beget Ullikummi, who rebels against Teshub.
Mount Casius is the site of a battle between Typhoeus and Zeus.	Mount Casius is the site of an emergency assembly of the gods to deliberate about Ullikummi's attack on Teshub.
The sickle used to castrate Ouranos is reused by Typhoeus to cut Zeus' sinews.	Teshub reuses the knife which divided heaven and earth to defeat Ullikummi.
Zeus' son Hermes steals back his sinews.	Teshub's son tricks Illuyanka into returning his father's heart and eyes.
The Fates trick Typhoeus into eating the ephemeral fruit which prepares. for his defeat at the hands of Zeus.	Tlnara tricks Illuyanka into overeating at a feast which prepares for his defeat at the hands of Teshub.

The differences look even stronger in other areas too. For example:

- Anu (Sky) has a predecessor, Alalu; Ouranos (Sky) does not;
- the 'father of the gods' is Kumarbi (Kronos) not Teshub (Zeus);
- Ullikummi is a stone monster, not a hybrid beast like Typhoeus;
- Genealogies, which are so central to Hesiod's *Theogony*, hardly appear at all in the Hittite tales.

From all this it looks as if Hesiod could have had some knowledge of Hittite mythology, but whether he drew directly on any of the surviving stories must remain doubtful. The issue of when, where and how the Greeks acquired a knowledge of tales from the Near East is fascinating, though the differences of detail suggest oral transmission was responsible, and we do know that Greeks lived and were active commercially in Cilicia in both the Mycenaean and the archaic periods. That said, it would be rash to argue that any Greek tale can be totally derived from a Hittite one, especially as there are also striking similarities between the myths of Babylon, Phoenicia and Egypt. For example, an Egyptian myth seems to explain the separation of Earth (Geb) and Sky (Nut) by an act of castration, although in this case Sky is female, and she also eats her children. This makes it unlikely that one basic story underlies the different variants: the tales might appear superficially similar, but in fact the differences suggest that we are probably witnessing the creative recycling of common, evolving clusters of mythical ideas. The relationships between these tales has been aptly described as being like a gene pool, where distinctive characteristics are maintained over a long period of time, but where, with the constant alteration of the genetic code, the members will frequently bear closer relation to one another at any point of time than to any particular ancestor.

These myths were extremely popular with ancient artists of all periods. A good case in point is the Gigantomachy, which was one of the favourite subjects for Greek temple decoration. The Archaic Siphnian Treasury at Delphi (*c*.525) displayed a fine Gigantomachy frieze, where the giants are armed hoplite warriors vainly struggling against the might of the gods; in the Classical era the west metopes of the Parthenon (built between 447 and 438) showed the same subject; and so did the magnificent Hellenistic Great Altar of Zeus at Pergamon (*c*.150), where the anguished Giants with their serpentine tails take on the calmly authoritative Olympians. In none of these cases is it ever in doubt that the gods will win, and that order and civilization will triumph over chaos and barbarity. In the post-Persian-invasion Greek world (after 479), that was a very significant message.

Interesting connections abound here: the Great Altar is mentioned in Revelation 2:13 as the 'Throne of Satan', and in Milton's *Paradise Lost* the downfall of Satan draws on many elements of Hesiod's *Theogony*, as does the *Titans' Fall*, which Rubens designed for Philip IV of Spain in 1636. Goya's bloody and nightmarish *Saturn* [Kronos] *Devouring one of his Children* (1821–3) vividly expresses his insight into human cruelty and self-destructiveness.

The less morbid side of these tales has also filtered through, with Aphrodite (Venus) becoming a very popular subject because of her associations with erotic beauty. Sculptors and painters were particularly attracted to the story of her birth. The Ludovisi throne of *c*.460 shows her rising from the sea and being clothed by two attendants on a pebble beach, and later in the fifth century an image of Eros receiving her from the sea was depicted on Pheidias' base of the statue of Zeus at Olympia. She regularly appears rising (*anadyomene*) from the waves, wringing her beautiful wet hair, and floating ashore on a seashell. Sandro Botticelli's *The Birth of Venus* (*c.*1490) is perhaps the classic version, placing the nude goddess in a modest pose that goes back to ancient Greek sculpture, being offered a cloak by one of the Seasons as Zephyr and Flora blow her towards the shore. The contrast between Botticelli's young, ethereal Venus and Hesiod's dangerous, primordial Aphrodite is a fine illustration of how different perspectives of what is essentially the same story can be depicted. This is what gives the Greek mythical tradition so much strength in its post-classical afterlife.

2

APOLLO AND ARTEMIS:
MUSIC, LOVE AND HUNTING

Key Characters

Latona/Leto	The mother of Apollo and Artemis
Apollo	The god of light and prophecy; musician; archer
Artemis (Diana)	The sister of Apollo; virgin huntress
Orpheus	An amazing musician
Eurydike (Eurydice)	Orpheus' beloved wife
Hyakinthos (Hyacinth)	A beautiful youth loved by Apollo
Marsyas	A satyr who challenged Apollo to a music contest
Midas	The King of the Phrygians; a maker of very bad choices
Orion	A mighty hunter, later transformed into a constellation

Zeus might have been King of the Gods, but his amorous advances were not always welcomed: in one tradition Asteria flung herself into the sea in the form of a quail to escape from him, and became the island of Ortygia (Quail Island), which was subsequently called Delos:

> Thy name of old was Asteria, since like a star thou didst leap from heaven into the deep moat, fleeing wedlock with Zeus.

Until then golden Leto consorted not with thee: then thou wert
still Asteria and wert not yet called Delos.[1]

Delos became the birthplace of Apollo in a tale best known
from the *Homeric Hymn to Apollo* by Pindar and Kallimakhos' *Hymn IV to Delos*. As a result of an intrigue with
Zeus, Asteria's sister Leto (or Latona) became pregnant with
twins, Apollo and Artemis. The response of Zeus' wife Hera
was to ban everywhere from sheltering her, and as the time
for the birth approached, Hera hounded her. In Kallimakhos'
narrative she cried out:

O burden of mine, whither shall I carry thee? The hapless sinews
of my feet are outworn.[2]

But Apollo, from inside his mother's womb, told Leto
that

'There is to be seen in the water a tiny
island, wandering over the seas [. . .] Thither do
thou carry me. For she shall welcome thy coming.'
   When he had spoken thus much, the other islands
in the sea ran away. But thou, Asteria, lover of
song, didst come down from Euboia to visit the
round Cyclades [. . .] since thy
heart was kindled, seeing the unhappy lady in the
grievous pangs of birth: 'Hera, do to me what thou
wilt. For I heed not thy threats. Cross, cross
over, Leto, unto me.'[3]

Leto then gave birth:

she
loosed her girdle and leaned back her shoulders
against the trunk of a palm-tree, oppressed by
grievous distress, and the sweat poured over her
flesh like rain. And she spake in her weakness:
'Why, child, dost thou weigh down thy mother?'[4]

Hera seemed to become resigned to the forces of fate: the swans sang seven times over the birth pangs, and

In that hour, O Delos, all thy foundations
became of gold: with gold thy round lake flowed all
day, and golden foliage thy natal olive-tree put forth
and with gold flowed coiled Inopos in deep flood.[5]

In Pindar's version four mighty pillars shod with adamant sprang from the bottom of the earth to anchor the floating island, so that Leto could give birth. Because Apollo, the god of light, was born there, the island Asteria, known until then as A-delos, 'the obscure', was renamed Delos, 'the brilliant'.

The version told by Apollodoros makes Latona come to Delos and first give birth to Artemis, and then, aided by her newborn daughter's midwifery skills, to Apollo. This myth seems to explain the paradox of why Artemis, a virgin goddess, was invoked by women in childbirth. The *Homeric Hymn to Apollo* differentiates Ortygia and Delos, and says that Apollo was born on Delos and Artemis was born on Ortygia, which may be identified with the uninhabited island close to Delos called Rhenia. At certain times in Greek history it was unlawful either to be born or to die on Delos, so expectant mothers and expiring people were ferried across to Rhenia.

Artemis devoted herself to hunting, while Apollo learned the art of prophecy from Pan and went to Delphi, where

Themis was said originally to have delivered the oracles.[6] When Python, the snake that guarded the oracle, tried to stop him approaching the oracular chasm where the priestess made her prophecies under the supposed influence of its divine exhalations, Apollo slew it and took over the oracle. It is said that the Pythian Games at Delphi were instituted in honour of the dead dragon.

Not long afterwards Apollo also slew Tityos, the monstrously sized son of Zeus and Elare (or Elara). The early mythologist Pherekydes of Athens related that Zeus hid Tityos under the earth in order to save him from Hera's outraged anger, so Tityos was commonly said to have been earth-born. He met his doom when he became overcome by lust for Latona and assaulted her on a visit she made to Delphi; she called Apollo and Artemis to her aid and they shot him down with their arrows. Tityos' punishment in the Underworld was one of the most notorious: vultures eternally feasted on his vital organs, and his sufferings were depicted by the great artist Polygnotos in a celebrated painting at Delphi, showing Tityos worn to a shadow, though no longer tortured by the vultures.

Apollo had a relationship with the Muse Kalliope, who had two sons by him: Linos,[7] who was killed by Herakles, and Orpheus,[8] the great musician who played a telling part in the voyage of the Argonauts and whose songs had the power to move animals, stones and trees.

Orpheus' wife, the nymph Eurydike (Eurydice), was being pursued by Aristaios, and died as a result of being bitten by a snake, so Orpheus went down to the Underworld to bring her back. The earliest mention of this is in Euripides' play *Alkestis* (*Alcestis*) (438), but more complete versions appear in the Roman writers Virgil and Ovid. Orpheus entered the Underworld at Tainaron in the Peloponnese and used the power of his music to charm Kerberos (Cerberus) the watchdog, and

Kharon (Charon) the ferryman, into granting him access. All the normal processes ground to a halt: the ghosts wept; Tantalos' hunger and thirst abated; the vultures stopped tearing Tityos' liver; Sisyphos sat down on his rock; Ixion's wheel stopped turning; the Furies were moved to tears; and Hades and Persephone were persuaded into allowing him to take Eurydike back to the world above. But they attached a condition: Orpheus should go first and should not turnaround until he had left the realms of the dead.

> In deadly silence the two of them followed the upward slope;
> The track was steep, it was dark and shrouded in black mist.
> Not far to go now; the exit to earth and light was ahead!
> But Orpheus was frightened his love was falling behind; he
> was desperate
> To see her. He turned, and at once she shrank back into the
> dark.
> She stretched out her arms to him, struggled to feel his hands
> on her own,
> But all she was able to catch, poor soul, was the yielding air.[9]

There was to be no second visit to the Underworld for Orpheus in his lifetime. He ended up in Thrace, singing to assuage his grief, and finally met his death by being torn in pieces by Maenads, either because the women were offended by his commitment to the memory of his late wife to the exclusion of their attractiveness, or because he preferred the love of boys. There is also a variant which holds that Aphrodite was responsible, motivated by anger over Kalliope's judgement in her dispute with Persephone over Adonis,[10] and a further one which says that Orpheus failed to honour Dionysos because he regarded Helios (the Sun) as the greatest of the gods: he would get up at dawn every day to watch the sunrise from the top of Mount Pangaion, a preference that angered Dionysos. Whatever prompted the Maenads to do it, each one wanted Orpheus for herself, and their tugging at him ended in a bloody death.

His severed head floated, still singing, down the River Hebros and drifted across the sea to Lesbos where, in an aetiology for the fine achievements of the great Lesbian poets such as Alkaios and Sappho, the local people buried it and received special talents in poetry and music. The remains of his body were buried by the Muses in Pieria, where the nightingale was felt to sing more sweetly than anywhere else. His instrument was placed in the stars by Zeus as the constellation Lyra, and his ghost was happily reunited with his beloved Eurydike.

Apollo was also involved in a complex, multi-faceted love-relationship centred on Hyakinthos (Hyacinthus), the son of King Amyklas of Sparta and Diomede (or of the Muse Klio and Pieros, son of Magnes). In the first inter-mortal homosexual relationship, a singer called Thamyris fell in love with Hyakinthos, as did Zephyros (the West Wind)[11] and Apollo. Hyakinthos liked Apollo best, but while the two of them enjoyed a discus contest, the Zephyros took revenge by blowing Apollo's discus so that it hit Hyakinthos' head with fatal results. The blood that poured from the wound gave rise to the hyacinth flower, which is said to be inscribed with letters that commemorate Hyakinthos' demise, though these can differ: Ovid read the cry 'AIAI' ('Alas, alas!') on them, and adds that Apollo promised that he would be commemorated through the great hero Aias too, whose name would also appear on the petals; others reckoned that they could see first Greek letter (Y) of Hyakinthos' name in the dark lines of the flower.

The other disappointed lover Thamyris was very beautiful and a fine musician, so good in fact that he challenged the

Muses to a musical contest. Inevitably this brought catastrophic consequences: in Homer he not only loses the competition, but also his vocal and instrumental talents as well; in Apollodoros there is extra spice, in that the rules of the contest are that if he won, he could have sex with all the Muses in turn, but if they won they could take from him whatever they liked. Duly defeated, he was deprived of his musicality and his eyesight.

Another foolish character to challenge a divinity to a music competition was the Phrygian satyr Marsyas, the son of Olympos. Athena had invented the *aulos*, a double-reeded wind instrument, in order to imitate the song the Gorgons sang to mourn their dead sister Medousa, but when a reflection showed how distorted her face became when she played it, she discarded it immediately. Marsyas found the *aulos* and acquired incredible virtuosity. He challenged Apollo on the basis that the winner could do whatever he liked to the loser. After the first performances, which were equally impressive, Apollo turned his lyre upside down and challenged Marsyas do the same. This proved impossible, so Apollo was declared the victor and killed Marsyas by fastening him to a tall tree and flaying him alive.

Another important mythical musical contest concerning Apollo involved the Phrygian King Midas. Midas' career started well: when a drunken old man was brought to him as a prisoner, he recognized him for who he was – Silenos, one of Dionysos' great companions-in-revelry. Having entertained him and returned him to Dionysos, the god granted Midas any one wish. Without thinking through the ramifications, he asked that everything he touched should be turned to gold. His delight at being able to transform sticks and stones into precious metal soon turned to horror when the same happened to his food and drink. Parched and starving, he begged Dionysos to revoke the badly selected gift, and the god obliged by giving him instructions to wash in the River Paktolos, which ever since has contained golden sand.

Having made one stupid decision, Midas now made another. Apollo and the god Pan were having a musical contest judged by the mountain god Tmolos, who favoured Apollo and his lyre over Pan and his pipes. But Midas queried the decision. In his fury at Midas' total lack of musical appreciation, Apollo transformed the offending ears into those of an ass – long, twitching and bristly. Midas was consumed with shame, and tried his best to conceal his embarrassment by wearing a turban, but he could not conceal the truth from his barber. The barber was afraid to disseminate the astonishing secret, but could not contain himself, so he dug a hole and whispered the truth into it. Eventually the hole became covered by reeds, which came to broadcast the barber's words (and still do): 'Midas has asses' ears.'

If challenging Apollo was a perilous thing to do, the same applied to his sister Artemis, who was responsible for the death of the great hunter Orion.

Orion was either earth-born or a son of Poseidon and Euryale. He was of gigantic stature, and could either walk on the surface of the sea, or wade through it because he was so tall. His first serious relationship was with the gorgeous Side, but she was misguided enough to claim that she rivalled Hera herself in beauty, and was cast into Hades as a result.

Orion then relocated to Khios, where he courted Merope, the daughter of King Oinopion ('Wine-Drinker'). Oinopion was happy to let the match go ahead if Orion would rid the island of wild beasts. This posed no problem for Orion, but Oinopion failed to deliver his side of the bargain, and in the end Orion's frustration got the better of him and he raped Merope. Oinopion responded by getting Orion incapacitated with drink and putting out his eyes. The hunter made his way over to Lemnos, where Hephaistos had his smithy, and snatched up a boy, put him on his shoulders, and told him to lead him to the sunrise. They moved in that direction, and once the sun's rays had healed Orion's vision, he set off to destroy Oinopion. However, he was stymied in this because Oinopion was safely accommodated in an underground residence built by Hephaistos. There is a version that says that Eos (Dawn) fell in love with Orion and took him to Delos – Aphrodite had inflicted Eos with insatiable sexual appetites because she had slept with her husband Ares.

Orion finally met his death in Crete, where he had taken to hunting with Artemis and Leto. He stupidly boasted that there was no animal on earth that he would not kill, so Gaia (Earth herself) sent a giant scorpion that gave him a fatal sting. In some versions it is Artemis who is responsible for his death, either sending the scorpion because he tried to rape her, killing him for challenging her to a discus match, or shooting him for violating the Hyperborean maiden Opis. Other myth-tellers say that Apollo engineered Orion's death because Artemis liked him so much and was contemplating marriage. Her brother lured her into an archery competition in which the far-distant target was, unknown to her, Orion's head. Orion and the Scorpion were both elevated to the stars as constellations.

Apollo and Artemis (who is Diana in her Roman form) are ubiquitous in Classical art, and incidents from their mythology have attracted artists, poets and playwrights ever since. They are readily recognizable in the visual arts, Apollo with his bow and arrow, lyre or other stringed instrument, laurel wreath, chariot of the sun and sometimes a halo; Artemis likewise equipped with bow and arrow and other hunting paraphernalia – spear, dogs, deer – and sometimes sporting a crescent moon.

Apollo's contest with Marsyas became a highly popular subject, especially in Hellenistic and Roman art, where Marsyas is regularly depicted tied to the tree with his hands above his head, his face contorted in anticipation of the agonizing pain to come, and often with a figure sharpening a knife in front of him. For Renaissance artists the rivalry between stringed and wind instruments symbolized that between sensual and intellectual types of music, and so acquired extra resonance beyond its classical model. The flaying scene appears in the Italian Ovid of 1497, where we see a succession of incidents: Minerva (Athena) performing to a table full of gods, who laugh her off stage; the goddess playing to her reflection in a pool; the contest itself; the flaying; and the exhibition of Marsyas' skin in a temple. The subject also features in the work of Raphael (1483–1520), Titian (c.1487/90–1576) and Guercino (1591–1666), to name but three. The contemporary artist Hughie O'Donoghue saw Titian's *Flaying of Marsyas*, where the satyr is shown upside down, at the 'Genius of Venice' exhibition at the Royal Academy in 1983. He has used it, along with the influence of his father Daniel, who owned a postcard of an ancient Greek sculpture of Marsyas, to striking effect in his *Crossing the Rapido* series of paintings (1999–2000). In O'Donoghue's work Marsyas can appear suspended with either his wrists or ankles uppermost, and he brings a subtext of silenced music that reflects the fact that his father lost a flute while crossing the Rapido in the Second World War. Daniel also owned a photograph of Mussolini hanging by his ankles after his execution in 1945 – a very Marsyas-like image – and Mussolini becomes part of the iconography of *Crossing the Rapido* VI, just as Marsyas does in *Crossing the Rapido* IV where he is juxtaposed with a photograph of a German soldier whose skin has been burned off. Ancient mythical cruelty touches on modern historical tragedy very powerfully here.

It is also interesting to see how the musical contest is sometimes confused with that between Apollo and Pan judged by Midas, since we do see Midas judging the Marsyas contest instead. Midas himself has always had great appeal as a subject for painters, with fine pieces produced by Veronese (*c.*1528–88), Rubens (1577–1640), Poussin (1594–1665) and Tiepolo (1696–1770). It is interesting that the consequences of Midas' golden touch are often forgotten in contemporary usage: football commentators frequently equate having the Midas touch with a degree of success and skill, and Ian Fleming's Auric Goldfinger is an excellent example from film media.

It has been suggested that the tale of Midas' ears may well have been the inspiration behind the scene of Bottom with his ass's head in *A Midsummer Night's Dream*, and a more recent and explicit dramatization of the myths of Midas and Pan and Apollo has featured in Ted Hughes' remarkable *Tales from Ovid*. Shakespeare also shows the power of Orpheus' music quite brilliantly in *Two Gentlemen of Verona*, with a possible nod towards Midas along the way:

> For Orpheus' lute was strung with poets' sinews,
> Whose golden touch could soften steel and stones,
> Make tigers tame, and huge leviathans
> Forsake unsounded deeps to dance on sands.[12]

The Orpheus myth came to Shakespeare via the Middle Ages, where the fourteenth-century Middle-English romance *Sir Orfeo* has the hero successfully recovering Queen Heurodis (Eurydike, from Fairyland, rather than from the Underworld), and poets and musicians were attracted by the message the myth held for them: music and love confer immortality. The power of Orpheus' music is eloquently expressed at the beginning of Rainer Maria Rilke's *Sonnets of Orpheus* (1923):

A tree rose from the earth. O pure transcendence –
Orpheus sings: O tall oak in the ear!
All was still. And then within that silence
he made the sign, the change, and touched the lyre.

One by one they crept out from the wood,
emptying each set and form and lair;
and looking in their eyes, he understood
they'd fallen quiet in neither stealth nor fear,

but in their listening.[13]

Opera seems to have had a special relationship with the myth, from Monteverdi's *Orfeo*, through to Gluck's *Orfeo ed Eurydice* (again with a happy ending) and Offenbach's entertaining send-up of the classical clichés in his *Orpheus in the Underworld*.

More recently film has incorporated the Orpheus myth to good effect. Marcel Camus's *Black Orpheus* (1959), with its excellent score by Antonio Carlos Jobim and Luis Bonfa, places the events in the Rio de Janeiro carnival, whereas in Jean Cocteau's landmark film *Orphée* (1950) the lyre-playing singer of Greek myth becomes a famous Left Bank poet in post-war Paris. Here Orphée has fallen out of favour and lost his inspiration, and is in love with Death, called the Princess, who claims the life of his wife Eurydice. In this hauntingly beautiful piece of cinema the entrance to the Underworld is via a dissolving mirror. Cocteau revisited the myth for his last film *Le Testament d'Orphée* (1959), where black motorcyclists and an erotic figure of death in a Rolls-Royce accompany the descent.

It is remarkable how these fragments of the Greek mythical tradition are still felt to be moving and resonant in an amazing array of media: these tales have won the hearts and minds of millions of people, wordwide, at many different times. An exquisite illustration of the way the different influences coalesce appears in William Schumann's song 'Orpheus with his Lute', which itself is a setting of verses from Shakespeare's *Henry VIII*, Act 3, scene 1:

Orpheus with his lute made trees
And the mountains that freeze
Bow themselves when he did sing.
To his music plants and flowers
Ever sprung, as sun and showers
There had made a lasting spring.

Every thing that heard him play,
Even the billows of the sea,
Hung their heads and then lay by.
In sweet music is such art,
Killing care and grief of heart
Fall asleep, or hearing, die.

3

THE CREATION OF MAN AND
WOMAN; THE GREAT FLOOD;
TRANSGRESSORS AND HEROINES

Key Characters

Zeus (Jupiter)	King of the Gods
Prometheus	('Foresight') Stole fire from the gods
Epimetheus	('Hindsight') Prometheus' stupid brother
Pandora	('Allgift') The first woman
Deukalion (Deucalion)	The 'Greek Noah'
Pyrrha	Wife of Deukalion
Pelasgos	The aboriginal Greek
Lykaon (Lycaon)	Killed by Zeus along with his sons for impiety
Kallisto (Callisto)	Turned into a bear; mother of Arkas
Arkas (Arcas)	Eponym of the Arcadians
Triptolemos	Taught mankind the cultivation of crops
Hellen	Son of Deukalion and Pyrrha; eponym of the Greeks ('Hellenes')
Meleagros (Meleager)	Son of Oineus; led the hunt for the Kalydonian Boar
Atalanta	Virgin huntress defeated in running thanks to a golden apple
Sisyphos	Extremely cunning; transgressed divine law; punished in Hades

Salmoneus	Arrogantly imitated Zeus; destroyed by a thunderbolt
Admetos	King of Pherai; is offered the chance to avoid death if he can find someone to take his place
Alkestis (Alcestis)	Admetos' wife, who agreed to die in his place

The Five Races of Mankind

In the *Theogony*, Hesiod told of the origins of the gods; in his poem *Works and Days*, he tells the myth of the five successive races of men and what happened, or what will happen, to them.

He opens by narrating how the Olympian gods created a golden race of men, who lived in the time of Kronos (which became a byword for the Golden Age). Life was perfect: they were happy, had no need to work or farm, did not endure old age, and feasted plentifully until death came to them in the form of sleep and they lived on as beneficent spirits.

The silver race that followed was way inferior: they existed as babies for 100 years, and on reaching maturity lived brief, anguished, stupid, reckless lives full of *hybris* (violent, arrogant pride) towards each other. Because they spurned the gods too, Zeus hid them away and they became spirits of the Underworld.

The age of bronze witnessed further deterioration. These men had a very puzzling relationship with ash trees: either they are made of ash wood, descended from ash-tree nymphs, or were 'made of ashen spears' in a sense rather like our phrase 'men of steel'. They used bronze for everything from weaponry to domestic architecture, were powerful, violent, and caused their own destruction.

The decline of humanity is not strictly linear, since things get better with the fourth race. These are the heroes who fight at Thebes and at Troy, and are described as better and more just than the bronze race. Some of them were allowed to live on the Isles of the Blessed after they died.

We then come to the race of iron. This is our world. Pessimistic Hesiod laments:

> I wish I were not of this race, that I
> Had died before, or had not yet been born.[1]

Ours is a time of toil, grief and death, and the future is even worse: might will be right, morality will disintegrate, evil will flourish, and Aidos (Shame) and Nemesis (Righteous Indignation), who inhibit outrageous behaviour, will abandon mankind.

Prometheus, Fire and Woman

Alongside this tradition runs another one in which the first human beings were created by the Titans and lived during the reign of Kronos. In some versions the Titan Prometheus appears as the benefactor of mankind, but later traditions represent him as their actual creator, moulding them out of water and earth.

Prometheus' great gift to humans was fire. But it came with a price. Prometheus was a great trickster (his name means 'Foresight'), but unfortunately he had a dim-witted brother, Epimetheus ('Hindsight'). Hesiod tells how at Mekone (said to be Sikyon, close to Korinth) there was an incident in which gods and mortals divided up an ox. Prometheus concealed the meat in the stomach of the ox and hid the bones in the tasty-looking fat. Zeus was then invited to choose, and, although he saw through the trick, he selected the inedible portion anyway, which explains in mythological terms why the Greeks burned the bones to the gods at sacrifices, and ate the meat.

Zeus did not allow this 'deception' to go unpunished: he denied humanity the benefit of fire. But Prometheus got up to his tricks again:

> [Prometheus] stole
> The ray, far-seeing, of unwearied fire,
> Hid in the hollow fennel stalk, and Zeus
> Who thunders in the heavens ate his heart,
> And raged within to see the ray of fire
> Far-seeing, among men.[2]

Zeus' comeback was to give men a balancing evil: Pandora, the first woman, 'an evil thing for their delight, and all will love this ruin in their hearts'.[3] Hephaistos made her out of earth and water, giving her a face like a goddess, and the lovely figure of a virgin girl; Athena adorned her with exquisite garments, and taught her the art of weaving; Aphrodite poured charm upon her head, but also painful desire and body-shattering cares; Peitho (Seductive Persuasion) and the Kharites (Graces) gave her golden necklaces; the Horai (Seasons) wove spring flowers into a crown for her; Hermes added lies, persuasive words and cunning ways, and named her Pandora ('Allgift'), after these divine gifts. The tender trap was complete:

> Amazement seized the mortal men and gods,
> To see the hopeless trap, deadly to men.
> From her comes all the race of womankind,
> The deadly female race and tribe of wives
> Who live with mortal men and bring them harm,

No help to them in dreadful poverty
But ready enough to share with them in wealth.[4]

Hermes was detailed to take Pandora to Epimetheus, who forgot Prometheus' advice to send back any gift from Zeus, in case it should injure men. He accepted Pandora, but understood too late.

Pandora does not have a 'box' in Greek. She has a huge earthenware storage jar called a *pithos*, here translated as 'cask':

But now the woman opened up the cask,
And scattered pains and evils among men.
Inside the cask's hard walls remained one thing,
Hope, only, which did not fly through the door.
The lid stopped her, but all the others flew,
Thousands of troubles, wandering the earth.[5]

This is enigmatic: is there now no hope, because she is shut in the jar, or do men at least have hope, if nothing else? However we interpret this, the incident was costly for all concerned: mankind received many evils, and Prometheus got a personal punishment for stealing fire, since Zeus ordered Hephaistos to nail him to Mount Caucasus in Scythia, where an eagle came and ate his 'deathless' liver, which grew back to its original state every night.

The Pandora myth often invites comparison with the Hebrew tale of Eve, found in Genesis. Both these stories have had far-reaching influence because they apparently reveal woman's real nature. Popular opinion usually holds that the Eve and Pandora tales exist to warn men about feminine evil, but in fact, although the two women are often conflated, they are quite dissimilar in original meaning, and over the centuries Eve appears to have been transformed into a Pandora figure.

Like the Old Testament, the Babylonian *Epic of Gilgamesh* and the mythology of cultures as far afield as North America, Greek mythology has a myth of a Great Flood. Apollodoros says that Prometheus subsequently had a son called Deukalion who married Pyrrha, the daughter of Epimetheus and Pandora. In his version, rather than letting the bronze race men destroy themselves, as they do in Hesiod, Zeus decides to eradicate them by means of a deluge. Deukalion, who is a champion of humanity like Prometheus, takes his father's advice, builds a chest, stocks it with provisions, and embarks in it with Pyrrha. Zeus' torrential rain floods most of Greece and overwhelms everywhere outside the Isthmus of Korinth and the Peloponnese, destroying everyone except the few who fled to the mountains. Deukalion floats in his chest for nine days and nights, and when the rain finally abates he makes landfall on Mount Parnassos. He sacrifices to Zeus, who sends Hermes to grant him whatever he wishes. Deukalion chooses to make humans, which he and Pyrrha do by taking stones and tossing them over their heads: his stones become men; hers become women.

Prometheus was only one of many important mythological culture-bringers, and the region of Arkadia had its own particular version of the arrival of civilization. Pelasgos was the aboriginal inhabitant of the country, although Pausanias comments: 'It seems likelier that there were other people with him, and not just Pelasgos by himself, or else who could Pelasgos have ruled over?'[6] He was a son of Zeus, tall, strong, beautiful and a great developer of social activity, inventing the first huts, teaching his people to wear sheepskin tunics, stopping them eating leaves, grass and inedible fruits, and discovering the nutritional value of acorns. His son, called Lykaon, subsequently reigned over the Arkadians and, by a variety of wives, had fifty sons. He continued his father's developments, at least until either he, or more usually his sons, tried to test or deceive Zeus by sacrificing a child and serving his flesh to Zeus in a hideous transgression of every precept of hospitality. Zeus was not deceived: thunderbolts blasted Lykaon's sons, Lykaon was turned into a wolf, or the very existence of mankind was imperilled in Deukalion's Great Flood.

Pausanias presents a different account in which Lykaon slaughtered a human child on the altar of Zeus on Mount Lykaios and was suddenly changed into a wolf. There is a possible link between myth and ritual here, since rather violent rites seem to have been performed on Mount Lykaios down to the second century CE. The worshippers partook (symbolically or actually) in an act of cannibalism, and whoever happened to taste human flesh was believed to metamorphose into a wolf, only reverting to human form if he had managed to abstain from eating human flesh for eight years. The wolf-man left the community, which possibly reflects an initiation rite in which young Arkadians would spend a period of time outside the boundaries of the community, before returning as fully integrated citizens.

Lykaon's daughter Kallisto[7] was one of Artemis' hunting companions and had sworn to remain a virgin. But Zeus fell in love with her:

> He reckoned: 'My wife will never discover this tiny betrayal; or else, if she does, oh yes, the joy will make up for the scolding!'[8]

When, inevitably, he did get caught, he transformed Kallisto into a bear,[9] but Artemis shot her down, either to please Hera, or because she had not preserved her virginity. Zeus sent Hermes to rescue the son that Kallisto had conceived from her womb, called him Arkas, and turned Kallisto into the constellation of the Great Bear.

Arkas continued the civilizing process. His people changed their name from Pelasgians to Arkadians, and he introduced the cultivation of crops, which he had learned from Triptolemos, another significant culture-bringer. When Demeter, goddess of cereal, was seeking her daughter Persephone, after Hades had abducted her, she had made her way to Keleus, who was either the ruler of the Eleusinians or a poor old peasant. He received her hospitably, and some women in the house invited her to sit with them, and the aged Iambe's jokes made the unhappy goddess smile (which became an aetiological story explaining why women made ribald jests at the Thesmophoria Festival in Athens). Keleus' wife Metaneira had a son called Demophon, whom Demeter intended to immortalize by putting him on the fire at night, to strip off his mortal flesh, and then anointing him with ambrosia by day. Demophon grew prodigiously, but one night Metaneira discovered him in the fire and screamed, prompting Demeter to cease the immortalization process (or indeed for the child to be consumed in the fire). However, Demeter gave Triptolemos, Demophon's elder brother,[10] a chariot of winged dragons, along with wheat, so that he could sow the entire inhabited world.

Some scholars see the innovations of these culture heroes as illustrating a pattern known as that of the 'first finder', where an object or practice felt to be typical of, or vital to, human life is attributed to a particular individual from the mythological past. Certainly, after Deukalion's flood the Greek mythological tradition then proceeds into a series of complex genealogies, which have numerous variants, but which lay down the basis for the Greek tribes (among other things). It is notable that almost all of these stories are aetiological, that is, they contain characters who give their names to regions, cities, rivers and so on.

Deukalion and Pyrrha's first child was Hellen,[11] who gives his name to the Greeks. In antiquity the Greeks referred to themselves as 'Hellenes', and according to a famous inscription known as the *Parian Chronicle*, this first occurred in 1521 BCE. Hellen's offspring, by a nymph called Orseis, were Doros, Xouthos and Aiolos (Aeolus),[12] and he divided the Greek territory among them:

- Doros received the country adjacent to Peloponnese and called the settlers Dorians.
- Xouthos got the Peloponnese. His sons Akhaios and Ion gave their names to the Akhaians (Latinized to Achaeans) and Ionians.
- Aiolos ruled the regions around Thessaly and named the inhabitants Aiolians (Latinized to Aeolians). He had five daughters and seven sons.

Although many interesting tales are clustered around the descendants of Aiolos, there is really no continuous narrative linking them, and from the 'A'-list celebrities such as Prometheus and Pandora we enter the 'B'-list world of myths with more limited, and often more local, significance. Aiolos' daughter Kanake's family by the sea god Poseidon included Aloios, who married his brother Triops' daughter Iphimedeia, who in turn fell in love with her grandfather Poseidon.[13] In her erotic yearning Iphimedeia would scoop up the waves and pour them into her lap, and, duly fertilized by this, she gave birth to Otos and Ephialtes, also known as the Aloadai. They grew prodigiously – one cubit (45cm) in breadth and one fathom (2 metres) in height per year – and when they were nine cubits by nine fathoms they decided

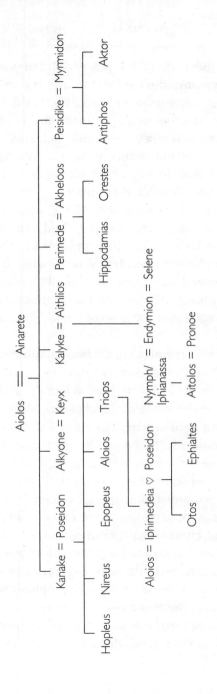

to assault the gods. They placed Mount Ossa on top of Mount Olympus, then piled Mount Pelion on Ossa, and threatened an inversion of the natural order by filling up the sea with the mountains to make dry land, and making the land into sea. They were only defeated when Artemis tricked them on the island of Naxos by changing herself into a deer and leaping between them. Throwing their missiles at her, they hit each other.

Alkyone, another daughter of Aiolos, was married by Keyx, son of the Morning Star, who, says Ovid, reflected his father's brightness in his face. But their pride led to their fall. When he foolishly claimed that Hera was his wife, and she boasted that her husband was Zeus, they found themselves metamorphosed into birds: Alkyone into a kingfisher (Greek *alkyon*, Anglicized via Latin as halcyon) and Keyx into a gannet (*keyx*).[14]

Alkyone's sister Kalyke had a famous son by Aithlios called Endymion,[15] who was so extraordinarily beautiful that Selene (the Moon) fell in love with him. When Zeus offered to grant him whatever he wanted, he chose to sleep for ever in a deathless and ageless state. His eternal sleep became proverbial. Endymion also had a son by the name of Aitolos, who gave his name to the region of Aitolia and became the ancestor of a number of intriguing individuals.

One particularly fascinating character in Aitolos' family group is his great-great-grandson Oineus, who was King of Kalydon and became the first to receive the vine plant from Dionysos (Greek *oinos*, 'wine'). He had a son named Toxeus, and in a motif reminiscent of (though not identical with) the Roman Romulus legend, in which he kills his brother Remus for leaping over the rising foundations of Rome, Oineus slew Toxeus as he leaped over a ditch. Toxeus' siblings included the formidable Deianeira, who was said to have been Oineus' wife Althaia's child by Dionysos. She drove a chariot, was adept in the art of war, and married Herakles after he won a wrestling match with Akheloos to win her hand.

The Kalydonian Boar Hunt

Althaia and Oineus also had a son named Meleagros (Latinized to Meleager), although according to some myth-tellers his father is the war god Ares. Meleagros' story crops up in Homer's *Iliad*, provides the theme for tragedies by Sophokles and Euripides, and belongs to a class of tales where someone's life is inextricably linked to some external object or animal. When Meleagros was seven days old the Fates decreed that he would die 'when the brand burning on the hearth was burnt out', so Althaia instantly extinguished it and put it in a chest for safe-keeping. Meleagros grew into a splendid hero, but there was no way he could cheat his destiny. The events leading to his death could be traced back to a ceremony in which Oineus dedicated the first fruits of the crops to all the gods, but failed to include Artemis. In her rage she sent the Kalydonian Boar, a massive beast of extra-ordinary strength, which caused widespread destruction to both livestock and humans and stopped anyone farming the land. Oineus' response was to call together a stellar line-up of heroes, with the promise that whoever slew the boar would get its skin as the prize. Various sources catalogue the heroes who responded, who were very much taken from the 'A' list: Theseus, Jason, Kastor and Polydeukes were all present.

Oineus entertained these mighty characters for nine days, but problems occurred on day ten when Kepheus, Ankaios and others refused to go hunting with Atalanta because she was a woman. Meleagros forced them to go, though, primarily because he wanted her to have his child, despite the fact that he was already married to Kleopatra, the daughter of Idas and Marpessa. [16] So the hunt went ahead, but began badly: the heroes surrounded the boar, but it killed two of them, and then Peleus hit Eurytion with his javelin by mistake. However, Atalanta shot it in the back with an arrow, after which Amphiaraos hit it in the eye, and Meleagros finished it off with a thrust in the flank. Meleagros got the animal's skin as his prize, but he presented it to Atalanta. This incensed the sons of Thestios, who were so appalled that a woman should get the prize that they took the skin from her, on the pretext that if Meleagros did not want it, it was theirs by right of birth. Meleagros' violent response then brought about his own death. He slew the sons of Thestios, who were his mother Althaia's brothers, and returned the skin to Atalanta, but, in grief and rage, Althaia relit the brand on which Meleagros' fate depended, causing his instant death.

Interestingly, there is a different version of Meleagros' death. In the *Iliad* it is told how the sons of Thestios claimed the skin on the grounds that Iphiklos had been the first to hit the boar. This sparked off a war in which the Kouretes besieged the city of Kalydon, from which Meleagros sallied forth to kill some of the sons of Thestios. His mother Althaia cursed him, so he remained seething at home, until the Kouretes were right at the walls and the Kalydonians begged him to come to the rescue. It was Kleopatra who finally persuaded him to take the field, and although he killed the rest of the sons of Thestios, he fell in the fighting himself. Meleagros' death prompted both Althaia and Kleopatra to hang themselves, and the female mourners at the funeral were turned into guinea-fowl, called *meleagrides* in Greek.

The Kalydonian Boar Hunt was a particular favourite subject with Greek vase painters, and is perhaps most famously rendered on the magnificent 'François Vase' of *c.*575, by Ergotimos and Kleitias, where the hunters and their dogs confront the mighty, bristling boar. Suetonius also tells us that the Roman Emperor Tiberius had a painting by Parrhasius, which had been bequeathed to him on condition that, if he disliked the subject, he could have 10,000 gold pieces instead. He chose to keep it, and hung it in his bedroom. It showed Atalanta committing a grossly indecent act with Meleagros.

Atalanta's mythology outside the boar hunt is fascinating. She had a traumatic childhood. Her father[17] only wanted male children, so she was exposed to die. However, a she-bear discovered her and suckled her until some hunters came across her and took her in. As an adult Atalanta lived rather like Artemis, a virgin hunting in the wilds. She was formidable, as Peleus found out when she beat him at wrestling at the wedding of Pelias, and the Centaurs Rhoikos and Hylaios discovered to their cost, shot down as they tried to rape her.

In due course she rediscovered her parents, and her father was keen for her to marry. But she had received an oracle that made her reluctant:

'No need of a husband
for you, Atalanta. Avoid all knowledge of men if you can.
But you shall not escape. You will lose yourself, without losing
your life.'[18]

Atalanta's response was to challenge her suitors to a foot race, with the prize being marriage if the suitor won, but death if he did not. Even so, she was well worth competing for:

[Hippomenes[19]] saw the bright-coloured ribbons attached to
her knees and her ankles
fluttering gaily behind her, while over her ivory shoulders

her hair streamed back in the wind. The white of her girlish
    skin was all suffused with a rosy glow, as a marble hall
will be steeped by the sun in counterfeit shade through a
    purple awning.[20]

Many had already perished when Hippomenes competed for her. He brought golden apples, either from Aphrodite or from the Hesperides, and deliberately dropped them during the chase. Atalanta could not resist them (and possibly Hippomenes' charms as well), and the delay in picking them up cost her the race:

Hippomenes, when he wished to wed
a maid, took apples in his hand
and ran a race. When Atalanta
saw him, how she lost her head!
Plumb into Eros took the leap![21]

But marriage was a difficult institution for a wild girl like Atalanta. When she and her new husband were out hunting and stumbled upon a precinct of Zeus or Kybele, they violated all religious taboos by having sex there. So that they could never repeat the offence, Zeus transformed them into a lion and lioness, which ancient mythographers explained according to a belief that lions mate with leopards, not lionesses. Kybele took pity on them and harnessed them to her chariot. A more modern interpretation is that this shows Atalanta reverting to her original wild state in a myth that examines Greek gender perceptions: women have a 'wild' side which must be tamed by men for society to function normally, and there can be no question of compatibility between the (female) roles of wife and mother with the (male) roles of hunter and warrior. The social significance of the Atalanta tale lies in the examination of the reality of women living out their potential wildness.

Atalanta was a popular figure in Greek art and appears either hunting the Kalydonian Boar – easily recognizable on the François Vase by her white skin among the black flesh of the men – or grappling with Peleus, sometimes clad in a short tunic or in a sporty bikini-like ensemble. In later art the Dutch painter Van Balen, who specialized in mythological subjects, produced *Atalanta and the Golden Apples* (1619), where Atalanta is in the process of picking up one of the apples as Hippomenes moves away with a furtive glance over his shoulder.

The Sons of Aiolos and Their Descendants

Through his male progeny Aiolos became the ancestor of a number of interesting characters: Athamas, Kretheus, and two of the great transgressors of Greek mythology – Sisyphos and Salmoneus.

Athamas was ruler of Boiotia. His wife Nephele bore him a son named Phrixos and a daughter called Helle, but the family equilibrium was upset when he married Ino, and sired Learkhos and Melikertes. The new wife plotted against the children of the old, and by persuading the local women to parch the wheat, she engineered the failure of that year's crops. Athamas consulted the Delphic Oracle about the problem, but Ino persuaded the messengers to say that the solution was for Phrixos to be sacrificed to Zeus. He was saved either by Zeus himself or by an eleventh-hour intervention by Nephele, who gave him and Helle a ram with a Golden Fleece, which she had acquired from Hermes.[22]

Phrixos and Helle flew off to the East on the ram, but Helle slipped off, fell into the sea, and was drowned in the waterway that has been called the Hellespont (the 'Sea of

Helle') ever since. Phrixos got safely to Kolkhis, the realm of Aietes, son of Helios (the Sun) and the nymph Perseis, and brother of the enchantress Kirke (Circe) and Pasiphae, the notorious wife of Minos. Aietes not only welcomed Phrixos but gave him his daughter Khalkiope for his wife; Phrixos reciprocated by sacrificing the ram to Zeus Phyxios (the god of escape), and donating its Golden Fleece to Aietes, who nailed it to an oak tree in a grove of Ares.

Back in Boiotia, things went from bad to worse for Athamas, since Hera drove him and Ino insane, causing them to kill their chidren.[23] Athamas was banished, but received an oracle telling him to settle where wild beasts would entertain him. When he encountered a pack of wolves devouring some sheep, he settled there and named the place Athamantia.

Euripides wrote a tragedy, *Ino*, which dealt with the third marriage of Athamas. Ino had gone to the mountains in the service of Dionysos, and Athamas, who thought that she was dead, married Themisto, and fathered two children called Orkhomenos and Sphingios. But Ino secretly returned, and informed Athamas of her presence. He disguised her as a servant and brought her into the palace, and though Themisto discovered that her rival was still alive, she could not find out her whereabouts. She decided to murder Ino's children in a scheme whereby Ino's children would wear black clothes and her own children white, so that they could be recognized in the dark. Themisto confided this to the new servant and, needless to say, Ino swapped the clothes. Themisto killed her own sons, and when she realized her mistake she killed herself too.

Another son of Aiolos was Sisyphos, an archetypal trickster who in some traditions is the father of Odysseus. He is renowned principally for his punishment in Hades where Odysseus (who is not his son in Homer) sees him:

I also saw Sisyphos. He was suffering strong pains
and with both arms embracing the monstrous stone, struggling
with hands and feet alike, he would try to push the stone upward
to the crest of the hill, but when it was on the point of going
over the top, the force of gravity turned it backward,
and the pitiless stone rolled back down to the level.[24]

Homer does not specify why Sisyphos was punished like this, but other sources say his crime involved Aigina, the daughter of Asopos, who had been secretly abducted by Zeus. Sisyphos betrayed the secret so Zeus destroyed him with a thunderbolt. He is also said to have prevented Odysseus' (more usual) father Autolykos from stealing his cattle by writing 'Stolen by Autolykos' on lead plates attached to their hooves. He was also able to trick Thanatos (Death) twice: first by chaining him up, so that nobody died until the gods intervened and made Sisyphos release him (Sisyphos was inevitably Thanatos' first victim); second by persuading Thanatos to allow him to return to the world above to punish his wife for not giving him a proper funeral. Sisyphos had, of course, told her not to do this, and he proceeded to live to a ripe old age. His punishment was designed to keep him permanently out of mischief.

The other transgressive son of Aiolos was Salmoneus, founder of the city of Salmone in Elis. He was incredibly arrogant, to the point of wanting to put himself on an equal footing with Zeus. In fact, he claimed that he *was* Zeus. He decreed that all sacrifices to Zeus should be offered to him instead, dragged dried hides and bronze kettles behind his chariot to imitate thunder, and hurled flaming torches at the sky to simulate lightning. This gross impiety obviously incurred the wrath of Zeus, who blasted him with a real thunderbolt and wiped out his city along with all its inhabitants.

Salmoneus and his partner Alkidike did have time to have a daughter before his death, and in the version transmitted by Apollodoros, this girl, Tyro, was raised by Salmoneus' brother Kretheus. She fell in love with the River Enipeus, who was

> the handsomest of all those rivers whose streams cross over
> the earth, and she used to haunt Enipeus' beautiful waters;
> taking his likeness, the god who circles the earth and shakes
>   it [Poseidon]
> lay with her where the swirling river finds its outlet,
> and a sea-blue wave curved into a hill of water reared up
> about the two, to hide the god and the mortal woman.[25]

Having lost her virginity in this way, Tyro gave birth in secret to twin sons, but then exposed them. They were discovered by some passing horsekeepers, one of whose mares kicked one of the children and left a livid mark on his face. One of the horsekeepers rescued the children and raised them, or in another version Pelias was suckled by a mare and Neleus by a bitch. The child with the livid mark was named Pelias (Greek *pelion*), and the other Neleus, and they were subsequently rediscovered by their mother. Aristotle tells us that Sophokles wrote a play called *Tyro*, where the recognition of the abandoned children was achieved through the chest in which they were found; Menander, in his comedy *Epitrepontes*, says that an old goatherd found the children, and that they were recognized by means of a little leather bag of tokens. In Apollodoros' version, having rediscovered their mother and found out that their stepmother Sidero, Salmoneus' second wife, had abused her, they attacked Sidero with lethal intent. She managed to take refuge in the precinct of Hera, but Pelias cut her down anyway, and treated Hera with disrespect from that moment on. Subsequently Pelias and Neleus had a quarrel over who should control the kingdom, as a result of which Neleus was exiled. Pelias continued to live in Thessaly, where he became the father of Alkestis.

These motifs of exposed twins with a divine father and a human mother, suckled by animals, reared by a peasant, and quarrelling about a kingdom, invite comparison with Romulus and Remus at Rome, and it has been suggested that this Greek tale lies at the heart of the Roman story, which was introduced into the Roman tradition by a Roman historian called Q. Fabius Pictor.

Salmoneus' brother Kretheus founded Iolkos, from where his grandson Jason sailed in search of the Golden Fleece. Two of his other grandsons were Bias and Melampous ('Black Foot' because as a child his mother had put him in the shade but left his feet in the sun). In front of Melampous' dwelling was an oak tree where there was a lair of snakes. When this was destroyed by his servants, Melampous cremated the dead snakes and reared the survivors. The reptiles later cleaned out his ears with their tongues, with the result that he started to understand the voices of the birds, and so predict the future. This process was not uncommon: both Helenos and Kassandra acquired their prophetic powers when as children they were left overnight in a temple of Apollo, and serpents were found licking their ears in the morning. Indeed, in the folk-tales of many cultures people obtain knowledge of the language of animals from serpents.

Melampous' brother Bias was among the heroes who courted Pero, the much sought-after daughter of Neleus at Pylos. In fact, there were so many suitors that Neleus imposed rigorous conditions on them: Pero would go to whoever brought him the cattle of Phylakos,[26] which were guarded by an incredibly ferocious dog. Bias asked his brother to help him out. Melampous prophesied that if he did, he would be caught in the act and would have to endure a year's imprisonment, but he still offered his assistance, and was duly caught and incarcerated. In the end, he heard the woodworms in the roof say that the roof was on the verge of collapse, foretold the impending accident, and got himself transferred to another cell. When the building caved in, Phylakos was so impressed by Melampous' powers that he released him and asked how his childless son Iphiklos might rectify that situation. Melampous offered the information in exchange for the cattle, and Phylakos accepted the deal. The soothsayer dismembered two bulls and, when a vulture descended he heard how, when Phylakos had been castrating rams, he had put the bloody knife down beside Iphiklos, which had scared the boy into running away. His father had then stuck the knife into a tree and the bark had grown right over it. The vulture said that if they could find the knife, scrape the rust off it, and give it to Iphiklos in a drink, he would father a son. Melampous managed to find the knife and followed the instructions, with the end result of a son for Iphiklos called Podarkes. Melampous drove the cattle back to Pylos, won Pero as promised, and presented her to Bias.

Another grandson of Aiolos' son Kretheus was Admetos, who became ruler of Pherai in Thessaly. When Zeus punished Apollo for killing the Cyclopes,[27] the god had to spend a year in thrall to Admetos at the exact time when Admetos was wooing Pelias' loveliest daughter Alkestis. Pelias had stated that the successful suitor would have to be able to yoke a lion and a boar to a chariot. This proved a relatively easy task for Apollo, who then gave them to Admetos, who in turn took them to Pelias and won his bride. Unfortunately Admetos forgot to include Artemis in a sacrifice at the wedding, so when he entered the marriage chamber he found it full of serpents. Apollo told him to appease Artemis, and also obtained a special dispensation from the Fates that when Admetos was about to die, he could avoid the inevitable if he could find someone voluntarily to take his place. After various people refused, including Admetos' elderly father Pheres, Alkestis offered herself.

The events that occur when the fateful day dawns are brilliantly dramatized by Euripides in his first extant tragedy, the *Alkestis* of 438. At the outset Apollo confronts the hideous, implacable figure of Thanatos (Death), before we get a very moving portrayal of Alkestis, 'the best of women'. She dies quite early in the play, leaving Admetos to come to terms with her loss. One of the main themes of this play is the relationship of man to woman, set in the fundamental institution of that relationship: marriage – and a marriage at its best. This relationship is symbolized by the marriage bed, to which Alkestis calls as she dies, and there is an accepted inequality at the heart of this relationship: by marrying, Alkestis has entered the central institution of a male-dominated society, represented in the play by Admetos and the Chorus of Pheraian Elders. Her decision to die is taken out of a sense of duty towards her husband, rather than for passionate love, and conforms to the contemporary idea of what society believed a household should be like, although it is made clear that she is brave, gentle and full of loving kindness. Obviously she loves Admetos – she wouldn't be willing to die for him if she didn't – but her death scene concentrates primarily on her disillusionment with marriage, as she expresses her regret for the impulsive promise she gave on her wedding night. Yet in fifth-century Athenian society, a woman's life was ultimately at the disposal of a man, so Admetos had simply accepted her offer as a matter of course. Euripides himself avoids passing judgement and prefers to examine the effects from two sides: the all-male chorus uphold the views of the society they represent, and are concerned with Admetos' hardship; the female side of the picture is put by the slave women and is soon forgotten.

However, no sooner has Alkestis died than Herakles arrives, and Admetos feels obliged to conceal his grief and offer his guest the normal hospitality. This in itself raises delicate questions of tact and morality, but the following scene, between Admetos and Pheres, takes this to a whole new level. Admetos feels bitter and resentful:

> What man on earth could match your cowardice? Though as old as you are, as close to life's end, you lacked the will, the courage to die for your son, renouncing this privilege to the woman who lies here.[28]

But Pheres is scornful of his complaints, and rejects them:

> I am under no obligation to die for you. I have inherited no such tradition from my ancestors, that fathers should die for their sons; it is not one recognised by the Greeks [. . .] You are happy to see the sun's light; do you imagine your father is not? It's a long time, I reckon, I'll be spending dead, a long time, and only a short one alive, but all the more precious for that [. . .] What a brilliant solution to the problem of dying – you simply persuade your wife of the day to die for you each time![29]

Meanwhile Herakles is drunk and inappropriately cheerful, at least until an outraged servant informs him of the truth of the situation. The mighty hero's response is to try to remedy the whole scenario, but in the meantime we see Admetos utterly devastated by grief. His error lies in accepting society's valuation of women. This has given him a false sense of deserved privilege, and so placed a contradiction in the basic concept of marriage: Alkestis may be 'the best of women', but she is still not worth the price of a man's life. Yet the extended life that Admetos has now achieved is utterly worthless:

> Friends, I count my wife's fate happier than my own, though it may not seem so. No pain will ever touch her now, nothing tarnish her good name, no more troubles weigh her down. But I, the man who cheated fate, who should not be living, will drag out my days in anguish. This truth has just come home to me.[30]

After the chorus have sung of necessity and death, Herakles reappears with a veiled woman, chides Admetos for not having been open with him, and teases him in order to delay the beautiful truth. He claims the woman is someone he has won in a contest, and asks Admetos to look after her. Admetos is distraught by this, because he had promised Alkestis that he would never remarry, but Herakles persists until he gives in. At that moment Herakles lifts the veil to reveal Alkestis, tells of how he fought a duel with Thanatos to win her back, and the overjoyed Admetos decrees public feasting and dancing.

Defining Humanity

Hesiod's tales of Pandora and Prometheus are by no means straightforward, and do not yield easily 'readable' underlying messages, but they do contain much of the Greek understanding of humanity's lot. In mythological terms, Hesiod presents us with a series of reasons for why life is as tough as it is. The events at Mekone also serve to explain the division of ancient Greek existence into the three areas of technology (fire and the arts derived from it), religion (sacrifice) and culture (Pandora and the family). Fire is at the heart of the story – it provides the wherewithal for technology, cooked food and sacrifice; and sacrifice illuminates the attitude of mortals towards the gods, coming across as both a shared act and also as an indicator of trickery, highlighting the cunning of the Greek mind on the human side, pitted against the deceptiveness of the world of the gods. We get to see the restraints that Hesiod sees to be operating on human behaviour, along with all the responsibilities and problems of (a Greek male's) life: sickness, old age, marriage, women. The Greeks generally regarded sacrifice, fire and marriage as fundamental characteristics of the human condition – they were key elements of civilization. They were felt to be missing in primitive times in Greece, when humans just lived like animals; and they were believed to be missing in historical times in Greece from the barbarians who inhabited the fringes of the known world. So what Hesiod is offering here is a definition of mankind under Zeus. Compared with this definition, the physical creation of mankind is less important: religious and cultural integration is what defines humanity.

The Afterlife of Prometheus

A totally different take on the Prometheus myth appears in the writings of Sigmund Freud. In many ways the tale lends itself very nicely to Freudian analysis, and, despite the fact that the names of Greek mythological characters (Oedipus, Cassandra, etc.) abound in his work, this was one of the few Greek myths that Freud actually did analyse.[31] In Freudian terms, the results of the analysis are straightforward enough at surface level:

- fire is a libido symbol;
- the fennel stalk in which Prometheus steals the fire is a phallic symbol;
- Prometheus' liver being devoured by the eagle of Zeus is a castration symbol.

But Freud is interested in why a hero who gives mankind fire and civilization should be so savagely punished. In his interpretation the myth is based on real people and events: fire could only be preserved if the 'natural' male instinct to urinate on fire (which he confirms by psychoanalysis) is repressed, and Prometheus was originally a law-giver who banned men from urinating on fire. The ban drew a mixed response: people liked having fire, but resented the repression of their libido, and so cooked up his punishment. For Freud the symbolism of the myth inverts fire and water: Prometheus gives fire, but forbids watering; the fennel stalk contains fire, but the penis it symbolizes contains water. When Herakles finally comes on the scene to slay the eagle and terminate Prometheus' punishment, Freud sees the inversion being inverted: Herakles broke the law, but he redeemed Prometheus by using his water to put out a dangerous fire.[32] So the ambivalent actions of Prometheus were compensated for by the unambiguously good deeds of Herakles. However, as one commentator has aptly observed, the analysis would carry more weight if man's 'natural impulse' to urinate on fire survived with sufficient vigour to extinguish our doubts as well.

Prometheus had a cult in ancient Athens, which celebrated his gift of fire to mankind with a torch race. In later times his role as a benefactor who suffers greatly on behalf of mankind invited analogies with Christ, along with more sinister connotations. In a fascinating *mélange* of pagan and

Christian ideas, the Church Fathers regarded Prometheus' sufferings as a mystical symbol of the Passion, and Tertullian described the crucified Christ as the 'true Prometheus'. On the other hand Emile Burnouf, the anti-Semitic director of the French School of Athens in the later nineteenth century, who was dedicated to proving that Christianity had an Aryan origin, not a Semitic one, published *The Science of Religions*, in which he derived the Christian cross from the swastika, a motif which Heinrich Schliemann, the excavator of Troy, said that he had 'recognized at first glance' as being connected with swastikas found on prehistoric pots in Germany – proof, for him, that Trojans belonged to the Aryan race. Burnouf asserted that it represented the two pieces of wood that were laid cross-wise upon one another in front of the sacrificial altars of the Aryans, before being rubbed together to produce fire, and proceeded to link the swastika with Prometheus, whose torment he understood as a prefiguration of the crucifixion of Christ: 'When Jesus was put to death by the Jews, this old Aryan symbol was easily applied to him.'[33]

In other less contentious post-classical traditions Prometheus' confrontation with Zeus came to symbolize resistance against tyranny, while his gift of fire was often equated with providing the spark of human intelligence. For the Romantic poets he was the human spirit tussling against priests and kings; Goethe interpreted him as a personification of doing good, not just dreaming of doing it; Vincenzo Monti's *Prometeo* of 1797 drew parallels between Prometheus and Napoleon as liberators from tyranny; and Byron saw Prometheus as a great enhancer of life. Shelley's drama *Prometheus Unbound* (1818–19) makes brilliantly creative use of the Greek tradition, with Prometheus not only championing mankind, embodying its highest moral and intellectual achievements, illustrating the struggle between good and evil, personifying the poet's creative energy, but also ultimately ushering in a golden age of love and beauty as Jupiter is overthrown.

Mary Shelley's horror story *Frankenstein, or The Modern Prometheus*, also draws on the Prometheus myth to engage with issues such as the creation of life and the limits of human ingeniousness, which are at the top of the modern debate over cloning and genetically modified foods ('Frankenfoods'). Wrestling with fundamental questions such as 'What would things be like if we really could create life?', the book and its adaptations in the cinema have given Frankenstein/Prometheus a very special status: the tale has now become traditional, and it is socially significant. It is a living myth.

4

JASON AND THE ARGONAUTS; MEDEIA

Key Characters

Pelias	King of Iolkos; sent Jason to find the Golden Fleece
Jason	Son of Aison; leader of the Argonauts
Hypsipyle	Queen of Lemnos
Herakles (Hercules)	The great hero; one of the Argonauts
Hylas	Herakles' companion
Medeia (Medea)	Daughter of King Aietes; lover, then wife of Jason
Aietes	King of Kolkhis; owner of the Golden Fleece
Kreon (Creon)	King of Korinth
Glauke (Glauce)	Kreon's daughter; Jason's second wife
Aigeus (Aegeus)	King of Athens

Aison, the son of Kretheus, had a son called Jason by Polymede,[1] daughter of Autolykos. Jason lived in Iolkos, which at the time was ruled by Pelias, who had received an enigmatic oracle:

> Beware and hold in all guard him of the single sandal
> when he comes down from the steep steadings
> to the sunny land of famed Iolkos,
> stranger be he or citizen.[2]

Pelias was offering a sacrifice to Poseidon and had sent for Jason, among others, to take part in it. Jason had to cross the River Anauros, and had lost one of his sandals, and when Pelias saw him he remembered the oracle. He asked Jason what he would do if he had received an oracle that he should be murdered by one of his citizens. Jason suggested ordering him to fetch the Golden Fleece. Pelias did just that, and, as it was at Kolkhis on the Black Sea, in a grove of Ares, hanging on an oak and guarded by a sleepless dragon, it seemed unlikely that Jason would return.

The tale of Jason's quest for the Golden Fleece is known from a number of sources, including Pindar, Diodoros, the Orphic *Argonautika*, Hyginus and Ovid, but the best-known version is that of Apollonios Rhodios, 'the Rhodian'. Apollonios, who was librarian of the Mouseion in Alexandria from around 261 to 246, is very much a poet of the Hellenistic Age.[3] He is learned, allusive and quite a difficult author for the modern reader, but after early career setbacks he became highly successful in antiquity, mainly as a result of his *Argonautika*, whose hero Jason is very different from the mighty heroes of Homer.

Apollonios starts by apologizing for not describing how Argos built the *Argo* under Athena's supervision – other poets have told the tale of how Jason called in Argos, son of Phrixos, who built a fifty-oared vessel named *Argo* after himself, and how Athena installed a speaking timber from the oak of Dodona at the prow. Once the Delphic Oracle had approved the mission, Jason assembled the finest crew that the Greek world could provide on the strand of Pagasai. Traditions concerning the precise make-up of the crew do vary, but there was no doubt that the Argonauts were a stellar group of heroes in all respects: 'the heroes shone like gleaming stars among the clouds'.

It could be that the mythical Argonauts reflect the sailors of the Greek Bronze Age, who journeyed into the Black Sea, and it is interesting that the core of the crew comes from the Minyans, who were based on Orkhomenos in Boiotia (a major Mycenaean city whose mythical founder was Minyas) and Iolkos in Thessaly. In the historical era, Greek cities justified their activities in the Black Sea area by claiming to have provided an Argonaut. This helps to explain the various irreconcilable rosters of the crew.

The Argonauts are not a generic, faceless 'crew' like the one that accompanies Odysseus: each one of them has his own specific motives for joining, they were united only for this one special task, they were specifically chosen, and they were specially competent to accomplish it.

Once the catalogue is complete, Apollonios moves in cinematic fashion from the heroes, through the crowd of admiring onlookers, to the female spectators who are lamenting the tribulations of Jason's mother and father, into the palace and finally to Jason. His leave-taking has a melancholy atmosphere at odds with his comrades' exuberance: theirs is the public arena of the Homeric hero; his is the private milieu so dear to Hellenistic poets. He tries to improve the depressing atmosphere in the room, which is not an easy task given that his mother is hanging on to him and the female servants are crying continually. He fails, then tries again, and his polite words cannot disguise his exasperation. Though the scene is charming, it is also rather chilling – a juxtaposition of beauty and the grotesque which Hellenistic taste was so fond of.

When at last Jason takes the public stage he is described in conventional terms and traditional wording.

And as Apollo goes forth from some fragrant shrine to divine Delos or Klaros or Pytho or to broad Lycia near the stream of Xanthos, in such beauty moved Jason through the throng of people; and a cry arose as they shouted together.[4]

This is Homeric. This is a hero. Yet a tinge of sadness deflates Jason's triumph when he is met by an ageing priestess of Artemis:

> And there met him aged Iphias, priestess of Artemis guardian of the city, and kissed his right hand, but she had not strength to say a word, for all her eagerness, as the crowd rushed on, but she was left there by the wayside, as the old are left by the young, and he passed on and was gone afar.[5]

This effect is repeated when Jason arrives at the shore. This is his first encounter with his crew, and Apollonios prepares to build him up:

> He came to the beach of Pagasai, where his comrades greeted him as they stayed together near the ship Argo. And he stood at the entering in, and they were gathered to meet him.[6]

The translation doesn't quite pick up the force of one of the Greek words used here: the main group stands *enantioi* ('in opposition') to Jason, and as he stands apart, we anticipate poetic clichés about his heroic qualities. Unfortunately, though, all his arrival has done is to turn his comrades' gaze up the beach:

> And they perceived Akastos and Argos coming from the city, and they marvelled when they saw them hasting with all speed, despite the will of Pelias. The one, Argos, son of Arestor, had cast round his shoulders the hide of a bull reaching to his feet, with the black hair upon it, the other, a fair mantle of double fold, which his sister Pelopeia had given him.[7]

Jason has been completely upstaged. Still, he asks the heroes to sit down and proceeds to address them, showing careful forethought and a strong sense of the responsibilities that will face the leader. Everything is ready, he says, except for one last thing:

> Now therefore with ungrudging heart choose the bravest to be our leader, who shall be careful for everything, to take upon him our quarrels and covenants with strangers.[8]

There really should be no choice here: this is Jason's moment; he has called them all together; they are on his family's soil; we know that he will win the Golden Fleece in the end; and he will be the leader. But that is not how it turns out:

> Thus he spake; and the young heroes turned their eyes towards bold Herakles sitting in their midst, and with one shout they all enjoined upon him to be their leader.[9]

This seems like a horrible betrayal of Jason, and things get worse:

> But [Herakles], from the place where he sat, stretched forth his right hand and said: 'Let no one offer this honour to me. For I will not consent, and I will forbid any other to stand up. Let the hero who brought us together, himself be the leader of the host.'[10]

It is as though Jason has been chosen simply because in the tradition of the myth he is formally the leader. Even though he will ultimately win the day, he seems very much second best now.

Still, as the *Argo* sets sail Jason's heroic qualities start to emerge. Apollonios' Jason is very much a new hero for a new age: un-Homeric, but modern and Hellenistic. Above

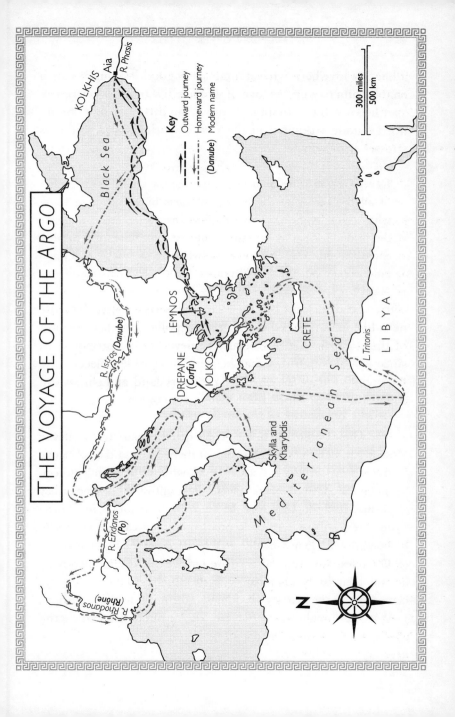

THE VOYAGE OF THE ARGO

Key

— Outward journey
--- Homeward journey
(Danube) Modern name

300 miles
500 km

KOLKHIS
Aia
R. Phasis

Black Sea

R. Istros (Danube)

LEMNOS

DREPANE (Corfu)
IOLKOS

Skylla and Kharybdis

CRETE

L. Tritonis

LIBYA

Mediterranean Sea

R. Eridanos (Po)

R. Rhodanos (Rhône)

N

all he is a love hero. He is fantastically good-looking,[11] which enables him to gain the love of women: his *arete* (effectiveness as a hero) is his sexuality. Beauty is an attribute that should not be underestimated in the Greek world, and Apollonios stresses it heavily:

> Never-yet had there been such a man in the days of old, neither of all the heroes of the lineage of Zeus himself, nor of those who sprung from the blood of the other gods, as on that day the bride of Zeus made Jason, both to look upon and to hold converse with. Even his comrades wondered as they gazed upon him, radiant with manifold graces.[12]

The effect of Jason's beauty on others is very noticeable, and he is likened in extended similes to Apollo or to the loveliest of the stars. In fact, his beauty achieves heroic proportions, since it is through this that he wins the Golden Fleece.

After five days at sea the Argonauts land at Lemnos, an island that was populated entirely by women:

> The whole of the men of the people together had been ruthlessly slain through the transgressions of the women in the year gone by. For the men had rejected their lawful wives, loathing them, and had conceived a fierce passion for captive maids whom they themselves brought across the sea from their forays in Thrace; for the terrible wrath of Kypris [Aphrodite] came upon them, because for a long time they had grudged her the honours due.[13] O hapless women, and insatiate in jealousy to their own ruin! Not their husbands alone with the captives did they slay on account of the marriage-bed, but all the males at the same time, that they might thereafter pay no retribution for the grim murder.[14]

The situation on Lemnos is one in which the 'natural order' of things has been inverted. The women, who resemble Amazons and find herding cattle, wearing armour and ploughing the fields easier than devoting themselves to the domestic arts, swarm down to the beach like raw-meat-eating followers of Dionysos. But here we see Jason 'in his element' as his *arete* becomes clear: his first important act in the narrative is to meet and acquire carnal knowledge of the Lemnian princess Hypsipyle.

When Jason goes for his initial interview with Hypsipyle he wears a gorgeous cloak that has been embroidered by Athene. It is clearly meant to be a counterpart to the shield of Akhilleus in Homer's *Iliad*, Book 18,[15] but the comparison is instructive: Akhilleus' shield is used in heroic combat; Jason's cloak is donned for amatory action. The cloak has many scenes: Cyclopes forging a thunderbolt for Zeus; Amphion moving rocks by singing on his golden lyre and Zethos lifting the peak of a mountain as they establish the foundations of Thebes; a triumphant Aphrodite looking like a tousled courtesan using Ares' shield as a mirror, her sexiness contrasted with the following scene where the Teleboai and the sons of Elektryon fight over some oxen, blood and death defiling the pastoral peace; the chariot contest between the lover Pelops and the implacable father Oinomaos (Oenomaus) for the hand of his daughter Hippodameia (Hippodamia);[16] Apollo shooting down the mighty Tityos who was attempting to rape Leto; and finally Phrixos, listening to the ram with the Golden Fleece.

Jason is totally successful on Lemnos, since the island is repopulated and restored to normality.[17] Apollonios is doing something very radical by showing a man in a heterosexual love relationship in an epic context. Homer's Odysseus, for instance, is a man who enjoys the company of women and deals with them confidently on the sexual level while remaining completely in control of every situation. Yet love means having to submit, and the Homeric ideology did not allow for that, except in the submission to one's own sex. However, the women of the *Argonautika* seem to be interested in Jason in a very deep and complex emotional way, and Lemnos anticipates Jason's exploitation of love as a means to his ends at Kolkhis.

From Lemnos the *Argo* journeys to Samothrace and thence to the Propontis and the land of the Doliones, who live in a society of perfectly ordered happiness that the Argonauts unwittingly shatter. Their newly married King Kyzikos has been told that when a band of heroes arrives, he should receive them kindly. This he does, but the following night adverse winds drive the *Argo* back to his territory, and taking them for a Pelasgian army (he was always being harassed by the Pelasgians) he leaves his bridal chamber to do battle, and is tragically killed by Jason in his first *androktasia* (man-slaying) of the poem. The tragedy of the termination of Kyzikos and Kleite's love is heavily emphasized:

No, nor was his bride Kleite left behind her dead husband, but to crown the ill she wrought an ill yet more awful, when she clasped a noose round her neck. Her death even the nymphs of the grove bewailed; and of all the tears for her that they shed to earth from their eyes the goddesses made a fountain, which they call Kleite,[18] the illustrious name of the hapless maid.[19]

Kyzikos was given a worthy burial, after which the Argonauts sailed away. At this point Jason's modern type of heroism is put perfectly into perspective by the removal of Herakles from the action. Apollonios was not forced by the tradition to include Herakles among the Argonauts, but he does so even though Herakles' heroic qualities are not necessarily essential to the success of the quest. His impressive feats of physical strength never really seem to further the cause – indeed they are usually useless or destructive. In short, Herakles is too anachronistic for this kind of Hellenistic narrative: in a story where seduction and magic are so powerful, violent physical exertion gets you nowhere. This is well illustrated when the Argonauts amuse themselves with a rowing contest in which the *Argo* speeds through sea so fast that not even the storm-footed steeds of Poseidon would have overtaken her, until the heroes have had enough. All except Herakles, that is:

> Herakles by the might of his arms pulled the weary rowers along all together, and made the strong-knit timbers of the ship to quiver. But [. . .] Herakles, as he ploughed up the furrows of the roughened surge, broke his oar in the middle. And one half he held in both his hands as he fell sideways, the other the sea swept away with its receding wave. And he sat up in silence glaring round; for his hands were unaccustomed to lie idle.[20]

The situation is essentially comical, but no one laughs. Herakles' abilities are closely circumscribed and do not usually extend beyond the deployment of brute strength, and the rowing contest is the prelude to the removal of Herakles from the narrative altogether. When the Argonauts land in Mysia, Herakles heads off to replace his oar, and finds an enormous pine tree:

> Quickly he laid on the ground his arrow-holding quiver together with his bow, and took off his lion's skin. And he loosened the pine from the ground with his bronze-tipped club and grasped the trunk with both hands at the bottom, relying on his strength;

and he pressed it against his broad shoulder with legs wide apart; and clinging close he raised it from the ground deep-rooted though it was, together with clods of earth.[21]

Meanwhile his companion Hylas had gone off to find water and discovered a spring called Pegai, where a water-nymph was captivated by his beauty,[22] and as he dipped his pitcher into the spring she pulled him into the waters. Polyphemos heard the boy's cry and set off in the belief that he was being abducted by robbers. He ran into Herakles and broke the news. The mighty hero broke into a frenzy, likened to that of a bull tormented by a gadfly, and was still looking for Hylas when dawn broke.

Weather conditions that morning were perfect for sailing, so Tiphys the helmsman urged them to embark. It was only when they were away at sea that the horrible realization that they had abandoned three of their companions hit them.[23] Amid the inevitable recriminations Jason was totally lost for words.

Apollonios' Herakles does not really belong in the Hellenistic world, but in a mythical age long past. He has the wrong kind of heroism, and the gulf that separates him from the Argonauts is stressed by his disappearance. From the outset he has been the foil by which Jason's special nature is illuminated. Jason is a romantic hero who will move out of the male-dominated context of traditional epic and into a new heterosexual milieu. His particular *arete* will triumph in the end, as Herakles – and the tradition for which he stands – withdraws in an outmoded pederastic pursuit.

From Mysia they moved on to the land of the Bebrykes, which was ruled by King Amykos, whose practice was to force strangers to have a boxing match with him, which invariably ended in fatality for the visitor. Amykos' challenge was taken up by Polydeukes (Pollux). The contest was one of

Amykos' bestial brutality (he is compared to a monstrous son of Typhoeus or Gaia) against Polydeukes' style and skill. The evenly matched bout was finally settled when Polydeukes dodged a haymaker from Amykos and shattered his skull with a counter-punch. Amykos' subjects immediately assaulted him, but the Argonauts were at his side in an instant, and, amid violent slaughter, they put the Bebrykes to flight. [24]

Jason's next port of call was Salmydessos in Thrace, the home of Phineus, a blind old seer[25] who was tormented by the Harpies, foul creatures graphically described by Virgil:

> No viler monstrosity than they, no pest more atrocious
> Did ever the wrath of god conjure up out of hell's swamp.
> Bird-bodied, girl-faced things they are; abominable
> Their droppings, their hands are talons, their faces haggard
>   with hunger
> Insatiable.[26]

Whenever a meal was presented to Phineus they flew down and snatched up most of the food, and whatever was left stank so badly that no one could go near it. So when the Argonauts asked him about the voyage, he said that he would advise them if they would rid him of the Harpies. Accordingly, the Argonauts set up a table as bait, and the shrieking Harpies swooped down and snatched the food away, leaving a hideous stench behind. Zetes and Kalais, the winged sons of the North Wind Boreas, immediately pursued the Harpies to the Floating Islands (Plotai), before Iris intervened and swore an oath that they would wrong Phineus no more, after which the islands were renamed the Strophades ('Islands of Turning') because that is where the sons of Boreas turned back. Other authors relate a version where the fate of the Harpies was to die at the hands of the sons of Boreas, and that one of the sons of

Boreas was to die when they could not catch a fugitive. In the chase, one of the Harpies (called Nikothoe or Aellopos) fell into the River Tigres in the Peloponnese, which came to be called Harpys after her; the other (called Okypete, Okythoe or Okypode) fled to the Echinadian Islands, which came to be called the Strophades because that was where she turned (Greek, *estraphe*) and collapsed with fatigue.[27]

Phineus gave the Argonauts instructions for their voyage, which hinged on being able to negotiate the Blue Rocks (Kyaneai), also known as the Wandering Rocks (Planktai) or the Clashing Rocks (Symplegades). These massive cliffs smashed together to close the passage, and no one had yet successfully navigated them. Phineus' advice was to let a dove[28] fly between the rocks, and, if it was able to pass through safely, row through the narrows at full speed, but they were not to make the attempt if it failed. Euphemos released a dove from the prow, and though the clash of the rocks sheared off its tail feathers, it was otherwise left unscathed. The rocks recoiled, and with Tiphys' brilliant steering, hard rowing, and the help of Athena, who held back one of the rocks with her left hand and pushed the ship through with her right, they managed to scrape through. Just the very end of *Argo*'s ornamented stern was damaged, and from that moment on the Clashing Rocks stood still, since as soon as a man in a ship had passed between them alive they became rooted fast to each other for eternity.

As the Argonauts sped on their way, they came to the desert island of Thynias, where Apollo appeared to them. At Orpheus' instigation, they built an altar in his honour and celebrated him with song and dance. Further along their journey they arrived among the Mariandynians, where King Lykos accorded them a warm welcome. But it was here that Idmon the seer died from a wound inflicted by a monstrous boar.

The beast was slain by Peleus and Idas, but Idmon died in his comrades' arms. It was also the destiny of Tiphys to die from sickness in that land and a crisis of confidence occurred until Ankaios undertook to take on the mantle of helmsman. He steered the ship on her way, touching on the territory of the Amazons at the mouth of the River Thermodon, and encountering ever weirder tribes such as the Khalybes, Tibarenoi and Mossynoikoi. Near Aretias, the island of Ares, they were attacked by birds whose used their feathers as arrows, but also met up with the sons of Phrixos (Kytissoros, Phrontis, Melas and Argos) who had been shipwrecked on the island. They issued dire warnings to the Argonauts about the enormity of the task ahead, but still agreed to sail with them to Kolkhis.

They continue to pass great landmarks of mythology: the spot where Ouranos and Philyra had made love and created the Centaur Kheiron; the Caucasian Mountains where the great eagle was still devouring the eternal liver of Prometheus; and finally the River Phasis in the land of Kolkhis.

Here, at last, Jason is able really to come into his own. Hera and Athena decide to ask Aphrodite to get her son Eros to work for the Argonauts. Hera has a long-term plan to use Aietes' daughter Medeia to destroy Pelias for violating her sanctuary and failing to honour her, and Eros promises to shoot Medeia with an arrow. Medeia's psychological subtlety goes far beyond that of a conventional Homeric heroine, and as both a young girl in love and also a dangerous witch, she will hold the key to Jason's success.

Jason's plan is to ask Aietes whether he will give up the Golden Fleece for friendship's sake. All men everywhere, even the most shameless, revere the ordinance of Zeus, god of strangers. Or so he thinks.

The Argonauts approve, and Jason sets off for Aietes'

rather amazing palace, taking the sons of Phrixos and two other comrades. As he enters Eros takes an arrow, strings his bow, and shoots Medeia:

> Speechless amazement seized her soul. But the god himself flashed back again from the high-roofed hall, laughing loud; and the bolt burnt deep down in the maiden's heart, like a flame; and ever she kept darting bright glances straight up at Aison's son, and within her breast her heart panted fast through anguish, all remembrance left her, and her soul melted with the sweet pain [. . .] coiling round her heart, Love the destroyer burnt secretly; and the hue of her soft cheeks went and came, now pale, now red, in her soul's distraction.[29]

Jason and his comrades secure an interview with Aietes and make their request. Aietes is singularly unimpressed: he suspects they want his kingdom as well as the Fleece, and says he regrets not having cut out their tongues and chopped off their hands. Jason asks again. Aietes then decides on a test, and dictates his terms. They must do something that Aietes himself can do:

> Two bulls with feet of bronze I have that pasture on the plain of Ares, breathing forth flame from their jaws; them do I yoke and drive over the stubborn field of Ares, four plough-gates; and quickly cleaving it with the share up to the headland, I cast into the furrows for seed, not the corn of Demeter, but the teeth of a dread serpent that grow up into the fashion of armed men; them I slay at once, cutting them down beneath my spear as they rise against me on all sides. In the morning do I yoke the oxen, and at eventide I cease from the harvesting. And thou, if thou wilt accomplish such deeds as these, on that very day shalt carry off the Fleece.[30]

Jason is speechless, but despite a real lack of self-belief ultimately he accepts the challenge.

Medeia is distraught because of her passion for Jason.
Now, on the advice of Argos, it is decided to apply for
Medeia's help through Khalkiope, who is Argos' mother and
Medeia's sister. Medeia agrees to help, but she remains racked
with indecision. Love and fear keep her awake at night:

> Fast did her heart throb within her breast, as a sunbeam quivers
> upon the walls of a house when flung up from water, which is
> just poured forth in a caldron or a pail maybe; and hither and
> thither on the swift eddy does it dart and dance along; even so
> the maiden's heart quivered in her breast.[31]

Should she give Jason charms to cast a spell on the bulls?
Should she take her own life? Helping Jason would alienate
her from her own family, but could she ever forgive herself
if she did not? After a night of tears she makes the decision:
she will give Jason a magic potion. She assembles her handmaids and sets out for a shrine to Hekate, where she intends
to meet Jason. His physical charms are particularly strongly
emphasized, and even his comrades are amazed by his radi-
ance. When the two of them finally meet, the air is electric:

> Soon he appeared to her longing eyes, striding along loftily, like
> Sirius coming from ocean, which rises fair and clear to see, but
> brings unspeakable mischief to flocks; thus then did Aison's son
> come to her, fair to see, but the sight of him brought love-sick
> care. Her heart fell from out her bosom, and a dark mist came
> over her eyes, and a hot blush covered her cheeks. And she had
> no strength to lift her knees backwards or forwards, but her feet
> beneath were rooted to the ground; and meantime all her hand-
> maidens had drawn aside. So they two stood face to face without

a word, without a sound, like oaks or lofty pines, which stand
quietly side by side on the mountains when the wind is still;
then again, when stirred by the breath of the wind, they murmur
ceaselessly; so they two were destined to tell out all their tale,
stirred by the breath of Love. And Aison's son saw that she had
fallen into some heaven-sent calamity, and with soothing words
[. . .] addressed her.[32]

The gist of what he says is that he needs her help very badly.
She is so in love that she willingly gives him the drugs he
needs, along with precise instructions on how to use them:
sacrifice to Hekate at midnight; ignore the sound of feet and
the baying of hounds; at dawn steep the charm in water,
strip, and anoint your body with it; you will feel a match
not only for men but for the immortal gods; sprinkle your
spear, shield and sword with it as well; you will just be invulnerable for that one day; do not flinch from the contest.
Then she gives instructions on how to deal with the events
of the coming day: the moment you have yoked the oxen,
ploughed all the field and sown the serpent's teeth, you will
find the Giants springing up; hurl a stone into their midst,
and like ravening hounds fighting over their food, they will
slaughter one another; jump into the thick of the conflict,
and the Fleece will be yours for the taking; then go. She ends
with a plea that he should not forget her:

Remember, if haply thou returnest to thy home, Medeia's name;
and so will I remember thine, though thou be far away.[33]

Jason promises not to forget her. In fact he does better: he
promises to marry her if she returns to Iolkos with him. They
each go back to their respective bases. Aietes gives the
Argonauts the dragons' teeth and Jason makes his preparations.

Interestingly he wears a garment that reflects his status as a love hero, though not one that indicates a great deal of commitment to his new love:

> And around him he placed a dark robe, which Hypsipyle of Lemnos had given him aforetime, a memorial of many a loving embrace.[34]

Jason duly completes the required rituals and the following morning he prepares for the contest. Every hero has his moment – his *aristeia* as it is known. This is Jason's. Medeia's charms make his weapons unbreakable, and a terrible, unspeakable, dauntless prowess enters into him. He looks like a cross between Ares and Apollo as he surveys the field, the bronze yoke and the adamant plough. The bulls rush from their lair, roaring and snorting fire, and though the heat plays around him, battering him like lightning, Medeia's salves protect him, and he proves equal to their onslaught. He throws the bulls to their knees, wrestles them into the yoke, and ploughs the field and sows the dragon's teeth before scaring the bulls off and returning to the ship to quench his thirst. His comrades are thrilled by the success of the day so far; Aietes marvels at his might.

By now the earth-born men are springing up over the entire field, armed with sturdy shields, double-pointed spears and shining helmets whose gleam reaches Mount Olympos. Jason seizes a huge boulder, which four strapping youths could not even have raised off the ground, and hurls it a long way into their midst. The earth-born warriors turn upon one another; Jason seizes the moment to attack, draws his sword, and mows them down until the furrows are filled with blood. As the day comes to a close, so does Jason's successful *aristeia*.

King Aietes went back to his city, but although Jason had done all that had been asked of him, he still would not surrender the Golden Fleece. Indeed, he wanted to destroy the *Argo* and her crew. But before he could do so, Medeia, who was in a terrible state, fled from the palace by night and joined the Argonauts. Her offer to lull the Fleece's guardian serpent to sleep and deliver it to the Argonauts was matched by an oath from Jason to marry her as soon as they all got back to Greece.

The Argonauts sailed to the grove of Ares where the Golden Fleece was kept. It was a wonder to behold, like a cloud blushing red with the beams of the rising sun, but right in front of it, hissing hideously, writhed the serpent with his keen, sleepless eyes. Medeia went up to him and a fearful Jason followed, but the serpent was already being charmed by her song, and was relaxing the long ridge of his massive spine, and stretching out his coils. There was still a chance that he might raise his grisly head and trap them in his murderous jaws, but she brought out her mystic brew, sprinkled his eyes with a freshly cut spray of juniper, and chanted her song. The serpent let his jaw sink down, and his countless coils stretched out all through the wood.[35]

Jason grabbed the Golden Fleece from the oak and they left the grove in high spirits, with Jason raising the Fleece in his hands, and its red flush settling on his face like a flame. With their mission accomplished the Argonauts set sail for home, but when the Kolkhians discovered what had happened, they set off in pursuit. The Argonauts made landfall in Paphlagonia, where Argos showed them the right route to take.[36] They sailed up the River Istros (Danube), and along one of its branches into the Adriatic, only to find their progress barred by the Kolkhians, who had anticipated them. At this point an agreement was proposed between the

Argonauts and Apsyrtos, Medeia's brother and the leader of the pursuing Kolkhians: the Argonauts could keep the Golden Fleece, but they must surrender Medeia. Predictably outraged, she reproached Jason, but offered to help entrap Apsyrtos, who was duly lured into an ambush, where Jason cut him down.[37] His blood spattered Medeia's dress and veil – a fact noted by the Fury – while Jason lopped off his victim's extremities. The Kolkhians with him were slaughtered by the Argonauts, who rowed off to the Isle of Amber at the mouth of the River Eridanos (Po). Zeus was outraged at the murder of Apsyrtos, and Hera sent a raging storm that drove them off course. The talking beam in the *Argo* then informed them that the wrath of Zeus would not abate until they were purified by Medeia's aunt Kirke (Circe).

They sailed along the Eridanos, past the outfall of the lake where Phaethon fell into the water from the chariot of the sun.[38] From there they made their way into the Rhône, avoided the Celtic and Ligurian tribes, voyaged through the Sardinian Sea past the Stoikhades Islands, bypassed Elba, skirted Tyrrhenia and finally reached Aiaia, where Kirke performed the purificatory rites: a sucking pig was held over the homicides; its throat was cut; and their hands were sprinkled with its blood; and Zeus was invoked. Only then does Kirke get to know the nature of the crime. She immediately dismisses Jason and Medeia.

By this stage of their journey the Argonauts are in territory familiar from Homer's *Odyssey*, or rather, we should say that the *Odyssey* makes use of incidents drawn from the *Argonautika*, since it speaks of 'celebrated *Argo*'.[39] They pass Anthemoessa ('Flowery'), the island of the Sirens, the singing enchantresses who bewitched sailors with their seductive melodies. The tradition surrounding them is very confused. Homer implies that there were two of them, as does Sophokles, who calls them daughters of Phorkys; Apollodoros says there were three of them – Pisinoe, Aglaope and Thelxiepia, daughters of Akheloos and the Muse Melpomene;[40] Tzetzes calls them Parthenope, Leukosia and Ligia, children of Akheloos and the Muse Terpsikhore, and so agrees with Apollonios' parentage;[41] other sources name four Sirens, namely Teles, Raidne, Molpe and Thelxiope (again offspring of Akheloos by Melpomene).

In Homer's *Odyssey* they sing a duet, but elsewhere one of them plays the lyre, one sings, and one plays the pipes, using their virtuosity to lure sailors to their deaths.[42] Homer says nothing about their physical form, but other sources, including the visual arts, make them human on top and birds from the thighs down. This hybrid form is explained in a number of ways: either they had been playing with Persephone when she was abducted, and they begged the gods to give them wings to facilitate their search for her; or the wings and feathers were a punishment imposed by Demeter for them allowing Hades to carry off Persephone; or the love goddess Aphrodite turned them into birds because they wanted to remain unmarried. The Argonauts successfully negotiated sailing past the Sirens thanks to the musical prowess of Orpheus, whose singing neutralized the power of their song. There was nearly one casualty, however: Boutes swam off to the Sirens, but Aphrodite rescued him and settled him in Lilybaeum.

The *Argo* next encountered the sheer cliff of Skylla and the seething roar of Kharybdis, followed by the Planktai or Wandering Rocks, above which flame and smoke had been seen rising.[43] Fortunately for Jason, the sea goddess Thetis and a host of other Nereids (sea-nymphs) steered the ship through the rocks, playing with it as though it were part of a girlish game.

Onward they sailed, past the Island of Thrinakia, where the milk-white, golden-horned Cattle of the Sun were pastured. Then it was on to Drepane,[44] the island of the Phaiakians (Phaeacians), whose ruler Alkinoos (Alcinous) welcomed them. Here a party of Kolkhians turned up, and demanded that Alkinoos should surrender Medeia to them. Alkinoos' response was that if Medeia was still a virgin he would send her back to her father, but if she was not, he would give her to Jason, and his wife, Queen Arete, forced the issue by arranging for Medeia to consummate her relationship with Jason in a sacred cave with the Golden Fleece on top of their bed.

With their marriage now official, they put to sea again, laden with gifts from Alkinoos and Arete, and were in sight of the Peloponnese when they were driven by a storm to Libya and the Syrtis. This was a lifeless wasteland, a gulf from which no shipping could escape, with shoals and seaweed everywhere, and sand stretching as far as the eye could see. When a tidal wave drove the *Argo* a long way inland, they would have perished if some local nymphs had not galvanized them into action with an enigmatic oracle:

'And when Amphitrite has straightway loosed Poseidon's swift-wheeled car, then do ye pay to your mother a recompense for all her travail when she bare you so long in her womb.'[45]

A monstrous horse then emerged from the sea and provided Peleus with a clue: Amphitrite had just unyoked Poseidon's horses; 'our mother' and her 'womb' was the *Argo*; and the 'recompense' meant that they should carry the ship. So they took the *Argo* on their shoulders to Lake Tritonis, near to the Garden of the Hesperides, where Herakles had performed his Labour of fetching the Golden Apples only the day before,[46] and had created a spring, where they slaked their raging thirst.

Two Argonauts met their deaths here: Kanthos, killed in a raid to steal sheep; and Mopsos, bitten by a deadly snake. The god Triton gave Euphemos a clod of earth as a gift, and then conducted the *Argo* back into the Mediterranean Sea.

Back on course, they were hindered from touching at Dikte on Crete by Talos,[47] a bronze giant descended from the men of the Bronze Age as told by Hesiod. Talos had been given to Europa by Zeus to guard the island, running around it three times every day and hurling massive rocks at approaching mariners. Medeia's magic caused him to graze his ankle, which was his one vulnerable spot, against a jagged rock, so that all the *ikhor* that filled the only vein in his body gushed out like molten lead.[48] He tottered and fell lifeless to the ground.

The following night the *Argo* encountered a violent storm, but Apollo came down from Olympos and flashed beams of light over the sea, which allowed them to pick out a nearby island and anchor safely. They called it Anaphe ('Revelation'), because it had been revealed to them by Apollo, and they founded an altar of Radiant Apollo; the twelve handmaids that Arete had given to Medeia engaged in some light-hearted ribaldry with the chiefs, as a result of which it was always customary for women to jest at the sacrifice to Apollo, Lord of Light and protector of the Isle of Revelation. The scholarly Apollonios often explains his stories aetiologically like this,[49] referring to ancient customs, conjectural derivations or rationalizations. In many ways this prefigures much modern scholarship, which since the nineteenth century has often tried to pinpoint the sources of myths, work out their dates and places of origin, and to connect them to religion, economics and social life.

Euphemos dropped his clod of earth in the sea just north of Crete, and it became the island of Kalliste (Thera/Santorini). They moved on from there to Aigine, where they stayed for a single night to draw water, and had a contest as to who could transport the water to the ship the quickest. And from there Apollonios brings them somewhat abruptly home:

> Be gracious, race of blessed chieftains! And may these songs year after year be sweeter to sing among men. For now have I come to the glorious end of your toils; for no adventure befell you as ye came home from Aigine, and no tempest of winds opposed you; but quietly did ye skirt the Kekropian land and Aulis inside of Euboia and the Opuntian cities of the Lokrians, and gladly did ye step forth upon the beach of Pagasai.[50]

They had successfully completed the whole voyage in four months.

The *Medeia* by Euripides

Back in Iolkos, Pelias never imagined that Jason could possibly return from the quest for the Golden Fleece, and so murdered Jason's father Aison. Aison chose the manner of his own death, and drank bull's blood.[51] Jason's mother cursed Pelias and hanged herself, [52] while Pelias completed the carnage by slaying her infant son Promakhos. On his return Jason gave Pelias the Golden Fleece, but waited before moving to avenge his family. He sailed to the Isthmus, dedicated the *Argo* to Poseidon, and then asked Medeia to find a way to punish Pelias. Hera had in fact brought her to Iolkos to do just that, and the sorceress performed a staggering feat of magic:

> The daughters [of Pelias] brought forward a sheep, a clapped-
> out creature
> of years untold, with its horns all twisted around its forehead.
> Medeia then thrust her Thessalian knife in its scraggy old
> throat

(the metal was hardly stained, as the blood was so thin), and
    plunged
the carcass into a cauldron containing her potent mixture.
The ram's frame shrunk and its years burned up along with
    its horns;
then a feeble bleating was heard right down in the depths of
    the cauldron,
and while they were all still frozen in wonder, a lamb jumped
    out
and friskily scampered away in search of an udder to suck.[53]

Medeia then persuaded Pelias' daughters that they could reju-
venate Pelias in the same way. When this inevitably resulted
in an agonizing death for Pelias, Jason and Medeia were
expelled from Iolkos. They went to Korinth, had children,
and lived happily for ten years, until Jason decided to upgrade
his marriage to Medeia in favour of a wedding to Glauke,
the daughter of King Kreon of Korinth.

This is the situation that we find at the beginning of Euripides' magnificent tragedy *Medeia* (*Medea*), performed in
Athens in 431, whose heroine is one of the finest creations
of Greek drama. From the outset it is obvious that she is no
average woman; she is a larger than life character whose
emancipated intelligence and indignant words have great
impact in their statement of the wrongs done to women. She
takes on the mantle of champion of oppressed women, which
is closely connected with her maternal role, and she has good
reason to feel aggrieved: when Jason betrays her, she loses
everything. Medeia's nurse tells us of the situation:

Poor Medeia! Scorned and shamed,
She raves, invoking every vow and solemn pledge
That Jason made her, and calls the gods as witnesses

What thanks she has received for her fidelity.
She will not eat; she lies collapsed in agony,
Dissolving the long hours in tears [. . .]
                    Poor Medeia! Now
She learns through pain what blessings they enjoy who are not
Uprooted from their native land. She hates her sons:
To see them is no pleasure to her. I am afraid
Some dreadful purpose is forming in her mind. She is
A frightening woman; no one who makes an enemy
Of her will carry off an easy victory.[54]

After these notes of impending disaster, Medeia's children
Mermeros and Pheres now appear with their Tutor, a
typically Euripidean cynic who is far from surprised that
Jason has been unfaithful. While the children stand silent,
he relates the current gossip that Kreon intends to banish
the boys as well as their mother. Then we hear Medeia's
voice offstage:

Oh, oh! What misery, what wretchedness!
What shall I do? If only I were dead! [. . .]
Do I not suffer? Am I not wronged? Should I not weep?
Children, your mother is hated, and you are cursed:
Death take you, with your father, and perish his whole house![55]

Drawn by Medeia's cries, the Chorus of Korinthian women
now enters. They offer resigned, sympathetic consolation,
but Medeia continues to rave:

Come, flame of the sky,
Pierce through my head!
What do I gain from living any longer?
Oh, how I hate living! I want

To end my life, leave it behind, and die [. . .]
Mighty Themis! Dread Artemis!
Do you see how I am used –
In spite of those great oaths I bound him with –
By my accursed husband?
Oh, may I see Jason and his bride
Ground to pieces in their shattered palace
For the wrong they have dared to do to me, unprovoked![56]

All this worries the Nurse and the Chorus, but when she actually enters the stage Medeia seems very self-controlled. Her isolation is emphasized by the fact that she is foreign, strange, slightly barbaric, and originates from the borders of the known Greek world. In antiquity Euripides was often regarded as a misogynist, but Medeia's breathtaking speech seems to give the lie to that prejudice:

Surely, of all creatures that have life and will, we women
Are the most wretched. When, for an extravagant sum,
We have bought a husband, we must then accept him as
Possessor of our body. This is to aggravate
Wrong with worse wrong. Then the great question: will the
    man
We get be bad or good? For women, divorce is not
Respectable; to repel the man, not possible [. . .]
                         If a man grows tired
Of the company at home, he can go out, and find
A cure for tediousness. We wives are forced to look
To one man only. And, they tell us, we at home
Live free from danger, they go out to battle: fools!
I'd rather stand three times in the front line than bear
One child.[57]

This justly famous outburst ends with a subtly ironic twist when Medeia reminds the women in the Chorus that the same arguments do not apply to them: they have a city and a home, whereas Medeia is a complete outsider. Yet Medeia actually chose her husband, so what she says is more relevant to the wives in the Chorus than it is to herself.

The Chorus are silenced by her eloquence, and she asks them to remain so as she seeks to gain her revenge on Jason. In this way, the Chorus become uneasy spectators, very ordinary people torn between sympathy and horror at what they witness. Medeia's violations of divine and human law stand out all the more against the background of these mundane women.

King Kreon now appears and confirms that Medeia has to go into exile. He is totally honest about his reasons:

> I fear you. Why wrap up the truth? I fear that you
> May do my daughter some irreparable harm.
> A number of things contribute to my anxiety.
> You're a clever woman, skilled in many evil arts;
> You're barred from Jason's bed, and that enrages you.
> I learn too from reports, that you have uttered threats
> Of revenge on Jason and his bride and his bride's father.
> I'll act first, then, in self-defence. I'd rather make you
> My enemy now, than weaken, and later pay with tears.[58]

Medeia hates the fact that her reputation for cleverness is dangerous. This idea that women are more devious than men and are constantly up to mischief is as old as Homer's Hera, and this type of characterization of women was particularly associated with Euripides, whose heroines are often seen as equal or superior to men in nobility and self-sacrifice or more ruthless, cunning and unscrupulous.

In his comedy *Thesmophoriazousai*, Aristophanes portrays
Euripides trying to evade a death sentence imposed on him
by the wives for revealing their intrigues in his plays: their
husbands would have been none the wiser had he not
done so.

Kreon is tough, not a tyrant, and he reluctantly grants
Medeia one concession: she can have twenty-four hours to
organize the details of her exile. He persuades himself that
one day is too short for Medeia to do any harm, but this
humanity will be his undoing: one day is all she needs. The
moment he has gone she metamorphoses from the cringing
suppliant into the sinister sorceress. She reveals her plan:
Jason and his new bride must die. It is just a question of
how: if she can find someone to protect her from any reprisals,
she will poison them and escape, but if not she will kill them
with her own hands and face the consequences. She prays
to Hekate, the dark spirit of witchcraft, and reminds the
audience of her divine ancestry:

> Come! Lay your plan, Medeia; scheme with all your skill.
> On to the deadly moment that shall test your nerve!
> You see now where you stand. Your father was a king,
> His father was the Sun-god: you must not invite
> Laughter from Jason and his new allies, the tribe
> Of Sisyphos. You know what you must do. Besides –
> > [*She turns to the Chorus.*]
> We were born women – useless for honest purposes.
> But in all kinds of evil skilled practitioners.[59]

The Chorus reply with a lament about the way women are
treated in the mythological tradition. It is so unfair to accuse
women of lies and deceit, when men behave like Jason has
done.

Legend will now reverse our reputation;
A time comes when the female sex is honoured [. . .]
Male poets of past ages, with their ballads
Of faithless women, shall go out of fashion;

For Phoebus, Prince of Music,
Never bestowed the lyric inspiration
Through female understanding –
Or we'd find themes for poems,
We'd counter with our epics against man.[60]

At last Jason enters. He is a clearly drawn, unreconstructed Greek male. Euripides has only shown him to us from the perspective of people who are biased against him, but we still wonder how he might justify himself. But he doesn't even try – his new marriage is obviously the right thing to do, and everything else is Medeia's fault. In his arrogant, self-righteous way he truly believes that what he has done is good for himself, and so must be right. He has offered Medeia financial support in her banishment and thinks that this has discharged his obligations. Issues of love, trust and honour count for nothing, and the man that Apollonios made into a romantic hero is here shown as selfish and unfeeling. Medeia is incensed by what she hears, and reminds him of everything she has done for him:

When you were sent
To master the fire-breathing bulls, yoke them, and sow
The deadly furrow, then I saved your life; and that
Every Greek who sailed with you in the *Argo* knows.
The serpent that kept watch over the Golden Fleece,
Coiled round it fold on fold, unsleeping – it was I
Who killed it, and so lit the torch of your success.

I willingly deceived my father; left my home;
With you I came to Iolkos by Mount Pelion,
Showing much love and little wisdom. There I put
King Pelias to the most horrible of deaths
By his own daughters' hands, and ruined his whole house.
And in return for this you have the wickedness
To turn me out, to get yourself another wife,
Even after I had borne you sons![61]

She makes the very valid point that there is absolutely nowhere she can go, yet Jason is amazed at her ingratitude. He tells her how much she has benefited from their relationship, and argues that, although she did indeed save his life, Aphrodite should really get the credit, because she made Medeia fall for him in the first place. He tells her to count her blessings:

You left a barbarous land to become a resident
Of Hellas; here you have known justice; you have lived
In a society where force yields place to law.
Moreover, here your gifts are widely recognised,
You are famous; if you still lived at the ends of the earth
Your name would never be spoken.[62]

It never occurs to him that Medeia's celebrity is a curse to her, or that his behaviour is hardly a brilliant example of Greek justice. Women, he says, are so unreasonable: they cannot tell what is good for them; they think it's the end of the world if their husband wants a new wife:

Was such a plan, then, wicked? Even you would approve
If you could govern your sex-jealousy. But you women
Have reached a state where, if all's well with your sex-life,
You've everything you wish for; but when that goes wrong,

> At once all that is best and noblest turns to gall,
> If only children could be got some other way,
> Without the female sex! If women didn't exist,
> Human life would be rid of all its miseries.[63]

Medeia and Jason descend into bickering, and he stomps off to the palace, with Medeia's angry words ringing in his ears. These exchanges introduce an interesting aspect of male–female relationships in tragedy: woman + *eros* (sexual desire) = bad. Women of a strongly sexual nature often come to bad ends in tragedy, as does Glauke in this play. Euripides has seen how a woman's reproductive function puts her at the mercy of man and demands qualities like consideration and mercy, which were often at a premium in fifth-century men. Also, women's sexual desires were as great as men's, but their pursuits were more difficult. To make matters worse, as a result of being physically weaker, the usual way out was through trickery: feminine power was not overt, and this made it seem all the more devilish and sinister. In this context, the Chorus of everyday 'women in the street' now sing of the mixed blessings of Love, and stress the classic Greek maxim that moderation is best:

> Let Innocence, the gods' loveliest gift,
> Choose me for her own;
> Never may the dread Cyprian[64]
> Craze my heart to leave old love for new,
> Sending to assault me
> Angry disputes and feuds unending;
> But let her judge shrewdly the loves of women
> And respect the bed where no war rages.[65]

An old traveller now appears on the stage. He is King Aigeus of Athens, and Medeia instantly throws herself on his mercy,

tells him her story, hints that she knows of drugs that will
put an end to his sterility, and begs him to shelter her.
Although he is somewhat circumspect, he still takes the bait:

> If you come
> Yourself to Athens, you shall have sanctuary there;
> I will not give you up to anyone. But first
> Get clear of Korinth without help; the Korinthians too
> Are friends of mine, and I don't wish to give offence.[66]

Aigeus' promise allows her to proceed with her plan, which
is to send her sons with a robe and golden diadem as presents
for Glauke. But the gifts are impregnated with deadly poison
and will bring a hideous death. And there is one other matter:

> I will kill my sons.
> No one shall take my children from me. When I have made
> Jason's whole house a shambles, I will leave Korinth
> A murderess, flying from my darling children's blood.
> Yes, I can endure guilt, however horrible;
> The laughter of my enemies I will not endure [. . .]
> He shall never see alive again
> The sons he had from me [. . .]
> From his new bride he never
> Shall breed a son.[67]

The Chorus are utterly horrified and in an effort to dissuade
her they sing an exquisite ode to the glories of Athens, and
wonder how a city standing for truth and justice will give
sanctuary to a murderess. But Medeia is adamant. She has
sent for Jason again, and when he returns her role-play is
chilling: she becomes humble, reasonable, submissive and
apologetic:

> I saw my foolishness;
> I saw how useless anger was. So now I welcome
> What you have done; I think you are wise to gain for us
> This new alliance, and the folly was all mine.
> I should have helped you in your plans, made it my pleasure
> To get ready your marriage-bed, attend your bride.
> But we women – I won't say we are bad by nature,
> But we are what we are. [68]

She calls out her sons and tells them to hug their father, and although she is in danger of breaking down as she thinks of what is going happen to them, she just about manages to keep control of herself. Jason is completely won over, and Medeia takes the opportunity to ask if the boys should take the gifts to the princess. Initially Jason is reluctant, but her arguments persuade him:

> Gifts, they say, persuade even the gods;
> With mortals, gold outweighs a thousand arguments.[69]

The boys follow Jason to Glauke's home, unwittingly taking the instruments of death with them, and so sealing their own fate and that of the princess. The Chorus lament their inevitable deaths, after which the Tutor hurries in to announce that the princess has accepted the gifts and pardoned the children. The children themselves return, and Medeia bids them farewell in one of the most moving scenes in the whole of Greek drama:

> All was for nothing, then – these years of rearing you,
> My care, my aching weariness, and the wild pains
> When you were born. Oh, yes, I once built many hopes

On you; imagined, pitifully, that you would care
For my old age, and would yourselves wrap my dead body
For burial. How people would envy me my sons!
That sweet, sad thought has faded now. Parted from you,
My life will be all pain and anguish. You will not
Look at your mother any more with these dear eyes.
You will have moved into a different sphere of life.[70]

She weakens and cuddles them, and then forces herself to be resolute again, fully aware of what she is about to do. They leave the stage for the last time, forlorn, silent, innocent victims ensnared in issues they know nothing about.

The atmosphere now veers from pathos to utter horror with the arrival of a messenger, who announces the death of the princess in brutal, vivid detail. She puts on the gown and the coronet, and alarm bells ring for us as she starts to admire herself in the mirror. Then Medeia's potions kick in. Glauke staggers, collapses, froths at the mouth, rolls her eyes and goes completely pale. When she comes to, the golden coronet discharges a stream of unnatural devouring fire, while the dress eats at her flesh. Her attempts to loosen the crown only make things worse, until she falls to the ground, grotesquely disfigured, barely recognizable, her flesh melted like gum-drops from a pine tree's bark.[71] That was not the end of the messenger's story, since when Kreon arrived on the scene and embraced his daughter's corpse he stuck fast to the dress, weakened with pain, and gasped out his life too.[72]

Medeia is exultant at the news, and now steels herself to murder her children. She goes inside, and a tense wait ends when cries are heard offstage, all the more poignant because these are the first sounds the children have made. Jason now enters, coming directly from the scene of Glauke's death, and in a state of panic about his children's safety, mainly because he fears that Kreon's kinsfolk will kill the boys in revenge. So he is doubly shattered when the Chorus tell him what has really happened.[73] Jason orders his men to unlock the door, and as the audience focus their attention on the central door, Medeia's voice is heard from over the roof: she is riding in a chariot drawn by serpents, and holds the children's bodies in her arms. Jason demands his sons; she refuses. As they taunt each other, Euripides introduces some aetiological material, with Medeia promising to create a festival at Korinth to expiate the murders. Her chariot then flies off, leaving Jason devastated and mourning for his sons as the Chorus reflect on the precariousness of life:

> Many are the Fates which Zeus in Olympus dispenses;
> Many matters the gods bring to surprising ends.
> The things we thought would happen do not happen;
> The unexpected God makes possible;
> And such is the conclusion of this story.[74]

Throughout the drama, Euripides has exploited mythological material to explore contemporary social questions like woman's status in a man's world, and the weakness of promises when opposed by self-interest. But he provides no answers: it has been well said that many Athenians in the audience would have seen their own problems reflected in the *Medeia* but would not have found them solved. The timelessness of those issues, and their sensitive handling by Euripides, are part of the reason for the continuing relevance of Greek myth to the modern world.

The story of the aftermath of these horrifying events is told by Apollodoros, in somewhat more prosaic style. Medeia went to Athens, married Aigeus, and bore him a son called Medos.

However, she was discovered to be plotting against Aigeus' son Theseus. In one account, Medeia was only thwarted in this when his father dashed the cup of poison from his lips. Medeia was consequently banished from Athens, along with Medos, who went on to conquer many barbarians, give his name to the Medes, and die fighting against the Indians. Medeia went back to Kolkhis, where she discovered that her father Aietes had been deposed by his brother Perses. Either she or Medos killed Perses and restored the kingdom to her father. In the version recorded by Hyginus, Medos gets to Kolkhis before Medeia, but is imprisoned by Perses, who has heard that he will be slain by a descendant of Aietes, even though Medos says he is Hippotes, son of Kreon. Kolkhis is smitten by famine as a result. When Medeia arrives, pretending that she is a priestess of Artemis, and discovers that Kreon's son is in Perses' hands, she sees a chance to take vengeance on Kreon by sacrificing the boy to stop the famine. But she recognizes her son in time, hands him the sacrificial knife, and he slays Perses.

The tradition has little to say on the death of Medeia. Hesiod implies that she was divine by including her in a list of goddesses who slept with mortal males;[75] Ibykos and Simonides suggest that she was married to Akhilleus in the Elysian Fields. Jason is sometimes said to have committed suicide in despair, but more usually he gets crushed to death by a rotting beam which falls off the *Argo*.

Legacy of Jason and Medeia

The *Argonautika* is really an agglomeration of myths and folk-tales. Stories like Jason's, where a hero is sent on a dangerous journey in order to get rid of him; he arrives at his destination; is confronted by tasks; and the daughter of the evil local ruler helps him to achieve his goal, appear the world over. The Norse *Mastermaid* and the Gaelic *Battle of the Birds* fit this pattern, and indeed Vladimir Propp, who analysed the Russian 'wondertale' and found that it consisted of thirty-one 'functions', applied this method to the *Argonautika* story and was satisfied that it fitted his scheme.[76]

The Golden Fleece itself has also attracted a good deal of speculation ever since antiquity. It is unquestionably the kind of generic treasure that heroes often go looking for, but the story was rationalized at a very early stage: one explanation was just that it became golden because there was gold at Kolkhis, and certainly the geographer Strabo thought that Jason was looking for gold. He introduced the explanation that it originated because the Kolkhians extracted gold dust using fleeces in the river; the Byzantine Suda says that the Fleece was actually a book explaining how to make gold by means of alchemy; and more recently Eric von Däniken has identified it as an alien flying machine . . .

Apollonios Rhodios was by no means the only author to deal with Jason and the Argonauts. The Argonauts' stay on Lemnos featured in plays by Aiskhylos and Sophokles, and some scholars have interpreted the Lemnian traditions as evidence that a local gynaecocracy, the rule over men by women, once existed. In Ovid's *Heroides*, which are poetic studies of distressed females, he explores the emotions of Hypsipyle after Jason abandoned her, and another Roman, Valerius Flaccus, wrote an *Argonautica* in the first century CE. The Renaissance also took to the story very well:

> Therein all the famous history
> Of *Iason* and *Medaea* was ywritt; . . .
> His goodly conquest of the golden fleece . . .
> The wondred *Argo*, which in venturous peece
> First through the *Euxine* seas bore all the flowr of *Greece*.[77]

The nineteenth century was equally receptive to the tale. Grillparzer's *Golden Fleece* carried the tradition into territory where myths were used simply as poetry, and they started to become merely vehicles for entertainment, particularly for children. Nathaniel Hawthorne's *Tanglewood Tales* (1853) made scintillating use of the Argonauts story, and, somewhat like Apollonios had done in his day, adjusted Greek mythology to fit the new age: 'These immortal fables are legitimate subjects for every age to clothe with its own garniture of manners and sentiments, and to imbue with its own morality.' [78] Charles Kingsley's *The Heroes* (1856) focused on the Argonauts and carried a heavy moral leaning towards courage and adventure: 'there are no fairy-tales like these old Greek ones, for beauty and wisdom and truth, and for making children love noble deeds and trust in God to help them through.'[79] The Argonauts also inspired William Morris into a poetic work half as long again as Apollonios', entitled *The Life and Death of Jason* (1867), where there is a strong element of medieval chivalry blended with the Greek mythology, and the tale emerges as an odd hybrid of Keatsian romance, Christian Socialist text, and mid-Victorian pornography, as when Jason betrays Medeia for Glauke:

> And once more on that night
> She stole abroad about the mirk of midnight,
> Once more upon a wood's edge from her feet
> She stripped her shoes and bared her shoulder sweet.
> Once more that night over the lingering fire
> She hung with sick heart famished of desire.
> Once more she turned back when her work was done;
> Once more she fled from the coming sun;
> Once more she reached her dusky, shimmering room;
> Once more she lighted up the dying gloom;

Once more she lay adown, and in sad sleep
Her weary body and sick heart did steep.[80]

In the twentieth century a brilliant adaptation of the tale was made in the iconic film *Jason and the Argonauts,* directed by Don Chaffey (1963), with some splendid special effects and a fine score conducted by Bernard Herrmann. On the other hand, the 2000 remake, directed by Nick Willing, fails to match up: a shabby collection of Argonauts; a love affair between the Argonaut-huntress Atalanta and Jason shoe-horned in; Poseidon appearing as a grisly giant; Phineus living in a Mycenaean-style *tholos* tomb; no Hylas episode, but Herakles forming a special bond with Jason and staying until the end; lousy acting; third-rate special effects; and embarrassing pronunciation of the classical names. Sometimes the Greek mythical tradition is best left well alone.

Medeia has also enjoyed a vibrant life outside Euripides and Apollonios. Scenes from her life appear regularly in Greek vase painting, whether she be perpetrating the death of Pelias, contemplating that of her own children, or flying away in her serpent-chariot. Pausanias gives a description of a cedar-wood chest, carved and adorned with figures of ivory and gold, known as the Chest of Kypselos, which was displayed at Olympia. On it, he says, was Medeia enthroned with Jason on her right and Aphrodite on her left, with the inscription 'Aphrodite commands: Jason marries Medeia'. The Roman playwright Seneca produced his own dramatization of the story, placing great emphasis on Medeia's violence and occult powers.

The post-classical arts also embraced Medeia's story in many different media. The French playwright Corneille, in Act 1, scene 5 of his *Medea* of 1634, gives her the memorable line:

NERINE: After such a disaster what do you have left?
MEDEA: Me, I tell you, me, and that's enough.

In the next century the Italian composer Luigi Cherubini was
inspired to produce his opera *Medea* (1797) whose demanding
title role was famously handled by Maria Callas, who sang
it in Florence in 1953, with Leonard Bernstein conducting.
In the nineteenth century Delacroix's powerful image of *The
Fury of Medea* (1862) depicted a distraught Medeia preparing
to kill her children. In 1913, somewhat ironically, given
Euripides' ancient reputation as a misogynist, excerpts from
his tragedy were recited at suffragette meetings, because they
seemed to resonate so strongly with the issues of the day. In
the *Médée* of 1953, Anouilh's heroine commits suicide on
her children's flaming funeral pyre after their murders; Maria
Callas made her only non-singing film appearance as Medeia
in Pasolini's compelling and controversial cinematic version
of *Medea* in 1970; and Euripides also lies behind *A Dream
of a Passion* (1978), directed by Jules Dassin, where Melina
Mercouri plays an actress who is both performing the role
of Medeia in a production of Euripides, and trying to understand a female prisoner who has murdered her children.
Earlier in her career, in *Never on Sunday* (1960) also directed
by Jules Dassin, Mercouri played Illia, a sassy, good-
humoured prostitute from Piraeus, who symbolizes modern
Greece's fall from its ancient greatness. She adores tragedy,
but constructs her own personal version of the myth,
complete with a happy ending. In the theatre she watches
Euripides' tragedy, and sobs bitterly until Medeia kills her
children, at which point she smiles and winks knowingly
at her companion, and confidently tells him, 'And every-
body's happy and they go to the seashore and that's all.'

5

ARGOS AND THE MONSTER-SLAYERS

Key Characters

Inakhos (Inachus)	Ancestor of the Argive rulers
Pelasgos (Pelasgus)	Founder of the mythical race known as the Pelasgians
Argos (1) (Argus)	Early ruler of the city of Argos
Argos (2)	'Panoptes', the all-seeing monster
Io	Daughter of Inakhos, beloved of Zeus, turned into a cow
Danaos (Danaus)	Egyptian, son of Belos, became King of Argos
Danae	Mother of Perseus
Akrisios (Acrisius)	Danae's father, killed by Perseus
Proitos (Proetus)	King of Tiryns
Bellerophontes (Bellerophon)	Sisyphos' grandson; tamed Pegasos; killed the Khimaira
Pegasos (Pegasus)	Winged horse, offspring of Medousa
Perseus	Son of Zeus and Danae; slew Medousa, married Andromeda
Medousa (Medusa)	The mortal Gorgon
Andromeda	Rescued by Perseus and became his wife

Argos and its environs play a major part in Greek mythology. The ancestor of the Argive rulers was Inakhos, the son of Okeanos and Tethys, and according to the first-century CE grammarian Apion, the flight of the Israelites from Egypt happened in his reign. He had a grandson called Apis who appears in Aiskhylos' play *Suppliant Women*, where he is a son of Apollo, a seer and physician who came from Naupaktos and eradicated monstrous snakes and plagues from the Peloponnese. Apollodoros tells us that he died without issue, and identifies him with the Egyptian bull god Apis, who was in turn identified with Serapis (Sarapis), an Egyptian deity combining the attributes of Apis and Osiris. Apis' sister Niobe was allegedly the first mortal woman with whom Zeus cohabited, and bore him a son named Argos, and also, according to one genealogy, a son called Pelasgos,[1] the eponym of the Pelasgians, the supposed aboriginal inhabitants of Greece.

This Argos was the great-grandfather of a monstrous multiple-eyed being, also called Argos,[2] who was known as Panoptes ('The All-seeing'). He had either an extra eye in the back of his head, two eyes front and back, or eyes over the whole of his body, which never slept all at the same time. He was incredibly strong, and generally cleaned up the Peloponnese region: he killed a bull that was ravaging Arkadia and dressed himself in its hide; he slaughtered a cattle-rustling satyr; and he destroyed Ekhidna, the half-woman, half-snake daughter of Tartaros and Gaia, who used to carry off passersby. However Argos Panoptes is best known as the guardian of Io, the ancestress of the royal houses of Argos and Thebes.[3] As a staggeringly beautiful virgin priestess of Hera at Argos, she attracted Zeus' amatory interests. He sent her suggestive dreams, which the oracles interpreted as meaning that her father should drive her out of the country. He obeyed, and Io was metamorphosed into a cow by either Zeus or Hera, and then driven all over the world by a gadfly, sent by Hera to prevent her staying in one place long enough for Zeus to have sex with her.

Io's tale is told differently, and more famously, by Ovid in his *Metamorphoses*. The King of the Gods told her to rest in some woods, but she fled in terror, and he threw a mantle of darkness over the earth and her. Hera's suspicions were aroused by the unnatural clouds: sensing that 'Either I'm wrong, or I'm wronged!'[4] she dispersed the clouds to find her husband in the company of a very beautiful white heifer, which had recently been Io. Hera cunningly asked for the beast as a present, and Zeus could not really refuse. Hera then detailed Argos the All-seeing to guard the girl/heifer, who was by now terribly distressed by her new appearance and voice. However, she was able to write her name in the dust with her hoof (the two letters iota and omega: I), and communicate the situation to her father Inakhos. Argos, however, moved her on to a more distant pasture.

Zeus found the situation intolerable, so he got Hermes to lull Argos to sleep with his pan pipes and then decapitate him.[5] Hermes then became known by the moniker Argeiphontes, 'Slayer of Argos', and Hera placed Argos' many eyes in the tail of the peacock, her royal bird. At this point the goddess sent a gadfly to torment Io the cow, and in Aiskhylos' tragedy *Prometheus Bound* she strayed to the crag where Prometheus was chained, and he predicted where she would wander: across what is now called the Bosphorus ('The Cow's Ford'), to Scythia, to the land of the Amazons, to the Graiai and the Gorgons, to the Griffins and the one-eyed Arimaspians, the dark-skinned Ethiopians, and finally to Egypt. In Egypt she recovered her human form and gave birth to a son named Epaphos (named after the touch, '*epaphe*', of Zeus that had led to his conception). Hera asked the Kouretes to steal Epaphos, and this they did, so Io set off once again and found him in Syria being nursed by the wife of the King of Byblos. She then returned to Egypt, where she married King Telegonos, and came to be worshipped as the goddess Isis,[6] and Epaphos as the bull god Apis.

The tale of Io's transformation into a cow appears in A.E. Housman's magnificent parody 'Fragment of a Greek Tragedy', where in a spoof of Aiskhylos and Sophokles, which also pokes fun at the style of many nineteenth-century translations of Greek tragedy, the Chorus sing:

> Why should I mention
> The Inachean daughter, loved of Zeus?
> Her whom of old the gods,
> More provident than kind,
> Provided with four hoofs, two horns, one tail,
> A gift not asked for
> And sent her forth to learn
> The unfamiliar science
> Of how to chew the cud.
>   She therefore, all about the Argive fields,
> Went cropping pale green grass and nettle-tops,
> Nor yet did they disagree with her.
> But yet, howe'er nutritious, such repasts
> I do not hanker after:
> Never may Cypris for her seat select
> My dappled liver!
> Why should I mention Io? Why indeed?
> I have no notion why.[7]

Io's son Epaphos later became ruler of Egypt and married Memphis, daughter of Nile, naming a new city after her; they had a daughter called Libya who gave her name to that region. Libya had twins by Poseidon: Agenor and Belos. Agenor migrated to Phoenicia, where he ruled Sidon or Tyre; Belos ruled Egypt and married Ankhinoe, daughter of Nile, who produced twin sons, Aigyptos and Danaos.[8] Belos settled Danaos in Libya and Aigyptos in Arabia, but Aigyptos was unhappy with this arrangement and so subjugated the tribe of the Melampodes ('Black Feet') and named it Egypt ('Aigyptos' in Greek) after himself. Each twin had fifty children by multiple wives: Aigyptos had sons, Danaos daughters. In the end they quarrelled, and Danaos, who suspected Aigyptos would take over Libya, took Athena's advice and built a ship (he was the first person ever to do this), put his daughters on board, and fled to Argos. On the way he put in at Rhodes where he set up the image of Lindian Athena.

When Danaos arrived in Argos a wolf appeared from nowhere and killed a prime Argive bull. This was interpreted as meaning that the outsider (Danaos) would prevail, and so the reigning King Gelanor surrendered the kingdom to him. He established a sanctuary of Apollo *Lykeios* ('Wolf-God'), solved the region's water crisis, and named the inhabitants Danaoi after himself: 'Danaans' became a generic name for 'Greeks' from Homer onwards.

Aiskhylos wrote a trilogy of tragedies on the daughters of Danaos. The first play, *The Suppliants*, now survives, but *The Egyptians* and *The Danaids* do not. In *The Suppliants* the sons of Aigyptos went to Argos in the hope of marrying Danaos' daughters, and though Danaos distrusted their motives, he was forced to agree to the match when the girls all threatened to hang themselves.

The marriages were arranged by a combination of drawing lots and matching partners who had similar names, and Danaos organized the wedding feast. However, he gave his daughters daggers, and told them to murder their new partners in the night. Forty-nine of them did this, but the eldest, Hypermnestra, spared Lynkeus, either because he had respected her virginity, or because she genuinely loved him. He escaped, but Danaos imprisoned Hypermnestra, while the rest of his daughters buried the severed heads of their husbands.[9] Finding new husbands for girls like this was obviously problematical, so Danaos promised to give them away as prizes in running races without the usual bride-gifts, and they did all eventually remarry. Lynkeus was reunited with Hypermnestra, reconciled with Danaos, and later became King of Argos,[10] although the Danaids themselves were punished in Hades by being made to pour water into leaky containers that had to be eternally filled.

Lynkeus and Hypermnestra stand at the head of a great royal line that includes Perseus and Herakles. Their grandson Proitos and his wife Stheneboia have a key role to play in the myth of Bellerophontes (Bellerophon). Bellerophontes was the son of Glaukos (sometimes Poseidon) and Eurymede (or Eurynome) and grandson of Sisyphos. He had to leave his native town, Ephyra (later called Korinth) because he had killed a tyrant of Korinth called Belleros:[11] his name means 'Slayer of Belleros'. He went to Proitos at Tiryns, who purified him, but Stheneboia (or Anteia) had less pure thoughts in mind. She fell in love with Bellerophontes,[12] but when he rejected her advances, she accused him of trying to rape her. Proitos believed her, and sent him to her father Iobates, King of Lykia, with a sealed letter containing instructions that he was to kill Bellerophontes. Iobates read the 'dire, life-destroying symbols',[13] but rather than kill his guest himself, he ordered Bellerophontes to slay the Khimaira ('She-goat', Latinized to 'Chimera'), believing that he would not survive the test. This monstrous creature was more than a match for many, let alone one, and Hesiod gives a vivid description of her:

Khimaira, who breathed awful fire,
Three-headed, frightening, huge, swift-footed, strong,
One head a bright-eyed lion's, one a goat's,
The third a snake's, a mighty dragon's head.[14]

The Khimaira's genealogy is hazy: Hesiod relates that it was
the child of Typhoeus and Ekhidna, or of the Hydra of Lerna
and an unnamed father, and she could possibly have been
the mother of the Sphinx and the Nemean Lion by Orthos,
the hound of Geryon. What was certain, however, was that
she devastated the country and its livestock. Most accounts
agree that Bellerophontes mounted his winged steed Pegasos,
the offspring of Medousa and Poseidon. He had seen this
fabulous horse by the spring of Peirene, and had tamed him
by following the instructions of Polyeidos the seer to sleep
on an altar of Athena, where he dreamt that the goddess
gave him a golden bridle plus orders to sacrifice a white bull
to Poseidon, Tamer of Horses. In the morning he found the
golden bridle beside him, sacrificed the bull, and Pegasos
willingly accepted him. They were a formidable team: with
Pegasos' aid Bellerophontes slew the Khimaira; when he
returned Iobates commanded him to fight the Solymoi single-
handed; then he ordered him to engage the Amazons in
combat; when Bellerophontes had conquered them as well,
Iobates sent the bravest of the Lykians to ambush him, but
he killed them too; finally Iobates showed him the letter,
asked him to stay, gave him his daughter Philonoe (or Antikleia or Kassandra), and bequeathed the kingdom to him.

In Euripides' tragedy *Stheneboia*, which no longer survives,
Bellerophontes took vengeance on Stheneboia by giving her
a ride on Pegasos and pushing her off when they were over
the sea. Another lost drama by Euripides, entitled
Bellerophontes, is wittily parodied by Aristophanes in his

comedy *Peace*: Bellerophontes attempted to ride Pegasos up to Olympos, but Zeus sent a gadfly to sting the horse, who threw his rider back to earth. Bellerophontes survived the fall, and he reappears in Euripides' play as a cripple wearing rags. Homer says that he ended up hated by the gods, eating his heart out and skulking away from the trodden track of humanity, but there is no tale that tells us how Bellerophontes died.

Perseus and the Gorgon Medousa

Back in the Argolid, when Akrisios ruled Argos, he received an oracle that his daughter Danae would produce a son who would kill him. So he had a bronze underground chamber constructed, complete with a small opening for air and light, and incarcerated Danae in it. Some authors say that Akrisios' brother Proitos seduced Danae and that this caused friction between them, but the best-known version is that Zeus had sex with her by turning himself into a shower of gold and pouring down into her lap. She gave birth to Perseus. Akrisios refused to accept that Zeus was responsible, and shut Danae and Perseus in a wooden chest and threw it in the sea. The chest floated to Seriphos, where Diktys, the brother of the island's King Polydektes, caught it in his fishing nets.

Perseus grew to manhood in Diktys' home, but Polydektes subsequently fell in love with Danae. Perseus hindered his attempts at courtship, though, so the king pretended that he was a suitor of Hippodameia, the daughter of Oinomaos,[15] and that he was collecting contributions towards the obligatory bride-gift. When Perseus boasted that he would bring him the Gorgon's head if he wanted, Polydektes felt that the chances of him returning were remote, and so gratefully accepted.

However, Perseus was aided on his mission by Hermes and Athena, who advised him to visit the Graiai – Enyo, Pemphredo and Deino – women who were daughters of Keto and Phorkys, and sisters of the Gorgons, and had been old since the moment of their birth. Between them they had one eye and a single tooth, which they took turns to share. Perseus grabbed the eye and the tooth, and promised to return them if they guided him to some nymphs who could help him in his quest. These nymphs gave him some winged sandals, the *kibisis* (a kind of bag) and the cap of invisibility; Hermes gave him a sickle made of adamant.

He flew to the river of Okeanos to the land of the three Gorgons, the immortal Stheno and Euryale, and the mortal Medousa. They had heads that were shrouded in writhing snakes, large boar-like tusks, bronze hands, golden wings, and they turned anyone who looked at them into stone. They were asleep when Perseus arrived, so he grabbed his chance. He averted his gaze and used a bronze shield to reflect their image, and while Athena guided his hand he severed Medousa's head. She was pregnant by Poseidon, and the winged horse Pegasos sprang forth from her neck, along with Khrysaor ('the Man with the Golden Sword'). Perseus stuffed Medousa's head into the *kibisis* and flew off, and though her sisters awoke and gave chase, it was to no avail: the cap of invisibility did its trick.

On his way back he passed through Africa. Ovid describes how he arrived in the land of the Hesperides and asked Atlas for hospitality. The consequences of his refusal were dire:

'Well, since you value my friendship
so little, here is a gift!' Then turning his face, he produced
from a bag on his left-hand side the loathsome head of
    Medusa.
The mighty Atlas was turned into a mighty mountain; his hair
and beard were transformed into trees, his massive shoulders
    and arms

to a line of ridges, his erstwhile head to a cloud-capped peak; his bones became rocks.[16]

Atlas the giant was now Atlas the mountain. Perseus then headed east to the somewhat vaguely located Aithiopia, where Kepheus was king. Here Perseus discovered Kepheus' daughter Andromeda chained to a rock by the sea-shore as food for a sea monster,[17] as punishment for the arrogance of Kepheus' wife Kassiopeia (Cassiopïa), who had boasted that she exceeded the Nereids in beauty. Poseidon empathized with the Nereids' anger, flooded the land and sent the monster. The oracle at Ammon pronounced that the situation could be rectified if Andromeda was sacrificed to the monster, and Kepheus was pressurized by the Aithiopians into doing this. For Perseus, though, it was love at first sight, and he promised Kepheus that he would kill the monster if he could have Andromeda's hand in marriage. Kepheus agreed; oaths were sworn; Perseus killed the monster by flying over it and attacking it with his sickle; and Andromeda was released. Unfortunately that was not the end of the matter, because Kepheus' brother Phineus was already engaged to Andromeda, and he now tried to prevent the wedding. Perseus simply showed Phineus and his supporters Medousa's head and turned them to stone, and so the marriage duly took place, and soon resulted in the birth of Perses, who was said to be the ancestor of the kings of Persia.

When Perseus arrived back in Seriphos, he found that his mother and Diktys had been subjected to violence by Polydektes, so he again unleashed the Gorgon's head and turned Polydektes and his cronies into stone. He installed Diktys as King of Seriphos, gave back the sandals, the *kibisis* and the cap of invisibility to Hermes, who returned them to the nymphs, and gave the Gorgon's head to Athena. She placed it in the middle of her shield, or in the centre of the *aegis* (aegis) – her goat-skin cloak with a fringe of snakes – to terrify her enemies. She also gave some of Medousa's blood to Asklepios, the god of healing: the blood from Medousa's left-side veins brought harm, but that from her right could raise the dead. Euripides tells a similar tale, whereby she gave two drops of blood to Erikhthonios, one a lethal poison, the other a powerful healing medicine. She also gave Herakles a lock of Medousa's hair in a bronze jar, which he used to protect Tegea, since it had the power to repel invaders.

Medousa is usually depicted in art as a very grisly creature, but she was not always really ugly: there is a tradition in which Medousa was beheaded because she had the arrogance to compare her beauty to Athena's, and Ovid says that it was her hair that was especially attractive, but that Athena turned it into snakes because she had sex with Poseidon in her temple.

Perseus finally returned to Argos with both Danae and Andromeda. His grandfather Akrisios was alarmed by their impending arrival because of the oracle that he would be killed by Danae's son, so he left Argos. Perseus continued on to Larissa, whose king, Teutamides, was holding funeral games in honour of his late father. Akrisios happened to be at the games as well, and, when Perseus entered the pentathlon, his discus throw accidentally hit Akrisios' foot and killed him outright. Realizing that the oracle had been fulfilled, Perseus was ashamed to return to Argos and claim his inheritance, even though it was technically his. Instead, he made an arrangement with Megapenthes, the son of Proitos, whereby Megapenthes became King of Argos and Perseus King of Tiryns. He also fortified and founded Mycenae, where he had more children by Andromeda: five sons[18] and a daughter named Gorgophone ('Killing of the Gorgon'). He and Andromeda were the great-grandparents of Herakles.

Patterns in the Myth

It is possible to detect some interesting symmetries under-lying the whole of this myth, which suggest that there is more to these tales than mere rollicking story-telling. For instance, there are some striking parallels between Danae and Andromeda.

Danae	Andromeda
Pursued by her paternal uncle (Proitos)	Pursued by her paternal uncle (Phineus)
Put into isolation by her father (Akrisios)	Put into isolation by her father (Kepheus)
Saved by Perseus from an unwanted marriage	Saved by Perseus from an unwanted marriage
Maternal	Sexy

There is a further significant female figure, which of course is Perseus' victim Medousa, whose name ('Ruler') has an inter-esting corollary in that of his prize, Andromeda ('Man-ruler').

The three pairs of twin brothers in the tale also exhibit interesting characteristics:

Akrisios	Proitos	Polydektes	Diktys	Phineus	Kepheus
Mutually hostile brothers		Mutually hostile brothers		Mutually hostile brothers	
Threatening	Benign	Threatening	Benign	Threatening	Benign
Turned to stone		Killed by a stone		Turned to stone	

To complete the symmetries, there are also three sets of sisters:

Graiai	Nymphs	Gorgons
Old and grey	Young and pretty	Hideous monsters
Lose their tooth and eye	Give Perseus the sandals, cap and *kibisis*	Lose the head of one of their number

This type of analysis, which can lead to a number of different conclusions, is very much the stock in trade of the psycho-analyst and structuralist approaches, although how the patterns might be interpreted will be determined by the intellectual school of thought that the myth analyst belongs to.[19]

Another interpretative approach is also possible here. The Mycenaean Age (roughly 1600–1200) has a crucial role to play in the formation of Greek mythology, since it provides the 'historical' setting for many tales. It is striking that the importance of a town in myth often correlates with its importance in Mycenaean times rather than in the historical era,[20] so there seems to be a kind of continuity between Mycenaean times, when places such as Mycenae, Tiryns and Pylos were powerful and influential, and the historical age, when they were not.

It is also worth observing that the mythical states are invariably ruled by kings, which again was not the norm in historical times. Greek writers seem to regard this as a reflection of history: 'Obviously in ancient times they had kings like everyone else, since kingship not self-government was the age-old tradition of the whole of Greece.'[21] In myth, kings are good to think with: they make apposite subjects for stories, but we should also acknowledge that it is almost impossible to find out anything about named important individuals of the Mycenaean period. The earliest written evidence we have in this respect comes from thousands of clay tablets written in a script known as Linear B, which were found at Knossos on Crete and at significant Mycenaean centres such as Mycenae, Tiryns, Pylos and Thebes. Linear B is a form of Greek, and the surviving tablets contain around seventy names that are recognizable from Homer (Hektor and Akhilleus included) and because names like these were not used in the historical period, it looks like Homer was using genuine Bronze Age names. One such tablet gives a list of landholders:

> *Theseus*, the servant of the deity, has a beneficial plot of land so much seed grain BARLEY 9.6 litres.
> *Hektor*, the servant of the deity, has a beneficial plot of land so much seed grain BARLEY 4.8? litres.[22]

Theseus and Hektor were not the names of mighty heroes, but of mundane Mycenaeans. There was nothing remarkable about the names of Homer's heroes, and this should make us cautious about trying to shoehorn too much history into the mythology: the view that myth is just damaged or distorted history goes right back to antiquity, and is still deployed by people with a vested interest in trying to make myth communicate more directly than it generally does. Reading myth as history is misreading its purpose.

The 'damaged historian' might see Danaos on his travels from Egypt to Libya to Rhodes to Argos and imagine he is a real historical person from Egypt. Alternatively, a wider view of the tale could read into it the movements of a tribe called the Danaoi, who could then be linked to the 'Denyen' (one of the so-called 'Sea-Peoples') who are mentioned in an Egyptian inscription of 1186, with the tribe of Dan in Genesis and Judges, or with 'Danaoi' in an Egyptian inscription of *c*.1380. But this puts the historicist on treacherous ground because mythical accounts of peoples and individuals are much more interested in constructing identities and making statements. There is an outside chance that Hittite records might be referring to someone called Eteokles, if the name Tawagalawos can be interpreted as such, who was making a nuisance of himself around Miletos, but the name actually seems closer to the Greek *tagos* ('commander in chief') of the *lawos* ('armed forces'), which would make more sense. The anti-historicist view is perhaps most strongly expressed by K. Dowden who argues: 'There is not a single individual in mythology in whose actual existence we can believe.'[23]

If this seems pessimistic and disappointing, it is still true that myth provides good evidence for the importance of certain places: Heinrich Schliemann was right to look for Mycenae, if not for the death-mask of Agamemnon and the treasury of Atreus: significant things happened at Mycenae, even though we do not know what they were (apart from the destruction of the site). And we can track down lost tribes like the Danaoi. In Homer the Danaoi were incredibly important: he used their name to mean 'the Greeks' as a whole, even though there was no trace of them left in historical times, other than the 'tomb of Danaos' in the centre of Argos, where he and his fifty daughters were said to have arrived, with Egyptians in pursuit. It is therefore possible, as Pausanias suggested, that 'Danaoi' was once the particular local tribal name of Greeks at Argos. It is also notable that Perseus' mother Danae has a feminine form of the tribal name, Perseus has links with nearby Mycenae, and the Danaids are said to have established the temple of Athene Lindia on Rhodes on their journey from Egypt. So although this does not tell us directly about the movements of historical individuals, the myth does imply that the Danaoi tribe existed at Argos, Mycenae and Rhodes, and that Rhodes was a Mycenaean colony from the Argolid. That implication is backed up by Strabo's narrative of colonists heading for Rhodes from Argos and Tiryns:

> When Tlepolemos had grown to manhood, 'he forthwith slew his own father's dear uncle, Likymnios, who was then growing old; and straightway he built him ships, and when he had gathered together a great host he went in flight.'[24] The poet then adds, 'he came to Rhodes in his wanderings, where his people settled in three divisions by tribes'; and he names the cities of that time, 'Lindos, Ialysos, and Kameiros white with chalk.'[25]

So although myth is not history, even in a damaged state, it does let us follow the footsteps of colonists and gain clues about the important sites of the Mycenaean era.

The adventures of Perseus, particularly his killing of Medousa and his escape from her sisters, can be found all over ancient art from as early as the seventh century. Pausanias describes the famous archaic Throne at Amyklai, which was covered in mythological scenes including Perseus' triumph over Medousa, and also the Chest of Kypselos, similarly crammed with motifs such as Perseus fleeing from the surviving Gorgon sisters. A fine graphic illustration of the myth also occurs on an archaic *dinos* (mixing bowl) and stand by the Gorgon Painter (*c*.600–590) now in the Louvre, where the decapitated Medousa collapses on the left while her sisters, all beating wings and lolling tongues, pursue Perseus on the right. Medousa also appears, with her head this time, on the pediment of the temple of Artemis at Corfu (*c*.590–580). She is shown running, presumably away from Perseus, and the artist violates strict chronology by depicting her with her offspring Pegasos and Khrysaor: clearly he was not bothered by the logic that Medousa could never exist alongside her offspring, given that they only appeared after her head was severed.

Post-classical art took very readily to the mythology of Perseus. Piero di Cosimo (c.1462–1521?) depicted the sea-monster advancing on the chained Andromeda as Perseus heroically assaults it with his sword while standing on its back; Titian (c.1485/90–1576) also picked up on this popular 'beauty and the beast' theme in his *Perseus and Andromeda* (1554–6); the bronze statue by Cellini (1500–71), which is now in the Loggia dei Lanzi in Florence, shows the hero brandishing the Gorgon's head in a stunning work of ghastly, grandiose beauty; Caravaggio produced a terrifying version of Medousa (1598–9) painted upon Cosimo II de Medici's tournament shield, placed there to scare the prince's opponents; Edward Burne-Jones' nineteenth-century painting *The Baleful Head* depicts a moment much closer to the conclusion of his adventures, where he and Andromeda are in a garden looking at a reflection of Medousa's head, which he is holding over the waters of a well.

The Perseus myth has held many meanings for many people. Francis Bacon interpreted Perseus' targeting of the mortal Gorgon as a symbol that only winnable wars should be attempted; Freud had a field-day with Medousa's snakes (phallic) and decapitation (castration);[26] and the British novelist William Sutcliffe described Iris Murdoch's *A Severed Head* (1961), a satirical novel about marriage, adultery and incest among a group of civilized and educated people, in these terms: 'Of all the lots-of-people-screwing-lots-of-other-people novels this is probably the best, and certainly the weirdest'[27]– one of the characters, Honor, is the Gorgon.

6

HERAKLES:
THE GREATEST OF THE HEROES

Key Characters

Amphitryon	The mortal father of Herakles
Alkmena (Alcumena)	Mother of Herakles
Eurystheus	Sent Herakles on his Labours
Herakles (Hercules)	The ultimate Greek hero
Iphikles (Iphicles)	Herakles' mortal brother
Iolaos (Iolaus)	Nephew and companion of Herakles
Megara	Herakles' first wife
Iole	Won by Herakles in an archery contest; indirectly caused his death
Omphale	Purchased Herakles as a slave
Laomedon	King of Troy
Deianeira	Wife of Herakles
Astydameia	Wife of Herakles

Of all the heroes of Greek mythology, Herakles is perhaps the hardest to see as a single character. He seems to be so many things: a heroic master of prodigious feats; a tragic figure; a buffoon; a philosopher; a civilization-builder. As a hero, then a god, by virtue of accomplishing his Twelve Labours, Herakles is the Greek hero par excellence, who achieves immortality through performance.

Apollodoros relates, in a story of strange chronology and odd genealogy, how when Elektryon was King of Mycenae the six sons of Pterelaos came with some Taphians and claimed the nearby kingdom of Tiryns, which had belonged to his ancestor Mestor. The consequences were illustrated on the marvellous cloak that Athena gave to Jason:

> A woodland pasturage was shown with oxen grazing. For these a battle was afoot. Elektryon's sons had been attacked by a band of Taphian raiders, who wished to walk off with the cattle. The dewy grass was drenched with blood. But the herdsmen were too few, and the larger force had got the upper hand.[1]

Casualties were high: Likymnios was the sole survivor out of Elektryon's sons, while the remaining Taphians sailed off with the cattle. Seeking revenge, Elektryon entrusted his daughter Alkmena, along with the kingdom, to Amphitryon, who swore to respect her virginity until his return. However, as Elektryon was retrieving the cattle one of them charged at him, and when he threw his club at it, it bounced off its horns, hit him on the head, and killed him.[2] His brother Sthenelos used this as a pretext to banish Amphitryon and to usurp the throne of Mycenae and Tiryns.

Amphitryon, Alkmena and Likymnios took refuge with Kreon at Thebes, and Alkmena promised Amphitryon that she would marry him when he had avenged her brothers' deaths. He agreed to do this, and asked Kreon to help him. Kreon agreed, providing Amphitryon would rid Thebes of the giant vixen that was ravaging the area.[3] He did, and in Ovid's *Metamorphoses* there is a vivid description of the chase:

The hound was released, and at once we had no idea where he
    was;
his footprints showed in the baking sand, but Whirlwind himself
had vanished, gone with the speed of a spear or of bullets hurled
from a whirling sling or an arrow shot from a Cretan bow
    [. . .]
The vixen one moment appeared to be caught, but the next
to escape from the hound's very jaws [. . .]
But the dog kept close on his quarry's heels; and yes, he had
    got her!
But no, he had not; he was only snapping at empty air.
    [. . .]
I looked away for a moment and then looked back to the same
    place.
There, in the midst of the plain, I saw with surprise two figures
in marble; you'd guess that one was in flight, while the other
    was barking.
I suppose, if a god was there with the runners, he must have
    decided
That neither should win that astonishing race, and neither should
    be beaten.[4]

Amphitryon now set off to ravage the islands of the Taphians,
supported by his allies, but the task was complicated by the
fact that Poseidon had made Pterelaos immortal by implanting
a golden hair in his head, and that as long as Pterelaos was
alive Taphos could not be taken. However, Pterelaos' daughter Komaitho fell in love with Amphitryon and pulled out
the golden hair, so Pterelaos died and Amphitryon subjugated
the islands. There was no happy ending for Komaitho, though,
because Amphitryon executed her for her treachery, and
sailed away back to Thebes.

An event of monumental importance took place just before

Amphitryon got home. Zeus assumed the likeness of Amphitryon, made the night last for three entire days, made love with Alkmena[5] and told her all about the expedition. The real Amphitryon received a rather frosty welcome from a slightly confused Alkmena, and it fell to the seer Teiresias to diffuse the tension by revealing the truth of the situation. The end result of all this was two sons for Alkmena: Iphikles by Amphitryon, and Herakles by Zeus, who was one night older. The delivery of Herakles was not an easy one for Alkmena: while she was in labour Zeus declared that the descendant of Perseus about to be born would reign over Mycenae, and Hera, irritated at the offspring of yet another of her husband's illicit relationships, persuaded the Eileithyiai (goddesses of childbirth) to postpone the birth,[6] and for Eurystheus, the son of Sthenelos and so also a descendant of Perseus, to be born at seven months. In Ovid's Roman version, the goddess Lucina, the Roman equivalent of Eileithyia, prevented the birth by sitting with crossed legs and clasped hands until she was tricked into relaxing her pose by Alkmene's slave-girl Galanthis, thus allowing the birth to take place. Galanthis was turned into a weasel (*gale* in Greek) by Hera.

Numerous authors tell how before the boys were one year old, two huge serpents appeared in their bedroom.[7] Alkmena screamed to Amphitryon to come, but when he arrived Herakles had already strangled the snakes with his bare hands. Some sources say Hera sent them to destroy Herakles, others that Amphitryon did it in order to find out which of the children was his.

There are chronological accounts of Herakles' life in both Diodoros and in Apollodoros, from which it appears that Herakles had a pretty standard heroic education in chariot driving, wrestling, archery, swordsmanship and lyre-playing.

When his music teacher Linos, brother of Orpheus, got frustrated with Herakles for his lack of musicality and hit him, Herakles killed him with his own lyre. Although he was acquitted of murder on the grounds that defending oneself against a wrongful aggressor was lawful, Amphitryon remained uneasy that he might do something similar again, and sent him to the cattle farm, where he matured magnificently. By his eighteenth year he was between six and seven feet tall, flashed a gleam of fire from his eyes, and never missed the target with either bow or javelin. It was obvious who his father was.

The chronology of his exploits differs widely from source to source, though the account given by Apollodoros provides a good framework. In that work his first major feat is to slay the lion of Kithairon (Cithaeron), which was harrying the livestock of Amphitryon and Thespios, King of Thespiai.[8] The king had fifty daughters by his wife Megamede. Thespios entertained Herakles for fifty days, and every night he sent one of his fifty daughters to sleep with him. Herakles thought he had had intercourse with the same girl fifty times, but in reality they all produced sons (and the eldest and youngest sometimes had twins).[9] The lion hunt was equally productive, and Apollodoros says that after Herakles had vanquished the lion, he dressed himself in its skin and wore the 'gaping mouth' as a helmet. The more usual version is that he acquires these attributes after slaying the Nemean Lion in the first of his great Labours. In art he is easy to identify, wearing the lion's skin, often with the lion's scalp as a hood.

An interesting event known as the 'Choice of Herakles' is placed at this point of his career.[10] At a road junction, Herakles met two women. One of them, a personification of Vice, who was sexy and alluring, offered him the easy path of pleasure; the other, Virtue, who was much more demure,

1. killing the Nemean lion;
2. killing the Hydra of Lerna;
3. capturing (or killing) the Kerynitian or Keryneian hind;
4. capturing the Erymanthian boar;
5. cleansing the stables of Augeias;
6. chasing away (or killing) the Stymphalian birds.

The next two sent Herakles to outlying areas of the Greek world:

7. capturing the Cretan bull (south);
8. fetching the man-eating horses of Diomedes from Thrace (north).

The final four sent Herakles to the ends of the earth and even beyond:

9. getting the belt of Hippolyte, Queen of the Amazons (east);
10. stealing the cattle of triple-bodied Geryon (west);
11. fetching the Golden Apples of the Hesperides;
12. bringing Kerberos up from the Underworld.

Eurystheus first ordered Herakles to bring the skin of the Nemean lion, an invulnerable beast with monstrous ancestry[15] that was ravaging the area around Nemea. He tracked the lion down, but when his first arrow bounced off its impenetrable pelt he gave chase with his club. The lion went to ground in a cave with two entrances, so Herakles blocked up one mouth and attacked via the other. He strangled it, sacrificed to Zeus the Saviour, dedicated the Nemean Games in honour of Zeus, and took the lion back to Mycenae. Eurystheus was so stunned by Herakles' capabilities that he not only told him never to enter Mycenae again and to display the fruits of his labours outside the gates, but also had a bronze jar made for him to hide in, and started to communicate his commands through a herald, Kopreus.[16]

In most traditions Herakles now flayed the lion using its own claws to cut its otherwise invulnerable hide, and began to wear the skin and the lion's scalp as his distinctive attributes. Zeus placed the lion among the stars as the constellation Leo, as a sign of his son's first great achievement.

The second Labour was to kill the Lernaean Hydra, the monstrous poisonous progeny of Ekhidna and Typhoeus that Hera herself had nurtured. It had a huge body with multiple heads (nine – eight mortal, the middle one immortal – according to Apollodoros; a hundred in Diodoros and Ovid; but just one in Pausanias), and was bred in the swamp of Lerna, from where it terrorized the local countryside. Herakles flushed the Hydra out of its den by shooting it with blazing arrows, and then grabbed it. It coiled itself around his feet, but although he kept smashing its heads with his club this only made matters worse, because the moment one head was destroyed two more grew up in its place. A massive crab also assisted the Hydra by biting Herakles' foot. He killed this, but Hera transformed it into the constellation of Cancer. Herakles now enlisted the aid of his nephew Iolaos, who took a firebrand and cauterized the neck stumps as Herakles severed the heads, and so prevented new ones sprouting. The severed immortal head had to be buried under a great rock, and Herakles finally cut open the Hydra's body and dipped his arrows in its venomous blood. Apollodoros says that Eurystheus, who initially gave Herakles ten Labours, refused to count this one on the grounds that Herakles only subdued the Hydra with the help of Iolaos.

Labour number three was to bring the Keryneian or

Kerynitian hind to Mycenae alive. It had golden horns and
was sacred to Artemis, and got its name either from Mount
Keryneia or the River Kernites. In his *Hymn to Artemis*, the
Hellenistic poet Kallimakhos says the hind was one of five
such animals, four of which Artemis had yoked to her chariot,
but this one had evaded her and had made its way to Mount
Keryneia. In Apollodoros' version Herakles wanted to avoid
killing or wounding it, so he tracked it for an entire year.
Eventually Herakles wounded the exhausted animal just as
it was about to cross the River Ladon in Arkadia. He caught
it, slung it on his shoulders and headed for Mycenae. On
the way he ran into Artemis and Apollo, and the goddess
would have taken the hind from him had he not pleaded
necessity and blamed Eurystheus.

Euripides gives a different version in his *Madness of Herakles*, where the hind is an aggressive beast and is killed by
Herakles. In the variant represented by Pindar's *Olympian*
3, the hind bore the inscription 'Taygete dedicated [me] to
Artemis'. Taygete was one of the Pleiades who had been
turned into a deer by Artemis in order to get her away from
the amorous attentions of Zeus. In this version Herakles
pursued the hind to the land of the Hyperboreans, 'the land
at the back of the cold north wind', leading to some rather
fanciful later identifications of the hind with a reindeer. He
is also said to have brought the olive wreath that formed the
victor's crown at the Olympic Games from the land of the
Hyperboreans.

For the next Labour Eurystheus ordered Herakles to bring
back alive the savage boar that lived on Mount Erymanthos
and was ravaging Psophis in Arkadia. On the way he was
entertained by the rather civilized Centaur called Pholos, who
served cooked meat to Herakles despite eating his own raw.
Pholos also broached a jar of wine, which had been presented

to him by Dionysos with orders not to open it till Herakles came, but the smell attracted the other Centaurs, who arrived at Pholos' cave armed with rocks, firs and a mighty thirst. When Herakles shot down Ankhios and Agrios, the rest sought refuge with the friendly Centaur Kheiron (Chiron), who had lived in the Peloponnese ever since the Lapiths had driven him from Mount Pelion.[17] Herakles shot Elatos, but to his great distress the poisoned arrow passed through his arm and into Kheiron's knee. Herakles applied a balm that Kheiron gave him, but the Hydra's deadly poison was incurable, so Kheiron retired to his cave to die. However this was not an option because he was immortal, at least until Prometheus offered to become immortal in his place. Kheiron died and the surviving Centaurs dispersed, but, sadly, when Herakles got back to Mount Pholoe he discovered that Pholos was dead as well: he had extracted one of Herakles' deadly arrows from a corpse, dropped it on his foot, and fallen dead on the spot. Herakles then proceeded to hunt the Erymanthian boar, and in a relatively unproblematic exploit he drove it out of its lair with his shouts, chased it into deep snow, caught it, and took it to Mycenae. A highly popular scene on Greek vases shows Herakles delivering the boar to Eurystheus, who cowers ignominiously in his pot.

The fifth Labour was somewhat different in style. Augeias, the King of Elis, who is sometimes an Argonaut, is most famous as the owner of many herds of cattle, whose stables had never been cleaned. Faced with Eurystheus' instruction to do this in a single day, Herakles proposed a deal: he would carry out the dung, if Augeias would give him 10 per cent of the cattle. When Augeias, with his son Phyleus as witness, agreed, Herakles breached the foundations of the cattle-yard, diverted the rivers Alpheios and Peneus into it, and sluiced out the filth. However, when Augeias discovered that

Herakles was acting on the orders of Eurystheus, he not only refused to pay up but also denied that he had promised anything in the first place. The dispute then went to arbitration, and when Phyleus testified against his father the expulsion of both himself and Herakles swiftly ensued. Herakles went to Dexamenos ('Welcomer') at Olenos, who betrothed his daughter Mnesimakhe to him. Herakles then departed on an expedition, only to return to find Mnesimakhe being forced into a marriage with the Centaur Eurytion. He slew Eurytion, but on his return to Mycenae Eurystheus refused to accept this Labour as one of the ten either, on the grounds that it had been performed for hire. The two disqualifications are what result in the eventual canon of twelve Labours.

The cleansing of the Augeian stables was never really popular with artists, possibly because it was a local event. Indeed, when it appeared on the temple of Zeus at Olympia it had never been represented before. A slightly more mature, bearded Herakles works industriously, while Athena provides calm, unobtrusive support.

The final Peloponnesian Labour was to chase away the Stymphalian birds, which Apollodoros says had flocked to the woods around Lake Stymphalis to avoid being preyed upon by the wolves. Other authors make them less benign: they are man-eating, bronze-beaked, as big as cranes, and shoot their feathers like arrows. In the *Argonautika*, Amphidamas tells the Argonauts how Herakles drove the birds from the wood by shaking a bronze rattle, sending them away screeching in flight. In some accounts Athena gave him the rattle, and as they fluttered away Herakles shot them down.

Again, this was not a particularly popular theme in art, especially after the sixth century. Herakles never deploys a rattle – he usually shoots the birds with arrows or slingshots, or batters them with his club.

Eurystheus now started to send Herakles much further afield, and the seventh Labour was to bring the Cretan bull, which some say was the same animal that Poseidon sent from the sea to Minos in support of his claim to the kingship of Crete. Minos had promised to sacrifice the bull to the god, but substituted a different one when he saw how beautiful it was. The snubbed sea god made Minos' wife Pasiphae fall in love with it, which is how it became the father of the Minotaur.[18] Poseidon had made the bull feral, and when Herakles arrived in Crete Minos asked him to catch it, which he did. He rode it across the sea to the Peloponnese and displayed it to Eurystheus, who simply let it free. The bull wandered through Greece to Marathon in Attica, where it harried the inhabitants until Theseus killed it.[19]

Herakles is often shown tussling with the Cretan bull in ancient art, using either his bare hands or his club. On the Olympia metope he appears in a striking X-shaped composition: the bull pulls away from him, but Herakles has managed to drag its head round and so create an exciting confrontation between him and the beast.

Herakles now moved north. Diomedes, a Thracian son of Ares and Kyrene, who was king of the extremely bellicose Bistones, owned some man-eating mares (or stallions in some traditions),[20] which were stabled in bronze mangers with iron chains. When Herakles was instructed to bring them back to Mycenae he overpowered their grooms and fed one of them to the mares before driving them down to the sea. When the Bistones came to retrieve the animals, Herakles entrusted them to his lover Abderos, but the horses dragged him to his death. Herakles was able to defeat the Bistones, though, and he slew Diomedes, according to Diodoros by feeding him to his own mares, which cured them of their man-eating proclivities. Herakles founded the city of Abdera in honour of his friend, and drove the horses back to Mycenae. Diodoros adds that Eurystheus dedicated them to Hera, and that their descendants lived on to the time of Alexander the Great.[21] This was not a Labour that proved especially attractive to ancient artists.

Herakles' ninth Labour involved going to the River Thermodon off the Black Sea to bring back the belt of the Amazon Queen Hippolyte for Eurystheus' daughter Admete. The Amazons were a race of mighty warrior women, who spurned the company of men, lived by hunting and cultivated the 'manly virtues'. On the occasions when they did happen to conceive children they only reared the females. Their name, Amazons, supposedly meant 'breastless' (the *a-* prefix in Greek means 'not', *mazos* means 'breast'), since they amputated their right breasts to avoid being hindered by them when throwing the javelin, but retained their left breasts in order to suckle their daughters. Interestingly, there is no trace of their one-breastedness in Greek art, where they frequently fight with perfectly formed exposed right breasts.

Hippolyte had been given a special belt by Ares as a token of her superiority to the other Amazons. Herakles took a single ship of volunteers, including Telamon and (in some sources) Theseus, and sailed into Amazon territory, where they put in at Themiskyra. Here Hippolyte asked Herakles why he had come, and promised to give him the belt. This was an unacceptable outcome for Hera, though, so she assumed the likeness of an Amazon and spread rumours that the strangers were abducting Hippolyte. Her sister Amazons attacked on horseback. Herakles either suspected treachery, killed Hippolyte and stripped her of the belt, or ransomed the belt by capturing Hippolyte's sister Melanippe. Having fought off the others, he sailed away to Troy, where some very significant events took place.

The walls of Troy had been built by Poseidon and Apollo for King Laomedon, or, in some accounts, by Poseidon as stone-mason while Apollo served as a herdsman. Pindar adds that Aiakos helped the gods: Troy was ultimately destined to be captured, so the immortals had to be assisted by a mortal, otherwise the walls would have been impregnable. At the end of a year Laomedon dismissed them without pay, and threatened to chop off their ears and sell Apollo into slavery. Feeling cheated and humiliated, Apollo sent a plague and Poseidon a sea-monster to ravage the Trojan plain. Oracles said that the remedy was for Laomedon to expose his daughter Hesione to be devoured by the sea-monster, so he fastened her to the rocks near the sea. In a story that corresponds closely to that of Perseus and Andromeda,[22] Herakles saw her plight and promised to save her if Laomedon would give him the mares that Zeus had given to Tros, the father of Ganymedes, in compensation for the boy's abduction.[23] Laomedon agreed. Herakles killed the monster and saved Hesione. An odd variant of the story says that Herakles leaped into the jaws of the sea-monster in full armour and hacked away at its innards for three days, after which he emerged with no hair on his head. However Laomedon refused to hand over the horses. Herakles threatened to make war on what Ovid memorably calls 'the twice-perjured walls of Troy', and sailed for Mycenae. Laomedon's days were numbered.

Herakles finally delivered Hippolyte's belt to Eurystheus as requested. Its acquisition was very popular in ancient vase painting, though many of the hundreds of surviving works name the queen Andromakhe.

For his tenth Labour Herakles was detailed to steal the cattle of Geryon from Erytheia, 'the Red Land' beyond the river of Okeanos in the far west. Geryon, the son of Khrysaor by the Oceanid Kallirrhoe, was, according to Hesiod, three-headed, but more usually he is triple-bodied, with the three elements joined at the waist. He owned great herds of red cattle, overseen by the herdsman Eurytion and the two-headed hound Orthos (or Orthros).

Herakles commenced this daunting task by clearing Crete of wild beasts, making Libya fertile and prosperous, and moving on to Tartessos in Spain, where he erected two pillars opposite each other at the boundaries of Europe and Libya: the Pillars of Herakles, which defined the Strait of Gibraltar. Herakles was oppressed by the heat, and so shot at the sun god Helios, who then gave him the golden bowl which, after sunset, carried Helios and his horses through the Ocean back to the east in time for sunrise. Okeanos sent wild waves to rock Herakles, until the hero menaced him into calmness with his bow.

On reaching Erytheia he slew both Orthos and Eurytion, but Menoites, another herdsman who was tending the cattle of Hades, saw the incident and reported it to Geryon, who ambushed Herakles as he was driving the cattle away. A tantalizing set of papyrus fragments now survives, which gives snatches of a poem by Stesikhoros describing the combat. Geryon might be a monster, but he has to defend his herds from this cattle rustler, and despite his mother's protestations, he decides to confront Herakles. Geryon says that he cannot really lose: as the son of Khrysaor he is either immortal, and so will win the fight, or mortal, and so will die a glorious death. Herakles seems to smash one of Geryon's heads with his club, knock the helmet off another with a stone, and shoot him with one of his venom-soaked arrows:

It cut through the flesh and bone [. . .] straight to the crown of his head, and stained his breastplate and bloody limbs with crimson gore. And Geryon drooped his neck to one side, like a poppy that suddenly sheds its petals, spoiling its tender beauty.[24]

Herakles herded the cattle into the bowl, sailed back to Tartessos, and then moved through southern Spain to Liguria in southern France, where he was attacked by a horde of belligerent natives who tried to take the cattle from him.[25] Herakles' supply of arrows started to run short, and there were no stones around to use as missiles, so he prayed to Zeus, who rained stones down from the sky. Duly supplied with ammunition, Herakles turned the tables on his assailants. The location of this adventure was said to be the Plain of Crau, west of Marseilles, which is covered with a vast number of rocks and stones.

As Herakles moved on to the forests north of the Black Sea, his chariot horses were stolen by a woman who was a snake from the waist downwards, who said she would only return them if Herakles made love to her. He obliged until there were three sons. Only the youngest, Skythes, proved able to draw a bow and put on a belt that Herakles left behind, which gave him the right to rule the kingdom, which took his name as Skythia.

In Tyrrhenia, at the future sight of Rome, he encountered Kakos, a fire-breathing monster who ate human flesh and nailed the heads of his victims to the doors of his cave. Kakos abducted four bulls and four cows, dragging them backwards by their tails to confound any pursuers, but the lowing of one of the cows gave them away. Herakles blocked the entrance to Kakos' cave with a massive boulder, then wrenched the top off the mountain and fought the fire and smoke of his adversary with branches and rocks. This proved unsuccessful, so he plunged into the inferno and strangled Kakos, to the eternal gratitude of the local inhabitants.

Further south at Rhegion a bull broke away, plunged into the sea, and swam over to Sicily. Apollodoros says that Italy was so named because the Tyrrhenians called the bull *italos*.[26] In Sicily Eryx, a son of Poseidon, concealed the bull among his own herds, and when Herakles finally tracked it down, he challenged him to a wrestling match, which Herakles won, killing him in the process. Inevitably, the goddess Hera then intervened and afflicted the cattle with a gadfly, causing them to disperse. Herakles rounded up some of them and finally delivered them to Mycenae, where Eurystheus sacrificed them to Hera. This Labour was relatively popular in art, with Herakles shown either in transit in Helios' bowl, or wielding his club, bow or sword and doing battle with Geryon.

Ten Labours had been performed in eight years and a month, but Eurystheus now insisted on two more, because he refused to count the Labour of the Hydra or that of the Stables of Augeias. Herakles had to fetch Golden Apples from the Hesperides, the 'Daughters of Evening', who lived in a garden beyond the sunset, where Atlas held up the sky.[27]

The apples themselves were a wedding present for Zeus and Hera, either from all the gods or from Gaia. Hera loved them so much that she had them planted in the garden of the Hesperides, but because the daughters of Atlas used to steal them, she stationed Ladon, an immortal serpent with a hundred heads, to watch over the tree. The Hesperides, whose numbers vary from between two and seven, also shared guard duties.

Herakles' first problem was to locate the land of the Hesperides. The ancient sea god Nereus, child of Pontos and Gaia, knew the way, but Herakles had to subdue him before he would divulge the information. He seized him while he slept, and though, like the other sea deities such as Proteus in his encounter with Menelaos and Thetis with her lover Peleus, the god metamorphosed himself into all manner of shapes, Herakles clung on and only released him when he had got the directions he needed.

The hero crossed Libya, which was at that time ruled by Antaios, son of Poseidon and Gaia, who used to kill strangers by forcing them to wrestle, and, according to Pindar, decorated the temple of Poseidon with the skulls of his victims. Antaios was invincible provided he stayed in contact with his mother Earth, so in the bout Herakles lifted him aloft, and crushed him to death above his head. From Libya he traversed Egypt, which was under the rule of Bousiris, another son of Poseidon, who was in the habit of sacrificing strangers to Zeus ever since Egypt had suffered a nine-year famine and the seer Phrasios said that it would stop if they adopted this practice. Bousiris started with Phrasios himself and continued to kill any foreigner who landed. Herodotos narrates what happened next in the myth, but then adds his own sceptical comments:

The Greeks have many stories with no basis of fact. One of the silliest is the story of how Herakles came to Egypt and was taken away by the Egyptians to be sacrificed to Zeus, [. . .] and how he quietly submitted at the altar, when he exerted his strength and killed them all. For me at least, such a tale is proof enough that the Greeks know nothing whatever about Egyptian character and custom. The Egyptians are forbidden by their own religion to kill animals for sacrifice [with a few exceptions]: is it likely, then, that they would sacrifice human beings? Besides, if Herakles was a mere man (as they say he was) and single-handed, how is it conceivable that he should have killed tens of thousands of people? And I hope that both gods and heroes will forgive me for saying what I have said on these matters![28]

Herakles resumed his travels and again utilized the bowl of Helios to cross the Ocean. En route, in the Caucasus Mountains, he shot the great eagle that had been devouring the eternally renewed liver of Prometheus for the last 30,000 years, and liberated Prometheus. Zeus consented to this because it increased the fame of his son, and fragments of a lost tragedy attributed to Aiskhylos suggest that Prometheus was released in return for a great secret told to him by Themis, namely that the sea deity Thetis was destined to bear a son greater than his father. Zeus accordingly abandoned his amorous pursuit of Thetis, who eventually married Peleus and gave birth to Akhilleus (Achilles).

Prometheus advised Herakles not to go after the apples himself, but to send Atlas to do it after relieving him of the job of holding up the sky. Acting on this advice, he arrived in the land of the Hyperboreans and shouldered the heavens, while Atlas collected three apples from the Hesperides. Atlas did not want to carry on supporting the sky, so he offered to carry the apples to Eurystheus himself. However, Herakles tricked Atlas by asking him to hold the heavens while he put a cushion on his head. Atlas agreed, put the apples on the ground and took the sky from Herakles, who simply picked up the apples and walked off. It was a popular theme in art; on the Olympia metope Atlas walks towards Herakles holding the wondrous fruits in his outstretched hands, while Athena stands at Herakles' side and casually raises one hand to help him shoulder his crushing burden.

A different tradition holds that Herakles killed the serpent Ladon with his poisoned arrows and picked the apples himself. In the *Argonautika* Jason and his companions find the snake dead but for its twitching tail, and the Hesperides in mourning. Orpheus sang to them and they turned into trees, while Ladon was immortalized as the constellation Draco.

Herakles delivered the Golden Apples to Eurystheus, who inspected them and gave them back to him. Herakles passed them on to Athena, who returned them to the Hesperides because it was not lawful for a mortal to own them.

The final Labour imposed on Herakles was to bring back Kerberos, the guard dog of the Underworld:

> A monstrous dog
> Stands pitiless guard in front, with evil ways:
> He wags his tail and both his ears for all
> Who enter, but he will not let them go.
> Lying in wait he eats up anyone
> He catches leaving by the gates of strong
> Hades and greatly feared Persephone.[29]

Kerberos had multiple canine heads (usually three, but also fifty or a hundred), the tail of a serpent, and snake heads all down his back. He was the offspring of Typhoeus and Ekhidna, giving him a number of monstrous siblings in the shape of the Hydra of Lerna, the Khimaira and Geryon's two-headed dog Orthos. Hesiod describes him as:

> Unspeakable Kerberos, who eats raw flesh,
> The bronze-voiced hound of Hades, shameless, strong,
> With fifty heads.[30]

Herakles was first initiated into the Eleusinian Mysteries,[31] and then, with Hermes as his guide, he descended through the entrance to Hades at Tainaron in Lakonia. Homer speaks of him wounding Hades, Lord of the Underworld, in the shoulder with one of his arrows, causing him such extreme pain that he had to go up to Olympos and be cured by Paieon. Down in the Underworld all the souls fled when they saw him, apart from Meleagros and the Gorgon Medousa. He brandished his weapons against them, but Hermes explained that they were harmless phantoms. Meleagros narrated the sad circumstances of his death, which moved Herakles to say that he would like to marry the sister of such a hero. Meleagros mentioned his sister Deianeira, and so the train of events that led to Herakles' death was set in motion.

Herakles also came across Theseus and Peirithoos, who were bound fast for trying to seize Hades' wife and niece Persephone (Proserpina in Latin, but also known as Kore, 'the Girl', in Greek), the Queen of the Underworld. She was the daughter of Zeus and Demeter, and Hades had fallen in love with her at first sight. Zeus helped Hades to abduct her while she was gathering flowers in a Sicilian meadow: as she stooped down to pick a wonderful narcissus, the earth opened and Hades burst out in his golden four-horse chariot, grabbed the terrified girl, and took her back to the Underworld. The water-nymph Kyane witnessed the events and dissolved into the waters of her own pool, such was her anguish. Utterly distraught, Demeter set off in search of her daughter, and, as the corn goddess, she withheld her fruits from the world, causing terrible famine. Zeus had to respond, so he ordered Hades to surrender Kore, which he did, but not before she had eaten some pomegranate seeds, either of her own volition, or having been tricked into doing so by Hades. The fact that she had eaten infernal food meant that Persephone was compelled to remain with Hades in the nether regions for either a third or a half of every year (which gave rise to Demeter's unhappiness, and hence the time when crops do not grow), and the rest of the time with the gods (when nature can once again flourish due to Demeter's rejoicing). Her return to the world, with its associated fertility, was the focus of great religious celebrations such as the Eleusinian Mysteries and the Athenian Festival of the Thesmophoria.

Regarding Herakles' attempt to rescue the two would-be

abductors of the Queen of Underworld, the general opinion was that Herakles rescued Theseus, but when he tried to free Peirithoos, the earth quaked and he let go. Hyginus, though, says that he brought them both up from the dead, while in Diodoros he brings up neither. Herakles also rolled away the stone that Demeter had placed on Askalaphos to punish him for divulging that Persephone had eaten the pomegranate seeds, whereupon Demeter promptly turned him into a screech-owl.

At last Herakles could ask for Kerberos. Hades said he could have the dog if he could master him without weapons. Herakles grabbed the monster in his arms, and even though he was bitten by the serpent in his tail, he wrestled Kerberos into submission. Herakles carried him off and ascended to the world of the living, where he exhibited the dog to Eurystheus, before returning him to Hades where he belonged. The Kerberos Labour is a common one to be illustrated by artists, who show Herakles attacking Kerberos, leading him away, or delivering him to Eurystheus, who cowers in his pot.

The Labours were complete.

After the Labours

With his Labours complete, and his obligations to Eurystheus fulfilled, Herakles gave his wife Megara to his nephew and companion Iolaos. Seeking a replacement, he was attracted by Iole, the lovely daughter of Eurytos, prince of Oikhalia,[32] who had offered her hand as the prize in an archery contest. Herakles won the competition, but did not get the girl, because Eurytos was concerned about a repeat of the incident when Herakles had killed the children he had by Megara. And Eurytos had good reason to be afraid of Herakles, since shortly afterwards, in an incident involving the theft of some cattle by Herakles (alleged or otherwise), he threw Eurytos'

eldest son Iphitos from the walls of Tiryns to his death, even
though Iphitos had supported Herakles' marriage to Iole.

Seeking purification after the murder Herakles went to
Neleus, King of Pylos. But Neleus was a friend of Eurytos
and so rejected his request. Herakles then contracted a terrible
disease and went to Delphi to ask the Oracle how to get rid
of it. Getting no response, he carried off the sacred tripod
and threatened to institute a rival oracle of his own. Apollo
stepped in to grab the tripod from him, and Zeus had to
throw a thunderbolt to separate them. This became a highly
popular subject for artists, with a fine depiction of the fight
portrayed on the sixth-century pediment of the Siphnian
Treasury at Delphi. The Oracle then decreed that Herakles
should be sold as a slave and serve for three years[33] in compensation for the murder.

Hermes became the slave dealer, and sold Herakles to
Omphale, Queen of Lydia, for three talents – an excellent
purchase, since he rid her realm of troublemakers. At Ephesos
he caught the two Kerkopes brothers trying to rob him,
bound them, and hung them by their heels from a pole which
he slung over his shoulders. They had been warned to beware
of a certain Melampygos ('Black Buttocks'), and as they hung
upside down they got a good view of Herakles' hairy, tanned
backside. They made so many hilarious bawdy jokes at his
expense that he released them.[34] He then slew a massive snake
that was ravaging Omphale's territory, defeated her enemies,
the Itonoi, and dealt with Syleus, a brigand who compelled
passing strangers to hoe his vineyard. Herakles killed him
with his own hoe, burned the vines, and took the life of
his daughter Xenodike, although another version makes
Xenodike become his lover and die of a broken heart when
he left. On the island of Dolikhe, Herakles found the body
of Ikaros washed up on the shore, buried it, and named the

island Ikaria after him. Ikaros' father Daidalos reciprocated by making a statue of Herakles which was so realistic that Herakles threw a stone at it because he thought it was alive. It was at this time that he sailed with the Argonauts.

An interesting aspect of Herakles' servitude to Omphale is that he is sometimes said to have fallen in love with her, allowed her to wear his lion skin and brandish his club, while he wore women's clothing and helped with the spinning. She bore him a son called Lamos (or Agelos) before she released him.

Herakles was now free to settle some old scores, and Laomedon was first on his list.[35] Herakles recruited a force of either six or eighteen ships and sailed for Troy, where he led his companions in an assault on the city. Telamon breached the walls, but Herakles hated the possibility of Telamon winning a greater share of the honour, so he drew his sword and advanced on Telamon, who responded by collecting a pile of stones. Puzzled, Herakles asked him what he was doing, to which Telamon responded, 'Building an altar to Herakles the *Kallinikos* ('the Glorious Victor').'[36] Herakles was touched by this and, after he had captured Troy and shot Laomedon and most of his sons, he awarded Laomedon's daughter Hesione to Telamon as a prize. He allowed Hesione to choose one of the captives to be released, and she chose her brother Podarkes, and ransomed him with her veil, which is why Podarkes came to be called Priamos ('Priam', supposedly derived from the Greek *priamai*, 'to buy'). Priamos ultimately became Troy's most celebrated ruler.

When Herakles left Troy, Hera sent terrible storms, which annoyed Zeus so much that he tied anvils to her feet and hung her from Olympos. The storms drove Herakles to Kos, where he was wounded in fighting with the locals, but Zeus spirited him away to safety, in what was a timely rescue, since Herakles then moved to Phlegrai in Thrace and played a crucial role in the gods' victory over the Giants.[37]

After the Gigantomachy he gathered a formidable army and marched against Augeias, who still owed him the fee for cleansing his stables.[38] Augeias appointed Eurytos and Kteatos as his generals. They were sons of Poseidon by Molione, and were called Moliones or Molionides,[39] and had either the form of two bodies joined in one like Siamese twins, or were individuals with one body, two heads, four hands, and four feet each. Herakles fell sick on this expedition and made a truce with the Molionides, but when they became aware of his illness they successfully attacked his army and, in one version, mortally wounded Iphikles. Herakles got his revenge, though, when he ambushed and killed the Molionides as they were going to take part in the third Isthmian Games. Herakles was then able to march on Elis, capture the city, kill Augeias and his sons, and allegedly institute the Olympic Games, athough this version conflicts with the tradition that the Olympic festival was started in 776.

Next on his list of paybacks was Neleus, who had refused to purify him of Iphitos' murder. He sacked Pylos, slew Neleus' shape-changing son Periklymenos, who, according to different traditions, had the power to change into a lion, snake, bee, eagle, ant, fly, or indeed any animal or tree he pleased. Herakles also accounted for Neleus and all his other sons apart from the young Nestor, who escaped because he was absent among the Geranians at the time. In a formidable feat of military prowess Herakles wounded Hades, Hera and Ares in the fight.

Then it was time for vengeance on Hippokoon at Lakedaimon (Sparta), who had also refused Herakles purification and, with his twelve or twenty sons, the Hippokoontids, had fought on Neleus' side. Herakles recruited Kepheus and his twenty sons at Tegea in Arkadia. Kepheus' reservations that Tegea might be attacked by the Argives if he left it were overcome when Athena gave Herakles a lock of the Gorgon's hair in a bronze jar, which he passed on to Kepheus' daughter Sterope, with instructions to repel any invaders by averting her gaze and holding it up three times from the walls. Lakedaimon was duly conquered, and Tyndareus restored to the Lakedaimonian throne, but Kepheus and his sons perished in the battle, along with Herakles' brother Iphikles in one tradition.

After these events Herakles was entertained by King Aleus of Tegea, whose daughter Auge was a virgin priestess of Athena. The story was widely used by writers and artists, and in one variation the Delphic Oracle had warned Aleus that his daughter would bear a son who would kill his sons Kepheus and Lykourgos, which is why he made her a priestess, with the additional sanction that if she had sex he would execute her. Herakles violated Aleus' hospitality by getting drunk and raping Auge. When Aleus discovered the inevitable pregnancy, he sent for a man named Nauplios and gave him instructions to drown his daughter, but on the way to the sea Auge gave birth to Telephos, and rather than drowning her Nauplios sold her to King Teuthras in Mysia, who married her and adopted Telephos. Another version says that Auge was sold to Teuthras, but Telephos, who had been born in secret and been deposited in the precinct of Athena, was exposed to die on Mount Parthenios, where a doe suckled him until shepherds took him in and called him Telephos, a name which Apollodoros seems to derive from the Greek *thele* ('a teat') and *elaphos* ('a doe').[40]

In Sophokles' lost drama, *The Mysians*, in which Auge was adopted by Teuthras as his daughter, Telephos arrived in Mysia looking for Auge 'silent and speechless',[41] but he failed to recognize her. However, he did accept the hand of the king's 'daughter' for helping him defend his realm. Auge baulked at marrying someone young enough to be her son, and tried to murder him on their wedding night, but she was thwarted by the gods, who sent a huge snake to intervene. She then owned up to her scheme, and Telephos was on the point of taking her life in revenge when she called on Herakles for protection, leading to a recognition scene and a happy ending. Telephos became King of Mysia, and was said to be the most like his father of all the sons of Herakles. Our sources do not tell us how Telephos fulfilled the oracle and killed the sons of Aleus.

Herakles now moved on to Kalydon, where he courted Deianeira, daughter of Oineus. He was forced to wrestle with her other suitor, the shape-changing river god Akheloos. Deianeira says that she was not too keen on Akheloos:

> Sometimes he came as a bull,
> Sometimes a gleaming writhing snake,
> Sometimes a man with a bull's forehead,
> Cascades of river water falling
> Down his thick dark beard.
> This was the husband I had to look forward to;
> No wonder I was always praying for death.[42]

In a vibrant account in Ovid, the river god tells Theseus how he first turned himself into a serpent:

> Herakles laughed and made fun of my magic:
> 'Dealing with snakes is a task I used to perform in my cradle!
> You may surpass other snakes, Akheloos, but really, a single
> Serpent is hardly a threat when compared with the Hydra of
> Lerna [. . .]

What do you think will happen to you, who are merely
   disguised
as a snake, in dubious form, with weapons not yours by
   nature?'[43]

Not having any success as a snake, Akheloos metamorphosed
into a bull, but Herakles wrestled him to the ground and
broke off one of his horns. Herakles married Deianeira, and
Akheloos recovered his horn by swapping the Horn of
Amaltheia for it. Amaltheia had been the nurse of Zeus, and
had a bull's horn that had the power of supplying whatever
you asked for (the Cornucopia).

Herakles helped his new father-in-law by campaigning
with him against the Thesprotians and helping him subjugate
King Phylas' city of Ephyra, although he was immediately
unfaithful to Deianeira and had sex with Phylas' daughter
and fathered Tlepolemos. After that he accidentally killed
Deianeira's father Oineus' cupbearer, and although it had
been an accident, Herakles felt he should follow strict
protocol and go into exile, so he set off to the court of
Keyx, the King of Trakhis, taking Deianeira with him. At
the River Euenos they encountered the Centaur Nessos, the
local ferryman:

But Nessos, the brutal centaur, was wholly destroyed by his
   passion
for Deianeira and shot in the back by a flying arrow.[44]

Herakles entrusted Deianeira to Nessos to ferry across, but
the Centaur attempted to rape her. Herakles shot Nessos
with one of his arrows, which were poisoned with the venom
of the Hydra, but as his blood mingled with the poison,

Nessos caught some of the mixture and whispered, 'You'll
   pay for my death!'
and then presented his blood-soaked tunic to Deianeira,
a gift which he told her could serve to excite the love of her
   husband.[45]

She kept it, just in case.

Herakles arrived in Trakhis and helped Keyx conquer the
Dryopes, a feral tribe of robbers, before moving on to assist
Aigimios, King of the Dorians, in a conflict over a boundary
dispute with the Lapiths. Then in Thessaly he was challenged
to single combat by Kyknos, a deeply unpleasant son of Ares,
who was building a temple to his father from the heads of
the passing strangers he decapitated. Herakles slew him also,
although some myth-tellers speak of the combat being
curtailed when Zeus hurled a thunderbolt between them.
There is also another tale, which serves to underline how
difficult it is to distinguish between different versions or variants of the myths, in which Ares got embroiled in the fight
on the side of his son and was wounded by Herakles (Kyknos
was still slain). The mighty hero added to his wife collection
at Ormenion at the foot of Mount Pelion, where King Amyntor tried to prevent him passing through and refused to give
him his daughter Astydameia in marriage: Herakles simply
slew him and took Astydameia anyway.

Finally, Herakles raised a force to claim Iole, his bride-
prize for victory in the archery contest, from Eurytos at
Oikhalia. Casualties were high, but it was mission accomplished for Herakles, who carried Iole away as his concubine.

The Iole story had a tragic end, beautifully dramatized in
Sophokles' tragedy *The Women of Trakhis*. Deianeira discovered
about Iole, and understandably felt that Herakles might love

this gorgeous woman more than her. But she also misguidedly imagined that the bloodstained tunic of Nessos really was a love potion that could win him round again. So she sent it to him. The instant he put the tunic on, the Hydra's ghastly venom started to attack his flesh. He tried to get the tunic off, but it clung to his body and his flesh came away with it. In this desperate state he was conveyed by ship to Trakhis. Meanwhile their son Hyllos informed Deianeira of what she had unwittingly done, as a result of which she took her own life.

Herakles instructed Hyllos to marry Iole when he came of age, then headed to Mount Oita in Trakhinian territory, where he constructed a pyre, climbed on to it, and gave Philoktetes orders for it to be set alight.[46]

> To him he entrusted his famous bow and quiver containing
> the arrows destined one day to revisit the kingdom of Troy.
> And while the flames were licking the sides of the funeral pyre,
> Herakles covered the piled-up wood with the skin of the lion
> of Nemea, then laid himself down on the pyre with his club for
>   a pillow,
> smiling as if he were gently reclining, a guest at a banquet,
> crowned with a garland and quaffing the unmixed juice of the
>   vineyard.[47]

As the pyre burned, a cloud passed under Herakles and a peal of thunder echoed in the heavens. He was taken up to Olympos, reconciled with Hera, married her daughter (and his sister) Hebe, the goddess of youth, and Zeus put a constellation named after him in the sky. Diodoros does not take the story at face value: his rationalization is that a thunderstorm occurred the moment the pyre was lit, and that when Herakles' companions came to collect his bones they couldn't find any, and so imagined that he had been spirited away to the gods.

Descendants of Herakles: The Heraklids and the Return of the Heraklids

Herakles had left a trail of offspring wherever he ventured, by a variety of different mothers: Hebe; the fifty daughters of Thespios; Deianeira, daughter of Oineus; Megara, daughter of Kreon; Omphale, daughter of Iardanos or Tmolos; Khalkiope, daughter of Eurypylos; Epikaste, daughter of Augeias; Parthenope, daughter of Stymphalos; Auge, daughter of Aleus; Astyokhe, daughter of Phylas; Meda, daughter of Phylas; Astydameia, daughter of Amyntor; and Autonoe, daughter of Pireus were all mothers of one or more sons, who were known collectively as the Heraklids. However, after Herakles' immortalization Eurystheus continued to persecute these descendants, and forced his children by Deianeira to flee to Keyx, King of Trakhis, who had been a good friend to their father. When Eurystheus demanded their surrender and threatened to invade, they fled to Athens, where they sought sanctuary at the altar of Mercy. An oracle declared that the Athenians would only be victorious if a virgin of noble background were sacrificed to Persephone, and a willing victim stepped forward in the person of Herakles' daughter Makaria. In Euripides' play *The Children of Herakles* Demophon is King of Athens at this time, but other versions make Theseus the champion of the Heraklids. This refusal to hand over the children of Herakles meant that Athens had to endure a war against Eurystheus, but they prevailed and Eurystheus' sons were slain, and as he himself fled in a chariot he was hounded down by Hyllos or Iolaos at the Skeironian Rocks. Hyllos decapitated him and gave the head to Alkmena, who gouged out his eyes with weaving-pins. In Euripides' play, on the other hand, Eurystheus was captured by Iolaos at the Skeironian Rocks and taken to Alkmena, who ordered his execution.[48]

Hyllos married Iole in accordance with Herakles' wishes, and after the death of Eurystheus he tried to re-establish the Heraklids in the Peloponnese. The invasion is often referred to as a 'return', because even though Herakles had been born in Thebes, he would have ruled Mycenae and Tiryns had it not been for Eurystheus, and he regarded them as his rightful home. Hyllos was relatively successful until a plague broke out, which an oracle attributed to the fact that the Heraklids had returned too soon. So they obediently retired to Marathon and took up residence there.

The Heraklids still wanted to know when they could rightfully return, and the Delphic Oracle said that they should wait for 'the third crop'. Hyllos waited three years, then invaded again, but he was slain in single combat by Ekhemos, King of Tegea, and the Heraklids retreated once more.

Further consultations of the Oracle established that 'the third crop' did not refer to the soil, but to generations of men. According to the traditional genealogy, the conquerors of the Peloponnese were Temenos and Kresphontes, great-great-grandsons of Herakles, who finally led the Heraklids and their allies, the Dorians, to victory in a campaign dated by Thukydides to the eightieth year after the capture of Troy, and by Pausanias to two generations after that event. Temenos assembled land and naval forces at Naupaktos, but before they could move on Aristodemos was killed by a thunder-bolt,[49] and Hippotes, a great-grandson of Herakles, killed a soothsayer, resulting in famine and destruction. The Oracle instructed them to banish Hippotes for ten years and to take 'the Three-Eyed One' as a guide. They discovered the Three-Eyed One in the shape of Oxylos sitting on a one-eyed horse, made him their guide, engaged their enemy on land and sea, and emerged triumphant.

The victors now drew lots to divide the spoils: Argos, Lakedaimon and Messene, in that order. A pitcher of water was prepared and the ballots were cast. Temenos and the Aristodemos' sons Prokles and Eurysthenes threw stones in, but Kresphontes, who wanted Messene and knew that he was going last, threw in a lump of earth, which dissolved in the water. Temenos drew Argos, the sons of Aristodemos drew Lakedaimon, and Kresphontes got Messene by default. Each one also received a sign on the altar where they sacrificed: Temenos found a toad, a creature that has no strength when it walks, signifying that he ought to remain in the city of Argos; the sons of Aristodemos found a snake, since Lakedaimon would be terrible in attack;[50] and Kresphontes found a wily fox.

Uses of Herakles' Mythology

It is interesting that Herakles is seldom portrayed in a group, and is notably written out of the Argonauts' expedition: his egotism is extreme; his violence and self-centredness at times verge on the insane; his lust was proverbial; he became a drunken, gluttonous butt of comedy, especially in Aristophanes; and yet, through motifs like the Choice of Herakles, he became important to fourth-century philosophers such as Isoktrates, who focused on his mind rather than his bodily strength, concentrating on the implications of a hero who had the cult-title 'guardian against Evil', and Diogenes the Cynic, who saw him as asserting the freedom of the individual against the artificial constraints of convention and tradition. Then in the third century the Hellenistic poet Theokritos made fascinating use of his mythology in his writings at the court of Ptolemy II Philadelphos of Egypt.

Theokritos adeptly subverted the archaic ideal to produce *Epyllia* ('little epics') with narratives based on episodes from the life of the hero, told so as to undercut or even mock the conventional heroic interpretation of the episode. He exploits strong contrasts between the epic setting of the various episodes and his own modern treatment of them. So, for example, in his *Idyll* 13, where he handles the Hylas episode of the *Argonautika* story,[51] Herakles' adventure does nothing to enhance his heroic reputation and his failure to sail on with the Argonauts leaves him greeted only by the derision of his companions. And in *Idyll* 24 his heroic strangling of the vipers as a child is set in an ordinary Hellenistic household.

The changes that Theokritos introduces to the myth are highly significant: in earlier tellings of the serpents story Alkmene rushes courageously to the aid of her child, but the Theokritean Alkmene merely wakes up her husband and tells him to find out what the matter is. Her nagging insistence makes her appear more like a housewife than a mythological heroine, and her affection for her husband is expressed in very conversational terms. Amphitryon himself has all the trappings of a Homeric hero – he is a heroic warrior, and the gear he puts on to investigate the cry is just what such a man would wear in battle, but his manner is far from heroic: when he gets up he is sluggish and reluctant; and his actions are prompted much more by his wife than by any sense of urgency; and his arming is over-careful and ultimately unnecessary. All this is underscored by interesting distortions of conventional heroic language: when Alkmene tells him not to put his shoes on, it is as though she knows the standard dressing procedures of Homeric heroes and is worried that he will waste too much time following the routine. And once the scare is over, rather than standing there rhapsodizing over the amazing powers of his son, as he does in Pindar, he puts the boy back to bed and then goes back to sleep himself. This is a very good example of how Hellenistic authors could treat the stories: the characters of the mythological world are made to behave like ordinary people in Hellenistic society. Apollonios Rhodios' Jason is another instance of this trend.

There is also an interesting significance in the ritual that follows the strangling of the serpents in the poem: what the snakes meant to inflict on Herakles is instead inflicted on them. The following morning Teiresias prescribes the ritual for getting rid of the dead snakes: they are to be burned at midnight in dry shrubs, their ashes collected and thrown beyond the boundaries by a servant who should not turn to look back. This is not scholarly pedantry on Theokritos' part, but indicates that the snakes have become scapegoats: Teiresias describes the typical details of a *pharmakos* (scapegoat) ritual – the snakes assume what was intended for Herakles (i.e. his mortality) and when they are disposed of properly he can be said to have truly escaped the death that they suffer. This seemingly ordinary domestic episode reflects the process by which Herakles will eventually achieve his immortality: the snakes come at midnight with a threat of funereal fire and endless sleep, but instead they are consumed in flames at midnight. They are appropriate scapegoats, taking upon themselves the forms of death that were intended for someone else.

Theokritos also makes the mythical narrative of Herakles work on another level. The snake-strangling story can be symbolic of the triumph of any good cause, and with the Ptolemies, who ruled Egypt throughout most of the last three centuries BCE, it was especially appropriate. These rulers actually traced their descent directly back to Herakles, and Ptolemy II assumed power on his birthday in April 285. The poem implies that Herakles was also born in April – a clever point to make to please the king. Not that it was hard to praise the Ptolemies, but to do it effectively was more tricky, especially using a mythical tradition which contained so many negative references to people like the Ptolemies who killed their brothers, married their sisters, tyrannized their fellow Greeks and practically assaulted Olympos. But by hedging about their own ascent to divine status with ancestors like Herakles, the Ptolemies influenced the ways in which poets used or avoided them, and as a discriminating and perverse audience, they continually shaped much of the tone and outlook of the poetry that was written in their lifetimes. It is no coincidence that most of the marriages mentioned in Theokritos' *Idylls* are incestuous.

As the Ptolemies formed their new society around a new mythology with themselves at the centre, the poets, who validated their status in myth, had a role of public and political consequence. Writers such as Theokritos were addressing myths as if they were comfortably dead, and so perfect to be catalogued, obfuscated and burlesqued, but yet the Ptolemies' self-interested tampering with Olympos marked a new generative stage of the myth, which responded to, and created, profound changes in private belief and public life. Theokritos seems to have joined the conspiracy to elevate the Ptolemies to Olympos by a subtle manipulation of traditional mythology. Theokritos has created a heroic ambience where the Ptolemies could feel comfortable; they needed a mythology that made them look normal, and he provided it brilliantly.

So once again we see how myths are seldom told without motives, and how their narration and reception change according to the needs of the teller and the audience.

Similarly, although in a very different context, the mythology surrounding the Heraklids brings out interesting issues

concerning the way the mythological tradition relates to
historical events. It is often stated that the myth of the
Return of the Heraklids has a strong connection with the
so-called Dorian invasion, when a group of outsiders, the
Dorians, conquered or drove out the existing pre-Dorian
population of Greece. It is by no means certain that such
an invasion did really take place, or, if it did, when it
occurred (archaeologica1 evidence to support it is very hard
to unearth), but the mythology was certainly used and
manipulated by later Greeks, especially in a political context.
The clash between Athens and Sparta that led to the
Peloponnesian War in the fifth century was regularly seen
as a conflict between Dorians on the Spartan side and
Ionians on the Athenian, and the use of myths and genealogies to score political points was common. The Athenian
tragedian Euripides did so in a play called *Ion*,[52] in which
the Ionians' ancestor Ion has a much stronger genealogy
than the Dorians' ancestor Doros: Ion is a son of Apollo
and Kreousa (Creusa), who herself is the daughter of
Erekhtheus, an earth-born King of Athens; Doros is the
son of Kreousa and an ordinary King of Athens called
Xouthos (Xuthus) – far less impressive. Just as Theokritos was
manipulating the tradition to make the Ptolemies purr with
pleasure, Euripides was indulging in some politico-
mythological one-upmanship in wartime Athens. Another
excellent example of myths being good to think with.

Post-Classical Herakles/Hercules

In visual art Herakles was incredibly popular, and it would
be futile to attempt here any sort of catalogue of the vast
array of images that still survive. Artists from all over the
Hellenic world used the Herakles tales, as did the painter of
the seventh-century amphora now in New York, which

depicts him slaying the Centaur Nessos by grabbing him by the hair, placing his foot in the Centaur's back, and running him through with his sword; or the sixth-century pediment of the Siphnian Treasury at Delphi, where he and Apollo contest possession of the Delphic tripod; or the early fifth-century east pediment of the temple of Aphaia at Aigine, where he kneels to draw his bow during the assault on Troy, his facial features beautifully framed by the lion headdress; or again the mighty, muscle-bound Hellenistic Farnese Herakles, who leans wearily on his club, presumably at the end of his Labours.

In post-classical art we can see the hero making his choice between Vice (identifiable by her artfully dishevelled diaphanous garments, an actor's mask and a musical instrument) and Virtue (more modestly attired, holding a sheathed sword and pointing up a rocky upward path) in Annibale Carracci's *The Choice of Heracles* (1596). He can exhibit a dramatically lit, muscular physique, framed by the lion-skin cloak, as in Guido Reni's image of him battering the multi-headed Hydra with his club (*Hercules and the Lernaean Hydra*, 1617). The abduction of his lover Hylas is shown by J.W. Waterhouse in *Hylas and the Nymphs* (1896), where seven alluring watery lovelies entice the boy into their world of idealized beauty. Cranach, Tintoretto, Rubens, Giordano, Boucher and Goya were all attracted to the theme of Herakles' servitude to Omphale, while Rubens also produced a glorious sketch of *The Apotheosis of Hercules* (1636) for Philip IV's hunting lodge near Madrid, where the hero finally ascends to Olympos out of the flames of his funeral pyre in a divine four-horsed chariot, as a putto places a victor's wreath on his head in a fitting gesture of triumph for Zeus' favourite son.

Herakles is equally popular in today's entertainment industry. The television series *Hercules: The Legendary Journeys* reworks the original mythological material to pretty good effect, and *The Xena Trilogy* in which Herakles enjoys a variety of adventures with the beautiful but deadly warrior princess Xena is no less entertaining. Disney's animated *Hercules* (1997) deploys the imagery of Greek vases and sculptures very adeptly as it both sends up and transforms the hero in a typically Disneyesque way in which the mythical tradition seems very alive, albeit with some interesting themes and variations: Herakles' blue-maned white charger Pegasos might be borrowed from the tale of Bellerophon, but he makes a brilliant cartoon character.

7

THEBES AND OIDIPOUS

Key Characters

Agenor	Ancestor of the Thebans, Phoenicians and Cilicians
Europa	Taken to Crete by Zeus in the form of a bull; mother of Minos
Kadmos (Cadmus)	Founder of Thebes
Harmonia	Daughter of Ares and Aphrodite; wife of Kadmos
Ino	Daughter of Kadmos and Harmonia
Semele	Mother of Dionysos
Dionysos (Bacchus)	God of intoxicated ecstasy
Aktaion (Actaeon)	A hunter, killed by his own dogs
Pentheus	Resisted Dionysos and was destroyed for doing so
Niobe	Boasted about her children; turned to stone
Oidipous (Oedipus)	King of Thebes; solved the riddle of the Sphinx; killed his father and married his mother
Kreon (Creon)	Ex-king of Thebes, brother-in-law of Oidipous
Teiresias (Tiresias)	A blind seer
Iokaste (Jocasta)	Queen of Thebes, mother and wife of Oidipous
Antigone and Ismene	Oidipous' young daughters
The Seven Against Thebes	Unsuccessful attackers of the city

The Epigonoi	'The Later Generation'; descendants of the Seven

The city of Thebes is the focus for one of the great cycles of Greek mythological stories, from its foundation by Kadmos, resistance to Dionysos, the events concerning Oidipous, and the conflicts with the rival state of Argos.

The convoluted nature of mythical genealogy is well illustrated by looking into the origins of the Theban royal family. Apollodoros says that Libya had two sons by Poseidon: Belos and Agenor. Belos ruled Egypt, while Agenor went to Phoenicia, married Telephassa, and fathered a daughter and three sons, who were the mythical ancestors of the Thebans, Phoenicians and Cilicians.

However, there is widespread disagreement about this:

- Some, including Homer, made Europa a daughter of Phoenix;
- Others said that Kadmos also was a son of Phoenix;
- There is also mention of Tityos as Europa's father;
- According to Hyginus, Agenor and Argiope were the parents of Kadmos and Europa;
- In Euripides, Agenor's sons were Kilix, Phoinix and Thasos, and Pausanias says that the inhabitants of the island of Thasos were descended from Phoenicians and traced their origins back to this Thasos. Herodotos adds that these Phoenician colonists discovered excellent gold mines on Thasos, and founded a sanctuary of Herakles there;
- Herodotos informs us that Kadmos, son of Agenor, founded a Phoenician colony in the island of Thera (Santorini);
- Diodoros reports that Kadmos founded a Phoenician colony

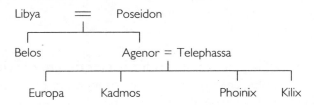

on Rhodes, and mentions that, in the sanctuary of Athena at Lindos, there was an ancient tripod bearing a Phoenician inscription. This has in fact been corroborated by an official record of the temple of Athena Lindia, which states: 'Kadmos [dedicated] a bronze tripod engraved with Phoenician letters, as Polyzalos relates in the fourth book of the histories.'

These myths seem to imply that the Greeks traced a blood relationship between the Phoenicians and Cilicians, and recognized a Phoenician element in some of the Greek islands and parts of the mainland.

Whatever her parentage, the best known tale about Europa is the one in which Zeus saw her gathering flowers by the seashore, and fell headlong in love with her. As Ovid remarked, love and regal dignity are not the best of friends, so he turned himself into a magnificent bull:

His hide was the colour of snow before it is trodden
by clumsy feet or turned to slush by the southerly rains.
The muscles stood out on his neck, he flaunted magnificent
    dewlaps,
his horns were curved in an elegant twist [. . .]

and were more transparent than flawless gems.
There wasn't a threat in his brow or a fearsome glare in his
    eyes;
His face was a perfect picture of peace.[1]

She was captivated by this astonishing creature, stroked him,
and put garlands on his horns.

Her lover was blissful and licked her hands as a prelude to other
and sweeter pleasures he barely, barely could wait for.[2]

Eventually she sat on his back, and he moved out into the
sea and conveyed his 'frightened prize' to Crete, where the
fruit of their lovemaking was the birth of Minos, Sarpedon
and Rhadamanthys.[3] Europa received some rather wonderful
gifts from Zeus: the bronze giant Talos, who repelled strangers
from Crete; a necklace made by Hephaistos, which she later
gave to Kadmos, and which he subsequently gave to Harmonia;
a javelin which always hit its target; and a hound called
Lailaps, who never failed to catch his prey.

Europa's father Agenor responded to her abduction by
sending his sons to track her down, but when they failed
they settled in various places which subsequently took their
names: Phoinix in Phoenicia; Kilix in Cilicia; Thasos on the
island of Thasos; and Kadmos initially in Thrace and then
in Kadmeia (later known as Thebes).

Following her relationship with Zeus, Europa married
Asterios (or Asterion), who brought up her children. Once
the boys reached the age when they started to become interested in sex they all fell in love with a beautiful young man
called Miletos. Sarpedon had the most success, which
prompted Minos to drive his brothers out. Miletos himself
fled to Karia where he founded the city of Miletos, while

Sarpedon helped Kilix defeat the Lykians and took over as King of Lykia. Sarpedon was one of Zeus' particular favourites, and was allowed to live for three generations until he was slain by Patroklos in the Trojan War. Rhadamanthys decamped to the islands of the southern Aegean, where he acquired a fine reputation for fairness and became a great law-giver. He later moved to Boiotia where he married Alkmene,[4] and because of his reputation he went to the Elysian Fields in Hades and became one of the judges of the dead.

The historian Herodotos, often known as 'the Father of History', narrated the events of the wars between Greece and Persia that occurred in the early years of the fifth century, and early in his narrative he commented on the way myths were often used to explain the origins of these wars. In a series of tit-for-tat actions Io was abducted from Argos by Phoenicians and was then taken to Egypt; Greeks (he says 'probably Cretans') then captured Europa from Tyre in revenge; the Greeks then upset the equilibrium by abducting Medeia from Kolkhis; some forty to fifty years after that, Paris abducted the Greek Helen; by this stage everyone was blaming everyone else, and the Trojan War broke out, resulting in a permanent division between Europe and Asia. That, says Herodotos, is how the Persians tell it, although he says that the Phoenicians have a different version: Io was not an unwilling victim – she had got pregnant by a sea captain, and in her shame she left with him. This is an interesting rationalization of the myths in the historicist mould, and Herodotos' verdict on it is illuminating:

> I have no intention of passing judgement on its truth or falsity. I prefer to rely on my knowledge, and to point out who it was in actual fact that first injured the Greeks; then I will proceed with my history.[5]

In other words, Herodotos is sceptical about the tales – for him as a fifth-century Greek, the distinction between myth and history was very clear-cut.

Europa's myth proved irresistible to artists and writers. A century or so before Herodotos, the abduction of Europa by the bull appears on a metope from Selinus in Sicily (540), which shows a dainty Europa riding side-saddle on a fine bull which turns to look front-on to the viewer, while the marine transit is indicated by dolphins around the bull's legs. In later times the *Rape of Europa* features as the title of paintings by Titian, Veronese and Hinderhout. Titian (c.1488–1576) also indicated the sea by the presence of dolphins, but his Europa is a much more abandoned (or desperate) figure, with swirling drapery and lots of exposed flesh, clinging to the bull's horn, while Cupids fly through the air and ride the dolphin, and Europa's distant companions call to her in vain. The Doge's palace in Venice sported Veronese's mannerist treatment of the theme (c.1570–80), of which there are also versions in the National Gallery in London and the Capitoline Museum in Rome, where her companions appear to be helping her on to the bull's back, unlike her distraught comrades who run into the sea as she and the bull move out of reach in Hinderhout's version from the 1680s.

The Early Myths of Thebes: Kadmos, Semele and Aktaion

When Kadmos' mother died he buried her and went to Delphi to enquire about his sister Europa. He was told not to worry about her, but to follow a cow with a white mark resembling the full moon on each flank, and to found a city wherever she lay down to rest. The cow finally stopped where the city of Thebes was established.[6] Kadmos wanted to sacrifice it to Athena and he sent some of his companions to get water from the nearby Spring of Ares, not realizing that a horrendous dragon, the offspring of Ares, guarded the spring. This monster

> flaunted a golden crest,
> fiery glinting eyes, a flickering three-forked tongue,
> three marshalled ranks of teeth and body swollen with venom.[7]

Undaunted by this, the mighty Kadmos killed it, and, on Athena's advice, sowed some of its teeth in the soil while she gave the rest to Aietes, King of Kolkhis. Armed men called the Spartoi ('the Sown Men') sprang up and Kadmos hurled stones at them. They all thought that they were being assailed by each other, and fell on one another with fatal results – there were only five survivors.

To atone for the slaughter of the dragon, Kadmos had to serve Ares for eight years, but after this he took possession of Kadmeia (later called Thebes), and, in a magnificent celebration attended by all the gods, he married Harmonia, the daughter of Aphrodite and Ares. Kadmos gave her a gorgeous robe and a fabulous necklace wrought by Hephaistos.[8] The fruit of this marriage was four daughters (Autonoe, Ino, Semele and Agaue) and a son (Polydoros).

Kadmos and Harmonia's family were the cause of much anguish to them. Zeus fell for Semele, who fell pregnant with Dionysos, and promised to grant her whatever she wished. When Hera discovered this, she preyed on Semele's insecurities by asking whether, when they made love, Zeus appeared to Semele as he did to her. He didn't, but Semele asked him to, despite his protestations. When Zeus appeared in all his Olympian majesty, in his chariot hurling thunderbolts, Semele was incinerated, although Zeus was able to save the premature child from her womb and sew it up in his thigh.

After the required gestation period, Zeus undid the stitches and gave birth to Dionysos, 'the Twice-born God'. He entrusted him to Hermes, who gave him to Ino and Athamas, who reared him as a girl to prevent Hera discovering him. The plan failed and Hera drove them insane: Athamas shot their elder son Learkhos thinking he was a deer, and Ino threw the younger Melikertes into a cauldron of boiling water before leaping into the sea and drowning with the dead child in her arms. Melikertes' body was carried ashore by a dolphin, and his uncle Sisyphos, King of Korinth, instituted the Isthmian Games in his honour. Dionysos transformed Ino and Melikertes into the sea divinities Leukothea ('the White Goddess'), and Palaimon, who protected storm-tossed mariners, Odysseus included. Zeus eluded the wrath of Hera by transforming Dionysos into a kid, and Hermes took him to the nymphs of Mount Nysa (which has many different possible locations), who brought him up and became part of his entourage of revellers. They were occasionally called the Hyades, and Zeus finally changed them into stars.

Further reasons for lamentation in Kadmos' family concerned his grandson Aktaion. He had been brought up by the Centaur Kheiron to be a hunter, but was tragically devoured on Mount Kithairon by his own dogs. According to the usual version, this happened because he stumbled upon the virgin goddess Artemis while she was bathing, and saw her naked. Embarrassed and furious, she transformed him into a stag. As he moved away in shock the fifty dogs in his pack caught his scent:

He fled from the dogs who had served him so faithfully, longing to shout to them,
'Stop! It is I, Aktaion, your master. Do you not know me?'

> But the words would not come. The air was filled with relentless
> baying.
> Blacklock first inserted his teeth to tear at his back;
> Beast-killer next; then Mountain-Boy latched on to his shoulder.[9]

His companions were completely unaware of the situation, and simply encouraged the dogs, which devoured him unwittingly. This assuaged Artemis' anger, while the dogs went in search of their master with heart-rending howls until Kheiron made an image of Aktaion for them to mollify their grief.

Dionysos, also known as Bakkhos or Iakkhos, the god of intoxicated ecstasy, ritual madness, the vine and drama, had a major role to play in Kadmos' life. Dionysos was driven mad by Hera, who was still angry about Zeus and Semele's liaison. He roamed through Egypt, Syria and Phrygia, where he was brought back to sanity by Rhea, who was sometimes identified by the Greeks with the Phrygian mother goddess Kybele.[10] Dionysos was accompanied by a revelling band of Satyrs and Silenoi (male, ithyphallic, mainly human creatures with some animal attributes and a healthy appetite for sex, alcohol, music and revelry, led by Silenos, the oldest, wisest and most inebriated of them all), plus nymphs and Mainads ('mad women', also known as Bakkhai or Bacchants). The Mainads entered a state of ecstatic frenzy brought on by wine, music, song and dance; dressed in fawn skins with wreaths of ivy, oak and bryony, plus sometimes girdles of snakes; brandished the *thyrsos* (a wand of fennel with a bunch of ivy leaves at the tip) and sometimes torches and branches of oak or fir; and worshipped Dionysos with activity that included *oreibasia* (mountain dancing) and wild rites that culminated in *sparagmos* (tearing animals apart) and *omophagia* (eating raw flesh).

Dionysos moved from Phrygia into Thrace, where Lykourgos gave him a hostile reception. The god was forced to take refuge with Thetis, and his Satyrs and Mainads were captured. But suddenly all Dionysos' followers were released, and Dionysos drove Lykourgos mad: thinking that he was lopping a branch off a vine with an axe, he was killing his son Dryas by chopping off all his extremities. Recovering his senses, he witnessed the horror of what he had done, before his subjects led him to Mount Pangaion, where he was torn to pieces by wild horses.[11]

Dionysos then journeyed over the whole of India, before returning to Greece. Oineus of Kalydon welcomed him, and received a vine, possibly as thanks for Dionysos enjoying his wife Althaia; the Attic farmer Ikarios similarly greeted Dionysos in a friendly way and was given a vine and knowledge of wine-making. However, when Ikarios gave some shepherds a taste of the revolutionary new beverage they drank vast quantities of it without water, thought they were bewitched, and battered Ikarios to death and buried him under a tree. When his dog Maira discovered the body, his daughter Erigone hanged herself and Maira jumped into a well and drowned. All three were immortalized as the constellations of Boötes (Ikarios), Virgo (Erigone) and Canis Minor ('the Lesser Dog' – Maira).

Those who resisted Dionysos paid heavily for it: the daughters of Minyas of Orkhomenos stayed working at their looms rather than joining the Bacchic revelry, and were terrified into sacrificing one of their sons before being turned into a bat and two owls (or three owls in Ovid); and the fate of Pentheus, son of Ekhion and Agaue, who succeeded Kadmos as King of Thebes, forms the basis for Euripides' awesomely compelling tragedy *Bakkhai*, produced posthumously in 405.

Dionysos, Pentheus and the Bakkhai

In the prologue Dionysos himself stands outside Pentheus' palace, and announces his intentions:

For Thebes, albeit reluctantly, must learn in full
This lesson, that my Bacchic worship is a matter
As yet beyond her knowledge and experience;
And I must vindicate my mother Semele
By manifesting myself before the human race
As the divine son whom she bore to immortal Zeus.[12]

Dionysos' physical appearance reflects his ambiguous nature: he is a god, but in human form; he was born in Thebes, but he wears Persian clothes; he is male, but his beauty is effeminate; he comes to punish, but his mask wears a smile. With Dionysos, the categories of divine/human, Greek/barbarian, male/female become blurred.

Semele's sisters opted not to worship Dionysos, so he has driven them insane. In fact he has driven all the women of Thebes on to Mount Kithairon, and out of their minds: they are not 'normal' Mainads, because their state has been forced upon them, but the Chorus of the play are. They enter the stage and summon everyone to worship Dionysos: the earth flows with milk, wine and honey, and their overriding emotion is joy; but Pentheus, whose regal authority is under threat, is suspicious, alienated and scared.

The blind prophet Teiresias now comes on to the stage, along with Kadmos. According to Kallimakhos' *Hymn to Athena*, Teiresias had lost his sight because, when he was roaming the hills with his dogs, he had seen Athena and Khariklo enjoying a refreshing dip in the fair-flowing spring of Hippokrene on Mount Helikon. Blindness was the fate of those who looked at the immortals without their consent, but in compensation Athena gave him the powers of prophecy, long life and the total retention of his mental faculties after death. Another tradition holds that he came across two copulating snakes on a mountain, struck them with his staff, and instantly turned into a woman. Some years later, he saw them copulating again, and a blow of his staff restored his maleness.[13] This experience put him in a good position to settle an argument between Zeus and Hera about whether a man or a woman gets more pleasure from making love. His response was categorical:

> Of ten parts a man enjoys one only;
> But a woman enjoys the full ten parts in her heart.

Annoyed that Teiresias had divulged woman's great secret, Hera blinded him, but Zeus gave him the art of soothsaying.

Teiresias and Kadmos are doddery old men, but they are wearing fawn skins, carrying *thyrsoi*, and they are going to dance. They worship Dionysos voluntarily and Teiresias advocates reverencing the divine in whatever form it appears, but Pentheus has a diametrically opposed response: he is incensed that the women of his city have headed off to the mountains, led by a foreign stranger, to venerate a new god.

After Kadmos and Teiresias exit, the Chorus sing an ode to holiness. Choruses in Greek tragedy tend to be quite neutral in their sympathies, but not so here: they strongly condemn Pentheus, whose forces have by now had Dionysos arrested. A soldier escorts the captive god on to the stage. Dionysos is still smiling, and the soldier emphasizes how gentle he is. We now witness the first of three confrontations between Pentheus and Dionysos, as they spar verbally in *stichomythia* – staccato, single-line sentences.

Things start to get uncanny in the next episode, when Pentheus' palace is rocked by a violent earthquake, and Dionysos' voice is heard from inside. Offstage utterances often emanate from characters who are being murdered, like Agamemnon in Aiskhylos' *Agamemnon* and Medeia's sons in Euripides' *Medeia*, but here the speaker is the perpetrator of the violence. Pentheus arrives looking for his prisoner, and we see the second of their meetings. Terrifying events are now happening all over the place, but Dionysos, who still appears in the form of his human cult leader, plays on Pentheus' curiosity. The king is both repelled and fascinated by the events on the mountain, and Dionysos manipulates him brilliantly. With one of the most expressive monosyllabic utterances in all of Greek tragedy ('*a*' at line 810) he stops cautioning Pentheus against going to spy on the Mainads, and proposes an alternative: Pentheus should dress as a woman to go to the mountain and see for himself.

Pentheus' appearance in female clothing, his craziness and vanity could easily make the audience laugh, if Dionysos' ambiguous words were not indicating dangers that Pentheus does not sense. Dionysos has already told the audience that he will punish Pentheus, and now he makes that threat explicit: Pentheus will not only incur the ridicule he fears from the Thebans; he will go to his death.

The Chorus now sing of the delights of Bacchic worship. They want to escape the oppression of the city, and they characterize themselves as a fawn in a simile where Pentheus is still the hunter. But he is about to become the hunted: the *peripeteia* (the term used by Aristotle to describe the turning point where the protagonist becomes the victim) is happening now. The fourth episode of the play stages the final encounter between Pentheus and Dionysos. The balance of power has changed totally: Pentheus is now possessed by Dionysiac madness, and as the episode ends, the Chorus sing an extremely violent song which foreshadows what is about to befall him.

Pentheus' grisly fate is now narrated in a messenger speech, a virtuoso display of horror-story narrative. The violence is extreme. Pentheus is torn limb from limb by the Mainads, led by his own mother Agaue, as Euripides plays with ideas of recognition: the man who originally failed to recognize the god is now not recognized for what he is – he is dressed as a woman, but not mistaken for one; and Agaue and the maddened women see him partly as a male spy, and partly as a wild animal.

As the audience recover from the news of Pentheus' hideous death, the Chorus sing of their delight. This response is unusual.[14] Pentheus was indubitably wrong to act the way he did, but the contrast between the messenger's anguish and the Chorus' exultation is stark and chilling.

The final section of the play, the *exodos*, is slightly incomplete, but still incredibly powerful. Pentheus' mother Agaue now enters the stage for the first time, still possessed by Bacchic madness, and carrying her son's severed head, thinking that it is a lion. This is a brilliant, grotesque visual completion of the reversal of power in the play: Pentheus threatened to behead Dionysos, and has been beheaded by his own mother. Kadmos now returns with the dismembered pieces of his grandson, creating a further macabre contrast with Agaue's crazy exhilaration. But the horror gets even worse when she recovers her wits and realizes what she has done.

Kadmos mourns the ruin of his house, his personal tragedy and the loss of his grandson. His fate is remarkable: earlier on Dionysos praised him, and he was ready to dance for the god, even if he was a bit cynical in his reasons for proclaiming Dionysos' divinity. Still, even the Chorus sympathize with him in the end.

Finally, we get the *deus ex machina*. Dionysos appears and foretells the aftermath of the tragedy, which is every bit as bizarre and terrifying as the on-stage events. In the period after that dramatized in the play, Kadmos and Harmonia left Thebes and became the rulers of Illyria, but ultimately both Kadmos and Harmonia were turned into serpents and sent away by Zeus to the Elysian Fields.[15] Euripides' predilection for tying up details of myth and history at the end of his plays reflects a strong contemporary interest in aetiology (explaining the origin of beliefs and traditions).

Having unequivocally exhibited his divinity at Thebes, Dionysos went to the Argolid, where again he was not honoured, whereupon the daughters of Proitos went mad,[16] and, according to Apollodoros, devoured the flesh of the infants they carried at their breasts. In the *Homeric Hymn to Dionysos* we get a tale of how Dionysos hired a Tyrrhenian pirate ship to ferry him to Naxos, but the pirates sailed past the island and made for Asia, with the intention of selling him into slavery. Once again weird things happened: the mast and oars turned into snakes; the vessel filled with ivy and flute music; the pirates went mad, leaped into the sea, and were turned into dolphins.

There was now no questioning Dionysos' divinity. He went to retrieve his mother Semele from Hades, but because he had never been there before, he had to ask the way. Prosymnos (or Polymnos or Hypolipnos) gave Dionysos directions in return for a promise of sexual favours. Hades said he would release Semele in exchange for whatever Dionysos held dearest in the world. This was ivy, the vine and myrtle, so he sent myrtle, which explained why Dionysiac initiates wreathed their brows with its leaves. The god renamed his mother Thyone, and ascended with her to Olympos, but on the way he discovered that Prosymnos had died, so to fulfil his promise he carved a branch of fig wood into the shape of a phallus, and performed an act designed to satisfy his ghost. The myth allegedly explained why *phalloi* figured prominently in Bacchic processions.

Oidipous

Traditions vary concerning the transition of power at Thebes after the reigns of Pentheus and Kadmos, and about the precise order of the rulers. One common version is given here.

Kings of Thebes

Kadmos	(son of Agenor or Phoinix)
Pentheus	(son of Ekhion)
Polydoros	(son of Kadmos and Harmonia)
Nykteus	(regent for the under-age Labdakos, his grandson)
Lykos	(regent after his brother Nykteus' death)
Labdakos	(son of Polydoros)
Lykos	(regent for the second time, for the under-age Laios. Killed by Amphion and Zethos)
Amphion and Zethos	(sons of Antiope and Epopeus)
Laios	(son of Labdakos)
Kreon	(son of Menoikeus)
Oidipous	(son of Laios)

Amid these regencies caused by premature deaths, Lykos was murdered by Amphion and Zethos. The reason behind this was that Zeus got Nykteus' daughter Antiope pregnant, for which her father expelled her, before committing suicide in despair. Antiope married Epopeus at Sikyon, but Nykteus' brother Lykos killed Epopeus, and captured Antiope. On the way back to Thebes she gave birth to twins on Mount Kithairon (Cithaeron), where they were exposed to die, but a herdsman found them and took them in, naming them Zethos and Amphion.

Zethos was adept at the 'manly pursuits' of agriculture, cattle-breeding and war, while Amphion was a brilliant musician who could make animals, trees and stones follow him.[17] Lykos and his wife Dirke (Dirce) treated the enslaved Antiope shamefully, until one day her chains miraculously fell away of their own accord and she made her way to the herdsman's cottage. Sadly, her sons did not recognize her, and so Dirke, who was in a Dionysiac frenzy on Mount Kithairon, recaptured her. She was going to murder Antiope by tying her to a raging bull, but at the eleventh hour the herdsman recognized Antiope, and Amphion and Zethos tied Dirke to the bull instead, and hurled her body into the spring that was called Dirke after her.[18] They also slew Lykos and took control of Thebes, which they fortified for the first time. The cloak which Athena gave to Jason in the *Argonautika* illustrated the tale: Zethos shoulders a mountain peak, and finds it really hard work; Amphion sings to his golden lyre while a boulder twice as large comes trundling after him. They also expelled Laios, who went off to Pelops in the Peloponnese, where he performed the very first homosexual act among mortals with Pelops' son Khrysippos. The boy killed himself in shame: Zeus decreed that Laios would be killed by his own son Oidipous as a result; Hera, goddess of childbirth, felt dishonoured by Laios' homosexuality, and sent the Sphinx to Thebes.

Zethos married Thebe, who became the eponym of Thebes, while Amphion married Niobe, daughter of Tantalos, sister of Pelops. There is considerable diversity in the ancient sources concerning how many children Niobe had: the figures range from ten sons and ten daughters to two males and three females, with the norm at seven of each. The prolific Niobe boasted that this made her superior to Latona/Leto who only had two children, but quality vanquished quantity since Latona's children were Apollo and Artemis, who respectively killed the males as they were hunting on Kithairon, and the females in their house.[19] Niobe went to Mount Sipylos where she was transformed into a rock from which tears flowed night and day.

After Amphion's death Laios returned to Thebes, took the throne, and married Iokaste (Latinized to Jocasta).[20] The marriage turned out childless, and when Laios consulted the Delphic Oracle, he received the dire prediction that if he did have a son, he would kill his father. He abstained from sex, but one night too much wine made Iokaste's attractions prove irresistible. When the inevitable child was born he pierced its ankles with brooches and gave it to a herdsman to expose on Mount Kithairon. Unfortunately for all concerned, a herdsman of King Polybos of neighbouring Korinth found the child and took it to the king's childless wife Queen Merope,[21] who raised him as though he were her own. They called him Oidipous ('Swollen-foot', Latinized to Oedipus) on account of his injuries.

When Oidipous was growing up, a chance remark to the effect that he was not really the son of Polybos and Merope set him on a quest to find his true ancestry. The Delphic Oracle did not answer his question, but did tell him not to go to his native land, because he would murder his father and marry his mother. So to avoid Polybos and Merope Oidipous set out on a journey that led to a chance encounter with Laios at the Triple Way where the road from Daulis and the road from Thebes and Lebadeia merge and ascend towards Delphi. Oidipous never discovered Laios' identity, because an incident of mythological road-rage caused Oidipous to turn violent and kill him. Oidipous continued on to Thebes, where Kreon became Laios' successor.

However, at this point Hera sent the Sphinx to terrorize the Thebans. She had the face of a woman, the breast, feet and tail of a lion, and the wings of a bird and had learned a riddle from the Muses whose wording varies, but whose content does not:

> What is that which has one voice and yet becomes four-footed and two-footed and three-footed?

Solving the riddle would rid the Thebans of the Sphinx, but the Sphinx devoured all unsuccessful guessers, and when Kreon's son Haimon became a victim, the king decreed that whoever could solve the riddle would receive both the kingdom and his sister Iokaste, the ex-wife of Laios. Oidipous stepped forward with the solution: man. As a baby he crawls 'four-footed', as an adult he stands 'two-footed', and as an old man with a walking stick he is 'three-footed'. In chagrin the Sphinx hurled herself from the citadel, and Oidipous claimed his reward. Thebes became his realm, and Iokaste his wife.

The ensuing events are dramatized in Sophokles' timeless tragedy *Oidipous Tyrannos* (*Oedipus Rex,* or *King Oedipus*). When the play starts, the Chorus of Theban elders are begging Oidipous to deal with a devastating plague that is afflicting the city. Conscientious and self-confident ruler that he is, Oidipous has already sent Kreon to the oracle to seek advice, which turns out to be to find the killer of Laios. At Oidipous' insistence Kreon publicly announces that the discovery and punishment of the murderer will end the plague, and Oidipous, unaware that he himself is the cause of the problem, swears to take instant action.

The Chorus sings an ode that vividly describes the plague. They beg the gods for deliverance, but are anxious about the sacrifice that may be demanded in return. Then, in the presence of the people of Thebes, Oidipous insists that anyone who has information must come forward. With tragic irony, he says that he will fight for Laios as he would for his own father, but he will be lenient – exile, not death for the murderer, plus a reward for information. But no one speaks. Enraged, Oidipous then curses the murderer and anyone who harbours him.

Teiresias, the paradoxically blind seer, now arrives. He has been summoned by Oidipous but does not want to be there, and when the king asks for his help he refuses. Oidipous is livid, and immediately accuses Teiresias of involvement in the murder. Teiresias' reaction is to state unequivocally that Oidipous is the murderer: 'The killer you are seeking is yourself.' Oidipous is even more incensed by this, and rejects the idea out of hand, but rejection of prophetic power is a very dangerous thing to do.

Things deteriorate into a slanging match: Oidipous boasts about his victory over the Sphinx, and even accuses Teiresias and Kreon of plotting against him. Teiresias replies with dark hints of incest, blindness, infamy and wandering, before Oidipous loses patience and dismisses him. The Chorus then ponder over Teiresias' allegations: they are horrified and confused, and they sense 'wings of dark foreboding' beating around them; but they will stay loyal to Oidipous unless the charges stick.

The following scene opens with Kreon denying the charges and Oidipous refusing to believe him. Their angry confrontation only subsides when Iokaste comes on and sends her brother home. When she hears what all the fuss is about, she dismisses the issue out of hand: she tells of a (false) prophecy that her son would kill her ex-husband. Unfortunately, as she explains how Laios exposed the child on Mount Kithairon and was murdered by a band of robbers at a crossroads, she jogs Oidipous' memory: he thinks back to the incident at the crossroads and wonders whether he, in fact, could be the killer. In an effort to reassure him, Iokaste stresses that Laios was killed not by one man but by many, but even so, Oidipous asks that a shepherd, who is the only surviving witness, be brought in for questioning.

Worries about the old oracle that he would kill his father and marry his mother now start to nag away at Oidipous, but his fears are almost instantly allayed by the arrival of a messenger from Korinth, with news that his father Polybos has died of old age. Iokaste is ecstatic – the falseness of Oidipous' oracle is confirmed – but Oidipous remains concerned about the possibility of marrying his mother, Merope. At this point the messenger steps in with some supposedly welcome information: Polybos and Merope are not actually Oidipous' real parents, so there is no need to worry. To confirm the good news, he says that he himself gave Oidipous to the royal couple when a shepherd offered him an unwanted child from the house of Laios. This comes as a complete bombshell to Oidipous, who becomes determined to track down the shepherd and learn the truth about his origins. But Iokaste already knows: Oidipous is her son, and the prophecy was correct. She begs Oidipous to abandon his enquiries, but when he refuses she runs into the palace in a frenzy of grief.

Oidipous still thinks that the worst he can find out is that he is low-born, and he awaits the shepherd with a degree of confidence. When the man finally does arrive, after a very apt choral interlude on the theme of Tykhe (Chance), he refuses say anything until Oidipous threatens him with torture and death. Then he divulges the truth: he disobeyed his orders and saved the child out of pity, and yes, he admits, it was the son of Laios and Iokaste.

Oidipous now knows that he has murdered his father and married his mother. It is his turn to rush wildly into the palace, and all that now remains is for the audience to witness the appalling consequence of this hideous knowledge. A choral lament on the fragility of human life prolongs the tension, which is finally released when a messenger arrives from the palace. He describes how Oidipous had careered into the palace to find Iokaste hanging from a noose.[22] In a tortured frenzy he took the pins from her dress and stabbed them into his own eyes, so that he would no longer have to look upon those he had defiled, particularly his daughters Ismene and Antigone. The violence diffuses Oidipous' fury, and he accepts his fate by becoming one with it: 'I am agony.'

At this point Oidipous appears in person on stage to elicit the classic tragic responses of horror and pity. He begs Kreon, who has resumed rule over Thebes, to have him put to death or banished, but Kreon says that he will consult the oracle first and insists on Oidipous' obedience. So the final resolution is the humbling of the once proud Oidipous, who must accept both blindness and submission to another's will. He accepts his fate, and the Chorus conclude the drama by lamenting Oidipous' fall from greatness with the warning to 'count no man happy till he dies, free of pain at last'.

Oedipal Aftermath: Eteokles, Polyneikes and the Seven Against Thebes

Oidipous was driven out of Thebes, but not before he had cursed his sons Polyneikes and Eteokles.[23] He went to Kolonos in Attika with Antigone.[24] King Theseus of Athens welcomed him but he died quite soon afterwards in mysterious circumstances. These events were also dramatized by Sophokles in his tragedy *Oidipous at Kolonos*.

Eteokles ('True Glory') and Polyneikes ('Much Quarrelling')

agreed to take it in turns to rule for a year at a time, but
Eteokles refused to relinquish power after his year. Polyneikes
found himself banished, and his exile took him to Argos,
with the necklace and the robe that Kadmos had given to
Harmonia at their wedding in his possession. Adrastos was
King of Argos at that stage, and as Polyneikes approached
his palace he got embroiled in a fight with Tydeus, who had
fled there from Kalydon. Adrastos separated them, and then
remembered an oracle telling him to yoke his daughters to
a boar and a lion. Since either Tydeus had a boar emblazoned
on his shield in reference to the Kalydonian Boar and
Polyneikes had a lion on his because of the lion-faced Sphinx
of Thebes, or because the two warriors wore boar and a lion
skin, Adrastos responded by marrying his daughters Deipyle
and Argeia to Tydeus and Polyneikes respectively. Adrastos
also promised that he would restore both of them to their
native lands, starting with Polyneikes.

The forces were assembled, but the seer Amphiaraos foresaw that everyone, himself included, would die in the war,
apart from Adrastos, and so tried to prevent it. However,
Adrastos found out that if Amphiaraos' wife Eriphyle
acquired the necklace of Harmonia, Amphiaraos could be
forced to go. This was because in the past, when Amphiaraos
and Adrastos had quarrelled and made up, Amphiaraos had
sworn to allow Eriphyle to arbitrate any future arguments.
Now, as Adrastos' sister and Amphiaraos' wife, Eriphyle
appeared to be a good unbiased choice to settle the current
dispute, but Polyneikes bribed her with the necklace into
deciding that her husband should march with Adrastos. With
no alternative but to go, Amphiaraos instructed his sons to
kill their mother and march on Thebes when they had come
of age.

Adrastos put together his mighty army with seven leaders,

the so-called Seven Against Thebes. Sources differ as to who the Seven were (and indeed as to whether there were Seven), but generally they are Adrastos or Eteokles, plus Amphiaraos, Hippomedon, Kapaneus, Parthenopaios, Polyneikes and Tydeus.[25]

When the army arrived at Nemea, where Lykourgos was ruler, Jason's old flame Hypsipyle showed them a spring. When the Lemnian women had discovered that she had spared her father Thoas from the massacre of the males on the island, she fled, was captured by pirates, and was sold to Lykourgos and became the nurse of his son Opheltes. However, Hypsipyle neglected the boy while she was taking Adrastos to the spring, and he was killed by a snake. Amphiaraos took this as a sign foreboding the future, and they renamed the boy Arkhemoros, 'the Beginner of Doom'. They celebrated the Nemean Games in his honour, and in historical times the judges at the Nemean Games wore dark-coloured robes as a sign of mourning for Opheltes.

On their arrival in Theban territory, they sent Tydeus to demand the abdication of Eteokles. Eteokles' rejection of the request did nothing to intimidate Tydeus, even though he was on his own among the Thebans:

[He] dared them to try their strength with him, and bested all
    of them
easily, such might did Pallas Athene give him.
The Kadmeians who lash their horses, in anger compacted
an ambuscade of guile on his way home, assembling together
fifty fighting men [. . .]
On these men Tydeus let loose a fate that was shameful.
He killed them all, except that he let one man get home
    again.[26]

So the Argives approached the walls. The assault on Thebes is described in two extant Greek tragedies: the *Seven against Thebes* by Aiskhylos, and the *Phoenician Women* by Euripides, and it also forms the subject of Statius' epic, the *Thebaid*, which was widely read in medieval and Renaissance times. Thebes had seven gates, and each hero was responsible for attacking one of them.[27]

Eteokles consulted Teiresias to discover how his Theban champions might emerge triumphant. The seer explained:

> In that den where the earth-born dragon lay on guard
> Watching the spring of Dirke, there your son must give
> His blood as a libation to the earth, and die
> To appease the anger which, in ancient times, Ares
> Nursed against Kadmos.[28]

Ares' grudge goes back to when Kadmos slew his dragon, and Kreon's son is Menoikeus, a descendant of the 'Spartoi'. Menoikeus accepts his own death voluntarily:

> Kreon's son, who died to save his native land,
> [. . .] stood on a high tower and through his throat [. . .]
>   plunged
> The deadly sword which brought deliverance to Thebes.[29]

He fell from the walls into the dragon's den, and battle was joined. Kapaneus made it as far as the walls of Thebes, and was scaling them with a ladder:

> Still, foot by foot, from rung to smooth rung, up he came;
> And at the moment when he topped the rampart's crest,
> Zeus stuck him with a thunderbolt.[30]

Given Kapaneus' earlier boasts, this was a classic punishment of *hybris* by Zeus, and his manifest hostility turned the Argives to flight. Hippomedon, Eteoklos and Parthenopaios all lost their lives, and Tydeus was dying of his wounds. Athena had intentions of curing and immortalizing him, but recoiled in horror and withdrew the intended benefit when Amphiaraos, who still hated Tydeus for making him come on the expedition, gave him the severed head of Melanippos[31] and Tydeus split it open and ate the brains.

Amid all the carnage Eteokles and Polyneikes fought a single combat. In Euripides' *Phoenician Women* a messenger describes how each wounded the other before Eteokles drove his sword into his brother's stomach. But he failed to check that his victim was dead, and as he triumphantly stripped the armour from the body, Polyneikes gathered enough strength for one last sword-thrust:

> There, side by side, biting the dusty earth they lie;
> And which has gained the victory is still unknown.[32]

Amphiaraos fled along the banks of the River Ismenos with Periklymenos hot in pursuit:

> But Zeus in all his strength, with lightning
> split the deep-bosomed earth for Amphiaraos and covered him
>   and his horses
> before, stabbed in the back with Periklymenos' spear, he must
>   be shamed
> in his warrior's spirit.[33]

Amphiaraos, his chariot and charioteer descended down to the Underworld, where Zeus made him immortal. Adrastos was the sole survivor, saved by his divine stallion Areion, the offspring of the rape of Demeter, who had turned herself into a mare, by Poseidon, who became a stallion in order to gratify his lust. Adrastos fled to Eleusis along with the mothers of his comrades.[34] The myth is dramatized by Euripides in his play *The Suppliants*, where, helped by Aithra, the mother of Theseus, they persuade the Athenians to march on Thebes, and force the Thebans to give up the dead Argives for burial. This successful mission secured the corpses of all except Polyneikes (buried already) and Amphiaraos (swallowed by the earth), and the proper rites were conducted at Eleusis.

At Thebes, the vacant throne now fell yet again to Kreon, who decreed that the corpse of Polyneikes should be left to rot, and that anyone trying to bury him should be stoned to death. This posed serious political and religious problems, which are explored in Sophokles' tragedy *Antigone*. Kreon's proclamation was motivated by a feeling that Polyneikes had been a traitor, but not to bury the dead was an offence against the gods, and relatives had a definite religious duty to make sure that they received the necessary rites. Kreon's decree placed Antigone, who was Kreon's niece and Polyneikes' sister, in an impossible situation. In the end Antigone threw three handfuls of earth on to Polyneikes' body, which fulfilled the minimum ritual requirement for burial, but Kreon was furious when he discovered what she had done. The exchanges between the two of them are electrifying:

KREON: Do you admit, or do you deny the deed?
ANTIGONE: I do admit it. I do not deny it.
KREON: Did you know the order forbidding such an act?
ANTIGONE: I knew it, naturally. It was plain enough.
KREON: And yet you dared to contravene it?
ANTIGONE: Yes

> That order did not come from God. Justice,
> That dwells with the gods below, knows no such law.
> I did not think your edicts strong enough
> To overrule the unwritten, unalterable laws
> Of god and heaven, you being only a man.[35]

Kreon ultimately decides that Antigone and Ismene, her (innocent) sister, should be put to death, but his son Haimon,
who is engaged to Antigone, tries to intervene. After an
acrimonious scene Kreon softens slightly: Ismene will live,
and Antigone will be entombed alive. But the seer Teiresias
appears and warns Kreon against offending the gods like
this. He makes a dire prediction:

> Ere the chariot of the sun
> Has rounded once or twice his wheeling way,
> You shall have given a son of your own loins
> To death, in payment for death – two debts to pay:
> One for the life you have abominably entombed;
> One for the dead still lying above ground.[36]

Kreon decides he will relent and bury Polyneikes and liberate
Antigone. But his decision comes too late. He reaches
Antigone's prison to find that she has hanged herself, while
Haimon, who has just discovered the grim situation, stabs
himself with his sword. To complete a hat-trick of personal
tragedies, Kreon's wife Eurydike, heartbroken at the death
of her son, commits suicide too, cursing Kreon as she does
so. Kreon is left a broken man.

Sophokles' handling of the myth allows him to dramatize
a very subtle series of issues, especially as the moral stand-
ings of Antigone and Kreon are not entirely clear-cut. Kreon
is not an out-and-out villain, since he is aware of his

responsibilities as ruler at the outset, and elicits some degree of sympathy as he carries Haimon's body on stage at the end. His proclamation is undoubtedly controversial (Teiresias certainly sees it as morally unacceptable; causing Polyneikes' body to be mutilated by dogs and birds is beyond the pale), but there was nothing abnormal in denying a traitor burial in his homeland. Many critics approve of Antigone, since her religious scruples are impeccable, but she is tough on her sister and can seem far too concerned with honour, and it would be a mistake to reduce the play merely to issues of city versus kin-bond, or state versus individual. The myth has too much substance to allow Kreon or Antigone to become the vehicle for one simple idea.[37]

The Epigonoi

Even after all this, there was still unfinished business at Thebes. A decade after the expedition of the Seven, their sons, known as the Epigonoi ('The Later Generation'), decided to avenge their fathers. The Epigonoi are identified as:

- Alkmaion (or Alkmeon) and Amphilokhos, sons of Amphiaraos;
- Aigialeios, son of Adrastos;
- Diomedes, son of Tydeus;
- Promakhos, son of Parthenopaios;
- Sthenelos, son of Kapaneus;
- Thersandros, son of Polyneikes;
- Euryalos, son of Mekisteus.

Amphiaraos had also instructed his sons, fruit of his difficult relationship with Eriphyle, to kill their mother for betraying him for the necklace of Harmonia, and to march on Thebes.

Apollo's oracle predicted victory under the leadership of Alkmaion.

Like his father before him, Alkmaion ended up embroiled in a war against Thebes due to the machinations of Eriphyle, who had received another bribe, this time the robe of Harmonia from Thersandros, son of Polyneikes. However, this time the campaign was a success. The Epigonoi defeated the Thebans on the battlefield, and advanced on the city. The Thebans fled with their women and children, Teiresias died during the evacuation, and the Argives sacked the city and demolished the walls.

If Alkmaion's entry into combat with Thebes mirrors that of his father, his domestic circumstances resemble those of Orestes.[38] When he found out that Eriphyle had been bribed again he killed her.[39] His matricide brought down the Erinyes (Furies) on him, and he went mad. His wanderings took him to Phegeus at Psophis, who purified him and gave him his daughter Alphesiboia in marriage,[40] who received the deadly necklace and robe of Harmonia as her dowry. Needing further purification, Alkmaion went to the river god Akheloos, whose purificatory powers were efficacious. Alkmaion then received Kallirrhoe, Akheloos' daughter, as his second, concurrent, wife. Pausanias comments that 'a lot of men run their lives on to the rocks of irrational desires, and women even more so', and tells how the family heirlooms started to exert their malign influence once again. The necklace and robe were still with Alkmaion's first wife Alphesiboia, but Kallirrhoe insisted that she would only live with him on condition that she had them. So Alkmaion went back to Phegeus and lied about how he could only lose his madness by dedicating the necklace and the robe at Delphi. Phegeus handed them over, but unfortunately for Alkmaion, he then discovered the truth of the situation and got his sons to murder him.

The cycle of vengeance continued when Alphesiboia articulated her disapproval at the killing of her husband. Her brothers shut her in a chest, took her Tegea, gave her to Agapenor as a slave, and falsely accused her of Alkmaion's murder. Kallirrhoe, who was now being wooed by Zeus, asked him if her sons by the late Alkmaion might immediately become fully adult in order to avenge their father. Zeus granted her request, and they slew Phegeus, his wife and his sons, took possession of the robe and the necklace, and dedicated them at Delphi.[41] The evil powers of the treasures were at last neutralized and the conflicts were over.

Sophokles' presentation of the myth of Oidipous has raised constant questions in the scholarly community, and continues to do so. Among the views expressed are: that Oidipous knew the truth all along; that he was just a helpless puppet devoid of free will; that the play proceeds from a set of coincidences so utterly improbable that we should be more afraid of being hit by a thunderbolt than getting involved in Oidipous' particular set of misfortunes; or that we can follow Freud and apply the 'Oedipus Complex' to the play.

These days you tend think of Oidipous if you think of Freud (and vice versa). Oidipous' quest for his identity really attracted Freud to Sophokles' tragedy: the hero single-mindedly pursues his own self-discovery, pieces together meagre scraps of information, delves back into the trauma of his earliest childhood, and finds out that his real relationships with his parents are totally at odds with the norms of society. Freud saw this entire process as comparable to a work of psychoanalysis, and both Oidipous and the Sphinx became powerful personal symbols for him. The Sphinx belongs to an impressively monstrous lineage. (See the diagram on p.222.)

But the Sphinx is not just scary; she is sexy too. There is

a red-figure vase in Kiel from around 470 that shows her as an alluring woman preying erotically on a young man while tearing him apart. In addition to this her tripartite nature (woman's face, lion's body and bird's wings) reflects her mythological function: she not only asks riddles, but she is also one herself. And if the Sphinx is composed of three elements, so is the answer to her riddle – the four-legged, two-legged, three-legged human being. The fact that the solution to the riddle is 'man' is perfect for the Freudian, because that solution solves the riddle of the Sphinx's nature: it is possible to interpret the Sphinx's combination of a bestial body with a human head as an allegory, with the lower animal parts representing the passions (the lion = crude and bestial; the wings = creative and divine), and the human head standing for the *superego*, which is what distinguishes human beings from other animals. The Greek word *Sphinx* might have a connection with the verb *sphingo* ('I bind fast'), which tempts the Freudian into seeing it as 'the Repressor', leading to a conclusion that the Sphinx symbolizes man trying to control his animal instincts, but finding it challenging because he is two-thirds animal and only one-third human. Interestingly, when Plato discusses the tripartite human soul, he makes the three parts our bodily appetites, our emotions and our controlling intelligence. However, he does not use the Sphinx as a model; he prefers the Khimaira, Skylla and Kerberos.

All manner of conclusions can follow once the Freudian has found the answer to his or her own riddle of the Sphinx. For instance, Oidipous' slaughter of the Sphinx might equal denial of his repressed desires for his mother and hostility to his father, a stance that rebounds on him with awful consequences. Yet because he also kills the human element of the Sphinx (the 'repressor'), he could be thought of as a man without repression. For the Freudian, even Oidipous' name,

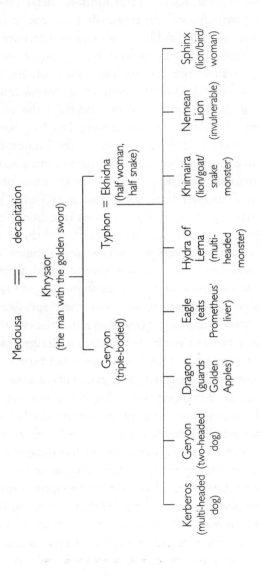

Medousa === decapitation
Khrysaor
(the man with the golden sword)

Typhon = Ekhidna
(half woman,
half snake)

Geryon
(triple-bodied)

Kerberos | Geryon | Dragon | Eagle | Hydra of | Khimaira | Nemean | Sphinx
(multi-headed | (two-headed | (guards | (eats | Lerna | (lion/goat/ | Lion | (lion/bird/
dog) | dog) | Golden | Prometheus' | (multi- | snake | (invulnerable) | woman)
 | | Apples) | liver) | headed | monster) | |
 | | | | monster) | | |

'Swollen Foot', can suggest out-of-control masculine sexuality: feet are the basis of the riddle of the Sphinx; Oidipous got his name from his ankles which were pierced by Laios – a Freudian symbol of the threat of castration by the father; Freud asserts that limping or crippling are castration symbols in dreams, which allows Oidipous' father and grandfather to enter the interpretation – *laios* means 'left' in Greek (and therefore indicates the uneven strength of the cripple?), and Labdakos may be connected to the letter *labda* (*lambda*), which was written λ, but with one long and one short stroke (and so indicates the man with the shortened foot, 'The Limper'?). Finally, Freud equates blinding with castration, and so Oidipous' self-blinding becomes the ultimate castration symbol.

And so, for Freud, Sophokles' *Oidipous Tyrannos* was the most powerful and universal tragedy of them all, because it told everyone's life story.

The Arts

Whether one's reaction to Freud's interpretation is 'comic or serious', there is no denying its influence. The myth of Oidipous did not really register in the popularity stakes prior to Freud getting hold of it.[42] One pre-Freud work, which exercised a great fascination for him, was Ingres's painting *Oedipus and the Sphinx* (1808), in which a heroically nude Oidipous stands outside her lair, which is littered with the bones of previous victims, looking her straight in the eyes, despite the artist highlighting her breasts and relegating her bestial elements to the shadows. Freud was mesmerized by it.

Gustave Moreau also produced an *Oedipus and the Sphinx* (1864), in an interpretation of the myth that draws heavily on Ingres's version, which was exhibited in Paris in 1846 and 1855. Like Ingres he focused on the moment when

Oidipous confronted the Sphinx in a rocky pass outside Thebes. Amid scattered human remains, Oedipus looks intently down at the explicitly amorous Sphinx as she clings to him with her rear claws either side of his genitals, and returns his gaze. The painting was a success at the Salon of 1864; it won a medal and established Moreau's reputation, though its acclaim was not universal: the cartoonist Daumier commented: 'a bare-shouldered cat with the head of a woman, so that's called a sphinx?'

The powerful pull of fate was what seems to have attracted Cocteau to the myth. In his play *La Machine Infernale* (1934) the machine of the title is 'one of the most perfect machines constructed by the infernal gods for the mathematical annihilation of a mortal', and the hero has no chance against the overwhelming divine intervention – events come to their conclusion regardless of what the characters do. For Cocteau, the Oidipous tale has become a great cosmic joke. The film *Edipo Re* by Pasolini (1967) has wider parameters than the Sophoklean tragedy, showing the exposure of Oidipous as a child, and the bloodthirsty encounter with Laios, and, by producing a version that is related to Freud's interpretation of the modern mind, he manages to keep the myth very fresh. One of the coolest renditions of the story has got to be Daniel Nussbaum's retelling through American-style car licence plates in PL8SPK:CALIFORNIA VANITY PLATES RETELL THE CLASSICS (1994). Here Oidipous tells of his discovery of the truth:

SUNLEE WEHEAR SHOCKING NEWS. WHEN IWASA TINY1 THISGRE8 4 SEER SED IWOOD OFF MY ROYAL OLDMAN THEN MARREE MYMAMA. SICKO RUBBISH NESTPAS? WHOWHO COULDBE

SOGONE? STILL MOMNDAD SENT MEEEEE
AWAY.

NOWWWWW GETTHIZ. MANY MOONS GOBY.
IMEET THISGUY ONATRIP. WEDOO RUMBLE.
WHOKNEW? ILEFTMY POP ONE DEDMAN.

UGET DAFOTO. MAJR TSURIS. JOJO
MYHONEE, MYSQEEZ, MYLAMBY, MIAMOR,
MYCUTEE. JOJOY IZZ MYMOMY.

8

FROM ATLAS TO HEKTOR

Key Characters

The Pleiades	The seven daughters of Atlas and Pleione
Hermes (Mercury)	Son of Zeus and Maia; trickster god of thieves; stole Apollo's cattle
Asklepios (Asclepius)	Son of Apollo and Koronis; god of medicine (Aesculapius in Latin)
Apollo	God of light, prophecy, archery, reason, intelligence, the sun
Helen	The 'face that launched a thousand ships'; wife of Menelaos
Menelaos (Menelaus)	Son of Atreus; husband of Helen
Kastor and Polydeukes	The 'Dioskouroi' (Dioscuri), 'Sons of Zeus' (Castor and Pollux in Latin)
Laomedon	King of Troy in the time of Herakles
Priamos (Priam)	King of Troy at the time of the Trojan War
Hekabe (Hecuba)	Wife of Priamos
Paris	Son of Priamos; made the 'Judgement of Paris'; abducted Helen
Kassandra (Cassandra)	Daughter of Priamos; prophesied the truth but was never believed
Hektor (Hector)	Son of Priamos; Troy's finest warrior

Atlas and the Oceanid Pleione had seven daughters[1] known collectively as the Pleiades, either after their mother or from the Greek *plein*, 'to sail', because in the Mediterranean the constellation of the Pleiades is visible during the sailing season. The most well-known explanation for their elevation to stellar status is that the hunter Orion fell in love and pursued them with his unwelcome attentions for anything up to twelve years, after which they were changed into doves. Zeus then turned both hunter and hunted into stars to continue an eternal pursuit.[2] Of the seven the star now called Celaeno is hard to see with the naked eye, a fact explained in myth by Elektra, the mother of the Trojan Dardanos, being so grieved at the fall of Troy that she hid her face in her hands, or by the Pleid Merope being so ashamed that she had married the mortal Sisyphos when all her sisters' partners were gods, that she did not want to reveal herself.

The eldest Pleiad Maia, 'the nymph with the beautiful hair, the shy goddess who lay in love with Zeus',[3] gave birth to Hermes in a cave on Mount Kyllene. He matured astonishingly quickly:

> She gave birth to a son who was versatile
> and full of tricks, a thief,
> a cattle-rustler, a bringer of dreams,
> a spy by night, watcher at the gate,
> one who was destined to bring wonderful things
> to light among the immortal gods.
> Born at dawn, he played the lyre in the afternoon
> and he stole the cattle of Apollo the Archer
> in the evening.[4]

This piece of thievery formed the subject of Sophokles' satyr play *The Trackers*, in which Apollo offers a reward for information leading to the animals' recapture. The old Satyr Silenos says that he and his fellow Satyrs will join the search, providing they are paid in advance. Apollo accepts, and the Satyrs soon find cattle tracks leading in various directions. They also hear a weird unfamiliar noise which turns out to be the muted tones of Hermes playing the lyre in the cave. The nymph Kyllene (Cyllene) emerges and gives the Satyrs a telling-off for disturbing the peace, but although they are suitably contrite, they still want to know about these alien sounds emanating from the bowels of the earth. Kyllene tells them that Maia has secretly given birth to Hermes, and describes how Hermes has grown at a staggering rate, and how he has made the lyre out of a tortoise shell. Being confined to the cave on Zeus' orders, he finds the instrument a great source of comfort, and he is in paroxysms of joy at the exquisite beauty of its sound. The Satyrs are unimpressed. They accuse Hermes of cattle-rustling. Kyllene denies the allegation: the boy is not genetically predisposed to criminality; you should go and look somewhere else; at your age, with your long beards and bald heads, you should know better. The Satyrs are stubborn, though. Hermes had used leather to build the lyre, so they put two and two together and stand firm until Hermes is handed over, at which point the tantalizingly fragmentary text starts to run out.

The Satyrs were definitely on the right track. The background to the fragment was that Hermes had stolen the cattle in Pieria, where Apollo was looking after the herds of Admetos but was preoccupied with a love affair with Hymenaios. Hermes worked hard to avoid detection:

> He did not forget the art of trickery
> when he reversed their hooves,
> making the front hooves backward

and the back hooves forward
while he himself walked backwards.[5]

He had driven the animals across Greece to Kyllene, where he
found the tortoise, made the lyre, and also invented the plectrum.[6]

Hot on Hermes' heels, Apollo finally caught up with him
at Kyllene and made his allegations. Hermes, who by this
time had snuggled back into his swaddling clothes, denied
everything, so Apollo appealed to Zeus, who told them to
seek the cattle together, with Hermes leading the way. In
due course Hermes returned the animals, but Apollo was still
enraged by the whole scenario. He was on the verge of punish-
ing Hermes when the young god started to play the lyre, and
he became so enamoured of its effect that he swapped the
cattle for it.

Apollodoros narrates a subsequent incident, in which
Hermes made himself a *syrinx* (pan pipes), which Apollo also
coveted. He offered Hermes a marvellous thing in exchange:

> I shall also give you
> A marvellous wand of blessing and fortune.
> A golden one, with three branches,
> Which will protect you and keep you unharmed
> As it accomplishes all the decrees
> Of noble words and deeds that I claim
> To know through the voice of Zeus.[7]

This wand, the *caduceus*, became one of Hermes' defining
attributes, and Zeus appointed Hermes 'the only consecrated
messenger to Hades': he became the messenger of the gods,
and the *psykhopompos*, the guide of the dead souls down
to the Underworld.

Another divine descendant of Atlas is Asklepios, the god

of healing. Although there are quite radically differing versions of his genealogy, Apollo was his father and there is a strong tradition that his mother was Koronis (Coronis), daughter of Phlegyas, and Pausanias quotes a statement from Apollo's oracle at Delphi in favour of her:

> O Asklepios,
> shoot of universal joy,
> whom Phlegyas' daughter bore to me
> beautiful Koronis
> with whom I mingled
> in love in rocky Epidauros.[8]

Epidauros was the site of a major sanctuary of Asklepios, and an inscription found there records a hymn to Apollo and Asklepios by an Epidaurian called Isyllos, in which the ancestry of Asklepios is given in detail.

The relationship between Apollo and Koronis, her affair with Iskhys and consequent death, and how Apollo rescued his child from the funeral pyre is told in Pindar's majestic 3rd *Pythian Ode*:

> Koronis, daughter of Phlegyas the great horseman,
> before with the ministration of Eleithyia she brought her
>   child to birth, was stricken
> by the golden bow of Artemis
> in a bedroom, and went down into the house of death
>   by design of Apollo. No slight thing
> is the anger of the children of Zeus. She, making little of this
> in her confused heart, accepted a second marriage, in secrecy
>   from her father,
> she who had lain before with Phoibos of the loose hair
> and carried the immaculate seed of the god.

Koronis went to bed with Iskhys, but Apollo discovered the 'graceless treachery', and sent his sister Artemis to exact vengeance on Koronis:

>   her angel
> shifted to evil and struck her down [. . .]
> But when her kinsmen had laid the girl in the wall
> of wood, and Hephaistos' greedy flame
> ran high, then spoke Apollo: 'No longer
> will I endure in my heart the destruction of my own child
> by a most pitiful death along with his mother's heavy suffering.'
> He spoke, and in the first stride was there and caught the boy
>   from the body,
> and the blaze of the pyre was divided before him.
> Carrying him to the centaur in Magnesia, he gave him to be
>   perfected
> in the healing of sicknesses that bring many pains to men.[9]

Pindar omits a part of the tale in which a raven, a bird that originally had snow-white feathers but was rather too fond of chattering, had witnessed Koronis' affair and relayed the information to Apollo. In this version Apollo shot Koronis, after which, rather than thanking the bird for revealing the truth, he cursed it for making him aware of the offence, and the raven ended up excluded from the white birds' ranks and condemned to be black.

The 'centaur in Magnesia' was Kheiron, under whose tutelage Asklepios developed into an unbelievably talented physician, who could not just prevent people from dying, but also raise them from the dead. Athena had given him some of the Gorgon Medousa's blood, which had the power either to do devastating harm or to raise the dead, depending on which side of her body it had flowed (left, lethal; right, beneficial).

So many people benefited from his death-defying talents[10] that the death rate went down so dramatically that Zeus became worried about the natural order of the universe and responded by blasting Asklepios with a thunderbolt.

Asklepios' death caused an angry backlash. Apollo slew the Cyclopes who had made the thunderbolt, or their sons, and Zeus would have hurled him into Tartaros had his mother Latona not intervened. Zeus commuted the sentence to servitude to a mortal for one or nine years, so Apollo served Admetos[11] as a herdsman at Pherai with remarkable results: the cattle increased in numbers, the she-goats never lacked young, the ewes always produced milk and lambs, and all the beasts invariably gave birth to twins.

Also tracing descent from Atlas is Helen of Sparta, the woman for whom the Greeks fought the ten-year war at Troy. The mythology that surrounds her is extremely complicated, and develops considerably as time goes on. Tracing her genealogy is problematical, since there is great confusion about the ancestry of her father Tyndareus, King of Lakedaimon.

Tyndareus was married to Leda, who had several daughters including Klytaimnestra (Latinized to Clytemnestra), who married Agamemnon, and Helen (Helene or Helena in Greek). Klytaimnestra's paternity is unclear, but as Helen herself explains, with an interesting note of circumspection, at the beginning of Euripides' tragedy *Helen*, she herself was the fruit of the union of Zeus and Leda:

> My home country is a place of some note – Sparta; and my father was Tyndareus. There is – you know – a legend which says that Zeus took the feathered form of a swan, and that being pursued by an eagle, and flying for refuge to the bosom of my mother, Leda, he used this deceit to accomplish his desire upon her. That is the story of my origin – if it is true.[12]

Rather appropriately after sex with a swan, Leda laid an egg. According to one account, the Dioskouroi ('Sons of Zeus') Kastor and Polydeukes, plus Helen, all hatched from one egg; according to another, Leda laid two eggs, the Dioskouroi hatching from one, and Klytaimnestra and Helen coming out of the other. Polydeukes and Helen are always regarded as offspring of Zeus, but Kastor and Klytaimnestra can be children of either Zeus or Tyndareus. There is also a variant in which Helen was a daughter of Zeus and Nemesis. When Nemesis changed herself into a goose to escape Zeus' unwanted advances, Zeus changed himself into a swan and took his enjoyment of her at Rhamnous in Attika.[13] The outcome of this avian intercourse was an egg, which was found by a shepherd, who gave it to Leda. Helen hatched after the due period of incubation, and Leda was so taken with her beauty that she brought her up as her own daughter.

Helen's astonishing loveliness carried through into childhood. One tradition holds that when she was seven, ten or twelve, the fifty-year-old Theseus and his friend Peirithoos fell for her and abducted her from the temple of Artemis Orthia in Lakedaimon.[14] They drew lots for who should have her, and Theseus won. He carried her off to Aphidnai near Athens and entrusted her to his mother Aithra. In some traditions he respected her virginity, but in others she became the mother of Iphigeneia (usually said to be daughter of Klytaimnestra). The agreement between Theseus and Peirithoos was that the loser should get Persephone, so the two then set off to abduct her from Hades, but while they were in the Underworld the Dioskouroi discovered Helen's whereabouts, rescued her and captured Aithra.

Once Helen was of marriageable age, the interest in her was considerable. Later in her life the Trojan elders would look at her in admiration:

Surely there is no blame on Trojans and strong-greaved Akhaians
if for a long time they suffer hardship for a woman like this one.
Terrible is the likeness of her face to immortal goddesses.[15]

A stellar line-up of Greek leaders made their way to Sparta to
try to win her hand, anything from twenty-nine to ninety-nine
in number. Pre-eminent among these individuals were: Aias
and Teukros, sons of Telamon from Salamis – Aias was particularly liberal in his offers of other people's property, promising
to give Helen many sheep and oxen which he proposed to loot
from the neighbouring territories; Aias, son of Oileus from
Lokroi; Diomedes, son of Tydeus, an awesome warrior;
Idomeneus, son of Minos, who trusted in the strength of his
own personal attractiveness to win her heart; Menelaus, son
of Atreus, ultimately the successful suitor; Odysseus, son of
Laertes, who did not bring any presents because he thought
he had no chance of winning Helen's hand; Podaleirios and
Makhaon, sons of the god Asklepios; and Patroklos, son of
Menoitios, the great friend of Akhilleus. The one conspicuous
absentee from the list is Akhilleus, who may have been too
young at the time. Tyndareus was worried that so many potentially disappointed heroes might create terrible conflict, but,
having secured a promise that Tyndareus would help him to
win the hand of Penelope, wily Odysseus advised him to make
all the suitors swear an oath to defend the chosen one against
any violation of the marriage. Tyndareus did just that, and the
suitors took the oath standing on the severed pieces of a horse.
Menelaos was the lucky man, and Odysseus subsequently
married Penelope. The oath was later invoked by Menelaos
when Paris abducted Helen and set the Trojan War in motion.

Homer says that Helen and Menelaos had one child, a
daughter Hermione, but other writers add various sons, and
there is even mention of Helen having a child by Paris. Being

married to the most beautiful woman in the world was obviously still not enough for Menelaos: extramarital liaisons resulted in sons by a female slave and a nymph.

Helen's brothers, the Dioskouroi, were 'A'-list heroes in their own right. 'Kastor, breaker of horses, and the strong boxer Polydeukes.'[16] They are credited with three key mythological adventures: the rescue of Helen from Aithra, sailing with the Argonauts (where Polydeukes defeats the barbaric Amykos at boxing),[17] and 'Rape of the Leukippidai', whose normal version was that Idas and Lynkeus, the sons of Aphareus, were engaged to their cousins Phoibe and Hilaira, the daughters of Leukippos, and invited their other cousins the Dioskouroi to the wedding. This, however, resulted in the abduction of the brides. The Hellenistic poet Theokritos describes the pursuit and fighting that ensued:

> [Lynkeus] was aiming a sharp thrust at the left knee, when
>   Kastor
> stepped back and chopped the top of his sword hand. Stricken,
> he dropped the weapon and started to flee to his father's tomb,
> where stout Idas was lying, watching his kinsman fight.
> But the son of Tyndareus darted after, and drove his blade
> clean through flank and navel, and straight the bronze parted
> the bowels within, while Lynkeus tottered and fell on his face,
> and the heavy sleep of death sped down to close his eyes.[18]

As Idas moved to intervene he was destroyed by one of Zeus' thunderbolts, leaving Theokritos to draw a somewhat brutal moral:

> And so it is no light matter to cross Tyndareus' sons,
> who are conquerors themselves, and sprung of a conquering
>   line.[19]

The Rape of the Leukippidai was a favourite subject in art, as was an incident that provided a different motivation for the conflict between the cousins, which was depicted on the sixth-century Treasury of the Sikyonians at Delphi. This was a dispute over the division of some cattle that they had stolen in a combined raid. Idas divided the booty by cutting a cow into quarters and saying that whoever ate his share first should get half the loot, with the second half going to whoever finished second. Before anyone had quite realized what was going on, Idas had devoured the entire beast and driven off the cattle. The Dioskouroi planned to set an ambush, but Lynkeus, who was exceptionally sharp-sighted, saw Kastor and pointed him out to his brother, who inflicted a mortal wound on him. Polydeukes avenged his brother by slaying Lynkeus, while Zeus exterminated Idas with a thunderbolt. When Polydeukes ran back to his dying brother and begged Zeus to grant him death too, his father offered him a choice:

> If you would escape death and age that men hate,
>   to dwell beside me on Olympos with Athene and Ares of the
>   black spear,
>   that right is yours. But if all your endeavour is for
>   your twin, and you would have in all things shares alike,
>   half the time you may breathe under the earth,
>   half the time in the golden house of the sky.[20]

Polydeukes did not give the matter a second thought, and from that point on Zeus allowed the Dioskouroi alternate days on Olympos and in Hades. They are frequently identified with the constellation Gemini, and they acted as saviours of those in peril at sea, appearing as the twin lights of St Elmo's fire.

When these events had run their course, Tyndareus transferred control of Sparta to his son-in-law Menelaos.

Troy: Foundation of the City and Celebrities Before the War

If the woman at the heart of the Trojan War could trace her ancestry back to Atlas, so could the founders of the city itself.

Iasion, son of Zeus and Atlas' daughter Elektra, had an affair with Demeter:

> And so it was when Demeter of the lovely hair, yielding
> to her desire, lay down with Iasion and loved him
> in a thrice-turned field, it was not long before this was made
> known
> to Zeus, who struck him down with a cast of the shining
> thunderbolt.[21]

Hesiod says that Ploutos (Wealth) was the offspring of this union. However, either overwhelmed by grief at his brother's death or driven by a flood, Dardanos left Samothrace for the mainland opposite, where he was welcomed by King Teukros (Latinized to Teucer). He founded Dardania (or Dardanos) in the foothills of Mount Ida, and had sons called Ilos and Erikhthonios. Erikhthonios became exceptionally rich, owning 3,000 horses, and he ultimately succeeded to the kingdom and fathered Tros. The country became known as the Troia or Tro(i)as ('Troad') after himself. His wife Kallirrhoe, daughter of Skamandros (Latinized to Scamander) bore him three sons, Ilos, Assarakos

> and godlike Ganymedes
> who was the loveliest born of the race of mortals, and therefore
> the gods caught him away to themselves, to be Zeus' wine-
> pourer,
> for the sake of his beauty, so he might be among the
> immortals.[22]

Ganymedes' abduction is said to have been perpetrated by Zeus himself, sometimes in the form of an eagle, or by an eagle on his behalf.[23] On Olympos he usually pours Zeus' nectar rather than wine, and in compensation for his abduction Zeus gave his father some divine horses or a golden vine made by Hephaistos. Ganymedes' brother Assarakos had a son called Kapys who had a son called Ankhises, whose affair with Aphrodite had a highly significant result:

> And fair-crowned Kythereia felt sweet love
> For the hero Ankhises, and she lay with him
> And bore Aineias on the mountaintop,
> In Ida, with its many wooded clefts.[24]

Ganymedes' other brother Ilos went to Phrygia, which is close to the Troad, to take part in some games where his prize for winning the wrestling included a dappled cow, along with instructions to found a city in the place where the animal lay down. This turned out to be at the Hill of Ate (Delusion) in Phrygia,[25] and there Ilos built his city and called it Ilion (the usual name for Troy).

A divine endorsement of Ilos' new city came in the form of the Palladion (Palladium), an ancient wooden image (a *xoanon*) three cubits high, with its feet joined together, brandishing a spear in its right hand and a distaff and spindle in its left. After Athena's birth from the head of Zeus she was brought up by Triton, whose daughter Pallas was also a warrior maiden, but during a falling-out Pallas was on the point of hitting Athena when Zeus held the aegis in front of her. Pallas was distracted and Athena dealt her a fatal blow. In her remorse Athena carved a wooden image of Pallas, and wrapped the aegis around it. The Palladion stayed on Olympos until Atlas' daughter Elektra took refuge by it when Zeus was raping her, prompting the King of the Gods to throw it down into Ilos' territory. Ilos built a temple to house it, and since it occupied its ritual position of its own accord (or fell into its proper place through the unfinished roof), he honoured it appropriately. So long as it remained in Troy the city could not be taken. [26]

Ilos was also the ancestor of the great Trojan heroes Laomedon (his son), Priamos (his grandson), and Hektor, Paris and Kassandra (his great-grandchildren). His wonderfully handsome grandson Tithonos got entangled in the numerous erotic intrigues of Eos (the Dawn).[27] She abducted Tithonos to Aithiopia, the land of the Sun, where their relationship produced two sons, Emathion and Memnon. Homer speaks of her daily routine:

> Now Dawn rose from her bed, where she lay with haughty Tithonos,
> to carry her light to men and to immortals.[28]

According to the *Homeric Hymn to Aphrodite*, Eos asked Zeus to make her lover immortal:[29]

> Zeus nodded and her wish was fulfilled.
> Foolish one, Dawn, the queen, did not think
> in her heart to ask for youth for him
> and to have deadly old age smoothed away.
> So as long as lovely youth possessed him
> he lived in rapture with early-born and golden-throned Dawn
> by the streams of Ocean at the ends of the earth.

However, when the first signs of ageing appeared, Eos stopped sleeping with him, and when old age completely incapacitated him

she laid him in a chamber and shut its shining doors.
His voice flows on endlessly, but the strength has gone
which once was his when his limbs were supple.[30]

In some versions Tithonos was turned into a cicada so that
Eos might always enjoy the resonance of her lover's voice.

In the reign of Laomedon, Ilion was captured by Herakles,[31]
after which Podarkes, who became called Priamos (Latinized
to Priam), came to the throne. Priamos' first marriage was
to Arisbe, but their son Aisakos, rather like Tithonos, achieved
unwanted immortality. In Ovid's account he was pursuing
the nymph Hesperia, who got bitten by an adder, ending
both her flight and her life.[32] Consumed with anguish, Aisakos

              jumped from a crag which the roaring waves had eroded
below, down into the sea. As he fell, he was gently caught
by pitying Tethys. She covered his body with wings as it floated
over the sea, and didn't allow him the death that he longed for.
The lover was deeply angry at being forced to live on,
and that obstacles had to be thrown in his way when he simply
      wanted
to die. As soon as his new-given wings had grown on his
      shoulders,
he dived and flung his body again to the water's surface.
His plumage lightened his fall. Then Aisakos furiously lowered
his head and plunged to the depths. He repeatedly tried to
      discover
a pathway to death and never stopped trying. His love made
      him thin,
and all of him lengthened out: his legs on their knotted joints,
his neck with the head so far from the body. He loves the sea,
and because he is constantly diving down it, we call him the
      diver.[33]

Priamos subsequently married Hekabe (Latinized to Hecuba), whose genealogy was particularly abstruse. The Roman Emperor Tiberius had a particular interest in Greek mythology, and would test scholars with difficult questions like, 'Who was the mother of Hecuba?'[34] Given that she variously appears as the daughter of Dymas and Eunoe, Kisseus and Telekleia, or the River Sangarios and Metope or Euagora, it was difficult to give a definitive answer. What we can say with confidence is that her first son by Priamos was Hektor, and that she had an uncanny dream when her second child was about to be born: she had brought forth a firebrand, whose fire devastated Troy. The interpretation of the dream was that the child would be the ruin of his country; the solution was that he should be exposed. Priamos' prophetic daughter Kassandra was particularly insistent:

> Kassandra cried, 'Kill him!' –
> Stood by the prophetic bay-tree, crying,
> 'Kill the destroyer of Priamos' city!'
> Kneeling to one after another,
> Entreating every elder and councillor,
> 'Kill that child!'[35]

The child was exposed on Mount Ida, but in one version he was reared by shepherds, who named him Alexandros, 'the Protected'[36] (Latinized to Alexander), or in another he was given to the servant Agelaos to expose, but then suckled by a bear. When Agelaos returned and found him alive, he brought him up as his own son, naming him Paris. As Paris matured he became stunningly handsome and very courageous. He married the nymph Oinone and lived on Mount Ida, where he earned himself the name Alexandros, 'the

Protector' – the name is ambiguous – because he defended the flocks very effectively against brigands.

Several years later Priamos held funeral games for the son he thought had died, and Paris, unaware of his true identity, went to Troy to compete. He was spectacularly successful, winning all the events and defeating his own brothers in the process. Angry and humiliated, Deiphobos drew his sword and Paris sought sanctuary at the altar of Zeus, where his sister Kassandra recognized him by her prophetic powers, or, in Euripides' lost play *Alexandros*, Hekabe recognized him at the eleventh hour and prevented the murder. Hekabe's ominous dream was forgotten for the moment, and Paris was welcomed back into his family.

Hekabe's beautiful daughter Kassandra was famous for having infallible prophetic skills that were never believed. One version of her acquisition of these powers is that as infants Kassandra and her twin brother Helenos fell asleep in the temple of the Thymbraian Apollo while their parents, somewhat the worse for wear after a lot of wine, had gone home and forgotten all about them. Having sobered up in the morning, they went back to the temple and found the sacred serpents licking the children's ears and mouths, and from that moment both Kassandra and Helenos had the gift of prophecy. A better-known tale narrates how Apollo fell in love with Kassandra and promised to teach her the art of prophecy in return for her sexual favours. She accepted the offer, acquired the powers, but failed to deliver her part of the bargain. This had disastrous consequences, as she explains to the chorus Leader in Aiskhylos' *Agamemnon*:

KASSANDRA: The prophet Apollo introduced me to his gift.
LEADER: A *god* – and moved with love?

KASSANDRA: I was ashamed to tell this once, but now . . .
LEADER: We spoil ourselves with scruples,
Long as things go well.
KASSANDRA: He came like a wrestler,
magnificent, took me down and breathed his fire through me and –
LEADER: You bore him a child?
KASSANDRA: I yielded,
Then at the climax I recoiled – I deceived Apollo!
LEADER: But the god's skills – they seized you even then?
KASSANDRA: Even then I told my people all the grief to come.
LEADER: And Apollo's anger never touched you? – is it possible?
KASSANDRA: Once I betrayed him I could never be believed.[37]

Priamos and Hekabe had a prodigious series of mighty sons (nineteen of his fifty sons were by her, including Hektor, Paris/Alexandros, Deiphobos, Helenos and Troilos (who is sometimes the son of Apollo and Hekabe) and beautiful daughters (including Kreousa, Polyxena and Kassandra) in addition to Priamos' various offspring by other wives. Without question, the finest of all these sons was Hektor, who married Andromakhe, daughter of Eetion, lord of Thebe in Kilikia, and became the great defender of Troy against the invasion led by Agamemnon.

Sophokles' fragmentary satyr play *Ikhneutai* (*Trackers*) has provided the inspiration for a remarkable piece of modern theatre by the British poet Tony Harrison, whose play *The Trackers of Oxyrhynchus* had a unique one-performance world premiere in the ancient stadium at Delphi in 1988. The play revolves around Harrison's free translation of Sophokles' play, which was found on papyrus scraps in Egypt in 1908. The actual archaeological dig by the Oxford papyrologists Grenfell and Hunt forms the first part of the play.

The middle section comes directly from Sophokles, and a chorus of satyrs look for Apollo's cattle exactly as they did in the original, except they clog-dance Yorkshire-style as they do it:

> Sniff, sniff
> sniff at the track
> we've got to get t' god's cattle back.
> [. . .]
> Hey, look at this! It's stupid, daft
> Their backlegs are forrad, their front legs aft.
>
> Blow me some bugger's done a switch.
> Head or arsehole, which is which?
>
> Eeh bah gum, and ecky thump
> This un's face must be its rump.[38]

In the final section Apollo refuses the satyrs access to high-quality music:

> NO! NO! NO!
> My advice is stick to being satyrs
> and don't go meddling in musical matters.
> You don't need lyres. You're natural celebrators
> stuck between animal and human status.
> You need no consolations of high art –
> your human pain's cancelled by your horse/goat part.[39]

Kyllene then distributes ghetto-blasters to the satyrs, who have no idea what they are. These suddenly start playing ear-shattering rock music, which terrifies the satyrs. Silenos smashes the machines and addresses the audience:

Civilization! Once man starts on that track
even for a satyr there's no going back.
The 'boucelloniphone', Apollo's lyre
leads, by leaps and bounds, to the amplifier,
the guts of cows and the tortoise-shell
to steel-plucked deafening decibel.[40]

The response of the satyrs to all this is to go on the rampage
as a group of lager-swilling football hooligans:

Aeschylus, Sophocles, gerroff our backs.
We're hijacking culture and leaving no tracks.[41]

In the end they set fire to the papyri that they came from,
make goalposts out of piles of fragments, and play six-a-
side football with a rolled-up bundle of papyrus. The play
comes to an end with Apollo speaking tiny fragments of
Greek.

This amazing piece of drama shows just what can be done
with mythological material in a modern theatrical context.
The Trackers of Oxyrhynchus is full of incongruities – you
wouldn't instinctively expect ancient Greek, ghetto-blasters,
papyrologists, football hooliganism, lyre-playing and clog-
dancing all in one play – but it works brilliantly, a perfect
example of how subversion, irony and deliberate anachronism
can turn Greek myth into effective modern drama.

If Harrison's satyrs were an embodiment of the earthy
ugliness of their ancient counterparts, Helen seems to embody
the opposite qualities. She was the mythological symbol of
surpassing sensual beauty par excellence, and nowhere is this
better expressed than in Marlowe's *Doctor Faustus*, published
in the early seventeenth century:

Was this the face that launch'd a thousand ships
And burn't the topless towers of Ilium?
Sweet Helen, make me immortal with a kiss!
Her lips suck forth my soul. See where it flies!
Come, Helen, come give me my soul again.
Here will I dwell, for heaven be in these lips,
And all is dross that is not Helena.[42]

Inevitably Hollywood has latched on to the most beautiful woman of all time, and there have been two significant versions of the tale of Helen, both entitled *Helen of Troy*. The 1956 version, directed by Robert Wise, prided itself on being archaeologically sound and deferent to Homer's *Iliad* ('this book was our challenge'), although its fine set was modelled on Minoan Knossos. It starred Rossana Podestá as Helen, with a pre-stardom Brigitte Bardot as her handmaiden, but the script never really lived up to the lavish production values. John Kent Harrison's 2003 *Helen of Troy* stars an artfully dishevelled Sienna Guillory as Helen, who seems uncertain whether she is making a shampoo advert or a soft porn film. The movie asserts its authenticity: 'Let me tell you the real story,' says Menelaos, and many of the mythical elements remain in place, such as the exposure of Paris and his return to Troy, and Helen's abduction by Theseus, but the further the story progresses, the further it strays from the tradition: Helen's suitors invent democracy; she anachronistically wears Schliemann's 'jewels of Helen', and negotiates with Agamemnon for the ransom of Hektor's body; Agamemnon gratuitously rapes Helen in front of Menelaos; and Klytaimnestra bonds with Helen and slays Agamemnon in his bath – at Troy. Unconvincing sets which mix Minoan, Mycenaean, Classical and Renaissance architecture, diabolical special effects and computer-generated images, atrociously choreographed fights, and laboured dialogue make this the kind of film that gives Greek mythology a bad name. In this case, all is dross that *is* Helena (Helen).

9

FROM ASOPOS TO AKHILLEUS

Key Characters	
Aiakos (Aeacus)	Father of Peleus and Telamon; honoured in Hades after his death
Telamon	Father of Aias and Teukros
Aias (Ajax)	'Great Aias'; formidable warrior
Peleus	Father of Akhilleus
Thetis	Sea deity; mother of Akhilleus
Kheiron (Chiron)	A wise Centaur; tutor to Akhilleus
Akhilleus (Achilles)	The mightiest of the Greek warriors at Troy
Patroklos (Patroclus)	Akhilleus' best friend (and more)

The Asopos River stands at the head of a genealogy that leads down to Hektor's great adversary Akhilleus, leader of the Myrmidons at Troy.

When Zeus carried off Asopos' daughter Aigina, Sisyphos informed the river god who the rapist was.[1] Zeus fended off Asopos' pursuit by hurling thunderbolts and took Aigina to the island of Oinone, which was renamed Aigina after her.[2] There Zeus had his pleasure of her, fathering a son called Aiakos. In a story based on a false etymology, which derived the name Myrmidons from the Greek *myrmekes*, 'ants', we hear that since Aiakos found himself all alone, Zeus transformed the local ants into humans for him. An interesting ancient response to this myth comes from the geographer Strabo, who rationalized the tale by saying that the Aiginetans were called Myrmidons because they had behaved like ants in excavating the earth to create cultivable land, and because they lived in the hollows that they had made.

Aiakos married a Centaur's daughter, who produced two sons, Peleus and Telamon,[3] but there was also an extramarital affair:

> A daughter of the Old Man of the Sea,[4]
> Psamathe, shining goddess, through the work
> Of golden Aphrodite, fell in love
> With Aiakos, and Phokos was her child.[5]

Some say that Phokos got his name because Psamathe turned herself into a seal (Greek *phoke*) trying to escape Aiakos' advances. Notwithstanding this, Aiakos acquired a great reputation for piety and justice. When Pelops had treacherously murdered Stymphalos and then scattered his mangled body over the land, Greece suffered a devastating drought,[6] but Aiakos responded positively to requests for him to intercede with his father, the sky god Zeus:

> And even while he prayed a loud clap of thunder pealed, and all the surrounding sky was overcast, and furious and continuous showers of rain burst out and flooded the whole land. Thus was exuberant fertility procured for the fruits of the earth by the prayers of Aiakos.[7]

After his death Aiakos became keeper of the keys of the Underworld. Plato depicts him as one of the judges of the dead alongside Minos, Rhadamanthys and Triptolemos, although elsewhere he is a more lowly character. In Aristophanes' comedy *The Frogs* he appears in a delightful parody as a jobsworth doorman in a scene where Dionysos, dressed as Herakles, is seeking access to the Underworld:

AIAKOS: Who's there?

DIONYSOS: Herakles the b-b-bold.

AIAKOS: Ah, so it's you, foul, shameless, desperate, good-for-nothing villain that you are. Ought to be ashamed of yourself, you ought! Coming down here, trying to throttle a poor little dog! Poor old Kerberos! I was responsible for that there animal, let me tell you. Well, you're caught now, see? Hah! I'll have you flung over the cliff, down to the black-hearted Stygian rocks, and you'll be chased by the prowling hounds of Hell and the hundred-headed viper will tear your guts out and the Tartessian lamprey shall devour your lungs and the Tithrasian Gorgons can have your kidneys and – just wait there a moment while I go and fetch them.[8]

The outburst makes Dionysos soil his clothing.

There was an unhealthy relationship between Aiakos' various sons. Phokos' athletic brilliance aroused the jealousy of Peleus and Telamon, and led to his death, sometimes accidentally, but more often by one or both of the brothers hurling a discus at his head and sometimes finishing him off with an axe. Aiakos exiled them, but according to Pausanias, Telamon soon returned to face trial, and was found guilty and banished in perpetuity. Elsewhere in the tradition Telamon went to King Kykhreus on Salamis, and Hesiod tells of Kykhreus rearing a snake which ravaged the island until it was expelled by a certain Eurylokhos, after which it was welcomed at Eleusis by Demeter, who made it one of her attendants.[9] Rationalist interpreters of this myth said that it was not a snake, but a cruel person nicknamed Snake who was banished by Eurylokhos, took refuge at Eleusis, and was given a menial job in the sanctuary of Demeter.

Kykhreus died childless and left his kingdom to Telamon, who accompanied Herakles on his expedition against Laomedon at Troy,[10] and had a formidable son thanks to Herakles' prayers:

> As he spoke, the god sent
> the lord of birds, a great eagle; and sweet delight troubled his
>   heart within,
> and he spoke aloud, as if he had been a seer:
> 'You shall have the child you ask for, my Telamon.
> For the bird that showed him forth, call him mighty Aias, to be
> in the tumult of armies a man of terror.'[11]

Aias (Latinized to Ajax) gets his name from the Greek *aietos*, 'an eagle'.

Telamon's brother Peleus was one of the premier league Greek heroes: he hunted the Kalydonian Boar;[12] sailed with the Argonauts; and wrestled with the athletic Atalanta at the Funeral Games of Pelias (though he lost). Astydameia (or Hippolyte), the wife of his friend Akastos, fell in love with him, but when Peleus spurned her she told his wife that he was about to marry Akastos' daughter Sterope. Peleus' wife hanged herself, while Astydameia told Akastos that Peleus had tried to rape her. Akastos then tried to engineer Peleus' death by organizing a hunting contest on Mount Pelion, abode of the Centaurs. It was desperately competitive: to save time, Peleus cut out the tongues of the animals that he slaughtered and put them in his pouch, and when Akastos' men derided him for returning empty-handed, he produced the tongues as his tally of kills. That night Akastos hid Peleus' sword in some cows' dung, and had it not been for the wise Centaur Kheiron, who returned his sword to him, Peleus would certainly have been savaged by the Centaurs. Peleus ultimately exacted terrible vengeance on Astydameia when he hacked her limb from limb, and led his army into the city of Iolkos through her scattered remains.

Peleus' second marriage was a particular privilege, however. Zeus and Poseidon had been rivals for the favours of Thetis, daughter of Nereus, but when it was prophesied that the son she bore would be mightier than his father, they backed off and Peleus entered the frame. As a sea deity, Thetis had the ability to change shape at will – fire, water, wind, tree, bird, tiger, lion, serpent, cuttlefish – but Peleus seized her and clung on until he finally subdued her and she consented to be his wife. They were married on Mount Pelion in a fabulous ceremony attended by the gods. The Muses (or the Fates in Catullus' brilliant Poem 64) sang, and the gods feasted. However, no good wedding would be complete without a major falling-out, and the goddess Eris (Strife), who had understandably not been invited, tossed a golden apple bearing the words 'for the fairest' into the assembled throng of goddesses. The ensuing catfight between Hera, Athena and Aphrodite led first to the 'Judgement of Paris', and ultimately to the Trojan War.[13]

Swift-Footed Akhilleus

The mightiest hero in the Trojan War was Akhilleus (Latinized to Achilles), son of Thetis and Peleus. His goddess mother wanted to make him immortal, and there is a tradition that Akhilleus was Thetis' seventh son, the first six having been destroyed by being thrown into fire or boiling water, either to ascertain whether they were immortal or to make them so. In one version Akhilleus was about to become the next victim when Peleus snatched him from the fire when just his ankle bone was burned, and replaced the missing bone with the ankle of Damysos, the speediest of all the giants. In the better known story, Thetis would put him in the fire at night, unknown to Peleus, intending to destroy his mortal elements, and smother him with ambrosia during the day. But everything went wrong when Peleus discovered what was going on:

> Peleus leapt up from his bed and saw his dear son gasping in the flame; and at the sight he uttered a terrible cry, fool that he was; and she threw him screaming to the ground, and herself like a breath of wind passed swiftly from the hall as a dream and leapt into the sea, exceeding wroth, and thereafter returned not again.[14]

Interestingly, the tale of the origin of the 'Achilles heel' is a late addition to Akhilleus' mythology. It is not found until the *Achilleid* by the Roman poet Statius (48–96 CE), where Thetis dipped him in the River Styx, holding him by the heel, making him totally invulnerable except in the heel where she held him.

Akhilleus' parents' separation was a painful one, Thetis living in the depths of the sea and Peleus dragging out a miserable old age at home. The single parent Peleus took his son to the Centaur Kheiron, who educated him in hunting, music and medicine, and fed him on a diet of entrails of lions and wild boars and the marrows of bears, fawns, or deer, which gave him the strength and courage of the aggressive animals and quickness of the others: he became a 'swift-footed' hero with 'manslaying hands'; the regime certainly worked.[15] Jean-Baptiste Regnault painted the *Education of Achilles by the Centaur Chiron* in the Louvre, which shows him having an archery lesson from Kheiron, with a dead lion, symbolizing Akhilleus' prowess as a hunter and alluding to his unusual diet, and a lyre in the foreground illustrating the more cultural side of his education.

As Akhilleus was growing up, the events leading to the Trojan War were coming to a head, and when he had reached the age of nine the seer Kalkhas prophesied that Troy would not fall unless he was present. However Thetis also foresaw that he would die if he went to fight, so she dressed him in female clothing and sent him to live among the women in the court of Lykomedes on Skyros. Rome's Emperor Tiberius famously used to ask experts on mythology, 'What name did Akhilleus assume when he disguised himself as a girl at the court of King Lykomedes?' The professors answered variously: Kerkysera, Issa and Pyrrha were the favourite responses. On Skyros Akhilleus had a dalliance with Lykomedes' daughter Deidamia, resulting in the birth of a son called Pyrrhos, who was later called Neoptolemos.

Ultimately wily Odysseus came to Skyros searching for Akhilleus and sprang his disguise in one of two ways. Either he displayed baskets of women's ornaments, with weaponry in among them, to Akhilleus and his female companions, and while the girls descended enthusiastically on the feminine fripperies, the macho hero revealed his gender by grabbing the military hardware. Or, while Akhilleus was browsing through the same merchandise, Odysseus caused a trumpet and a clash of weapons to be heard, at which point Akhilleus stripped off his girly garments and grabbed a spear and shield. This incident was popularized in art by Polygnotos in an influential work displayed at the entrance to Athenian Akropolis, and later attracted the artist Nicolas Poussin, who painted the theme more than once (*Discovery of Achilles on Skyros*, 1649–50, in the Museum of Fine Arts, Boston; *Achilles and the Daughters of Lycomedes*, 1656, in the Virginia Museum of Fine Arts). He depicts a rather androgynous hero eagerly examining a sword amid a group of girls haggling over the price of jewellery. Once Akhilleus had been found, he went willingly to war, in the full knowledge that he would go to an early grave.

He took fifty ships of Myrmidons to Troy, and was joined by two important companions, both of whom were refugees. The first was Phoinix, who had been blinded by his father Amyntor over an accusation of seduction by his father's concubine (false, says Apollodoros; true, says Homer – he had been put up to it by his mother, who was jealous of the concubine). Kheiron had restored his sight, and Peleus made him King of the Dolopians. The second refugee was Akhilleus' dearest companion of all: Patroklos, son of the Argonaut Menoitios. The two normally share a common ancestry that goes back to Aigine, with Patroklos' father Menoitios said to be Akhilleus' grandfather Aiakos' half-brother. (See the diagram on p. 256.)

On the other hand, a fragment of the Hesiodic *Catalogue of Women* makes Menoitios the son of Aiakos, and therefore the brother of Peleus. Hence Akhilleus and Patroklos are cousins. (See the diagram on p. 257.)

Patroklos ended up meeting Akhilleus because Patroklos had killed a friend in a quarrel over a game of dice, and had fled with his father to the house of Peleus. The relationship

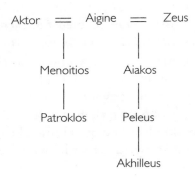

between the two heroes was pertinently defined by Menoitios in the *Iliad* when he offered these words to Patroklos:

> My child, by right of blood Akhilleus is higher than you are,
> but you are the elder. Yet in strength he is far the greater.
> You must speak solid words to him, and give him good counsel,
> and point his way. If he listens to you it will be for his own
>   good.[16]

Together they set off for a war that Patroklos was not destined to survive. After Patroklos' death Akhilleus was to lament his optimism:

> Ah me. It was an empty word I cast forth on that day
> when in his halls I tried to comfort the hero Menoitios.
> I told him I would bring back his son in glory to Opous
> with Ilion sacked, and bringing his share of war spoils allotted.

But Zeus does not bring to accomplishment all thoughts in men's minds.[17]

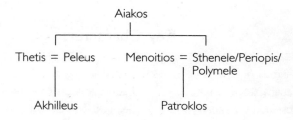

In fact neither of them was fated to return: Patroklos' death led directly to that of Akhilleus.

10

ATHENS: THE EARLY KINGS

Key Characters

Kekrops (Cecrops)	First real King of Athens
Athena (Minerva)	Patron goddess of Athens
Poseidon (Neptune)	Sea god; contested the possession of Attika with Athena
Phaethon	'Shining' son of Helios and Klymene; drove Helios' chariot with a catastrophic outcome
Adonis	Beloved of Aphrodite; killed by a boar
Erikhthonios (Erichthonius)	'Earth-born' Athenian king
Prokne (Procne) and	
Philomela	Sisters metamorphosed into birds
Erekhtheus (Erechtheus)	Ruler of Athens
Aigeus (Aegeus)	Ruler of Athens; father of Theseus

One of the defining elements in the self-image of the ancient Athenians, which was eloquently expressed in their mythology, was the notion that they were autochthonous, i.e. the aboriginal inhabitants of their land, in contrast to the Dorians, whose mythology expressed their nature as incomers equally strongly. The genealogical material here is complex, and there is an enormous catalogue of variant versions of these tales. The tradition is highly fluid, and was always open to manipulation by those who wanted to alter the mythology for their own

Athenian Kings

(Aktaios)
Kekrops I
Kranaos
Amphiktyon
Erikhthonios
Pandion I
Erekhtheus
(Xouthos)
Kekrops II
Pandion II
The Metionids
Aigeus

purposes. The recounting of these tales is rarely objective or unbiased.

There is dispute from the outset. Pausanias asserts that an aboriginal named Aktaios was the first King of Attika (the region of which Athens was the main city), which was called Aktike (*sic*) after him. Others deny the existence of such a person, whereas the Hellenistic inscription known as the *Parian Chronicle* says the first King of Attika was Kekrops, who assumed the throne by marrying Aktaios' daughter Agraulos (or Aglauros) I.

Kekrops was a son of the earth, and had a human body with a serpent's tail. One of the most important incidents in Athenian mythology took place in his reign – the contest between Poseidon and Athena for possession of Attika, a sculptural version of which later adorned the Parthenon and whose remains now reside in the British Museum. Poseidon thrust his trident into the acropolis and a salt-water spring

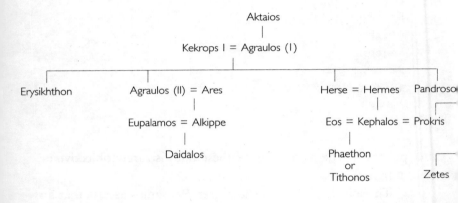

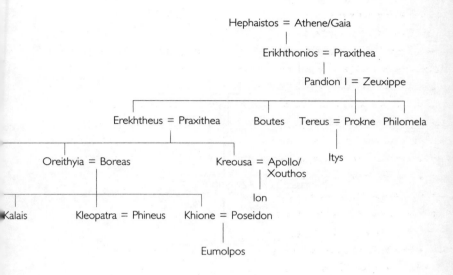

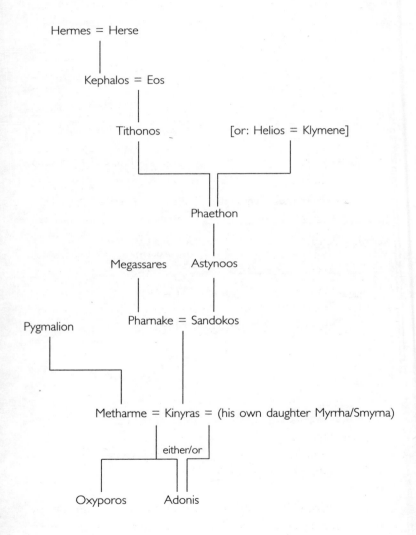

came into being.[1] Athena proceeded to plant an olive tree,[2] which was felt to be a more beneficial gift, so she took possession of the land and called the city Athens after herself.

Kekrops and Agraulos had a son and three daughters, Aglauros (or Agraulos) II, Herse and Pandrosos. Agraulos II had a daughter named Alkippe by Ares, and when Poseidon's son Halirrhothios tried to rape her, he was caught and killed by Ares, for which the god was impeached by Poseidon. Here we see mythological events being connected with real-life institutions, since Ares was tried (and acquitted) in the new court called the Areiopagos, from which time the name Areiopagos was believed to mean 'the crag of Ares'; it was Athens' main homicide court.

Kekrops' daughter Herse had a number of significant descendants, including Phaethon and Adonis. (See opposite family tree.)

Herse's son Kephalos[3] became one of the erotic conquests of Eos, the Dawn. In one version she abducted Kephalos, took her pleasure, and produced a son called Tithonos, who in turn had a son Phaethon ('Shiner'). Hesiod, however, makes Phaethon the son of Kephalos and Eos:[4]

> To Kephalos she bore a brilliant son,
> Strong Phaethon, a man much like the gods.
> When he was young and had the fragile bloom
> Of glorious youth, and tender, childish mind,
> The laughter-loving Aphrodite seized
> And took him to her shrine and made him serve
> As temple-keeper, bright divinity.[5]

Ironically, given the uncertainties surrounding his genealogy in the mythical traditions, Phaethon wanted reassurance about his parentage, and in Ovid's brilliant account of the tale in his *Metamorphoses*, where Klymene is his mother and Helios (the Sun) his father, Helios not only confirmed that he was indeed his son, but promised to give Phaethon anything his heart desired.

> Phaethon answered at once. He asked for his father's chariot,
> With leave to control the wing-footed horses, for just one day.[6]

It was a crazy request. Driving the chariot of the Sun needed specialist divine skills. But Phaethon was adamant, and Helios could not renege on his promise. With convoluted instructions from his father ringing in his ears, Phaethon mounted the chariot pulled by Fiery, Dawnsteed, Scorcher and Blaze, and almost instantly lost control: the chariot set the heavens alight and created the Milky Way, before searing the earth with heat so intense that forests burned, rivers dried up, the seas contracted, the skins of the Aithiopians were turned black, and North Africa became a desert. With the world on the brink of total destruction, Zeus stepped in. He fought fire with fire, hurling a thunderbolt at Phaethon, and the boy's flaming body fell like a comet into the River Eridanos (the Po). His sisters the Heliades mourned so intensely that they turned into poplar trees, and their tears became drops of amber exuding from the trees. When Phaethon's friend and kinsman Kyknos came to mourn for him, he was transformed into a swan (Greek *kyknos*, 'swan').

In another tale of resinous metamorphosis, Phaethon is the great-great-grandfather of Adonis, via Kinyras, who is the father of Adonis by incestuous intercourse with his own daughter Myrrha or Smyrna.[7]

> It's a shocking story. Daughters and fathers, I strongly advise you
> to shut your ears! Or if you cannot resist my poems,
> at least you mustn't believe this story or take it for fact.[8]

Myrrha was courted by suitors from all over the East, but no one aroused her interest like her father did. With the complicity of her nurse and alcohol, she lured Kinyras into an illicit affair with a mysterious admirer of 'about Myrrha's age' when his wife was celebrating a nine-night religious festival with a 'no sex' taboo.

> The father welcomed his flesh and blood to that bed of
>   uncleanliness,
> gently calming her virginal fears with words of assurance.
> Perhaps, because of her age, he even called her 'my daughter'
> and she said 'father', to put the finishing touch to their
>   incest.[9]

After several nights of this Kinyras' curiosity got the better of him, and he brought a lamp so that he could see who his (now pregnant) mistress was. When the hideous truth dawned, he drew his sword and, though she escaped, she prayed to the gods, who turned her into a myrrh tree (*smyrna*). The drops of resin that oozed from it were said to be her tears.

Myrrha's child Adonis was born either when a wild boar gored the tree, or when the goddess of childbirth facilitated his delivery. He was a really beautiful child – so much so that Aphrodite wanted him for herself. She hid him in a chest which she entrusted to Persephone, but Persephone was also captivated and refused to give him back. The goddesses took their dispute to Zeus for arbitration. He judged that Adonis should stay with each goddess for one third of the year and decide for himself where to spend the rest of it. He always chose Aphrodite,[10] and the time that Adonis spent with Persephone was seen as the winter time, when the seed was dormant, while the time he spent in the arms of Aphrodite was the fecund time of spring and summer.

Adonis met his death in an echo of his birth, gored by a wild boar while hunting. In her grief, Aphrodite promised annual rites in his honour (the Adonia Festival), and transformed his blood into a deep red flower:

> This new flower only has a short life:
> flimsy and loose on its stem, it's easily shaken and blown
> away by the winds which give it the name of anemone –
> wind-flower.[11]

The red rose was also said to originate from Adonis' death, because as Aphrodite ran to her dying lover she pricked her foot on a white rose, which was for ever after stained red.

Back in Athens, when Kekrops died, another son of the earth called Kranaos succeeded to the throne. The Great Flood associated with Deukalion was said to have taken place in his reign, after which he was deposed by Amphiktyon, who was either a son of Deukalion, or earth-born. After a twelve-year reign Amphiktyon was expelled by Erikhthonios, whose name also carries earth connections (Greek *khthon*, 'earth'). The most common tale of his birth is that Athena visited Hephaistos' forge to have some weapons made, but Hephaistos had been spurned by his wife Aphrodite and was overwhelmed with lust for the virgin goddess. Despite his lameness he got close to her and attempted to have intercourse, but she refused to submit, and his premature ejaculation landed on her thigh. Disgusted, she wiped his semen off with some wool, which she then threw away. The moment it touched the ground, the ever-fertile Gaia (Earth) produced Erikhthonios, and gave him to Athena. The goddess put him in a chest, which she entrusted to Aglauros II, Herse and Pandrosos, with strict instructions not to open it. But one, two, or all three of the girls did open it, and when they saw the terrifying apparition, either of a snake or two coiled about the child, or a child who was half-snake, they were either killed by the serpent, or went mad and hurled themselves off the Akropolis.

When Erikhthonios reached adulthood he expelled Amphiktyon and became King of Athens, actively promoting the cult of Athena by setting up the ancient olive-wood image of Athena on the Akropolis and instituting the Panathenaia Festival.[12] He is sometimes credited with inventing the four-horse chariot in order to conceal his reptilian lower parts, and he was immortalized as the constellation of Auriga (the Charioteer). His child Pandion I was to be the next ruler of Athens.[13]

Pandion I had two daughters, Prokne and Philomela, and twin sons, Erekhtheus and Boutes. His reign witnessed a boundary dispute with Labdakos, the King of Thebes, in which he called in the help of Tereus, son of Ares. After the Athenian victory, Pandion rewarded Tereus with a wedding to Prokne, but it was not an auspicious occasion:

> The wedding wasn't attended
> by Juno [Hera] as bridal matron, the Graces or jovial Hymen.
> Furies provided the escort with torches snatched from a
> funeral;
> Furies prepared the nuptial couch; and a sinister screech-owl
> swooped on the palace and came to rest on the roof of the
> bedroom.[14]

The union brought an ill-starred son: Itys.

After a while Tereus conceived an erotic longing for Prokne's sister Philomela. He engineered an opportunity to rape her in a secluded forest, imprisoned her there, and to prevent her telling anyone about what had happened, he cut out her tongue. He told Prokne that Philomela was dead. However, Philomela spent her incarceration weaving a tapestry in which she depicted the events, and managed to send it to Prokne, who tracked her down, and then exacted a sickening revenge. She stabbed her own son Itys to death, and then cooked him up and served him to Tereus for supper.

> So Tereus sat on the throne of his fathers high on a dais
> and started to gorge himself on a dish of the fruit of his own
>   loins.
> Blind to the truth, he actually called out, 'Go and fetch
>   Itys!'[15]

Itys' severed head was sufficient to reveal the literally stomach-churning ghastliness of the situation. Tereus grabbed his sword and made for the sisters, but the gods changed the three of them into birds: Prokne became a nightingale, Philomela a swallow, and Tereus a hoopoe:[16] Prokne the nightingale still called the name of her dead son, *Itu! Itu!* (the vocative case of *Itys* in Greek); and Tereus the hoopoe cried, *Pou! pou!* ('Where? Where?').

In the division of the inheritance on Pandion's death Erekhtheus got the kingdom plus the priesthood of Athena.[17] The *Parian Chronicle* records that it was in his reign that Demeter first came to Attika, the first corn was sown by Triptolemos, and the Eleusinian Mysteries were first celebrated.[18] Dionysos was also said to have been received at this time by Ikarios,[19] and the arrival of these two deities can be seen as a mythical expression of the first cultivation of corn and vines in the Attika region.

Erekhtheus' daughter Prokris had a tragic relationship with Kephalos, famously told by Ovid in the *Metamorphoses*.

Shortly after the wedding, the sexually predatory Eos abducted Kephalos, but her lust was unrequited, and feeling disrespected she looked for revenge by persuading him to test his wife's chastity. Kephalos disguised himself, made persistent advances until she gave in, and then revealed his identity. Prokris headed for the mountains in shame, and devoted herself to hunting with the virgin goddess Artemis, where she acquired the infallible hound Lailaps, and a javelin that never missed.[20] Kephalos came to see the stupidity of his behaviour, and the two were ultimately reunited.

Kephalos would now go hunting armed with the miraculous javelin, and at the end of the day he would call on a breeze (*aura* in Greek) to come and cool him off: 'Relieve me I beg you as only you can . . . You give me such pleasure! Oh *aura*, your refreshing caresses! . . . Yours is the breath that I'm always longing to catch in my lips.'[21] Unfortunately Aura was also a girl's name. An eavesdropper heard him and reported the 'affair' to Prokris. She shadowed him when he next went out, but when he uttered the words, 'Come, beautiful *aura*,' she moaned and rustled some leaves. He thought there was an animal in the undergrowth, threw his javelin, and scored a direct hit. Prokris was just able to clarify the misunderstanding before she died in his arms.

Apollodoros gives a totally different version in which Prokris is mercenary and unfaithful. She went to bed with Pteleon, who had bribed her with a golden crown, and fled to Crete when she was found out.[22] She had an affair with Minos there, before fear of his wife Pasiphae prompted her to return to Athens and make up with Kephalos. The couple then went out hunting together but he killed her in a freak accident, after which he was tried in the Areiopagos and banished indefinitely.

Erekhtheus had to face a major challenge from within his

own family in the form of his great-grandson Eumolpos ('Good Singer'),[23] who in his infancy had been saved from the sea by Poseidon and brought up by his daughter Amphitrite in Aithiopia. When a war broke out between the Eleusinians and Athenians, Eumolpos responded to the Eleusinians' request for help and invaded Attika, laying claim to the kingdom of Athens by referring back to Poseidon's contest with Athena and arguing that Poseidon had gained possession of Attika first.

Erekhtheus found out from the oracle that his only chance of victory lay in sacrificing one of his daughters, and when he did so, the others killed themselves as well, since they had sworn an oath to perish together.[24] In the ensuing battle either Erekhtheus killed Eumolpos, for which Poseidon retaliated by destroying Erekhtheus (or got Zeus to do it with a thunderbolt) or the Athenians gave the supreme command to the exiled Ion, and though Erekhtheus killed Eumolpos' son, he himself fell in battle. Eumolpos survived and stayed on at Eleusis.

Kekrops II, the eldest of the sons of Erekhtheus, was the next to occupy the throne of Athens. He achieved this position not by birthright but through the decision of his brother-in-law Xouthos, who had been appointed arbiter of the issue. Kekrops' disappointed brothers drove Xouthos out.

Xouthos is a key character in Euripides' play *Ion*, where he appears as King of Athens, having succeeded Erekhtheus. Ion, who is Xouthos' wife Kreousa's son by Apollo, had been abandoned at birth but rescued on Apollo's instructions, and then brought up at Delphi as a temple attendant, thinking that he was an orphan. As the drama unfolds, Xouthos and Kreousa make their way to Delphi to consult the oracle about their childless relationship, and Xouthos is led to believe that Ion is his son. This makes Kreousa jealous, and a combination of this with her grief for her own long-lost child leads her to try to assassinate Ion. Fortunately she fails and the truth is revealed marginally before Ion can kill her in retaliation. There is a joyful mother-child reunion, Xouthos remains blissfully misguided, thinking that Ion is really his son, and they all return happily to Athens.

Outside Euripides' version, Kekrops II fathered Pandion II. This Pandion was expelled by the sons of his uncle Metion (the 'Metionids') in a *coup d'état*, and sought refuge at Megara, where he married Pylia, daughter of King Pylas,[25] and had four sons. Pandion II later became ruler of Megara in his own right when Pylas was exiled to the Peloponnese, where he founded the city of Pylos, and when Pandion II died, his son Nisos took over in Megara while the other three, Aigeus,[26] Pallas and Lykos, marched on Athens, expelled the Metionids, and installed Aigeus in power.

Aigeus' first two marriages turned out childless, which made him worry about his status as king. So he consulted the Delphic Oracle and got this response:

> The bulging mouth of the wineskin, O best of men,
> Loose not until thou hast reached the height of Athens.[27]

Baffled, Aigeus headed back to Athens. On the way he stopped in on the wise Pittheus at Troizen. Pittheus understood the oracle immediately, got Aigeus drunk, and enticed him into sleeping with his daughter Aithra. Before Aigeus left, he placed a sword and some sandals under a stone, and instructed Aithra that if she had a son who could one day roll away the stone, she should send him to Athens with the tokens of recognition. She did have a son: the greatest Athenian hero, Theseus. However it was also said that Poseidon was his father, having had sex with Aithra on the same night as Aigeus.

Fertility problems solved, Aigeus made his way back to Athens where he not only gave refuge to Medeia after she had perpetrated the murders of her children, but also married her and had a son by her.

Postclassical Echoes

A great many of the episodes arising out of this phase of the mythology have been picked up by later ages and used for artistic inspiration. Phaethon's tale was never especially attractive to ancient artists, but there are post-classical versions of *The Fall of Phaethon* in the drawings of Michelangelo (1475–1564), and the paintings of Rubens, whose 1605 version shows the earth in flames and the heavens in crisis as Phaethon is smitten by a dazzling lightning strike and tumbles head first from the Sun's uncontrollable chariot. Humorously, the misguided hero became the eponym of the light, swift-moving, two-horsed open carriage – the phaeton.

Adonis has engendered some vigorous scholarly debate which goes back to the anthropological work of J.G. Frazer, who made a large-scale comparatist study and developed the idea of Adonis as an image of the succession of the seasons and their relevant agricultural activities. For Frazer he was a kind of vegetation spirit, but more recently the French scholar Marcel Detienne has deployed structuralist techniques to argue against this view, and posit the idea that Adonis is indicative of impermanence, fragility and barrenness. This well illustrates how the meaning of myths is constantly being redefined under the influence of fresh intellectual thinking: the myths do not remain static, and neither does their interpretation.

Adonis is a familiar figure in ancient art, and probably more so in later times. Rubens' *Venus* [Aphrodite] *and Adonis* (*c*.1635) in New York shows the young man ignoring the attempts of his clinging lover to prevent him going hunting. Her black cloak has ominous resonances, and the Cupid who holds on to his leg leaves his bow and arrows symbolically on the ground (so no more love) as Adonis and his faithful hound set off for the last time. Ovid's version proved inspirational to Shakespeare in his *Venus and Adonis*, where the anemone springs from Adonis' blood and the goddess puts it to her breast:

> Here was thy father's bed, here in my breast;
> Thou art the next of blood, and 'tis thy right.
> Lo, in his hollow cradle take thy rest;
> My throbbing heart shall rock thee day and night;
> There shall not be one minute in an hour
> Wherein I will not kiss my sweet love's flow'r.[28]

The Prokne and Philomela myth has a fascinating reverberation in Peter Greenaway's film *The Cook, The Thief, His Wife and Her Lover* (1989). The story explores the problems of Georgina, whose gangster husband Albert Spica is possessive, abusive and culturally challenged. Mr Spica owns a restaurant whose chef, Richard, helps Georgina in an affair with a customer called Michael. Inevitably Mr Spica finds out about her dalliance, and has Michael tortured to death. When Georgina discovers her husband's crime, she persuades Richard to prepare Michael's corpse as her husband's last supper. The film's climax comes when Mr Spica is forced to eat Georgina's lover, and her final word to him perfectly states how she has metamorphosed him: 'Cannibal!'

There are interesting relationships between the main characters of both myth and film: the husband (Tereus, Mr Spica), his wife (Prokne, Georgina), an object of the wife's affection (Philomela, Michael), and the cooked or cook (Itys,

Richard). Both husbands do violence to someone dear to the wife (Philomela: raped and mutilated; Richard: tortured and killed); the wives' discoveries reverse the balance of horror; both wives serve cannibal food to their husbands; and the revenge is exacted by means of cuisine: the cooked Itys provides the substance for Prokne's; the cook Richard provides the services for Georgina's. Further comparisons between Tereus and Mr Spica come to mind: they are both watchers (Tereus predatory; Mr Spica voyeurist); they both have voracious appetites (Tereus for sex and food; Mr Spica just for food); they are both very controlling; and they are both violent (Tereus is sexually motivated; Mr Spica is just barbaric).

The structural parallels do not end here, either, since both wives diminish their husbands' status (Tereus was a king; Mr Spica was a gangster boss), and each husband's crime leads to a reversal in the balance of power, and a denouement of discovery and revenge. The tales differ in the way the revenge fits the crime, and in the level of the avenger's guilt: Prokne and Philomela remain sullied by the crime, and their metamorphosis into birds leads to an eternity of searching and grief; Georgina simply reverts to her normal life. The husbands' afterlives similarly diverge: Tereus is metamorphosed, sometimes into a bird of prey, but Mr Spica just dies and remains powerless to hurt Georgina any more. The film as a whole provides a fascinating illustration of the way similar motifs can be combined to create new tales: there is much in here to interest the comparatist, the psychoanalyst and the structuralist.

THESEUS AND THE MINOTAUR

Key Characters

Minos	King of Crete
Pasiphae	Wife of Minos; mother of the Minotaur
The Minotaur	Half-man, half-bull; offspring of Pasiphae and a bull
Theseus	Athenian hero; slayer of the Minotaur
Aigeus (Aegeus)	Theseus' tragic father
Ariadne	Daughter of Minos; helped Theseus defeat the Minotaur; later abandoned by him
Daidalos (Daedalus)	The great artist of mythology; built the Labyrinth
Ikaros (Icarus)	Foolish son of Daidalos
Hippolytos (Hippolytus)	Son of Theseus; died of too much chastity
Phaidra (Phaedra)	Hippolytos' stepmother; fell in love with him with disastrous consequences
Centaurs	Half-man, half-horse creatures

As we enter the realm of the Minotaur, we find a nexus of connections between Theban, Athenian and Cretan myths, whose climax is the encounter between the hybrid monster and the great hero Theseus.

Minos, the son of Zeus and Europa,[1] lived on Crete, where

he married Pasiphae[2] ('All-Shining'), daughter of the sun god Helios and sister of Aietes, owner of the Golden Fleece, and Kirke the enchantress. They had numerous offspring, and Minos also enjoyed fruitful affairs with a couple of nymphs, but his nine-month pursuit of the virgin huntress Britomartis ended when she hurled herself over a cliff into the sea. She was caught in some fishermen's nets and was made a goddess by Artemis, coming to be known as Diktynna (either 'the Lady of the Nets', or a reference to Mount Diktys on Crete which was associated with her cult). In an effort to frustrate his promiscuity, Pasiphae gave Minos drugs that made him ejaculate snakes, scorpions and millipedes during sex, but he still managed to get Kephalos' wife Prokris into bed, since she had an antidote to Pasiphae's potion – the so-called 'root of Kirke'.

When Europa's partner Asterios died childless, Minos sought to establish sole rule over Crete, but ran into opposition. He claimed divine support, and tried to substantiate this by praying to Poseidon that a bull should appear from the sea, and vowing to sacrifice it when it did.[3] The sea god sent a particularly magnificent white bull, and Minos secured the kingship and also became the first to obtain dominion over the sea, but he could not bring himself to slaughter the fabulous bull. Poseidon's angry response was to turn the animal feral, and to instil an erotic passion for it in Pasiphae.

Pasiphae needed an accomplice to help her realize her monstrous desires, and she found one in Daidalos. Typically, his family roots vary according to tradition, but he is descended from Erekhtheus, with his father named as Eupalamos, Palamaon or Metion (names all associated with skill and knowledge). Daidalos' name also carries connotations of ingeniousness, and he is credited with being the 'inventor of images' – indeed Homer refers to artistic works as *daidala*. He is also credited with making a fortress and a temple platform in Sicily, along with a golden ram or honeycomb, a statue of Aphrodite, steam baths, 'living' statues, the walking pose for male statues, and the 'dancing ground' of Ariadne, which a Linear B tablet from Knossos reading *da-da-re-ja* ('Daidalos' place'?) could conceivably refer to. His Cretan connections were established as a result of feeling threatened by Talos, Kalos or Perdix (Partridge), one of his own pupils who had worked out how to saw a thin stick using a snake's jawbone, and then had used this (or the bones on the back of a fish) as the inspiration to invent the iron saw, as well as inventing the compasses. Daidalos pushed him off the Akropolis, was tried before the Areiopagos, and was condemned.

He fled to Crete, where he exercised his ingenuity on Pasiphae's behalf by constructing a hollow wooden cow on wheels, covering it in a genuine cowhide, and pasturing it with the bull. Pasiphae climbed into it, the bull took it for the real thing, and the inevitable happened. The fruit of this union was the Minotaur, a hybrid creature with a bull's head on a human body: *Minotauros* means 'Bull of Minos' in Greek, although his real name was Asterios. Horrified, Minos shut the Minotaur up in the Labyrinth, an underground structure designed by Daidalos 'that with its tangled windings perplexed the outward way'. There it remained until it was slain by Theseus.

Among Minos' more normal offspring was Androgeos, who was an outstanding athlete. When Aigeus celebrated the Panathenaia Festival at Athens, Androgeos performed brilliantly. Yet his prowess led to his death: some say he was murdered by jealous competitors; others that Aigeus had him assassinated because he feared he might usurp his throne; others again that Aigeus sent him to deal with the bull of

Marathon – the very animal that had mated with Pasiphae, and which had been the object of one of Herakles' Labours[4] – which destroyed him. Minos sought revenge, and, being the dominant naval power in the region, he took the offensive with his fleet. In an early success he took Megara, which was ruled by Nisos, who had a purple hair in the middle of his head. An oracle held that he would die if anyone pulled it out, and his daughter Skylla fell in love with Minos and did just that, although after Minos' victory he tied her feet to the stern of his ship and drowned her.[5] The conflict dragged on indecisively until Minos prayed to Zeus to secure his vengeance some other way. Plague and famine then struck Athens, to which the Athenians' first response was to slaughter the Hyakinthides (daughters of Hyakinthos or Erekhtheus) on the grave of the Cyclops Geraistos, in obedience to an ancient oracle. This failed to produce the desired effect, so they consulted the oracle, which told them to grant Minos whatever satisfaction he might choose. Minos ordered them to pay a tax of seven youths and seven maidens as fodder for the Minotaur, to be delivered annually or at nine-year intervals.

Theseus: Labours on the Road to Athens

While these events were taking place on Crete and at Athens, Aithra's son Theseus was being educated by Pittheus at Troizen. A hint of his future prowess came when Herakles came to visit and took off his lion skin: the other children thought that it was a real animal and fled; Theseus attacked it with an axe. At the age of sixteen, he easily rolled away the stone and took up the sword and sandals, the tokens of paternity left by his human father Aigeus,[6] and headed for Athens on foot. (See map, p. 279.)

The mythology of Theseus has many resemblances to that

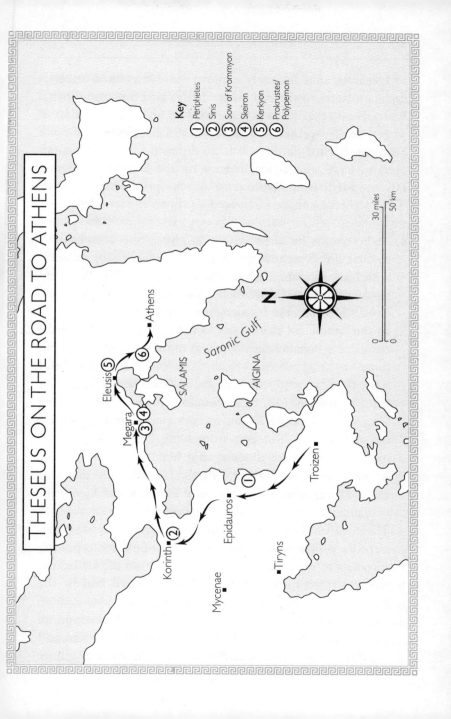

THESEUS ON THE ROAD TO ATHENS

Key
① Periphetes
② Sinis
③ Sow of Krommyon
④ Skeiron
⑤ Kerkyon
⑥ Prokrustes/ Polypemon

Athens
⑥
⑤ Eleusis
③④
Megara
Saronic Gulf
SALAMIS
AIGINA
② Korinth
① Epidauros
Mycenae
Tiryns
Troizen

N

30 miles
50 km

of Herakles, and his early exploits involve eradicating evil-doers en route to the city where he became a national hero. Plutarch says that Theseus performed these deeds in emulation of Herakles' monster-slaying feats, and they may well have been constructed on this model in order to fulfil an Athenian need to have a non-Dorian hero on the Heraklean model. His road-trip from Troizen to Athens provides a cycle of 'Labours' that can be compared to those of Herakles:

1. At Epidauros he came across Periphetes 'the Club-bearer', so nicknamed because he used to batter passers-by to death with his iron club. Theseus wrested the club from him and gave him a brutal taste of his own medicine. He kept the club, which became his signature attribute.

2. At the Isthmus of Korinth he slew Sinis ('Destroyer'), nick-named 'the Pine-bender', who was in the habit of murdering travellers using pine trees. Either he would make them bend a tree to the ground with his help, and then release it, hurling them to their deaths; or he would bend two pine trees to the ground, bind his victim to both trees, and then release the trees to tear him limb from limb. Theseus killed Sinis by using his own methods against him.[7]

3. At Krommyon he saw off a dangerous wild sow that was called Phaia, either the offspring of Ekhidna and Typhoeus, or named after the old woman who bred it.[8]

4. Theseus then despatched Skeiron, who resided in Megarian territory on the Skeironian rocks. He would force passing travellers to wash his feet and kick them into the sea below, where a giant turtle ate them. Theseus seized him by the feet and threw him off the cliffs to his doom.

5. Coming to Eleusis, Theseus killed Kerkyon, whose favourite pastime was to compel passers-by to wrestle with him and kill them in the process. Sadly for him, Theseus was a finer

wrestler and pulled a move in which he lifted him into the air and then smashed him to the ground.

6. Just after the bout with Kerkyon, Theseus encountered Prokrustes (also known as Damastes or Polypemon), who lived beside the road. On the face of it he was hospitable. He had two beds, one short and one long, and would offer passers-by accommodation. But he put short people on the long bed and hammered them out to make them fit, and laid the tall ones on the small bed and adjusted them to size by sawing off parts of them that hung over the end. [9] Again, Theseus made the punishment fit the crime by making Prokrustes fit his own bed.

With the road now safe for travellers, Theseus arrived at Athens, where Aigeus was now living with the sorceress Medeia as his wife.[10] This was always going to make life difficult for Theseus, especially since Medeia felt that his arrival threatened her position and that of her son Medos. Furthermore, Aigeus did not recognize Theseus straight away, but Medeia did. She set out to eliminate him by playing on Aigeus' insecurities, and he became deeply suspicious of the incomer – so much so that he sent him to deal with the Marathonian bull that was still wreaking havoc in the countryside, fully expecting that he would never return. But Theseus slew the bull, and he did return. Medeia responded by preparing a cup of poison that Aigeus would have administered to Theseus had he not recognized his own sword, which Theseus happened to be wearing. He dashed the cup from Theseus' hands, the two were properly reunited, and Medeia was expelled. Aigeus named Theseus as his successor.

The Athenians were, at this point, still paying their tribute of seven youths and seven maidens as Minotaur food. When the third selection departed for Crete, Theseus was among them, either as a volunteer, chosen by lot, or handpicked by Minos himself. Whatever the method of his selection, Theseus intended to terminate both the Minotaur and the tribute. The vessel in which he travelled had a black sail as a sign of mourning, but Theseus promised his father that if he returned alive, he would display white or scarlet sails on the way home.

On the journey Minos assaulted the maiden Eriboia. When Theseus intervened, Minos prayed to Zeus to confirm that he was Minos' father (which would essentially allow Minos to behave however he liked), and a lightning flash confirmed the issue. Minos then challenged Theseus to verify that he was the son of Poseidon. The poet Bakkhylides (c.520–450) wrote about how Minos tossed a golden ring into the sea, and Theseus retrieved it, along with a crimson cloak and a garland 'dark with roses besides', gifts from Poseidon's wife Amphitrite:

> The crowd of young
> Athenians had trembled when
> the hero leapt into the sea, and from
> their lily-lustrous eyes they shed
> tears, expecting compulsion's heavy grip.
> Dolphins, meanwhile, those salt-dwellers,
> quickly carried the great Theseus to the home of his
> father, the god of horses; and he came
> to the sea god's hall. [. . .]
> He [. . .] saw the dear wife of his father
> there in the lovely house, august
> ox-eyed Amphitrite,
> who clothed him in a mantle of sea-purple
> and set upon his thick-curled locks
> a plaited garland without flaws,

which earlier, at her marriage,
deceitful Aphrodite had given her, dark with roses.[11]

On arrival in Crete, Theseus attracted the amorous interest of
Minos' daughter Ariadne, who proposed to help him, on condition that he took her back to Athens and made her his wife.
Theseus agreed, and cemented the deal with an oath, while
Ariadne persuaded the Labyrinth designer Daidalos to reveal
how to find the exit. And at his suggestion she gave Theseus a
ball of thread. He was to attach one end to the lintel of the
door on entering the Labyrinth, and then unwind the thread as
he penetrated into the heart of the structure, until he found the
Minotaur.[12] Theseus did as he was told and found the Minotaur
in the bowels of the Labyrinth. They fought to the death. Theseus
won, and the thread enabled him to find his way out again.
He assembled his compatriots, and set sail with Ariadne.

Their first landfall on the return journey was the island
of Dia (identified with Naxos), where Theseus abandoned
Ariadne either forgetfully, deliberately (another girl, Aigle,
is mentioned), or at the behest of the gods:

    Here are the never-silent sands of Naxos
here Theseus vanishes towards the north,
a woman watches from the empty beach
unflagging grief in her heart,
Ariadne doesn't yet believe, quite,
she is witnessing what her eyes see –
she's only just woken from a trap
(of sleep)
found herself alone on the island.
And Theseus, heedless as storm & wind
carves up the waves as he goes
And throws their love-words overboard.[13]

However, in the normal tradition her situation immediately improved with the arrival of Dionysos, who fell in love with her and carried her off to be his wife. She found solace in his arms and bore a number of children.[14]

Theseus sailed onwards to Delos, where he made a sacrifice to Apollo and his companions danced the 'Crane Dance', whose twisting steps imitated the architecture of the Labyrinth, and which was danced by Delians in the historical era. From there it was a short voyage to Athens, but someone forgot to spread the white/scarlet sail as the ship came into port. Aigeus assumed that Theseus was dead, and threw himself down either from the high bastion of the Akropolis where the temple of Athena Nike still stands (the Greek tradition) or the sea cliffs (the Latin tradition, from which the Aegean Sea gets its name).

When Minos discovered how Theseus had escaped, he incarcerated Daidalos and his son Ikaros in the Labyrinth. But the ever ingenious Daidalos fabricated wings, demonstrated their use, and gave his son instructions:

'Now, Ikaros, listen carefully!
Keep to the middle way. If you fly too low, the water
will clog your wings; if you fly too high, they'll be scorched
    by fire.
Fly between sea and sun.'

Like a bird leading its fledgling from the nest Daidalos tried to keep an eye on Ikaros as he flew, but

All this adventurous flying went to Ikaros' head.
He ceased to follow his leader; he'd fallen in love with the sky,
and soared up higher and higher. The scorching rays
    of the sun

grew closer and softened the fragrant wax which fastened his
    plumage.
The wax dissolved; and as Ikaros flapped his naked arms,
deprived of the wings which had caught the air that was
    buoying them upwards.
'Father!' he shouted, again and again. But the boy and his
    shouting
were drowned in the blue-green main which is called the Icarian
    Sea.[15]

Daidalos flew to the court of Kokalos in Sicily,[16] where Minos
eventually tracked him down by a neat trick. He carried a
spiral shell and promised a huge reward to whoever could
pass a thread through it, knowing full well that only Daidalos
had the ingenuity to do this. In Sicily he publicized his challenge, and Kokalos accepted it. Kokalos gave the shell to
Daidalos, who attached an ant to a thread, bored a hole in
the shell, and induced the ant to do the rest. When Minos
received the threaded shell, he immediately demanded custody
of the great inventor, and Kokalos promised to hand him
over. However, Kokalos' daughters killed Minos by scalding
him to death in his bath, with either boiling water or pitch,
possibly administered through a pipe constructed by Daidalos
himself. There is no reliable tradition for Daidalos' life or
death after this.

Theseus assumed the vacant throne of Athens. When Aigeus
had been childless, his brother Pallas and his fifty nephews
had hopes of succeeding him, but once Theseus appeared on
the scene with Aigeus' sword and sandals, they were frustrated,
although they challenged his claim on the grounds that he was
a foreigner. When Theseus took the crown there was a rebel-
lion, but Pallas and his sons were eliminated, along with any
other potentially subversive elements.

The ancient Athenians attributed some major political reforms to Theseus, most notably the *synoecism* of Attika, i.e. the amalgamation of all the small independent communities of the region into one state, with Athens as its capital. Theseus is also credited with establishing the Panathenaia Festival,[17] reinstituting the Isthmian Games at Korinth which Sisyphos had originally founded, sailing with the Argonauts, and hunting the Kalydonian Boar.[18] The latter exploit also involved Theseus' great friend Peirithoos, King of the Lapiths of Thessaly. The two had met when Peirithoos raided Theseus' cattle, but respect rather than hostility developed between them, and they swore an oath to be lifelong friends. When Peirithoos got married,[19] Theseus was a wedding guest, and so got involved in the 'centauromachy', the battle between the Lapiths and the Centaurs.

The origin of the Centaurs goes back to Peirithoos' father Ixion, one of the four great violators of the divine order who was eventually punished in perpetuity in Tartaros.[20] He made a bad start by becoming the first person ever to shed a kinsman's blood when he lured his father-in-law into a pit of fire. Zeus purified him of this, but Ixion simply repaid him by attempting to rape his wife Hera, who reported the matter to Zeus. In order to verify the accusation, Zeus made a cloud-likeness of Hera, Nephele ('Cloud'), and put it in Ixion's bed. Ixion ravished Nephele, so Zeus bound him to a blazing wheel, or one entwined with snakes, on which he was whirled by winds through the air for eternity as a warning to mankind. Ixion did, however, manage to impregnate Nephele first. She gave birth to Kentauros.

Kentauros became the father of the feral, raw-flesh-eating, half-man-half-horse Centaurs by having sex with wild mares on Mount Pelion. When Peirithoos became King of the Lapiths, the Centaurs claimed a share in the kingdom because they were Ixion's grandchildren. That particular dispute was settled amicably, but things got ugly when the Centaurs were invited to Peirithoos' wedding. They did not usually drink wine, but on this occasion they got riotously drunk and very sexually aroused. They tried to carry off the Lapith women – Eurytion even had a go at the bride – and in the brawl that followed the body count was high. On the Lapith side was Kaineus who had once been a woman, but following intercourse with Poseidon was now an invulnerable man:

> Bards relate that Kaineus, though still living perished at the hands of the Centaurs, when apart from the other chiefs he routed them; and they, rallying against him, could neither bend nor slay him; but unconquered and unflinching he passed beneath the earth, overwhelmed by the downrush of massy pines.[21]

Eventually, though, in a classic victory of civilized order over chaotic barbarity, Peirithoos and the Lapiths, aided by Theseus, finally prevailed.

Theseus and Peirithoos also made a pact that they would marry daughters of Zeus (Peirithoos' Lapith wife was no longer alive by this time). With Peirithoos' help Theseus abducted Helen from Sparta,[22] and then they went down to Hades to get Persephone for Peirithoos. In Theseus' absence the Dioskouroi recovered Helen and abducted Aithra to be Helen's slave, and installed Menestheus, a great-grandson of Erekhtheus, as ruler at Athens.

Down in the Underworld things went badly. Hades invited the two friends to take a seat, but they could not get up, either because they were chained to their chairs, seated in the Chair of Forgetfulness (which removed any desire to return to the world above), or had physically grown into the rock of their seats. Peirithoos usually remained in Hades for eternity, though he is eaten by Kerberos in one tradition and released in another, whereas Theseus was rescued when Herakles performed the Labour of Kerberos,[23] and returned to Athens. An amusing version said that Theseus stuck so fast to his seat that when Herakles wrenched him away, he left a piece of his anatomy still on the rock, which explained why the Athenians had remarkably small bottoms.

Theseus also made an expedition against the Amazons, and carried off Antiope (or Melanippe, or Hippolyte). The relationship resulted in the birth of Theseus' son Hippolytos, but the abduction provoked a backlash from the warrior women, who invaded Athens and were able to get as far as the Areiopagos before they were beaten off. Despite the birth of Hippolytos, Theseus later entered into a marriage with Ariadne's sister Phaidra.

When Theseus and Phaidra's wedding was under way, the spurned Amazon appeared with her armed companions, threatening death to the guests. Again there was violence at a wedding, this time with the Amazons being defeated and Antiope killed. Phaidra bore Theseus two sons, but then the marriage disintegrated in horrible circumstances as Phaidra fell in love with Theseus' son by the Amazon, her stepson Hippolytos, whose name ominously means 'Torn Apart by Horses'.

Apollodoros says that in order to be purified of blood-guilt relating to the eradication of the sons of Pallas, Theseus undertook a year-long exile with his wife Phaidra at Troizen. There Phaidra conceived a fatal passion for her stepson Hippolytos. As the tale was normally told, she was a shameless, predatory seductress, who, when she was rejected, both feared the ramifications and wanted revenge on the innocent Hippolytos. However, Euripides produced a brilliantly dramatized version in his tragedy *Hippolytos*, performed in 428, where Hippolytos essentially dies from too much chastity.

He is so utterly devoted to the virgin goddess Artemis that he openly spurns the love goddess Aphrodite. This is an incredibly dangerous thing to do, and Aphrodite adapts the punishment to the crime by making Phaidra fall in love with him, doing so in the full knowledge that Phaidra will be destroyed too, despite the fact that she is essentially powerless. Having succumbed to her divinely inspired passion, Phaedra tries unsuccessfully to suffer in silence. She shares her feelings with her nurse, who tries to facilitate the love affair by telling Hippolytos what is going on. He is utterly horrified, and responds with an incredibly angry, eloquent and misogynistic tirade:

> O Zeus! Why have you established in the sunlit world
> This counterfeit coin, woman, to curse the human race?
> If you desired to plant a mortal stock, why must
> The means for this be women? A better plan would be
> For men to come to your temples and put down a price
> In bronze, or iron, or weight of gold, and buy their sons
> In embryo, for a sum befitting each man's wealth.
> Then they could live at home like free men – without women.
>   [. . .] For an easy life
> At home, to marry a cipher might be best – except
> That no good comes of inanity on a pedestal.
> Yet a clever woman, with more wit than becomes a woman,
> I abhor; I would not have such a woman in my house.
> The sexual urge breeds wickedness more readily
> In clever women; while the incompetent are saved
> From wantonness by lack of wit.[24]

Hippolytos' outburst is all the more unfair for being untrue in Phaidra's case: she is not guilty of the things he accuses her of. 'How cruel a curse it is to be born a woman!' is her response, and after hurling bitter recriminations at the nurse, she leaves the stage intending to destroy both herself and Hippolytos. When Theseus enters, he finds that his wife has hanged herself, and that there is a note fastened to her hand, which reads:

Hippolytos has dared to affront the holy eye
Of great Zeus, and with violence to enter my bed.[25]

Theseus happens to have been granted three curses by Poseidon, and he prays for his son's death. He rages against Hippolytos, who tries to deny the accusation in a rather adolescent way:

My body is innocent to this day of sexual love.
Except by hearsay, or from pictures I have seen.[26]

Theseus is adamant: Hippolytos must go into exile, and as he does a terrifying bull appears from the sea, which causes his chariot-horses to stampede. Hippolytos is fatally injured, and is brought onstage to live out the last moments of his life. There is just enough time for Theseus to discover the grim truth from Artemis, and to effect a reconciliation with his son.

Theseus was very much the Athenian hero par excellence, illustrating strongly that myths are seldom told without a motive. Despite the fact that Athens could be chillingly brutal in its dealings with other states, Theseus came to embody aspects of the way in which the city wanted to see itself and be seen: generous, noble and a champion of the oppressed – Oidipous, Herakles and the mothers of the Seven Against Thebes all came to him in time of need and got a positive response. His words in Euripides' *Suppliant Women* epitomize the values he stood for in fifth-century Athens, not unlike the way that certain contemporary powers present their role in the world today:

I have, by honourable deeds,
Chosen and claimed this character amongst the Greeks,
To be always the punisher of injustice.[27]

In the end, he died a rather banal death. He was driven out of Athens, and his power was usurped by Menestheus, who appears in Homer as the leader of the Athenian contingent at Troy. He went to Skyros seeking refuge, but the local king Lykomedes threw him to his death in an abyss. In the historical period, as Athens started to build its empire in the 470s, the general Kimon manipulated the mythology by locating the 'bones of Theseus' on Skyros and transferring them back to Athens, both to symbolize the city's links to the heroic age, and to bolster its claim to leadership over the Ionian Greeks.

Nachleben

These tales of Theseus, the Minotaur, Ariadne, Daidalos and Ikaros have all had long and vibrant afterlives.

Theseus' 'Labours' occur in two important classical settings that reinforce his special relevance to Athens. Athenian ceramic drinking cups called *kylikes* frequently depict all his exploits in sequence. A fine red-figure example from 475, now in the British Museum, has Kerkyon, Prokrustes, Skeiron, the Marathonian Bull, Sinis and the Sow of Krommyon around the outside, and the Minotaur in the centre. Interestingly, the bull substitutes for Periphetes here, who only appears in the cycle of Labours after 475. On a more public scale, the Athenian Treasury at Delphi (*c.*500) displayed images of his exploits from the road to Athens on its metopes, and the temple now called the Hephaisteion (*c*.450), which used to be called the Theseum because of its decoration, also featured these stories in its sculptural programme. Theseus also crops up in post-classical literary contexts as diverse as the *Knight's Tale* of Chaucer, Shakespeare's *A Midsummer Night's Dream* and Mary Renault's excellent novels *The King Must Die* (1958) and *The Bull From the Sea* (1962).

Theseus' adversary the Minotaur is unquestionably one of antiquity's most memorable and powerful creations. Much has been made of possible links between the Minotaur tale and the Minoan 'Palace' at Knossos, where there were frescoes of bull-leaping, 'horns of consecration', 'labyrinthine' architecture, and frequent representations of the double axe (*labrys*), but whether it is possible to make explicit historical connections between Knossos and the myths is open to debate. Even so, there are still far-reaching influences emerging from the Labyrinth. Archaeology suggests that Minoan priestesses may have used the *labrys*, and many interpret axes wielded by women as indicative of a powerful position for women in Minoan society. Feminist interpreters also view the *labrys* as a symbol associated with female power, and as a symbol of the mother goddess, and it is frequently employed as a symbol of lesbianism: *Labrys Atlanta*, for instance, describes itself as a magazine for gay women, lesbians and women everywhere. But the *labrys* is a multivalent image. Between 1936 and 1941 the Greek Fascist Youth movement adopted it, and it is also used by 'Black Metal' rock music fans in Greece as a symbol of Greek paganism.

The creature itself can also stand for many things. In a piece now in Tate Britain, London, entitled *The Minotaur* (1885), the English artist George Frederic Watts, who painted the work in only three hours in an outburst of disgust against prostitution, depicted a superbly melancholic Minotaur, gazing enigmatically out over the sea with what appears to be intense sadness, maybe longing for liberation from either its monstrous form or from the Labyrinth, yet at the same time it crushes a bird under its hand in an unpleasant undertone of senseless violence. Picasso depicted the Minotaur for the cover of Albert Skira's first edition of *Minotaure* (25 May, 1933), the magazine of surrealism. He made extensive use of the creature's dark side to express his feelings towards the Spanish Civil War. The English artist Michael Ayrton had a lifelong preoccupation with Greek mythology and produced a great many works inspired by the beast. His *Arkville Maze* (1968) is built of tall brick walls and houses life-size sculptures of the Minotaur and Ikaros and still stands in the estate of Armand Erpf in the Catskill Mountains, New York, and his bronze sculpture *Minotaur* (1973) on the Highwalk above London Wall, seems to empathize with a creature torn between its human mind and bestial form. Once again, we see that the power of the Greek myths to influence the modern mind lies, in some sense, in the way they blend humanity with monstrosity.

Ariadne's abandonment and rescue can make an effective allegory of good things coming out of bad, and composers of opera have exploited this with fine results. Richard Strauss' *Ariadne auf Naxos* (1912) presents an interesting take on the myth. In the second half Princess Ariadne has been deserted by Theseus and has shut herself off from human contact. She feels unable to leave Naxos, and she is determined to be eternally faithful to Theseus. The happiness of her imagination is directly proportional to the loneliness of her waking hours. Her companions Naiad and Dryad, as well as the unsympathetic Echo, are alert to her suffering, as is an itinerant troupe of comic actors including Zerbinetta and Harlequin. The latter sings to her about the importance of turning pain into new life, but she prefers to glorify the realm of death: she is waiting for Hermes to escort her to the land of the shades. The comedians cannot comprehend this, but their attempts to lighten the mood only make Ariadne back off further still. Zerbinetta talks to her woman-to-woman about the astonishing diversity of her own romantic liaisons, and admits that although she tries hard to be faithful to her lovers she invariably fails. Ariadne then sees Zerbinetta's dating strategy in action, as the comedienne allows herself to be wooed, and chooses Harlequin, somewhat contrary to expectations. This baffles Ariadne, who is now helped by Naiad and Dryad to prepare for the arrival of Bacchus (Dionysos), who Ariadne mistakes for Hermes, thinking he will accompany her into the Underworld. Bacchus has just had a dalliance with the enchantress Circe, and is fascinated by Ariadne, but is reluctant to enter a new relationship. Ariadne still takes him for an infernal deity, but becomes increasingly alluring to him, and she eventually succumbs to someone who promises her life rather than death. She bids adieu to her sorrows and follows Bacchus into new love.

Ariadne's collaborators Daidalos and Ikaros have also provided a rich vein of inspiration for artists and musicians. Their myth was rationalized both by Diodoros, who said that really Pasiphae provided them with a ship in which they escaped, but when they landed Ikaros fell into the sea and drowned, and by Pausanias who viewed the myth as indicating that the two of them sailed swiftly before the wind in separate ships with sails, which Daidalos had just invented. Later approaches were less mundane, as they become symbolic of the flight of humanity's inventiveness and aspirations, or in Ikaros' case, the stupidity of youth. Pieter Breughel the Elder produced a brilliantly quirky version entitled *Landscape with Fall of Icarus* (1558), where, in a broad landscape, a ploughman, a shepherd and a fisherman seem unaware of the splash as the tiny figure of Ikaros hits the water. As the proverb goes, 'No plough stops for the man who dies.'

Contemporary rock and jazz music has embraced Ikaros as a suitable subject too: 'Icarus Ascending' (Steve Hackett), 'Flight of Icarus' (Iron Maiden), and 'Icarus, Borne on Wings of Steel' (Kansas) represent a good sample of rock versions, while Stekpanna's 'Ikaros' paints a jazz portrait by means of a harmonic progression which rises until it can rise no more, then tumbles back to the sea.

Daidalos' role as the seminal artist has always earned him a special significance. There are those who are tempted to take a historicist view of him as a mythical embodiment of the vagabond artist, talented and versatile like Leonardo da Vinci, but as unscrupulous as Benvenuto Cellini. He has certainly become a strong emblem of artistic creativity, perhaps most powerfully expressed in James Joyce's *Portrait of the Artist as a Young Man* (1916), whose hero is the aptly named Stephen Dedalus, or in *Ulysses* (1922), where Stephen Dedalus again appears as an explorer of unknown arts. Joyce concludes *Portrait of the Artist as a Young Man* by invoking the mythical Daidalos in a way that underscores the strong connection that the ancient characters still have with our modern world:

April 27. Old father, old artificer, stand me now and ever in good stead.

CURSES AND CANNIBALISM: THE HOUSE OF PELOPS

Key Characters

Tantalos (Tantalus)	A great transgressor; punished by being 'tantalized' in Hades
Pelops	King of Elis; won Hippodameia in a chariot race; eponym of the Peloponnese
Oinomaos (Oenomaus)	Father of Hippodameia
Hippodameia (Hippodamia)	Beloved of Pelops
Atreus	King of Mycenae; father of Menelaos and Agamemnon
Thyestes	Son of Pelops; ate his own children; cursed Atreus
Agamemnon	Son of Atreus; leader of the Greeks at Troy
Menelaos (Menelaus)	Son of Atreus; husband of Helen

The family of Pelops contains some of Greek mythology's most important individuals and some of its most violent incidents. These stories often centre on issues of honour, power and sexual jealousy, where the bonds between human beings are incredibly strong but the competing claims on the individual are often totally irreconcilable. The ramifications

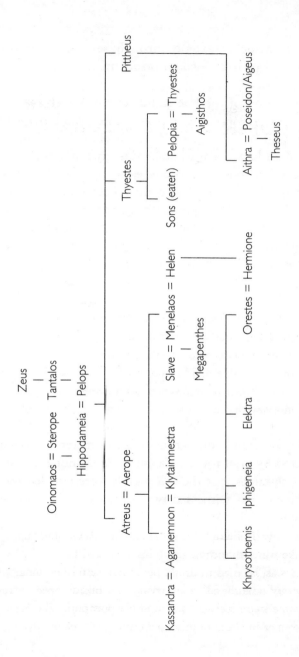

of these incidents extend through several generations of heroes, and provide inspiration for many great literary and artistic works.

At the head of the line stands one of Greek mythology's great transgressors, Tantalos. He came from Sipylos in Asia Minor, and was a son of Zeus, privileged enough to dine with the gods, and yet he violated many fundamental boundaries between gods and mortals, either by divulging the secrets of the gods to mankind, stealing nectar and ambrosia to share with mortals, or perpetrating a crime so grotesque that Pindar was loath to believe the story, even though he still recounts it. At a banquet of the gods Tantalos tried to test the gods by killing his own son Pelops and serving him to them:

> Some one of the spiteful neighbours whispered,
> how they took you and with a knife
> minced your limbs into bubbling water,
> and over the table divided and ate
> the flesh of your body, even to the last morsel.
> I cannot say that any god could gorge thus; I recoil.[1]

One deity certainly did 'gorge thus': Demeter,[2] who was still distracted by grief for her daughter Persephone, ate some of Pelops' shoulder, but the other gods were not deceived. His punishment was witnessed by Odysseus in the *Odyssey*:

> And I saw Tantalos also, suffering hard pains, standing
> in lake water that came up to his chin, and thirsty
> as he was, he tried to drink, but could capture nothing;
> for every time the old man, trying to drink, stooped over,
> the water would drain away and disappear, and the black earth
> showed at his feet, and the divinity dried it away. Over

> his head trees with lofty branches had fruit like a shower
> descending,
> pear trees and pomegranate trees and apple trees with fruit
> shining,
> and figs that were sweet and olives ripened well, but each time
> the old man would straighten up and reach with his hands for
> them,
> the wind would toss them away toward the clouds
> overhanging.[3]

Other sources add a great stone that loomed over his head, always on the point of crushing him. Having been killed, dismembered, cooked and partly eaten, Pelops was eventually restored to life by being put back into the cauldron and being given an ivory shoulder to replace the part that Demeter had eaten. The rejuvenated Pelops was so incredibly beautiful that Poseidon fell in love with him, and took him up to Olympos, where he spent most of his childhood.

When he grew up he decided to woo Hippodameia, daughter of King Oinomaos of Pisa in Elis. This was a daunting assignment, given that Oinomaos either had an incestuous passion for his daughter, or had been warned by an oracle that he would die at the hands of the man who married her. Either way, he was not going to let her marry if he could help it, and numerous suitors had perished in the process. Oinomaos had weapons and horses which Ares had given him, and every suitor was challenged to a chariot race to the altar of Poseidon at Korinth. The suitor would set off with Hippodameia in his own chariot, while Oinomaos sacrificed to Zeus before setting off in pursuit. Having caught the suitor up – easy enough with a chariot pulled by divine horses – Oinomaos would spear him through the back and take Hippodameia home again. A dozen or so young men had died in this way, and their severed heads adorned Oinomaos' house.

The situation changed somewhat when Pelops came seeking Hippodameia's hand, because she took one look at him and decided that she would like to marry him. Instrumental in the success of the relationship was Myrtilos, Oinomaos' charioteer. Either Hippodameia enlisted his help, which he gave because he was in love with her, or Pelops did, by offering Myrtilos half the kingdom and the first night with Hippodameia.[4]

The moments before the race are marvellously sculpted on the east pediment of the mid-fifth-century temple of Zeus at Olympia. All is tension and nerves: Oinomaos, hand confidently on hip, explains the terms of the contest; Pelops, head bowed, listens attentively; Zeus stands between them; Hippodameia is next to Pelops, nervously adjusting her veil in a bridal gesture; and Oinomaos' wife Sterope is there too, arms folded, at her husband's side. The figures do not physically touch, but the crackling emotions of the scene bind them together, while on the fringes indifferent servants sit or kneel by the horses (one is bored and absent-mindedly playing with his toes), and river gods, who establish the location of the event, flow past in the corners.

There are at least two versions of what happened next. According to Pindar, Poseidon gave Pelops a golden chariot with winged horses faster than those of Oinomaos, and so he won the race, but the more usual, less edifying tale, is that Myrtilos changed the bronze linchpins in the boxes of Oinomaos' chariot wheels for wax ones, or simply failed to insert them, and that Pelops won when the wheels fell off Oinomaos' chariot and he got entangled in the reins and dragged to his death. The incident was depicted on the cloak that Jason was given by Hypsipyle in the *Argonautika*:

And therein were fashioned two chariots, racing, and the one
in front Pelops was guiding, as he shook the reins, and with him
was Hippodameia at his side, and in pursuit Myrtilos urged his
steeds, and with him Oinomaos had grasped his couched spear,
but fell as the axle swerved and broke in the nave, while he was
eager to pierce the back of Pelops.[5]

As he died, Oinomaos cursed Myrtilos for his treachery.

So Pelops had his bride, but he was now faced with the
issue of Myrtilos. In some versions Pelops was simply not
prepared to let him sleep with Hippodameia, and in another
Myrtilos jumped the gun and tried to rape her. Either way,
Oinomaos' curse came to fruition, since Pelops threw Myrtilos
into the sea. But Myrtilos still had time to curse the house
of Pelops. Pelops sought purification by Hephaistos, promoted
the worship of Myrtilos' father Hermes, and erected a mound
in Myrtilos' honour next to the racetrack at Olympia, but
try as he might to appease the ghost of Myrtilos, he could
not shake off the curse, which brought misery for generations.

Pelops took over the kingdom of Oinomaos, and subjugated the entire region, which came to be called 'Pelopon-
nesos' (the Peloponnese, or 'Island of Pelops') after him.

Varying lists of the sons of Pelops and Hippodameia appear
in our sources, but they all include Atreus and Thyestes,[6]
who descended into a bitter animosity that had drastic ramifications of adultery, incest, murder and cannibalism.

There were few problems during Pelops' lifetime, but on
his death a significant prize came up for grabs: an oracle
said that on the death of Eurystheus Mycenae would be ruled
by a descendant of Pelops. But who? Atreus had married
Aerope, who became the mother of his famous sons Agamemnon and Menelaos,[7] but she was also having extramarital
sex with his brother Thyestes. To substantiate his claim over

Mycenae, Atreus vowed to sacrifice the finest lamb in his flocks to Artemis; but when a golden lamb appeared, he reneged on his promise by choking the lamb and keeping it hidden in a box.[8] Aerope, however, secretly ensured that Thyestes got hold of it, and when negotiations about the kingship began, Thyestes suggested that it should go to whoever owned such an animal. Atreus agreed; Thyestes produced the lamb and was appointed king. However, Zeus intervened, and told Atreus to propose a more definitive criterion for kingship: Atreus could be king if the sun went backwards through the sky and set in the east. Thyestes agreed; Zeus made it happen; Atreus took the kingdom; and Thyestes was banished. [9]

Atreus might have won the public battle, but Thyestes was still winning the domestic one, at least until Atreus found out about his affair and proceeded to a monstrous and macabre act of revenge. Atreus drowned Aerope, but then sent a herald to Thyestes to propose reconciliation. Once he had lured his brother back to Mycenae, Atreus slaughtered Thyestes' sons, [10] butchered their bodies, cooked them, and served them to him at a banquet. When Thyestes showed his appreciation for the food, Atreus showed him the heads, hands and feet of his children, and told him that he had already had what he could not see. Thyestes called down unspeakable curses on Atreus, and the so-called Curse of the House of Atreus would haunt all the later developments of the family.

When Thyestes started to seek revenge, an oracle told him that he could achieve his goals by having intercourse with his own daughter Pelopia and fathering a son. This is exactly what happened. Thyestes' daughter Pelopia had initially been sent to Sikyon for her own safety. Thyestes found her there. She was conducting a nocturnal sacrifice to Athena, and during the ceremony she slipped in the sacrificial blood and soiled her dress, so she went down to the river to wash it off. Concealing his identity, Thyestes pounced on her and raped her, although in the struggle she managed to take his sword from him. A little while later, Atreus was travelling in Thesprotia in southern Epeiros, and he met with Pelopia by chance, although he thought she was the daughter of the local king, Thesprotos. He asked if he could marry her, and Thesprotos agreed, though he omitted to say that Pelopia was not his daughter, or that she was pregnant. The marriage went ahead, and in due course Pelopia gave birth to a baby boy, whom she exposed to die. However, the child was found by shepherds and suckled by a she-goat, and when Atreus discovered his existence, he took him in and raised him as his own, naming him Aigisthos (Greek *aix, aigos*, 'goat').

Atreus' sons Agamemnon and Menelaos subsequently encountered Thyestes at Delphi, arrested him, and took him to Atreus, who summoned Aigisthos. The Latin writer Hyginus concludes the story:

> When Thyestes saw Aigisthos and the sword he was carrying, he recognized it as the one he lost during the rape. So he asked Aigisthos where he had got it from. He responded that his mother, Pelopia, had given it to him and ordered someone to go get her. She responded to their inquiry: she had taken it from someone – she did not know who – during a sexual encounter one night, and from that encounter she conceived Aigisthos.

Pelopia now became aware of the truth about her incest, and she could not face it:

> Then Pelopia took the sword (pretending to make sure it was the right one) and thrust it into her own chest. Aigisthos took the bloody sword from his mother's chest and took it to Atreus,

who was delighted because he thought that meant Thyestes was dead. Aigisthos killed Atreus while he was performing a sacrifice on the shore and returned with his father, Thyestes, to their ancestral throne.[11]

Atreus' sons Menelaos and Agamemnon, who were known as the Atreidai ('Sons of Atreus'), were banished by Thyestes, but Tyndareus later brought them back to Mycenae and drove Thyestes out. Agamemnon took over as King of Mycenae, and Menelaos reigned over Sparta after Tyndareus ceded the kingdom to him. The Atreidai married Tyndareus' remarkable daughters: Agamemnon got Klytaimnestra; Menelaos got Helen.

The Curse of the House of Atreus continued to drive events in Greek mythology throughout the generations of Agamemnon and his children Orestes, Elektra and Iphigeneia (Iphianassa). The head of the family line Tantalos gives us the English word 'tantalize', in reference to his devilishly frustrating punishment in Hades, and dedicated wine-drinkers will recognize a mythological allusion in the 'tantalus', which is a case for storing alcohol where the locked contents are still visible . . .

The contest between Atreus and Thyestes in which the sun reversed its path received rationalist explanations in some ancient scholars, who asserted that Atreus was really an astronomer who first calculated an eclipse, and so overshadowed his less scientific brother, or who first pointed out that the sun appears to revolve in a direction contrary to the motion of the stars.

We know that the Atreus and Thyestes story was dramatized by several tragedians in the fifth century, including Sophokles and Euripides, but these plays have now been lost. However, the first-century CE Roman playwright Seneca produced a

Thyestes, which covers the myth from the moment when the fury Megaera predicts to Tantalos that Thyestes will eat the flesh of two of his sons. As the drama unfolds, that is exactly what he does do, lulled into a drunken stupor by an exultant Atreus. Thyestes' drunken revelry soon turns sour as Atreus offers him a cup of wine and blood and displays the heads of the children on a platter. When Thyestes begs for the bodies to bury, Atreus tells him that he has eaten them. All that Thyestes can do is to predict total vengeance for Atreus' heinous acts. Other versions have continued to be produced, including John Wright's 1674 *Thyestes [. . .] to which is added Mock-Thyestes, in burlesque,* and Voltaire's *Les Pélopides* (printed in 1771), which radically rewrites the myth, and the Belgian playwright Hugo Claus' mid-twentieth-century adaptation of *Thyestes*, which represents a thorough rethinking.

Perhaps the loudest echo of the myth of the house of Atreus comes in the shape of a 1999 heavy metal album *House of Atreus – Act I* from Virgin Steele, whose twenty-two tracks form the soundtrack to what is described as a one-act Barbaric-Romantic opera, supplemented in 2000 by *The House of Atreus – Act II* (not quite so heavy, but more melodic than Act I).

Many visitors to the archaeological site of Mycenae are shown one of the finest architectural achievements of the Mycenaean world in the shape of the *tholos* (or 'Beehive') tomb, which is known as the Treasury of Atreus, but it should be stressed that there is no connection whatsoever between the structure and the hero.

THE TROJAN WAR

Key Characters

Paris	Trojan; son of Priamos; adjudicated the 'Judgement of Paris'; abducted Helen
Helen	Spartan; wife of Menelaos; 'the face that launched a thousand ships'
Odysseus (Ulysses)	Cunning hero; one of the Greeks' finest warriors and strategists
Telephos (Telephus)	Son of Herakles and Auge; wounded and healed by Akhilleus
Iphigeneia (Iphigenia)	Daughter of Agamemnon; sacrificed to ensure favourable winds
Troilos (Troilus)	Trojan; son of Priamos; killed by Akhilleus
Philoktetes (Philoctetes)	Got Herakles' bow and arrows; bitten by a snake on Lemnos
Akhilleus (Achilles)	Son of Peleus and Thetis; mightiest warrior on the Greek side

Menelaos might have become King of Sparta and married the most beautiful woman on earth, but he did not have a trouble-free reign or marriage, mainly because the Trojan Paris stole his wife. The abduction triggered the Trojan War, and it had its origins at the wedding of Peleus and Thetis,[1] where Eris (Strife) had maliciously instigated an impromptu beauty contest between Hera, Athena and Aphrodite by throwing an apple with the words 'for the fairest' among the guests. These three extremely beautiful goddesses each claimed the prize, so Zeus ordered Hermes to take them to Paris on Mount Ida in the Troad, who was given the task of making the impossible and inevitably catastrophic decision. Each goddess offered him an apposite bribe, and in the end it boiled down to a choice between power or sex, as Helen herself explains to Menelaos, in Euripides' tragedy *The Trojan Women*:

> Athena's bribe
> Was this: that he should lead the Phrygians to war
> And destroy Hellas [Greece]. Hera promised him a throne
> Bestriding Asia and Europe, if he placed her first.
> Aphrodite, with extravagant praise of my beauty,
> Promised him that, if he judged her the loveliest,
> I should be his.[2]

True red-blooded Trojan male that he was, Paris chose Helen, and therefore Aphrodite.

The 'Judgement of Paris' was always an attractive subject to artists, who give it some interesting twists. Lucas Cranach the Elder produced a small-scale *The Judgement of Paris* in oils in *c.* 1528, which really exploits the potential of three goddesses posing naked. Paris actually appears as a rather overweight Renaissance knight in a foppish hat, and confers with Hermes, who is an elderly warrior. The three gorgeous goddesses all adopt flirty attitudes (particularly Aphrodite) and Cupid draws his bow and takes aim. Joachim Wtewael (1615) and Rubens (1635–8) also produced versions, as did Claude Lorraine with his *Landscape with the Judgement of Paris* (1645–6).

Paris sailed to Sparta where Menelaos entertained him for nine days. However, on the tenth day he had to go to his grandfather's funeral on Crete, and so, with Aphrodite's assistance, Paris took his opportunity to go to bed with Helen and then elope with her. The tradition explores Helen's motives in great depth: she was wicked; it was the unstoppable power of persuasion; she was abducted by force; it was all Aphrodite's doing; or it was not really Helen that Paris abducted, but a phantom version of her made out of clouds, with the real Helen ending up in Egypt until Menelaos collects her after the Trojan War. This tradition seems to go back to the sixth-century poet Stesikhoros, who developed it as an apology to Helen for speaking negatively about her in an earlier poem; he had lost his eyesight, attributed this to her vengeance, and so sought to propitiate her by retracting his slanders. But whatever Helen's motives might have been, Paris was violating the fundamental rules of Greek hospitality: abducting another man's wife was always likely to incur dire consequences.

Helen abandoned her nine-year-old daughter Hermione, loaded a large amount of Menelaos' property on board, and she set sail with Paris by night. Their journey to Troy was either difficult, because Hera was still smarting from the outcome of the Judgement of Paris and so sent a severe storm which forced them to spend time in Sidon and Cyprus, or relatively straightforward, taking just three days across calm seas. Helen received a generous welcome at Troy, and she and Paris were formally married.

When Menelaos became aware that Helen and Paris were missing, he went to Agamemnon and asked him to put together an expeditionary force to go to Troy. His brother responded positively, and reminded the kings of Greece about the oath they had sworn to support Helen's husband in precisely such circumstances as these.[3]

Most of the potentates freely enlisted in the expedition, but not all. Odysseus pretended to be mad in order to avoid sailing, and yoked an ox and a horse or an ass to a plough and started to sow salt in the furrows. Greek envoys arrived, led by Palamedes, son of Nauplios, who immediately saw through the deception and called Odysseus' bluff by putting his baby son Telemakhos down in front of the plough or by snatching Telemakhos from Penelope's bosom and threatening him with a sword. Both tactics forced Odysseus to admit that he was not crazy, and he duly went to war, but he never forgave Palamedes, and later framed him of a capital offence by making a Phrygian prisoner write a letter full of treasonable material that had supposedly been sent to Palamedes by Priamos. He also hid a considerable amount of gold in Palamedes' tent, before casually dropping the letter in the Greek camp.[4] Agamemnon read the letter, found the gold, and Palamedes was stoned as a traitor. It was an incident whose ramifications would cause the Greeks much heartache on their way home.[5]

Odysseus also secured the involvement of Akhilleus by uncovering his disguise on Skyros,[6] and the expedition was bolstered by other mighty warriors such as the 'Greater' Aias, son of Telamon, 'Lesser' Aias, son of Oileus, Diomedes, son of Tydeus, and the wise old counsellor Nestor.

The coalition forces finally assembled at Aulis on the northeast coast of Boiotia. In historical times it was incredibly important to the various Greek states to be able to claim a hero who fought at Troy, and in Homer's *Iliad* there is a great Catalogue of Ships, which, although tedious to the modern reader, was a vital element in the Trojan myth, giving details of the 1,106 ships, 43 chieftains and 29 states that took part.

A remarkable omen occurred at Aulis. Next to an altar was a plane tree with a bird's nest in it; a snake slithered from the altar, ate the eight chicks in the nest, along with the mother bird, and was then turned to stone. The seer Kalkhas interpreted this as a sign that Troy was destined to hold out for nine years and be taken in the tenth.

The mighty force then sailed under the personal command of Agamemnon,[7] but they got lost and landed fairly close to Troy at Mysia, which they ravaged in the mistaken belief that it was Troy. Herakles' son Telephos, who was King of the Mysians, launched a counter-attack, and drove the Greeks back to their ships. But then he was confronted by Akhilleus, brandishing the awesome spear that his father Peleus owned:

> Huge, heavy, thick, which no one else of all the Akhaians
> could handle, but Akhilleus alone knew how to wield it,
> the Pelian ash spear which Kheiron had brought to his father
> From high on Pelion, to be death to fighters in battle.[8]

Telephos fled, got entangled in a vine branch, and Akhilleus wounded him in the thigh.[9]

After leaving Mysia, the Greeks were hit by a savage storm, and were driven back to their homelands, remaining none the wiser as to the precise whereabouts of Troy. In the meantime, Telephos' wound had not healed, but Apollo had told him that it could be cured by the one who inflicted it. So, dressed in rags, he begged Akhilleus to heal him, and promised to point out the way to Troy in return.[10] Akhilleus was not a medical man, but Odysseus observed that the one who had inflicted the wound was the spear, not the warrior, so Akhilleus scraped some of the rust off his spear into Telephos' wound, which soon cleared up.[11] Telephos kept his part of the bargain, and the fleet regrouped at Aulis once again.

Things now went seriously awry for the Greeks as the fleet found the elements against it, with either contrary winds or no winds at all. This was down to the anger of Artemis against Agamemnon, first because when he had shot a deer he had blasphemed 'Not even Artemis could have shot like that', and second because his father Atreus had not sacrificed the golden lamb to her.[12] Kalkhas then interpreted another omen as indicating that they would not be able to sail unless Agamemnon's daughter Iphigeneia was sacrificed to the goddess. To do this would be a terrible inversion of society's basic structures: animal sacrifice was normal; human sacrifice was hideously abnormal. Yet Agamemnon could not shirk the choice: either he should give up the expedition to avenge Paris' adultery (not an option), or he should sacrifice his daughter (not an option either). It was the classic tragic choice, and he knew it:

> Obey, obey, or a heavy doom will crush me! –
> Oh but doom *will* crush me
> once I rend my child,
> the glory of my house –
> a father's hands are stained,
> blood of a young girl streaks the altar.
> Pain in both ways and what is worse?[13]

To avenge Paris' transgression, Agamemnon must transgress. Of the two wrong choices available to him, he opted for the military one:

> Desert the fleets and fail the alliance? No.[14]

Agamemnon sent for Iphigeneia, on the pretext that she was to be married to Akhilleus. It was a terrible betrayal, eloquently judged by the Roman writer Lucretius:

It was her fate in the very hour of marriage to fall a sinless victim
to a sinful rite, slaughtered to her greater grief by a father's hand,
so that a fleet might sail under happy auspices. Such are the
heights of wickedness to which men are driven by superstition.[15]

Iphigeneia's sickening fate was graphically described by the
Chorus of Aiskhylos' *Agamemnon*:

Yes, he had the heart
  to sacrifice his daughter,
  to bless the war that avenged a woman's loss,
   a bridal rite that sped the men-of-war.

'My father, father!' – she might pray to the winds;
no innocence moves her judges mad for war.
Her father called his henchmen on,
  on with a prayer,
    'Hoist her over the altar
like a yearling, give it all your strength!
She's fainting – lift her,
  sweep her robes around her,
  but slip this strap in her gentle curving lips . . .
   here, gag her hard, a sound will curse the house' –

and the bridle chokes her voice . . . her saffron robes
pouring over the sand
         her glance like arrows showering
wounding every murderer through with pity
  clear as a picture, live,
she strains to call their names . . .[16]

Iphigeneia's death set in motion another sequence of brutal
revenge killings that would later account for Agamemnon,

his wife Klytaimnestra and her lover Aigisthos. Yet there is an alternative tradition, represented by Euripides' plays *Iphigeneia in Aulis* and *Iphigeneia in Tauris*, in which Artemis miraculously substituted a deer at the altar and spirited Iphigeneia away to Tauris on the Black Sea, where she installed her as her priestess.

Once Iphigeneia had been sacrificed, the winds turned in the Greeks' favour. Following Telephos' route they made landfall in Tenedos in the north-eastern Aegean, where Tenes held sway.

Here Akhilleus' fate was finally sealed. His mother Thetis knew that he would go to an early grave if he killed Tenes, and had specifically warned him about this. In fact she had detailed one of Akhilleus' servants to see that he remembered her warning, but on the island Akhilleus came across Tenes' very attractive sister and made love to her. When Tenes tried to defend her honour, Akhilleus killed him.[17] When he discovered who he had killed, Akhilleus slew the servant who should have warned him, but it was all too late: his fate was sealed.

At Tenedos[18] there was a further setback when Philoktetes was bitten by a water-snake. Quite what he had done to deserve this varies, but the bite refused to heal, and it festered so foully and caused him so much agony that no one could tolerate the stench or his screams. On Odysseus' suggestion he was put ashore on the island of Lemnos, where he used his unerring bow and arrows to provide himself with a means of subsistence on what is described as a desert island. Philoktetes was often said to have obtained the bow and arrows of Herakles, as a reward for his service in kindling the pyre on Mount Oita,[19] and indeed in one account Philoktetes received his terrible injury not from a water-snake but from one of these arrows, which were tipped with the venom of the Hydra. When Herakles was on the pyre he instructed

Philoktetes never to reveal the location of his ashes, and though Philoktetes gave his word, and never articulated it in words, he betrayed the secret by stamping on the grave with his foot. On his way to Troy, one of the arrows fell on the perfidious pedal extremity.

Arrival at Troy

The expedition made its way inexorably towards Troy, but before hostilities commenced there was one last attempt at negotiation. Odysseus and Menelaos made a direct appeal for the restoration of Helen plus Menelaos' property.[20] The Trojans did debate the issue, but they rejected the Greek demands, and the lives of the envoys were only saved by the intervention of Antenor. The diplomatic channels had been exhausted. It was time for war.

The Trojans tried to prevent the Greeks from establishing a beachhead, and since there was an oracle that the first Greek to come ashore would also be the first to die, there was a general reluctance to engage, until Protesilaos ('First of the Army') leaped from his ship, slaughtered several Trojans, and fell under Hektor's onslaught.[21] When his wife Laodameia[22] heard of his death, she successfully asked the gods for three hours in which to speak to him, but when their time was up, and he died again, she could not endure the pain. Hyginus tells us this version:

She made a golden statue in the likeness of her husband Protesilaos, put it in her chamber under the pretence it was a religious statue, and began to worship it.

Early one morning a servant of hers brought her some fruit for her sacrificial offering. He peered through the crack in the door and saw that she, far from Protesilaos' embrace, was holding and kissing the statue. Thinking that she was keeping a lover other than her husband, he reported it to her father, Akastos. When he arrived and burst into her chamber, he saw that it was a statue of Protesilaos; but in order to prevent her from prolonging her torture, he ordered that a pyre be built and that the statue and the sacred objects be burned. Laodameia, unable to endure the pain any longer, threw herself into the pyre and was consumed by fire.[23]

The Greeks now swarmed ashore. Akhilleus landed with the Myrmidons and claimed the first of his many victims, the invulnerable Kyknos, by strangling him with the straps of his own helmet. This terrified the Trojans, who fled to the city, allowing the Greeks to draw their ships up on the beach and pitch camp. The ten-year siege had now begun.

Any attempt to reconstruct an accurate 'historical' chronology of the Trojan War is doomed to failure.[24] There are so many different sources in so many different media that deal with the war, often introducing variant traditions of their own, and so many works that we know about, but which only exist in fragments, if at all. For instance, the motif of Akhilleus and Aias playing a game on a board, which features on a stunning Attic black-figure vase by Exekias, appears only in that medium and is not mentioned in Homer; a work of unknown date called the *Kypria*, by Stasinos of Cyprus, but also attributed to Hegesias or Homer, tells the story from the decision of the gods to cause the Trojan War, down to the quarrel between Akhilleus and Agamemnon, but in a highly fragmentary way; and Homer himself only deals with a relatively short period within the conflict.

There are a number of key incidents, however, and one extremely important victim of Akhilleus was Troilos, the young Trojan prince. It had been prophesied that Troy would survive if Troilos lived to the age of twenty, but he was

ambushed and slaughtered in a sanctuary of Apollo in what
vase painters often depicted as a fight between a tiny defence-
less boy and a huge and mighty warrior. The story of the
romance between Troilos and Cressida (which is a corruption
of the name Khryseis) comes from a much later tradition,
going back to the *Roman de Troie* of Benoît de Sainte-Maure
in the twelfth century CE, through Boccaccio's *Filostrato*
(1340–41), Chaucer's *Troilus and Criseyde* (1385) and into
Shakespeare's *Troilus and Cressida* (1602).

Akhilleus also captured Priamos' son Lykaon. He

> led him unwilling from his father's gardens
> on a night foray. He with sharp bronze was cutting young
>   branches
> from a fig tree, so that they could make him rails for a chariot,
> when an unlooked-for evil came upon him, the brilliant
> Akhilleus, who that time sold him as a slave in strong-
>   founded Lemnos.[25]

Akhilleus also ravaged the countryside around Troy, and
went to Mount Ida where he raided Aineias' (Aeneas) herds
and drove the hero off the mountain. Akhilleus was quick
to remind Aineias about this when they met in combat later:

> Do you not remember when, apart from your cattle, I caught
>   you
> alone, and chased you in the speed of your feet down the hills
>   of Ida
> headlong, and that time as you ran you did not turn to look
>   back.[26]

Akhilleus' conquests stretched far and wide: Lesbos, Phokaia,
Kolophon, Smyrna, Klazomenaei, Kyme, Aigialos, Tenos,

Adramyttion, Side, Endion, Linaion, Kolone, Thebes below Plakos, Lyrnessos, Antandros and many other cities were all taken. Crucially, it was at the sack of Lyrnessos that Akhilleus captured his concubine Briseis: she was at the centre of his feud with Agamemnon that lies at the heart of Homer's *Iliad*.

The Trojans were not without their allies, however. Homer arranges them in five geographical groups: the contingents from the Troad; those from across the Hellespont; troops from south of the Black Sea; allies from the south-east of the Troad; and contingents from south-western Anatolia.

Questions of History

In his commentary on his translation of Apollodoros, Sir James Frazer says: 'I agree with [W. Leaf in his book *Homer and History*, London, 1915] in the belief [. . .] that the Trojan war was not a myth, but a real war, "fought out in the place, and at least generally in the manner, described in Homer," and that the principal heroes and heroines recorded by Homer were not faded gods, but men and women of flesh and blood, of whose families and fortunes the memory survived in Greek tradition, though no doubt in course of time many mythical traits and incidents gathered round them.'[27] And it is hard not to want to do the same: we all want Homer to be true.

However, the idea of a unified Greek coalition assaulting Troy will not hold water. Such a notion was perceptively seen by the historian Herodotos, as early as the fifth century, as resembling the way in which the Persian Wars of 490–79 were seen in terms of Greek v. Barbarian. The myth of the expedition to Troy became a crucial tale that not only gave a positive, militaristic spin to Greekness, but also vindicated Greek movements into Asia Minor. It provided a justification for the whole process of the colonizing movement, and that is where the essence of the myth's relationship to history lies.

It may well be that a Greek force captured Troy: Greeks undoubtedly took it over at some stage, and, as Strabo tells us, Aulis was where the colonists from Aiolia traditionally set off from. But the notion of a 'real' Agamemnon coming from Mycenae far away to the south and collecting an invincible armada there is deeply unconvincing. Troy looks far more like a general representative of all the settlements that were overrun by Greek colonists, a kind of mythological shorthand.

If myths are socially significant traditional tales, and 'good to think with', the Trojan War stories can tell us a lot. These tales emphasize the way in which meanings of myths can change depending on the outlook of their tellers, and the way in which the opposition between the Greeks and Trojans was perceived at different historical periods is very illuminating. In Homer we can see no sign of ethnic or cultural opposition between Greeks and Trojans – Troy is a fine, civilized city, both sides worship the same gods, and there is no clear-cut distinction between 'goodies and baddies'. However, in the aftermath of the Persian invasions of Greece at the start of the fifth century, Troy acquired an incredibly negative image (especially at Athens, which led the resistance to Persia), and the Trojans were transformed into generic representatives of barbarism: Homer's noble Priamos becomes an arrogant, luxurious despot in Aiskhylos' *Agamemnon*, where Klytaimnestra persuades Agamemnon, just back from Troy, to revel in his triumph. She tells her maids to bring out rich tapestries and strew them from his chariot to the palace door. Initially Agamemnon is shocked:

What am I, some barbarian peacocking out of Asia?
Never cross my path with robes and draw the lightning.
Never – only the gods deserve the pomps of honour

and the stiff brocades of fame. To walk on them . . .
I am human, and it makes my pulses stir
with dread.

But Klytaimnestra lures him to his doom by playing on his vanity, and by inviting comparisons with Priamos:

> KLYTAIMNESTRA: But Priam – can you see him if he had your success?
> AGAMEMNON: Striding on the tapestries of gold, I see him now.[28]

Agamemnon is implicitly confirming the stereotype of Priamos as a typical barbarian. In the fourth century, the Spartan King Agesilaos attacked Persian possessions, and sacrificed at Aulis before he did so, in what was an obvious nod towards mythological precedent. Alexander the Great then pushed the idea to its limit. In his day the city of Ilion sat right on the interface between the Greeks and barbarians. On the one hand Alexander saw himself as the new Akhilleus (he claimed to be descended from him), and when he crossed into the Troad in 334, he paid homage at the supposed tomb of Akhilleus, and he allegedly carried a copy of the *Iliad* everywhere he went. Yet he had a broader vision than Akhilleus ever had, and dreamt of uniting west and east by his conquests. So his attitude towards Troy became inclusive, as is perfectly illustrated by the fact that he sacrificed at the same altar where Priamos was said to have been slaughtered by his ancestor Neoptolemos, son of Akhilleus.

14

HOMER'S *ILIAD*:
THE WRATH OF AKHILLEUS

Key Characters

Akhilleus (Achilles)	Mighty Greek warrior whose wrath motivates the *Iliad*
Agamemnon	Leader of the Greeks
Hektor (Hector)	Troy's greatest warrior
Priamos (Priam)	King of Troy
Odysseus (Ulysses)	Wily schemer, tactician and warrior
Great Aias (Ajax)	Formidable Greek warrior
Paris	Son of Priamos; abductor of Helen
Menelaos (Menelaus)	Husband of Helen
Helen	Abducted by Paris; the cause of the war
Hekabe (Hecuba)	Wife of Priamos, mother of Hektor
Andromakhe (Andromache)	Wife of Hektor

Part of Homer's colossal importance lies in the fact that he both represents the first real European literature, and stands at the heart of the Greek mythological tradition, in which the tale of the Trojan War is pre-eminent. We don't know precisely who 'Homer' was, and whether he was also the poet of the *Odyssey*, but judging by the fact that very few definitively post-eighth-century customs, practices and arte-facts appear in the poem, it seems likely that the *Iliad* was committed to writing some time in the eighth century. The tradition of oral poetry that underlies the *Iliad* seems to go back to the Mycenaean Age (*c.*1600–1100), which forms part of the Greek Bronze Age, and though by the eighth century Greece was firmly in the Iron Age, Homer's heroes use bronze weaponry. This suggests that the tradition of oral recitation goes back to Mycenaean times, when Greece was under the control of great palace-cultures based on places such as Mycenae and Pylos (which were insignificant in the Classical era), information about the economies and organization of which, again unlike anything in Homer, comes down to us in records written on clay tablets in a script called Linear B, an early form of Greek. In Xenophon's *Symposion*, a character called Nikeratos is reputed to know the entire work of Homer by heart. Nikeratos' knowledge is an extraordinary feat of memory, but it was by just such means that the tales were transmitted. It probably went through many different versions before it arrived in the form in which we know it. An oral poet embarking on a recitation is a bit like a jazz musician taking part in a jam session: the musician knows the tune, where the piece starts and ends, and will never deviate from the underlying structure and harmony, but because he has played the piece many times before, he will take many twists and turns in his improvisation. Finding a satisfactory route (the word *oime*, 'path/song-way', is used for a poet's song) through the tale is essential to the oral poet's craft.

Homer's *Iliad* is quite a simple story in outline, but it is crucial to be aware that Homer does not narrate the entire Trojan War, and that the Greek tradition does not allow us to create a continuous narrative of the events. Homer picks up the story in the tenth and final year of the conflict, which is still no closer to a resolution. The *Iliad* is written in 15,693 lines of dactylic hexameter poetry, which in ancient times were divided into 24 books, one for each letter of the Greek alphabet, whose endings signify critical moments in the narrative. The action is incredibly intense: chronologically the entire poem covers just fifty days, with only fourteen of those featuring narrated events, and three days taking up fourteen books.

When the *Iliad* starts, the Greek coalition is still besieging Troy.[1] Khryses, a Trojan priest of Apollo, comes to the Greek camp to ransom his daughter, Khryseis, who has been captured in a raid and allocated to Agamemnon as a concubine. When Agamemnon rejects his overtures and insults him, Khryses prays to Apollo to avenge him. Apollo inflicts a plague on the Greek army, and things get so desperate that Akhilleus convenes an assembly to debate what to do. Much to Agamemnon's displeasure, the soothsayer Kalkhas explains the reasons for Apollo's actions, but the leader still agrees to return the girl. This puts an end to the plague, but Agamemnon demands that he should receive a replacement for Khryseis. Akhilleus, who is unquestionably the finest Greek warrior but has less standing than Agamemnon, opposes this, prompting Agamemnon to seize Briseis, who had been awarded to Akhilleus as a prize. In essence Agamemnon has publicly announced that Akhilleus is surplus to requirements, and that he will do precisely what he likes with Akhilleus' hard-won property. Akhilleus' honour is now gravely affronted:

> I for my part did not come here for the sake of the Trojan
> spearmen to fight against them, since to me they have done
>   nothing.
> [. . .] but for your sake,
> O great shamelessness, we followed, to do you favour,
> you with the dog's eyes, to win your honour and Menelaos'
> from the Trojans. You forget all this or else you care nothing.
> And now my prize you threaten in person to strip from me,

for whom I laboured much, the gift of the sons of the Achaians.
[. . .]
Always the greater part of the painful fighting is the work of
my hands; but when the time comes to distribute the booty
yours is far the greater reward, and I with some small thing
yet dear to me go back to my ships when I am weary with
    fighting.
Now I am returning to Phthia, since it is much better
to go home again with my curved ships, and I am minded no
    longer
to stay here dishonoured and pile up your wealth and your
    luxury.[2]

Akhilleus is only narrowly prevented from killing Agamemnon by the Athene. He is a volunteer, so he withdraws from the conflict, retires to his tent accompanied by his best and very intimate friend Patroklos, nurses his heroic anger, and appeals for help to his mother, the sea goddess Thetis, who appeals to Zeus. She wants the Greeks to be defeated in Akhilleus' absence, so that their suffering humiliates Agamemnon and enhances Akhilleus' own value.

Now give honour to my son short-lived beyond all other
mortals. Since even now the lord of men Agamemnon
dishonours him, who has taken away his prize and keeps it.
Zeus of the counsels, Lord of Olympos, now do him honour.
So long put strength into the Trojans, until the Akhaians
give my son his rights, and his honour is increased among
    them.[3]

This is how the first book finishes, and once Akhilleus' wrath has been incurred, and his refusal to fight confirmed, the poem explores the consequences. In the second book

Agamemnon's army, minus Akhilleus, engages in combat with the Trojans. Fortunes vary during the first day's fighting, which is framed by indecisive duels between Menelaos and Paris in Book 3 and between 'Great' Aias and 'manslaughtering' Hektor in Book 7. Mighty feats of heroism take place, as when the Greek hero Diomedes wounds the goddess Aphrodite and the war god Ares, but even though events are inconclusive, the Greeks decide to build a defensive wall to protect their camp and ships.

The fighting now resumes after a day's interval. Before Hektor re-enters battle we are introduced to his wife Andromakhe and their baby son. He tells her that he cannot bear the

> thought of you, when some bronze-armoured
> Akhaian leads you off, taking away your day of liberty,
> in tears; and in Argos you must work at the loom of another,
> and carry water from the spring Messeis or Hypereia,
> all unwilling [. . .]
> But may I be dead and the piled earth hide me under before I
> hear you crying and know by this that they drag you captive.[4]

Hektor is not a mindless fighting machine. He and the other heroes would rather not fight at all. But under his leadership the Trojans start to get the upper hand, and at nightfall at the end of Book 8 they are sufficiently confident to bivouac on the plain so that next day they can storm the Greek encampment.

On the Greek side Agamemnon and his chieftains are pessimistic. He publicly acknowledges that the quarrel with Akhilleus was his own fault, and at the suggestion of his senior adviser, the aged and highly experienced Nestor, he despatches an embassy to Akhilleus consisting of Aias,

Odysseus and Akhilleus' old tutor, Phoinix. Agamemnon offers to give back Briseis in pristine condition, along with many other valuable gifts. Phoinix relates the tale of the anger of Meleagros, in the hope of persuading Akhilleus that he may lose the recompense if he delays too long.[5] Akhilleus entertains the ambassadors as friends, but he angrily rejects their offer:

> I hate his gifts. I hold him light as the strip of a splinter.
> Not if he gave me ten times as much, and twenty times over
> as he possesses now, not if more should come to him from
>   elsewhere,
> or gave all that is brought in to Orkhomenos, all that is
>   brought in
> to Thebes of Egypt, where the greatest possessions lie up in
>   the houses,
> Thebes of the hundred gates, where through each of the gates
>   two hundred
> fighting men come forth to war with horses and chariots;
> not if he gave me gifts as many as the sand or the dust is,
> not even so would Agamemnon have his way with my spirit
> until he had made good to me all this heartrending insolence.[6]

Akhilleus declares that he will not enter the fray again until the Trojans are setting fire to the Akhaian ships. These events take up Book 9, and Book 10 narrates a scouting expedition by Odysseus and Diomedes that takes place the same night.[7]

Dawn rises from her bed at the start of Book 11 to herald a day of intense fighting that only ends at Book 18. The Greeks get the better of the early exchanges, but many of their key fighters – Agamemnon, Diomedes, Odysseus, Eurypylos, Makhaon – are rendered *hors de combat*. With 'Great' Aias the only top-flight Greek warrior left in the field, the Trojans storm right into the Greek camp itself. The Greeks recover momentarily when Zeus allows his attention to be diverted elsewhere: Poseidon gives the Greeks the upper hand, and Hera makes love to Zeus to keep him occupied and then sleepy. But the Greek ascendancy is only temporary. Zeus wakes up seething and threatens the other gods with violence; Apollo smashes the Greek defences and Hektor's onslaught leaves the Greeks fighting to save their ships.

By now no offer of reparation from Agamemnon can appease Akhilleus' wrath, but the impasse leads to a catastrophic loss. Akhilleus has been monitoring the fighting, and Patroklos has become increasingly uneasy at the Greek reverses. He tries to talk Akhilleus round, and although no amount of pleas and reproaches can change Akhilleus' position, he does allow Patroklos to borrow his armour and lead out the Myrmidons to save the ships, adding one significant caveat:

> But obey to the end this word I put upon your attention
> so that you can win, for me, great honour and glory
> in the sight of all the Danaans, so they will bring back to me
> the lovely girl, and give me shining gifts in addition.
> When you have driven them from the ships, come back; although later
> the thunderous lord of Hera might grant you the winning of glory,
> you must not set your mind on fighting the Trojans, whose delight
> is in battle, without me. So you will diminish my honour.[8]

The idea is an instant success: Patroklos is wearing the fabulous armour of Akhilleus; the Myrmidons are rested and up for the fight; the Trojans are battle-weary; they think that the newcomer is Akhilleus himself; Patroklos saves the ships and routs the Trojans, killing, among dozens of others, Sarpedon, an especial favourite of Zeus. Unfortunately, though, Patroklos forgets Akhilleus' instructions. He pushes his success too far and Apollo intervenes to disorient him, allowing Euphorbos to hit him in the back with a spear, and Hektor to finish him off beneath the walls of Troy. Once again the conflict turns in the Trojans' favour. Hektor strips Akhilleus' armour from Patroklos' body, although the Greeks retrieve the corpse itself. By the end of Book 17 they are in headlong retreat.

Akhilleus' response is such a frenzy of grief, remorse and fury that when Thetis tells him that he will die almost immediately if he takes revenge on Hektor, he accepts the price. His motivation is to avenge his friend rather than to champion the Greek cause, but he cannot go into action immediately because he has no armour. However, the gods transfigure him, and simply by showing himself and shouting his awesome war cry he turns the Trojans back. Thetis gets Hephaistos, the blacksmith god, to forge superb new armour for Akhilleus, including a magnificent shield depicting various scenes of war and peace.[9]

The previous day's events have been a life-changing experience for Akhilleus. His anger towards Agamemnon is now replaced by a far more savage hatred for Patroklos' killer. He calls an assembly, announces an end to his feud with Agamemnon, and tells of his keenness to rejoin the battle. The Greeks are relieved and Agamemnon responds favourably, justifies his conduct, and offers reparations:

> I am not responsible
> but Zeus is, and Destiny, and Erinys the mist-walking
> who in assembly caught my heart in the savage delusion

on that day I myself stripped from him the prize of Akhilleus.
Yet what could I do? It is the god who accomplishes all things.
Delusion is the elder daughter of Zeus, the accursed
who deludes all; her feet are delicate and they step not
on the firm earth, but she walks the air above men's heads
and leads them astray. She has entangled others before me. [. . .]
So I in my time [. . .]
could not forget Delusion, the way I was first deluded.
but since I was deluded and Zeus took my wits away from me,
I am willing to make all good and give back gifts in
     abundance.[10]

Akhilleus now sets out to kill Hektor, in the clear knowledge
that this will hasten his own death – a fact prophesied to
him by his own horse Xanthos:

When he had spoken so the Furies stopped the voice in him,
but deeply disturbed, Akhilleus of the swift feet answered him:
'Xanthos, why do you prophesy my death? This is not for you.
I myself know well it is destined for me to die here
far from my beloved father and mother. But for all that
I will not stop till the Trojans have had enough of my
     fighting.'[11]

Meanwhile Hektor has latched on to the hope that a decisive
Trojan victory is in sight, and has spurned some sound advice
to retreat back to Troy, given that Akhilleus has returned to
the field. Zeus tells the gods that they may now enter the
fray, and Akhilleus leads a violent onslaught in which Poseidon has to save Aineias and Apollo rescues Hektor.

As inhuman fire sweeps on in fury through the deep angles
of a drywood mountain and sets ablaze the depth of the timber

and the blustering wind lashes the flame along, so Akhilleus
swept everywhere with his spear like something more than a
   mortal
harrying them as they died, and the black earth ran blood.[12]

So many Trojans are killed that the river god of Skamandros
tries to drown Akhilleus because he has clogged up his channels with so many corpses. Hephaistos intervenes on
Akhilleus' behalf, and the other gods engage: Athene defeats
Ares and Aphrodite; Poseidon wins a war of words with
Apollo; and Hera makes Artemis burst into tears. With the
exception of Hektor the Trojans are driven inside their walls.
Ashamed and deeply aware of the sanction of public opinion,
he now stands outside the city to face Akhilleus, watched
from the walls by his parents and fellow citizens with agonized
apprehension. The sense of pressure of what other people
might say is so strong that he *has* to fight, even against hope-
less odds:

   Now, since by my own recklessness I have ruined, my people,
   I feel shame before the Trojans and the Trojan women with
      trailing
   robes, that someone who is less of a man than I will say of me:
   'Hektor believed in his own strength and ruined his people.'
   Thus they will speak; and as for me, it would be much better
   at that time, to go against Akhilleus, and slay him, and come
      back,
   or else be killed by him in glory in front of the city.[13]

Isolated at the crucial moment, he suffers a failure of nerve.
He makes a run for safety and Akhilleus gives chase for three
circuits of the walls. But one of Akhilleus' defining epithets
is 'swift-footed', and when Zeus places the 'fateful portions

of death' of each protagonist on a pair of golden scales, Hektor's is heavier. Apollo deserts him, and Athene tricks him into standing his ground. In an outstanding simile Homer blends horror and violence with beauty and tranquillity:

> And as a star moves among stars in the night's darkening, Hesper, who is the fairest star who stands in the sky, such was the shining from the pointed spear Akhilleus was shaking in his right hand with evil intention toward brilliant Hektor.[14]

Hektor is no match for Akhilleus, and he goes down fighting. Akhilleus strips Hector's body and drags it behind his chariot in front of the walls of Troy and back to the Greek camp.

The fighting of the *Iliad* is essentially over,[15] but the death of Hektor now takes the *Iliad* into some very moving emotional territory. Rather than celebrating the achievements of the victors, Homer moves from the horrors of the battlefield to the formality of two funerals, which stand either side of a personal confrontation quite without parallel in all of Greek literature.

Patroklos' ghost appears to Akhilleus, asking for burial, and in Book 23 he gets his wish: a magnificent send-off complete with sacrifices of animals and Trojan prisoners. It is all celebrated with a series of athletic contests – chariot-racing, boxing, wrestling, foot-racing, armed combat, throwing a huge weight of pig-iron, archery – which are much more about winning than taking part, and the level of the heroes' commitment in this public arena is intense.

After the games Homer focuses on a very private scene. Akhilleus' violent feelings towards Hektor still remain strong, and he refuses to return Hektor's body for burial and attempts to mutilate it by dragging it behind his chariot, although Apollo prevents any damage to the corpse. Ultimately Zeus stamps his authority on the situation, and with the help of the god Hermes, Hektor's father Priamos makes his way through the Greek camp and into Akhilleus' tent to try to ransom Hektor's body.

This electrifying confrontation between the victim and the victor is made even tenser because there are really no ground rules for this type of encounter. The emotions felt by both men are incredibly raw, Akhilleus is still a chillingly violent and dangerous man, and the elderly Priamos is extremely vulnerable. Yet Akhilleus just about manages to control his wrath. He is reminded by Priamos of his own father Peleus, another old comfortless man, and he takes pity on the aged king. His wrath turns to sympathy, and he grants Priamos his wish with kindness and courtesy:

Honour then the gods, Akhilleus, and take pity upon me
Remembering your father, yet I am more pitiful;
I have gone through what no other mortal on earth has gone
    through;
I put my lips to the hands of the man who has killed my
    children.

    So he spoke, and stirred in the other a passion of grieving
for his own father. He took the old man's hand and pushed him
Gently away, and the two remembered, as Priam [Priamos] sat
    huddled
at the feet of Akhilleus and wept close for manslaughtering
    Hektor
and Akhilleus wept now for his own father, now again
for Patroklos. The sound of their mourning moved in the house.
    Then
when great Akhilleus had taken full satisfaction in sorrow
and the passion for it had gone from his mind and body, there-
    after

he rose from his chair, and took the old man by the hand, and set him
on his feet again, in pity for the grey head and the grey beard,
and spoke to him and addressed him in winged words: 'Ah, unlucky,
surely you have had much evil to endure in your spirit.
How could you dare to come alone to the ships of the Achaians
and before my eyes, when I am the one who have killed in such numbers
such brave sons of yours? The heart in you is iron. Come, then,
and sit down upon this chair, and you and I will even let
our sorrows lie still in the heart for all our grieving.'[16]

Homer now takes us back to Troy, and to Hektor's funeral, whose emotional content is no less traumatic than the scene in Akhilleus' tent. We hear lamentations from three women who have had a special place in Hektor's life. Predictably his wife Andromakhe and his mother Hekabe have moving things to say, but so, rather surprisingly, does Helen:

'Hektor, of all my lord's brothers dearest by far to my spirit
   [. . .]
I have never heard a harsh saying from you, nor an insult.
No, but when another, one of my lord's brothers or sisters, a fair-robed
wife of some brother, would say a harsh word to me in the palace,
or my lord's mother – but his father was gentle always, a father
indeed – then you would speak and put them off and restrain them
by your own gentleness of heart and your gentle words. Therefore
I mourn for you in sorrow of heart and mourn myself also

and my ill luck. There was no other in all the wide Troad
who was kind to me, and my friend; all others shrank when
   they saw me.'[17]

Not for nothing has the *Iliad* been described as 'the tragedy
of Hektor'.

This sequence of incidents provides a perfect conclusion
to Homer's tale. He opened by appealing to the Muse to
help him sing of the wrath of Akhilleus, and the wrath and
the *Iliad* are now over. But the Trojan War is not: hostilities
will resume once Hektor's funeral is over, bringing death to
Akhilleus and destruction to Troy.

Understanding the Heroes: Honour, and the Wrath of Akhilleus

A common modern complaint about the *Iliad* is that it is a
poem for men about men, all about male physical prowess.
Yet it is not a record of triumphant military achievements –
Troy is still standing, and large parts of the narrative concern
Greek defeats. So it is not purely about the grand heroic
achievements of the ancestors of the Greeks. For instance,
Hektor's impending return to the battlefield in Book 6
provides a very powerful moment in the poem, but one that
is clearly not concerned with male dominance:

So speaking glorious Hektor held out his arms to his baby,
who shrank back to his fair-girdled nurse's bosom
screaming, and frightened at the aspect of his own father,
terrified as he saw the bronze and the crest with its horse-hair,
nodding dreadfully, as he thought, from the peak of the helmet.
Then his beloved father laughed out, and his honoured mother,
and at once glorious Hektor lifted from his head the helmet
and laid it in all its shining upon the ground. Then taking

up his dear son he tossed him about in his arms, and kissed
  him,
and lifted his voice in prayer to Zeus and the other immortals
  [. . .]
So speaking he set his child again in the arms of his beloved
wife, who took him back again to her fragrant bosom
smiling in her tears; and her husband saw, and took pity upon
  her,
and stroked her with his hand, and called her by name and
  spoke to her.[18]

Similarly, Akhilleus' exchanges with his mother Thetis are
delicately handled, providing a sensitive counterpoint to the
horror of the fighting.

'But what pleasure is this to me, since my dear companion
  has perished,
Patroklos, whom I loved beyond all other companions,
as well as my own life. I have lost him, and Hektor, who
  killed him,
has stripped away that gigantic armour, a wonder to look on
and splendid, which the gods gave Peleus, a glorious present,
on that day they drove you to the marriage bed of a mortal.
I wish you had gone on living then with the other goddesses
of the sea, and that Peleus had married some mortal woman.
As it is, there must be on your heart a numberless sorrow
for your son's death, since you can never again receive him
won home again to his country; since the spirit within does
  not drive me
to go on living and be among men, except on condition
that Hektor first be beaten down under my spear, lose his life
and pay the price for stripping Patroklos, the son of
  Menoitios.'

Then in turn Thetis spoke to him, letting the tears fall:
'Then I must lose you soon, my child, by what you are saying,
since it is decreed your death must come soon after Hektor's.'
   Then deeply disturbed Akhilleus of the swift feet
     answered her:
'I must die soon, then; since I was not to stand by my
   companion
when he was killed. And now, far away from the land of his
   fathers,
he has perished, and lacked my fighting strength to defend
   him.[19]

The *Iliad* is about much more than warriors' heroics.

In fact, the *Iliad* tells us what it is about in the very first word of the poem: 'wrath' (*m nis* in Greek) – the Wrath of Akhilleus. The crucial issue at stake here is *tim* , a Greek word that has associations with value, honour, recompense, or paying a penalty. Honour demands recompense, so *tim* becomes a person's social value, hence its critical importance to the heroes. The ultimate goal of the heroes is to win eternal fame (*kleos* in Greek), and although they have a strong sense of their own self-worth, what really matters is the opinion of their peers. Defeat and insult are taken very hard. So when Odysseus talks to Agamemnon about his quarrel with Akhilleus, he says that he doesn't blame the other Greeks for being anxious: Agamemnon has behaved in a way that is likely to lead to failure; this is reprehensible; if the Greeks return empty-handed from a ten-year war they will incur shame; and it will all be Agamemnon's fault. Odysseus doesn't really care about the rights and wrongs of the quarrel, but he does care about its consequences. Outcome is everything.

In Book 3, when Paris ducks out of a possible duel with Menelaus, Hektor feels ashamed:

Surely now the flowing-haired Akhaians laugh at us,
thinking you are our bravest champion, only because your
looks are handsome, but there is no strength in your heart,
   no courage.
Were you like this that time when in sea-wandering vessels
assembling oarsmen to help you you sailed over the water,
and mixed with the outlanders, and carried away a fair woman
from a remote land, whose lord's kin were spearmen and
   fighters,
to your father a big sorrow, and your city, and all your people,
to yourself a thing shameful but bringing joy to the enemy?
And now you would not stand up against warlike Menelaos?[20]

The contrast Hektor draws is illuminating: *now* Paris is a coward, but *then*, making off with Helen from under Menelaos' nose, he was to be admired for doing heroic deeds. Paris' current action is a source of sorrow to the Trojans and joy to the Greeks, therefore Hektor feels he ought to be ashamed. The heroes' behaviour is judged partly in terms of stereotypes of how men *should* behave and partly in terms of *consequences*.

Akhilleus is likewise pre-eminently concerned about his own status. To modern readers he seems to be motivated by personal vendetta, lacking social responsibility, or just plain childish. C.S. Lewis described him as 'little more than a passionate boy', sulking because his woman, like a child's toy, has been taken away. But there is a more fundamental reason for Akhilleus' anger: his *tim* , his value/worth/honour, has been negated. He is obsessive about this and exhibits a powerful drive towards self-assertion, taking things much further than anyone else, and responding to things much more violently:

Father Zeus, Athene and Apollo, if only
not one of all the Trojans could escape destruction, not one
of the Argives, but you [*Patroklos*] and I could emerge from
the slaughter
so that we two alone could break Troy's hallowed coronal.[21]

Tim can also have a very concrete sense. When Sarpedon explains to his companion Glaukos why the various heroes are at Troy at all, he illustrates how the heroic value-system centres on the way that society needs the warrior, and is prepared to reward him with material gifts and public acclaim, which in turn are reciprocated by the warrior's duty of fighting in the front line:

Glaukos, why is it you and I are honoured before others
with pride of place, the choice meats and the filled wine
cups
in Lykia, and all men look on us as if we were immortals,
and we are appointed a great piece of land by the banks of
Xanthos,
good land, orchard and vineyard, and ploughland for the
planting of wheat?
Therefore it is our duty in the forefront of the Lykians
to take our stand, and bear our part of the blazing of battle.[22]

This explains why Akhilleus' old mentor Phoinix tries to persuade him not just to return to the fighting but to accept Agamemnon's compensatory gift as well:

No, with gifts promised
Go forth. The Greeks will honour you as they would an
immortal.
But if without gifts you go into the fighting where men perish,

Your honour will no longer be as great, though you drive back
the battle.[23]

Without concrete evidence of compensation, the Greeks
would simply assume that Akhilleus had given in.

There is an incredibly strong element of competitiveness
between heroes. At the heart of the dispute between
Agamemnon and Akhilleus is the issue of who should get
public rewards: should it be the best fighters, or the leaders
(regardless of whether they are right or wrong)? Wise old
Nestor attempts to find a middle way through the quarrel:

You [*Agamemnon*], great man that you are, yet do not take
the girl away
But let her be, a prize as the sons of the Greeks gave her
First. Nor, son of Peleus [*Akhilleus*], think to match your
strength with
The king, since never equal with the rest is the portion of
honour
Of the sceptred king to whom Zeus gives magnificence. Even
Though you are the stronger man, and the mother who bore
you was immortal,
Yet is this man greater who is lord over more than you rule.
Son of Atreus [*Agamemnon*], give up your anger; even I
entreat you
To give over your bitterness against Akhilleus, he who
Stands as a great bulwark of battle over all the Greeks.[24]

So in Homer's world excellence in fighting was only one of
a number of qualities that demanded *timé*. Wealth, the
number of a man's subjects or the quality of advice one gave
were all rival claims to status.

A helpful model for understanding Greek cultural values

is that of any team game. In this environment there always is a permanent tension between individual stardom and the needs of the team. There is never any doubt about the identity of the opposition – you treat them as people to be defeated, and they do the same to you – and when games are played in public, the game becomes a vehicle for conspicuous displays of success. And, of course, at the end of the day, excuses count for nothing: winning is the only thing that matters.

When Akhilleus and Hektor finally commence their single combat, Hektor knows from the outset that his chances are slim, but he still decides to face Akhilleus so as not to lose *timé*. Earlier in the epic, in a response to his wife Andromakhe's efforts to persuade him to stay with her and their child, he said this:

> I would feel deep shame
> before the Trojans and the Trojan women with trailing
> garments,
> if like a coward I were to shrink aside from the fighting.[25]

Public approval was an enormous positive motivation, and the possibility of public disapproval ensures that Hector fulfils his obligations. He is moved by what he imagines other people think about him.

Hektor's death should have brought satisfaction to Akhilleus, but in fact it does nothing of the sort. The hideous consequence of his decision to avenge Patroklos is that he will die shortly after, and he knows this. Hektor was essentially taken unawares by his fate, but Akhilleus confronts his head on. So, what is a man's life worth? Akhilleus tells us:

> Thus it is destiny for us both to stain the same soil
> here in Troy; since I shall never come home, and my father,

Peleus the aged rider, will not welcome me in his great house,
nor Thetis my mother, but in this place the earth will receive
   me.
But seeing that it is I, Patroklos, who follow you underground,
I will not bury you till I bring to this place the armour
and the head of Hektor, since he was your great-hearted
   murderer.[26]

Akhilleus values his life at the price of revenge on the person
who killed his beloved companion. He imposes his own death
sentence, not to win everlasting *kleos*, but because he feels
responsible for Patroklos' death. But killing Hektor fails to
assuage his anguish, which is why the moment where
Akhilleus and Priamos look upon each other in admiration
is so astonishing: it brings home the fact that there is more
to life than revenge, and more to manhood than slaughtering
other men.

The Afterlife of the *Iliad*

Troy's special aura actually has nothing to do with 'history'
and everything to do with what has been imagined and made
out of it over the centuries. At the end of Euripides' tragedy,
Trojan Women, Troy is incinerated, and the women call on
Troy itself:

Soon you will fall and lie
With the earth you loved, and none shall name you! . . .
All has vanished, and Troy is nothing![27]

Every time these words are performed, they become false.

The *Iliad* certainly enshrined a past to which the Greeks
could look back, but not necessarily a triumphant one. The
finest things in the *Iliad*, Hektor, Akhilleus and Troy, are all

Our efforts are like those of the Trojans.
We think we'll change our luck
by being so resolute and daring,
so we move outside ready to fight.

But when the big crisis comes,
our boldness and resolution vanish;
our spirit falters, paralyzed,
and we scurry around the walls
trying to save ourselves by running away.

Homer's power and relevance were brought home very strongly with the onset of the First World War, most notably during the Gallipoli campaign. Troy was located near the Gallipoli combat zone, which was a point not lost on Rupert Brooke:

They say Achilles in the darkness stirred . . .
And Priam and his fifty sons
Wake all amazed, and hear the guns,
          And shake for Troy again.[30]

Patrick Shaw-Stewart also faced the horrors of Gallipoli with the *Iliad* in mind:

O hell of ships and cities
          Hell of men like me
Fatal second Helen
          Why must I follow thee?

Achilles came to Troyland
          And I to Chersonese:
He turned from wrath to battle,
          And I from three days' peace.

Was it so hard, Achilles,
      So very hard to die?
Thou knowest and I know not –
      So much the happier I.

I will go back this morning
      From Imbros over the sea;
Stand in the trench, Achilles,
      Flame-capped, and fight for me.[31]

But as the First World War progressed, Homer seemed to become less appropriate: in John Buchan's words, 'to speak of glory seemed a horrid impiety. That was perhaps why I could not open Homer.'[32]

In the aftermath of the Second World War Homer was felt once again to have deep resonance. In George Steiner's opinion:

Every time we destroy a city, every time we see people under burning roofs fleeing for their lives, Homer becomes immediate. In the first production of (sic) the Berlin stage in 1945 against a photo-background of the great gutted city and of fire bombs, they read the *Iliad* because there was no contemporary text even half as contemporary.[33]

The *Iliad* certainly never backs down from confronting the horrors of war, but as Simone Weil argues, it is always aware of the victim as much as the victor, which means that force does not triumph:

Nothing the peoples of Europe have produced is worth the first known poem that appeared among them. Perhaps they will yet discover the epic genius, when they learn that there is no refuge from fate, learn not to admire force, not to hate the enemy, nor to scorn the unfortunate. How soon this will happen is another question.[34]

Not everyone shares Weil's view, though. George Steiner states:

> There is something in the descriptions of battle, the sheer beauty of combat, the sheer choreography of the great swordsman or javelin man or a man leaping from his chariot, the marvellous supple beauty of a young body in a mortal encounter . . . of Nürnberg Stadium marching under Hitler – the sheer maddening, very Greek beauty of that occasion, with the great torches in the night – a very Greek moment, that. It embarrasses us, yet we have to face it in order to read Homer rightly.[35]

Anselm Kiefer, an artist for whom Greek mythology is one of many diverse and esoteric sources of inspiration, has produced vast, charred, panoramic landscapes (some 7.60 metres across), which invite comparison with the poppy fields of the First World War. In *Nachricht vom Fall Troja* (2005–6) eight large fires burn across a vast open plain scattered with either reddish flowers or further fires, with text indicating place names on the horizon. As the fires burn we are reminded of the destruction of the city, but also of the beacon fires taking the news home to Klytaimnestra, and the sickening events still to come at Mycenae.[36] In *Die Nachricht vom Fall Troja* (2006), although there is less fire, the beacon's message is made more explicit by place names strewn across the land-scape, connected by a thick strip of white, illustrating the journey which starts at Ilion (top left) and ends at the 'Haus des Atrides' at the far right.

Parallels have been drawn between the recent Hollywood

blockbuster *Troy*, directed by Wolfgang Petersen (2004), and
the US-led assaults on Iraq, although it seems unlikely that
the director intended it to be seen that way, and the further
one pushes the analogies, the less convincing they seem: Iraq
is a much weaker opponent than Troy; Homer's adversaries
share a common culture, language and religion; Herakles'
sack of Laomedon's Troy bears little resemblance to the First
Gulf War; and Helen's abduction by Paris hardly mirrors the
search for WMD that sparked the second. However, the will-
ingness to look for these parallels says much about the
contemporary relevance of Homer's themes. Petersen tries to
read the *Iliad* rightly, but makes a number of interesting
modifications to the story, presumably in the interests of
commercial success. Akhilleus' relationship with Patroklos is
transmuted, possibly on the basis of a pseudo-Hesiodic fragment which bucks the trend of the usual tradition, to that
of 'cousin',[37] and we are left in no doubt as to his heterosexual
proclivities by the fact that he wakes up with two women
in his bed in his first scene. Briseis is also 'cousin' to Paris
and Hektor (there is no Khryseis): she is captured when the
Greeks first land, and is subsequently seduced by Akhilleus
when she tries to murder him in his tent. The Atreidai 'have
the look, attire, and manners of over-aged, overweight pirat-
ical Vikings'.[38] Agamemnon is an out-and-out imperialist,
and Menelaos wants revenge for the abduction of Helen;
unfortunately for him Hektor slays him early in the film.
Patroklos borrows Akhilleus' armour without his knowledge
– thereby absolving him (a) of any responsibility for his
cousin's death and (b) of the need to feel remorse.

The scene between Akhilleus and Priamos tries hard to
evoke the events of Book 24, and includes some near-verbatim
quotations from the *Iliad*, alongside the liberation of Briseis.
But the quarrel between Akhilleus and Agamemnon still

remains, and in the sack of Troy, Agamemnon kills Priamos, and Briseis kills Agamemnon before Paris shoots Akhilleus in the heel and escapes with her. Odysseus, with his muck-and-brass Yorkshire accent, finally cremates Akhilleus, bringing Homer's ten-year war to a close in a matter of a few weeks, and resolving a rather anodyne swords-and-sandals movie, lacking in the types of depth and complexity in which Greek mythology revels. For although his stereotype might be otherwise, Akhilleus still finishes on a note of reconciliation and has some sensitivity for the human condition. In searching for a contemporary Akhilleus there are those who look towards the action heroes played by the likes of Sylvester Stallone, Arnold Schwarzenegger and Jean-Claude Van Damme. But Rambo does not die young, the Terminator does not weep, and the Universal Soldier does not eat with the father of his victims.

THE WOODEN HORSE
AND THE SACK OF TROY

Key Characters

Penthesileia	Amazon queen, slain by Akhilleus
Memnon	King of the Aithiopians, slain by Akhilleus
Akhilleus (Achilles)	The finest Akhaian warrior
Paris	Slayer of Akhilleus; slain by Philoktetes
'Great' Aias (Ajax)	Mighty Greek hero; lost the contest for Akhilleus' arms; committed suicide
Odysseus (Ulysses)	Cunning Greek hero; won Akhilleus' arms; instrumental in Troy's fall
Neoptolemos	Son of Akhilleus
Kassandra (Cassandra)	Trojan prophetess: always told the truth; never believed
'Lesser' Aias (Ajax)	Raped Kassandra
Laokoon (Laocoon)	Tried to warn the Trojans of the dangers of the Wooden Horse
Priamos (Priam)	King of Troy; killed in the city's destruction

As the *Iliad* draws to its close, the outcome of the Trojan War is by no means settled. Troy's greatest son might have died, but the city itself still stands. A variety of sources take the tale through towards its conclusion: for instance, the

Aithiopis by Arktinos of Miletos narrates the period from the coming of the Amazons to the suicide of Aias, and a work known as the *Little Iliad* takes us from the death of Akhilleus down to the fall of Troy and the departure of the Greeks. In addition to these works, the various episodes appear as subjects across a variety of media ranging from tragic drama to vase painting.

Akhilleus became involved in fighting against Trojan allies who came from the ends of the earth: the Amazons from the north, and the Aithiopians from the south. The beautiful Amazon Queen Penthesileia was a very effective combatant, but in the end she succumbed to Akhilleus' superior might. Yet there was a twist to the story which is beautifully illustrated on an Attic black-figure amphora by Exekias, now in the British Museum: as Akhilleus thrust his spear into her throat, their eyes met, and for that fleeting moment the two fell in love. Thersites, the lame, bandy-legged, hunchbacked, balding, pointy-headed man who was the only commoner to play a part in the Iliad,[1] jeered at Akhilleus because of this, or even gouged out Penthesileia's eyes, but he paid the price of this behaviour with his life.

Memnon, the son of Eos and Tithonos, who was the most handsome man that Odysseus had ever seen, brought a significant contingent of Aithiopians to Troy, and, clad in magnificent armour manufactured by Hephaistos, he slaughtered a great number of Greeks. When he came up against Akhilleus the two men's mothers sought Zeus' help, but it was Akhilleus who emerged triumphant in an *androktasia* ('slaying of a man') that ranked among his most glorious. Herodotos tells us that Memnon became conflated with Sestriotis, King of Egypt, and there certainly were shrines to Memnon at Thebes and Abydos, with perhaps the best-known monument being the so-called Colossus of Memnon on the site of the mortuary temple of

Amenhotep III. It got its name because it gave out a musical note whenever the dawn's rays struck it, and it greeted its mother's appearance in this way until it was repaired in the third century CE.

The *androktasia* of Memnon was the prelude to Akhilleus' own death. In pursuing the routed Trojans towards the city, he was shot close to the Skaian gate. The arrow hit him in the heel, his one vulnerable area.[2] The identity of the archer varies according to who is the myth-teller: Homer twice says that Apollo and Paris are jointly responsible, once when Akhilleus' talking horse Xanthos prophesies that he will be killed by a god and a mortal, and again in Hektor's very last words, where the names and the location are specified; elsewhere in the *Iliad*, Akhilleus himself speaks of his knowledge that he will be slain by the shafts of Apollo alone, and this version seems to have been picked up by Aiskhylos, Sophokles and Horace; Hyginus makes Apollo transfix his ankle, but he does so disguised as Paris; Virgil and Ovid both say that Paris unleashed the arrow, but that Apollo guided it; yet again, other authors, such as Euripides and Plutarch, speak of Paris as the slayer of Akhilleus with no divine assistance.

A totally different version linked the death of Akhilleus with a romantic attachment to Priamos' beautiful virgin daughter Polyxena. He first saw her on Troy's towers, throwing down bracelets and earrings in order to ransom Hektor's body, and Priamos offered Akhilleus marriage with her in return for abandoning the siege of Troy. In the ensuing negotiations Akhilleus went unarmed and unaccompanied to the temple of Thymbraian Apollo (where he himself had murdered Troilos).[3] Priamos' son Deiphobos embraced him, while Paris either stabbed him with a sword, or fired the fatal arrow from behind the cult statue.

An intense struggle took place for possession of Akhilleus'

body, but 'Great' Aias made sure he managed to get the corpse back to the Greek ships with help from Odysseus, who covered his rear. In the *Odyssey* Agamemnon's ghost describes the magnificent obsequies to the ghost of Akhilleus. His mother Thetis came, accompanied by sea-nymphs, and all nine Muses sang:

> Nor would you have then seen any one of the Argives
> not in tears, so much did the singing Muses stir them.
> For ten and seven days, alike in the day and the night time,
> we wailed for you, both mortal people and the immortals.
> On the eighteenth day we gave you to the fire, and around you
> slaughtered a great number of fat sheep and horn-curved cattle.
> You were burned in the clothing of the gods, and abundant
> ointment and sweet honey, while many Akhaian heroes
> moved in armour about the pyre where you were burning,
> with horses and on foot, and a great clamouring rose up.[4]

The bones of Akhilleus were then placed with the bones of Patroklos in a golden urn, made by Hephaistos, and buried in a mound at the headland of Sigeion. Even though Akhilleus had, in a sense, embraced death by the way he lived his life, his *post mortem* existence led him to share some very memorable reflections with Odysseus, who finds him on his own in the Asphodel Meadow in the Underworld:

> O shining Odysseus, never try to console me for dying.
> I would rather follow the plough as thrall to another
> man, one with no land allotted to him and not much to live on,
> than be a king over all the perished dead.[5]

In a later tradition, Akhilleus receives a better afterlife, immortalized and living on Leuke ('the White Isle'), a wooded island off the mouth of the Danube, with Helen as his wife and

Patroklos and Antilokhos as his comrades. There he recited Homer, and sailors often heard ghostly singing drifting across the water, while those who anchored off the coast could make out the noise of horses and warring warriors. The poet Ibykos also generated a tale that Akhilleus married Medeia in the Elysian Fields.

With the death of Akhilleus the ruthlessly competitive Greek leaders needed to re-establish the hierarchy and determine which of them was the most worthy to take possession of his weaponry. Funeral games were held, with magnificent performances in chariot-racing, running, quoit throwing and archery.[6] But the fiercest competition came when the arms of Akhilleus were offered as a prize to the bravest, and 'Great' Aias and Odysseus claimed them. Homer tells us that the Trojans and Athena were the arbiters, and awarded the arms to Odysseus (the Trojan prisoners felt that Odysseus had inflicted the most damage on them, which is why he was chosen); in another account, Nestor's spies overheard two Trojan girls debating their respective merits, and he was swayed by the arguments of the one who spoke in favour of Odysseus; according to Pindar, the Greeks decided in Odysseus' favour in a secret ballot.

Aias was devastated. He planned a night raid on the Akhaian army, but Athena drove him mad, and he perpetrated incredible carnage among a herd of cattle instead. Aias' madness forms the theme of Sophokles' tragedy *Aias*, in which his exultant madness gives way to despair when he recovers his sanity. In a field littered with bloody carcasses, he laments his transition from a fearless warrior against men into a slayer of innocent animals; and he cannot bear the shame. As a hero his very existence was governed by the code of honour, but now there is no possibility of honour left. He decides to take his own life:

> Honour in life,
> Or honour in death; there is no other thing
> A nobleman can ask for. That is all.[7]

His concubine Tekmessa, who is the mother of his little son Eurysakes, does her level best to talk him out of it, but he is adamant. He soothes her fears, and those of his men, saying that he will learn to accept the blows of fate, but once he is on his own he curses his enemies and falls on his sword. This was a weapon that carried strong reminiscences of his illustrious past: Hektor had given it to him after they had fought a duel. Aiskhylos told how, because of Aias' invulnerability, the sword doubled back in the shape of a bow, until the precise point to apply the blade was made clear to him.[8]

Once his body was discovered, Menelaos and Agamemnon were in favour of throwing it to the dogs and birds; Odysseus, whose animosity towards Aias had now subsided, rather graciously insisted that it would be wrong violate Aias,

> Or refuse to admit
> He was the bravest man I ever saw,
> The best of all that ever came to Troy,
> Save only for Akhilleus.[9]

Agamemnon relented, and the drama concludes with preparations for Aias' burial with full heroic honours. He was the only hero who fell at Troy to be buried in a coffin.

Earlier in the play, Athena had asked Odysseus if he knew of any hero who was greater than Aias. His response was unequivocal:

> Never. He was my enemy, but I'm sorry
> Now, with all my heart, for the misfortune

Which holds him in its deadly grip. This touches
My state as well as his. Are we not all,
All living things, mere phantoms, shadows of nothing?

She replies:

Therefore beware of uttering blasphemy
Against the gods; beware of pride, puffed up
By strength or substance. Know that all things mortal
Hang in the scales; one day can tilt them up,
Or down. The gods love goodness, and I abhor
All that is evil.[10]

In many ways this exchange can be seen as the last word on
the whole heroic tragedy of the Trojan War.

In Homer's *Odyssey*, Odysseus meets Aias' ghost in Hades
and tries to patch up their quarrel, but to no avail: Aias will
not speak to him, and Odysseus does not have the time to
devote to winning him round. Pausanias records a tradition
in which Akhilleus' arms were washed ashore at Aias' tomb
after Odysseus was shipwrecked on his travels, and it is also
said that, like Akhilleus and others, he lived for ever on
Leuke, the White Island. Ovid relates a tale in which the
hyacinth flower sprang up where Aias' blood spilled on to
the ground.[11] Its petals were marked with the letters AI,
appropriate because they are the first letters of Aias' name
and because the Greek word *ai* means 'alas!'.

The war had now lasted for the predicted ten years. Kalkhas
(or the Trojan seer Helenos, who had been captured by
Odysseus for this very purpose),[12] divined that Troy could
not be captured unless the Akhaians had the bow of Herakles
in their possession, so wily Odysseus sprang into action and

went to Lemnos, where Philoktetes was using the bow to hunt for food. Sophokles' tragedy *Philoktetes* dramatizes the events of the embassy, with Odysseus devious and ruthless but Akhilleus' son Neoptolemos gaining sympathy for the wounded hero, and the whole issue having to be sorted out by Herakles as *deus ex machina*. Philoktetes sailed to Troy, where his wound was finally cured. He then shot Paris.

Before the Judgement of Paris, Helen's abduction and the Greek invasion, Paris had been married to Oinone,[13] a nymph who had the gift of prophecy. She had been unable to talk him out of the whole idea of abducting Helen, although she had told him to visit her if he were wounded, because only she would be able to heal him. Paris went to Oinone on Mount Ida, but her grievances now ran so deep that she refused to treat him. He was taken back to Troy, where he died. Oinone had a last-minute change of heart and brought the necessary drugs, only to find it was too late. Overcome by anguish, she hanged herself.

After the death of Paris there was a quarrel between his brothers Helenos and Deiphobos over who should now marry Helen. Deiphobos was the lucky man, and the spurned Helenos left the city to live on Mount Ida. Helenos knew the oracles that protected Troy, so Odysseus ambushed him and forced him to give the Greeks the necessary information. In addition to the bow of Herakles, they needed:

1. The bones (or shoulder blade) of Pelops;
2. Neoptolemos to fight with them;
3. Possession of the Palladion,[14] because while it was inside the walls, Troy could not be captured.

The Greeks immediately acted on this intelligence: the bones of Pelops were fetched; Neoptolemos was recruited from

Lemnos, and proceeded to fight formidably in his father's armour; and plans were put in place for stealing the Palladion.

It seems to have been a two-stage operation, but it varies in detail from source to source, and Apollodoros seems to conflate the two incidents. In the first stage Odysseus disfigured himself, dressed himself in rags, and went to Troy as a beggar. He was recognized, but not betrayed, by Helen. Stage two involved Odysseus and Diomedes. In one account the two heroes entered the city through a sewer, while in another Diomedes climbed on to Odysseus' shoulders to scale the walls, but then refused to pull his comrade up after him. Diomedes got hold of the Palladion and returned with it to Odysseus, but as they were heading back to camp Odysseus decided to murder him and take all the credit for the mission. He dropped back behind Diomedes, but his sword caught the light of the moon. Diomedes accused Odysseus of cowardice, and drove him back to camp while beating him with the flat of his sword.

The Palladion was now safely in Greek hands. Odysseus' cunning intelligence had successfully created the conditions for Troy's demise. Just one more act of deception was needed.

The Wooden Horse

It is interesting that the Wooden Horse motif, which is now one of the incidents most commonly associated with the Troy story, did not play a particularly significant part in the Greek tradition. There are allusions to it in Homer's *Odyssey*, although not in the *Iliad*, and references in authors of the lost Epic Cycle, but it really assumes massive importance through the work of the Roman poet Virgil, who brilliantly relates the definitive version in his *Aeneid*.

The idea for the Wooden Horse came from either Odysseus or Athena, and it was designed and constructed by the architect Epeios. It was an image of a horse built from local timber, with a hollow interior and an opening in the sides, and on the outside was the inscription:

> For their return home, the Greeks dedicate this thank-offering to Athena.

Inside the horse were a number of warriors: 3,000, 100, 50, 30-something, 23, or 12 are all suggested.

> ## The Twelve Occupants of the Wooden Horse, According to Eustathius:
>
> Menelaos, Diomedes, Philoktetes, Meriones, Neoptolemos, Eurypylos, Eurydamas, Pheidippos, Leonteus, Meges, Odysseus and Eumelos

Quintus Smyrnaeus, who names thirty occupants, says that Epeios got in last and sat by the door because he knew how to open the trapdoor. All the heroes had an anxious time of it, apart from Neoptolemos, if Odysseus' words to the ghost of his father are to be believed:

> The other leaders of the Danaans and men of counsel
> were wiping their tears away and the limbs were shaking under
> each man of them; but never at any time did I see him
> losing his handsome colour and going pale, or wiping
> the tears off his face, but rather he implored me to let him
> sally out of the horse; he kept feeling for his sword hilt
> and spear weighted with bronze, full of evil thoughts for the
>   Trojans.[15]

The remainder of the invasion force set fire to their camp and sailed away by night to Tenedos, leaving behind Sinon, who was detailed to signal to them with a beacon.

At daybreak the Trojans saw the abandoned Greek camp and the Wooden Horse, and assumed that their invaders had gone for good. However, the priest Laokoon was deeply suspicious, and tried to prevent them from taking the horse into the city. It was he who told the Trojans to beware of Greeks bearing gifts, and he thrust his spear into the horse to prove that it was hollow. However, Sinon, pretending to be a deserter, persuaded them that it was a *bona fide* offering, and his evidence seemed to be corroborated when two massive serpents rose from the sea and strangled Laokoon and his sons.[16] The two most renowned ancient versions of the scene are the magnificent sculptural group of the Hellenistic baroque tradition which is now in the Vatican, and that of Virgil in the *Aeneid*.

> Over the tranquil deep, from Tenedos, we saw –
> Telling it makes me shudder – twin snakes with immense coils
> Thrusting the sea and together streaking towards the shore:
> Rampant they were among the waves, their blood-red crests
> Reared up over the water; the rest of them slithered along
> The surface, coil after coil sinuously trailing behind them.
> We heard a hiss of salt spray. Next, they were on dry land,
> In the same field – a glare and blaze of bloodshot eyes,
> Tongues flickering like flame from their mouths, and the
>   mouths hissing.
> Our blood drained away at the sight; we broke and ran. The
>   serpents
> Went straight for Laokoon. First, each snake knotted itself
> Round the body of one of Laokoon's small sons, hugging him
>   tight
> In its coils, and cropped the piteous flesh with its fangs. Next
>   thing,
> They fastened upon Laokoon, as he hurried, weapon in hand,
> To help the boys, and lashed him up in their giant whorls.

With a double grip round his waist and his neck, the scaly
    creatures
Embrace him, their heads and throats powerfully poised above
    him.
All the while his hands are struggling to break their knots,
His priestly headband is spattered with blood and pitchy venom;
All the while, his appalling cries go up to heaven –
A bellowing, such as you hear when a wounded bull escapes
    from
The altar, after it's shrugged off an ill-aimed blow at its neck.
But now the twin monsters are gliding away and escaping
    towards
The shrine of relentless Athena, high up on our citadel,
Disappearing behind the round of the goddess' shield, at her
    feet there.[17]

To the Trojans it looked like Laokoon's fate was punishment
for spearing the goddess' offering, so they joyfully dragged
the horse into the heart of their city. In Homer's *Odyssey*
the singer Demodokos relates how there were still discussions
about whether to open it up, throw it down a precipice, or
dedicate it to the gods, and Menelaos describes Helen walking
round it imitating the voice of each man's wife, which would
have lured the men into giving themselves away, had Odysseus
not had the presence of mind to restrain them.

Kassandra issued warnings of disaster too, but as usual
no one believed her. So the Trojans spent one last doomed
day putting garlands of thanksgiving on their shrines, and
when night fell they enjoyed a short, blissful sleep before
awakening to devastation and terror. The Greek fleet moved
in from Tenedos; Sinon kindled the beacon; and the warriors
in the horse made their move and opened the city gates.
There is a certain irony in Troy being sacked by means of a

Wooden Horse, in that Hektor and the Trojans are consistently known as 'Tamers of Horses'.

The Greeks had completely infiltrated Troy, and countless acts of brutality now occurred, as the once mighty stronghold suffered the standard fate of any defeated city: murder, rape and enslavement.

Neoptolemos slew Priamos, who had taken refuge at an altar of Zeus; Menelaos mutilated Helen's current Trojan husband Deiphobos and led her back to the ships; 'Lesser' Aias raped Kassandra in Athena's temple, causing the cult statue to avert its eyes from the sacrilege; Hektor's young son Astyanax was hurled to his death from the battlements;[18] and Polyxena was sacrificed on the grave of Akhilleus at his behest. Her noble final words are reported in a memorable messenger speech in Euripides' tragedy *Hekabe*:

> [Neoptolemos] grasped
> His sword by the gold hilt, drew it from the sheath, and signed
> To the young men appointed, to take hold of her.
> Polyxena saw; and this is what she said: 'You Greeks,
> Who laid my city in ruins, I die willingly.
> Let no one lay hands on me; I will give my neck
> Steadfastly to the sword. So, in the name of God,
> Let me stand free, and kill me; then I shall die free.
> Since I am royal, to be called slave among the dead
> Would be dishonour.' The whole army roared consent;
> And Agamemnon told the youths to set her free.
> When she heard this, she took hold of her dress, and tore it
> From shoulder-knot to waist, and showed her breasts, and all
> Her body to the navel, like the loveliest
> Of statues. Then she knelt down on one knee, and spoke
> The most heroic words of all: 'Son of Akhilleus,
> Here is my breast, if that is where you wish to strike;

included. One serpent envelops Laokoon's shoulders as he falls back on the altar, ensnares those of his elder son, and slithers round to bite him in the side; the other serpent entangles the legs of all three figures and seems to have suffocated the younger son; Laokoon's face is contorted with pain as he struggles to get free. William Blake used the ancient group as the bouncing-off point for a magnificent etching, although he reinterpreted it as a copy of an original Hebraic work and named it *Jehovah and his Two Sons Satan and Adam* (1826–7). Charles Dickens described Scrooge as 'making a perfect Laocoon of himself' when he got tangled up in his stockings at the end of *A Christmas Carol* (1843). And the exhibition 'Towards a New Laocoon' at the Henry Moore Institute in Leeds (2007) displayed Edward Paolozzi's aluminium *Poem for a Trio M.R.T.* (1964), which is indebted to the Laokoon's sinuous forms, alongside Turner Prize-winner Tony Cragg's *George and the Dragon* (1988), whose serpentine plastic pipework's formal echoes are abundantly clear, and Richard Deacon's monumental *Laocoon* (1966), constructed out of steamed wood and aluminium, which omits Laocoon himself but concentrates on the writhing snakes by intertwining straight and curved sections into a continuous spiral.

Greek pottery shows Aineias escaping with his father Ankhises on his shoulders, and among memorable post-classical renditions are Adam Elsheimer's superb evocation of *The Burning of Troy* (*c.* 1604), where Aeneas strides heroically with his human burden away from the flaming city, and Federico Barocci's *Study for 'Aeneas' Flight From Troy'*, in which a tightly grouped ensemble of Aineias, Ankhises and Askanios are separated from Aineias' wife Kreousa amid confused shapes of Greeks and Trojans, and a small dog adds a touch of pathos as they make their escape.

Andromakhe taken into captivity; Astyanax thrown to his death from the walls of Troy; Helen preventing Menelaos from killing her by baring her astounding breasts; Aias' rape of Kassandra; and Priamos hacked down by Neoptolemos (Pyrrhus): all figure in the arts, sometimes in combination. A large attic red-figure *kylix* from around 500 in the J. Paul Getty Museum in Malibu shows Kassandra's rape, Priamos' death and Helen's breasts all together, while Eros hovers between Helen and Menelaus as he drops his sword. However, by the time of Shakespeare's *Hamlet* the death of Priamos had become a vehicle for old-fashioned ham acting:

First Player:
When she saw Pyrrhus make malicious sport
In mincing with his sword her husband's limbs,
The instant burst of clamour that she made –
Unless things mortal move them not at all –
Would have made milch the burning eyes of heaven,
And passion in the gods.
Polonius:
Look! wh'er he has not turned his colour and has tears in's eyes.[20]

This prompts Hamlet's famous question:

What's Hecuba to him or he to Hecuba
That he should weep for her?[21]

Hekabe's (Hecuba's) fate has been bewailed too, from Euripides through to Hector Berlioz's *Les Troyens*, to Michael Tippett's *King Priam*, and, likewise, Andromakhe's in Martha Graham's dance work *Andromache's Lament* with music by Samuel Barber (1982).

So the destruction of Troy has exerted a powerful allure

ever since antiquity. In Shakespeare's times there was a popular ballad that went:

Waste lie those walls that were so good
And corn now grows where Troy Town stood.

Byron spent seventeen days at anchor off the Troad in 1810, and walked the pain of Troy, and he picked up the same conceit in *Don Juan*, Canto IV.77:

High barrows, without marble or a name,
A vast, untill'd, and mountain-skirted plain,
And Ida in the distance, still the same
And old Scamander (if 't is he), remain;
The situation seems still form'd for fame –
A hundred thousand men might fight again
With case; but where I sought for Ilion's walls
The quiet sheep feeds, and the tortoise crawls;

Many a visitor to Troy can feel that way today. And Byron encapsulated the whole issue of how much myth matters to people in a diary entry of 11 January 1821:

We *do* care about the authenticity of the tale of Troy [. . .] I venerated the grand original as *the truth of history* [. . .] and of place; otherwise it would have given me no delight.

The Discovery of Troy and the Historicity of the War
The myth has endured partly due to the stunning quality of the *Iliad*, and partly because vast quantities of vases, paintings, sculptures, poetry, drama and opera, not to mention Hollywood films, deal with the same theme.[22] As far as the Greeks were concerned, the Trojan War really happened: the *Parian*

Chronicle[23] dates the Fall of Troy to exactly 5 June 1209. But not all Greeks regarded the historicity of the war in the same way: Thukydides accepted that the Trojan expedition took place, but queried, corrected and rationalized certain aspects of it; Pausanias also accepted the historicity of the war, but rationalized the Wooden Horse into a siege engine. Yet approaches like these could not dilute the imaginative power of a story so gripping that it still feeds the modern public's enthusiasm to confirm that mythical events really happened, discover the location of Homer's Troy, and verify the existence of the heroes. The big problem with these historicist investigations is that, although they often make engaging television, they can devalue the ancient works in favour of sometimes rather facile questions about historical and material 'truth'.

These days the discussions centre on the mound of Hisarlik, which is in the north-west corner of modern Turkey, and which was identified with Homer's Ilion by the Greeks. Indeed, we know that it came to be inhabited by Aiolian Greeks, who had been expanding eastwards into that region, from around 700 onwards, and many scholars now believe not only that Hisarlik was the setting for the *Iliad*, but also that it was the centre of the kingdom called Wilusa in Hittite texts.

The correct name of the city is in fact Ilion (earlier Wilion) rather than 'Troy', but its inhabitants are Troes (Trojans), named after the hero Tros, and their territory is known as the Troia or Tro(i)as (Troad). The discovery of Hisarlik was one of the most exciting moments in archaeology, but anyone visiting the site expecting something resembling the 'topless towers of Ilion', a 'broad city' with 'lofty gates', 'fine towers', and 'wide streets', will be disappointed. Not many people would visit the site were it not for the Homeric associations. It was not until the nineteenth century that excavations were undertaken, thanks first to the American Frank Calvert (1828–1908) and then to Heinrich Schliemann (1822–90), the banker, enthusiast, egotist and fantasist who made six campaigns between 1870 and 1890. His intuition that Priamos' Troy was to be found at Hisarlik seemed to be corroborated by his impressive finds of walls, gateways and fabulous jewellery. He was convinced: 'In the name of divine Homer, I baptise [this sacred locality] with that name of immortal renown, which fills the heart of everyone with joy and enthusiasm: I give it the name of TROY and ILIUM.'[24] In the level known as Troy II he found the famous 'Jewels of Helen', which are now in the Pushkin Museum in Moscow, but unfortunately for his desire for this to be Homer's Troy, level II dates from 2500–2300,[25] roughly a thousand years adrift of the dates we find in documents like the *Parian Chronicle* and archaeological evidence found elsewhere.

In 1882 Schliemann gained the expert collaboration of Willhelm Dörpfeld, who distinguished nine levels of civilization on the site, Troy I to IX, covering the lifespan of the city from *c*.3000 BCE to the end of the Roman Empire. He surmised that Troy VI (*c*.1700–1280), which was contemporaneous with Mycenaean Greece, was the city of the *Iliad*. The catalogues of troops in the *Iliad* certainly echo many aspects of the Bronze Age period, and Linear B tablets found at Thebes in the 1990s show interesting correlations with the Greek forces described there. The American archaeologists who carried out excavations under Carl Blegen in the 1930s further elaborated these archaeological divisions, and refined Dörpfeld's nine layers into forty-six different strata. Blegen felt that Troy VI had been destroyed by earthquake rather than by human agency, and suggested that the Troy sacked by the Greeks was Troy VIIa (1280–1180), which seems to have been destroyed by fire.

Manfred Korfmann's *Troia-Pojeckt* has consolidated and expanded the picture. Korfmann infers from his findings (which not all archaeologists interpret as he does) that Hisarlik was merely the fortified citadel of an extensive city which was one of the largest in the entire Near East, with somewhere between 5,000 and 10,000 inhabitants from around 1250 onwards. The agricultural nature of Hisarlik's economy is reflected in Homer's poem: even Akhilleus' shield has scenes of reaping, viticulture, ox-herding and sheepfolds. Hisarlik was wealthy, impressively fortified, strategically located, provided a good harbour in an awkward area for navigation, and was a good base for trading in metalwork, textiles and horses. It also had good links to the Greek world, and references to Trojan topography suggest that Homer knew it quite well, even down to the prevailing winds, although he is surprisingly quiet about its fleet. However, the coastline of the area had altered significantly between the putative date of the war and Homer's time – a gap of almost 500 years: he doesn't know the Bronze Age locality, and although his heroes lived in walled palaces, used bronze weaponry, fought from chariots, and Mycenae was 'rich in gold', there is no mention of the Linear B tablets that were so crucial to the palace economies, and boar's-tusk helmets, which were ten-a-penny in Mycenaean times, get singled out for special description as if they were extraordinary. Really the *Iliad* represents what Homer *thought* the heroic world should look like: he took tradition and adapted it to make his tale, but the fact that he located the Trojan War at Ilion does not automatically mean that it really was the site of such a war; it is the site for a story.

That said, in the records of Hittite King Tudhalija I (*c*.1440–1410 BCE) we discover names that could be realized as Tariusa (Troy?) and Wilusiya (Ilion?). There is also a treaty from the reign of the Hittite King Muwattalli II (1296–1272), where we find Wilusa being ruled by Alaksandu. The similarity between Alaksandu and Alexandros (Paris' alternative name) is fascinating. A fragmentary letter also shows that a notorious insurrectionist called Piyamaradu (Priamos?) may have captured Wilusa, prompting Muwattalli to despatch an army to restore his authority over it:

> [Gassus (the Hittite commander) . . .] arrived and brought along the Hittite troops. [And whe]n [they . . .] set out again(?) to the country of Wilusa in order to attack (it),[26] [I, howe]ver, became ill. I am seriously ill, illness holds me [pro]strated.
> [*A paragraph divider occurs here*]
> When [Piyam]aradus had humiliated me, he set Atpa [against me(?) (lit. he brought Atpa [u]p [before] me) . . .

This greatly excites those who wish to convert myth into history, but although the letter proves the presence of Hittite troops in the area, it is not clear whether they had come to liberate Wilusa from Piyamaradu: the paragraph divider may indicate that Piyamaradu's activities have nothing to do with Wilusa whatsoever. The mythical tradition might have preserved the name of an actual ruler of Troy, but it does not confirm the historicity of the *Iliad*.

Western Asia Minor was an unstable place in the mid-thirteenth century, and there is circumstantial evidence for identifying the Hittite Ahhiyawa (Akhaians, i.e. the Greeks?) with a mainland Mycenaean kingdom. Furthermore, there is a letter from the Hittite King Hattusili III to the King of Ahhiyawa in which Ahhiyawa, Wilusa and a conflict are all mentioned together. Hattusili writes that he and his Ahhiyawan 'Brother' had once had bad relations over Wilusa in around 1250, but: 'Now [. . .] we have reached agreement on the matter of Wilusa over which we fought.' Could the letter indicate that Akhaian forces had attacked Wilusa? Possibly. The Hittites certainly acted to support their vassal, and had a direct confrontation with the Ahhiyawans, which might also explain Troy VI's extensive fortifications. On the other hand, this could have been merely a diplomatic crisis, or there may have been military action over the control of Wilusa, but without Wilusa itself being involved in the fighting. Whatever, this falls woefully short of anything resembling a conflict on a Homeric scale, and Troy was definitely not abandoned.

One later thirteenth-century letter from the Hittite King Tudhalija IV says that the Wilusan King Walmu had been deposed and that Tudhalija was reinstating him. Again, this might have been the result of Ahhiyawan activity, but Ahhiyawa is not mentioned in the letter and Walmu might just as likely have been ejected by his own subjects. So this particular incident could be totally irrelevant to the Trojan War question.

A number of factors therefore tell against finding historical origins of the Trojan War tradition:

1. Wilusa may have had a turbulent history, but so did many other places in the Late Bronze Age. A state of war was the status quo.
2. None of the theories seem to take into account the tradition of Herakles' sack of Laomedon's Troy.
3. A one-off conflict involving a ten-year siege is not documented anywhere, and the longest siege we know of only lasted a few months.
4. There is no evidence for an enormous Akhaian invasion which resulted in the destruction of an Anatolian kingdom.
5. It is by no means certain that what might be Priamos' Troy

was destroyed by humans and not by an earthquake. There are arrowheads and weapons in Troy VI, but not enough to prove that the city fell to enemy attack, and those theories that propose destruction by both human and environmental agencies fail to take into account that there is no earthquake in Homer, even though Poseidon is on the Greek side.

6. Troy VI was destroyed but not abandoned. Troy VIIa is much less impressive, but there is no break in the culture.

7. Troy was eventually destroyed and abandoned, but not until the end of Level VIIb, around 1080, a period when Greece itself also had to cope with invaders. Troy's destruction could be down to the so-called Sea Peoples who crop up in Egyptian records.

It need not be a straight choice between fiction and history, and there might, of course, be fragments of historical truth buried in Homer's *Iliad*, but his genius lies in telling his story so brilliantly that his characters seem to be real people taking part in real events. All that the dogged 'Search for the Truth of the Trojan War' achieves is to reveal a vassal city controlled by the Hittite empire that constantly needed baling out of trouble by the Hittite king. This is most un-Homeric.

There are other factors that tell against Homer's Trojan War as a 'genuine' event. We know that Greek is a descendant of an earlier language known as Indo-European,[27] which has left traces in later languages such as Latin, English, Welsh, Russian, German, Sanskrit, Persian, Hittite and many others. For instance, in the Vedas, written around 1450 BCE, the name of the sky god, Dyaus, comes from the Sanskrit root *diut* ('to beam') and *diu* ('sky' and 'day'). *Dyaus pita* ('father Dyaus') and *Zeus pater* ('father Zeus') could derive from the same Indo-European root, and so could the Latin Jupiter, which has an older form Diespiter, and the Nordic sky god,

Tiw, who gives his name to Tuesday. The same root gives Latin *deus* ('god') and *dies* ('day'). So the Indo-Europeans may have had an important sky god named Dyaus, and the Greek sky god Zeus is most likely of Indo-European origin.

And, just as different cultures may share similar words, there are those who argue that they may share similar myths due to a parallel process.[28] A good example of this is the Indo-European myth of twin horsemen who rescue their sister or wife. In the Sanskrit, the twin Asvins ('horsemen'), Divo napata ('sons of Dyauh'), jointly woo and marry Suryā, daughter of the Sun Surya; in Latvian songs, the horsemen, Dieva deli ('sons of Dievs'), woo Saules meita ('the sun's daughter'); in Greek mythology the twin horsemen Kastor and Polydeukes, the Dioskouroi ('sons of Zeus'), rescue their sister Helen,[29] whose name might be related to *helios* ('sun') and hence to the Sanskrit Surya and Latvian Saule. But there may be another descendant of this tale: the twins Agamemnon and Menelaos going to recover Menelaos' wife Helen from Troy. The story of the Trojan War may be more traditional, and not be quite as historical, as it seems: it could perhaps be an ancient Indo-European myth: 'real history is unsuited to memory, myths are not.'[30]

The overall focus of the *Iliad* on heroism in action is by no means unique either. Oral poets aren't ancient historians, and the *Iliad* exhibits many generic themes common to oral poetry: introduction; supplication; prayer; divine visitations; summoning an assembly; dismissing it; journey by ship; sacrifice; meals and entertainment; arming scenes; dressing scenes; battles; messenger scenes; reception scenes; omens; and sleeping. The Babylonian *Epic of Gilgamesh*, which pre-dates Homer, is also very similar, and Akhilleus and Gilgamesh each have goddess mothers, lose their dearest companions, are devastated by the loss, and go to extremes to compensate for it.

Finally, the Greek historian Herodotuos[31] makes the telling point that Priamos would never have risked the devastation of his kingdom, the death of his children or the destruction of his people for the sake of a foreign woman. It could be that Ilion did fall to a Greek force: Aiolian Greeks certainly took over Hisarlik at some point, but we might add that there is no evidence that Greeks ever sacked Hisarlik. Even Korfmann is prepared to admit that 'Homer only used Troy as a poetic background for a tale about the conflict between and among humans and gods'.[32]

M.I. Finley concluded that 'we are confronted with this paradox that the more we know, the worse off we are' and he argued that 'Homer's Trojan War must be evicted from the history of the Greek Bronze Age'[33]. Unfortunately this has led to some rather bizarre reactions. Completely missing the point about how myth operates, I.J. Wilkens sees only two options: (a) the Trojan War never took place at Hisarlik and therefore the *Iliad* is the fruit of pure imagination, or (b) the war did take place, but in another country.[34] Citing the relationship between Galateia, Keltos and Akhilleus as 'irrefutable proof' that Homer's epics are of Celtic origin, he locates the 'holy city' just outside Cambridge on the Gog Magog Hills. Peter Jones, reviewing B. Strauss' 2007 publication, *The Trojan War, A New History* ('This slippery book is a disgrace to the historical profession'), makes the apt analogy of someone reading a James Bond novel 3,000 years from now, finding that Dunhill, Martini, White's and Boodles all actually existed, and concluding that *You Only Live Twice* was history, not fiction.[35] This entire process seems reminiscent of the episode 'The Myth Makers' in the BBC TV series *Doctor Who* (1965), where the Doctor, having initially dismissed the Wooden Horse as a fiction of Homer's, is forced to 'invent' it himself, and give the Greeks the wherewithal to defeat the Trojans.

16

THE RETURNS OF THE HEROES

Key Characters

Nestor	Venerable Greek warrior
Diomedes	Mighty Greek warrior
Menelaos	Husband of Helen
Aias (Ajax)	The 'Lesser' Ajax; killed for committing sacrilege
Nauplios	Wrecker of Greek ships and marriages
Neoptolemos	Son of Akhilleus
Agamemnon	Murdered by his wife Klytaimnestra on his homecoming
Klytaimnestra (Clytemnestra)	Killed Agamemnon in revenge for the sacrifice of their daughter Iphigeneia
Orestes	Son of Agamemnon; killed Klytaimnestra
Elektra (Electra)	Sister of Orestes
Aigisthos (Aegisthus)	Klytaimnestra's lover; killed by Orestes

The return home from Troy was a painful one for many of the Greek heroes, if indeed they made it at all. We now witness a great diaspora of Greek heroes all over the Mediterranean, and it may be that the tales in some way reflect the colonizing movement that took place from the eighth century onwards, as the heroes settle in Crete, Thessaly, Epeiros, Macedonia, Libya, Italy, Sicily, the Iberian islands, Asia Minor and Cyprus. Our word 'nostalgia' comes from the Greek *nostos* ('return journey', plural *nostoi*) plus *algos* ('pain'), and the *nostoi* of Troy's conquerors were full of it.

Agamemnon and Menelaos disagreed about whether to make sacrifices to Athena before setting off, so they decided to travel home separately. Menelaos travelled with Diomedes and Nestor, both of whom reached home safely, but he got separated from them, ran into a storm, and ended up in Egypt, although he did accumulate plenty of treasure on the way. He would have to subdue Proteus, the Old Man of the Sea, in order to find out how to secure his homecoming, and it would be eight years before he saw Sparta again.

Euripides clearly enjoyed the potential of this tradition. In *Helen* he dramatized the story where Helen was taken to Egypt while the Greeks and Trojans fought over a phantom. She was treated kindly by Proteus, King of Egypt, but after his death his son Theok.ymenos became more predatory towards her, and tried to force her to marry him. But then Menelaos arrived, recovered from his confusion at meeting an identical Helen, enjoyed his reunion with his beautiful wife, and escaped to a happy-ever-after existence in Sparta. In Euripides' *Orestes* they do not have it so easy, however. In this play Agamemnon's son Orestes and his friend Pylades attempt to kill Helen the moment she gets home, but Apollo immortalizes her as a protectress of sailors, like her brothers, the Dioskouroi. Homer makes Proteus prophesy that Menelaos would not die, but would be taken to the Elysian Fields for a happy eternity, because, as Helen's husband, he was an in-law of Zeus.

Kalkhas did not make it home. His fate was to die when he met a better seer than himself, and this materialized in the figure of Mopsos, who had an impressive pedigree (son of Apollo, grandson of Teiresias). Kalkhas challenged Mopsos to say how many figs were on a nearby tree. 'Ten thousand, plus one bushel, and one fig extra,' came the correct reply. Mopsos then indicated a pregnant sow, and asked Kalkhas, 'How many piglets are in her womb, and when will she give birth?' Kalkhas' answer was eight, but Mopsos' 'Nine, all male and due to be born without fail tomorrow at the sixth hour' was precisely correct.[1] Kalkhas died of shame.

Agamemnon sacrificed to Athena before putting to sea and touching at Tenedos. Thetis persuaded her grandson Neoptolemos to wait there for a couple of days[2] before embarking, and he took this advice. The rest of the Greeks were engulfed in a storm at Tenos, which was ultimately the responsibility of 'Lesser' Aias, rapist of Kassandra in Athena's temple. With the aid of Zeus the storm god and Poseidon the sea god, Athena wrought havoc among the ships. She hurled a thunderbolt at Aias' vessel, but he managed to swim to the safety of a rock, and would have survived had he not boasted that he had defied the will of the gods. Indeed, he had; but once too often:

> Poseidon heard him, loudly vaunting,
> and at once with his ponderous hands catching up the trident
> he drove it against the Gyrean rock, and split a piece off it,
> and part of it stayed where it was, but a splinter crashed into the water,
> and this was where Aias had been perched when he raved so madly.
> It carried him down to the depths of the endless and tossing main sea.
> So Aias died, when he had swallowed down the salt water.[3]

The survivors of the storm made their way to the island of Euboia, where further disaster awaited them. The cause of their difficulties was Nauplios. Tradition records two heroes of this

name who are often confused with one another. The elder
Nauplios (son of Poseidon and Amymone) was the founder of
the town of Nauplion, and had a rather better-known descendant for whom Apollonios Rhodios provides a full genealogy:

> Next to him came a scion of the race of divine Danaos, Nauplios.
> He was the son of Klytonaios son of Naubolos . . . son of Lernos
> . . . son of Proitos son of Nauplios; and Amymone daughter of
> Danaos, wedded to Poseidon, bore Nauplios, who surpassed all
> men in naval skill.[4]

This younger Nauplios was an Argonaut, and became the
pilot of the *Argo*. He was the father of Palamedes, who is
credited with numerous important inventions such as the
order of the Greek alphabet, money, number, weights and
measures, and the games of dice and draughts to alleviate
boredom at the siege of Troy. However Palamedes was the
man who exposed Odysseus' attempt to dodge the draft for
the Trojan War, and had been stoned to death through the
cunning hero's machinations.[5] Nauplios exacted revenge for
his son's death by kindling a beacon on Mount Kaphareus
and wrecking the Greek fleet. This unpleasant incident is
well dramatized by Euripides:

> The lone sailor Nauplios
> Lit his false fire on the Kapherian Cape –
> A star turned liar, that lured ten thousand more
> To ram the sunk rocks like fierce jaws agape;
> And watched men die amid the Aegean's roar.[6]

Prior to wrecking the fleet, Nauplios had also tried to subvert
the marriages of the absent heroes by encouraging their wives
into adulterous affairs. He succeeded with Agamemnon's wife

Klytaimnestra (with Aigisthos), Diomedes' wife Aigialeia[7] (with Kometes), and Idomeneus' wife Meda (with Leukos).

There are differing accounts of the *nostos* of Neoptolemos. In one of these he went on foot with Phoinix (who died on the way) and Helenos to Epeiros, subdued the locals, ruled as their king, and sired Molossos on Andromakhe. Henceforth the people were called Molossians. A different tradition says that Neoptolemos sailed across to Thessaly and took Helenos' advice to settle where he found a house with iron foundations, wooden walls and a woollen roof, which turned out to be at Lake Pambotis in Epeiros, where he encountered some people camping under blankets supported by spears whose blades were stuck into the earth. The Molossians were ruled by Neoptolemos' ancestors for generations, and Alexander the Great's mother Olympias claimed to be one of them. Other versions make Neoptolemos reassert control over the kingdom of his grandfather Peleus, who had been expelled from Phthia during the siege of Troy. Homer states that he returned to Phthia and married Hermione, daughter of Menelaos.

Neoptolemos' death also comes in a wide range of variants, although they all agree that he died at Delphi, and died violently. One reason behind his death was a dispute over Hermione with her cousin Orestes, who was engaged to her before the Trojan War. In Euripides' play *Andromakhe*, Menelaos had promised Hermione to Neoptolemos, if Neoptolemos should succeed in capturing Troy, despite the fact that she was already married to Orestes. Neoptolemos duly claimed his bride at the time when Orestes was being pursued by the Furies following the murder of his mother Klytaimnestra. Orestes protested, but to no avail, as he explains to Hermione:

He was insolent
He abused me as a matricide and victim of
The gory-eyed goddesses. My family circumstances
Forced me to take a humble tone.[8]

Orestes had to surrender Hermione to Neoptolemos, but he avenged himself by murdering his rival at Delphi. According to Euripides, Neoptolemos made two visits there: the first to seek redress from Apollo for shooting Akhilleus at Troy; the second to apologize to the god for doing this. It was on the latter occasion that Neoptolemos was ambushed in the temple of Apollo, although the death-blow was delivered 'with a sharp sword-blade wielded by a Delphian',[9] not by Orestes himself.

In another account Neoptolemos was at Delphi seeking redress from Apollo, but started to ransack the offerings and then set the temple on fire, at which point he was cut down by a man named Makhaireus. Pausanias mentions the hearth at Delphi where the priest of Apollo slew Neoptolemos and recounts that

> the Pythian priestess ordered the Delphians to kill Pyrrhos
> [Neoptolemos], son of Akhilleus.[10]

Pindar gives a very different version of events:

> He came to Apollo
> bringing gifts out of the spoil of Troy.
> There, in a quarrel over the meats, a man with a knife
> stabbed him.[11]

It was said that after his death Neoptolemos inhabited the sacred precinct and presided over the heroic processions and sacrifices. Pausanias was shown his grave when he visited the site in the second century CE.

The Homecoming and Murder of Agamemnon

One particular return, that of Agamemnon to Mycenae, where he was murdered by his wife Klytaimnestra and her lover Aigisthos, provided the raw material for Aiskhylos' mighty tragedy *Agamemnon*. The play is the first in a trilogy called the *Oresteia*, produced in 458, unquestionably one of the most powerful dramas ever staged in Athens. It is an awesome example of how myth can be narrated, and its subject is the unfortunate events following Thyestes' Curse of the House of Atreus.[12] Aiskhylos could take it for granted that his audience knew the background: it was common mythical currency and is mentioned several times in the *Odyssey*, although in the Homeric version Klytaimnestra is just Aigisthos' accomplice; on the other hand, the Hesiodic *Catalogue of Women* makes her mainly responsible for Agamemnon's murder.

Tragedy has a tendency to select one critical episode in the myth, and so Aiskhylos does in *Agamemnon*. We see a sleepy watchman who has been waiting an entire year for the beacon that will announce the fall of Troy. And as he speaks, it appears:

> There's your signal clear and true, my queen!
> Rise up from bed – hurry, lift a cry of triumph
> through the house, praise the gods for the beacon,
> if they've taken Troy . . .[13]

He exits in a festive frame of mind, though not without hinting that things have not been 100 per cent perfect while Agamemnon has been away, and is replaced on stage by a

Chorus of 'old, dishonoured, broken husks of men', who sing of the senselessness of the war they were too old to be involved in:

> So towering Zeus the god of guests
>> Drives Atreus' sons at Paris
> All for a woman manned by many
>> The generations wrestle, knees
>> Grinding in the dust, the manhood drains
>> The spear snaps in the first blood rites
>>> That marry Greece and Troy.[14]

There is an acute awareness in Aiskhylos' work of the horrible reality of war, and the Chorus remind the audience of how Agamemnon sacrificed his daughter Iphigeneia in order to secure the favourable winds needed for the expedition.

Klytaimnestra has entered the stage while the Chorus have been singing, and her opening words include reflections on the fortunes of war, but from the Trojan perspective:

> They are kneeling by the bodies of the dead,
> Embracing men and brothers, infants over
> The aged loins that gave them life, and sobbing,
> As the yoke constricts their last free breath,
> For every dear one lost.[15]

The tensions are manifest: on the face of it there is cause for celebration – the Greeks are victorious and Agamemnon is returning – but the characters have created a very uneasy atmosphere, and we keep hearing about the kind of reversal of roles that make any tragic audience nervous. At the end of Klytaimnestra's speech the Chorus comment:

Spoken like a man, my lady, loyal
Full of self-command.[16]

In the time of Aiskhylos, a woman's entire life took place
under the authority of a male: usually her father, then her
husband, and eventually her son. So by describing Klytaimnestra as a figure of male authority the Chorus are implying that
something is seriously wrong. She should not be behaving like
a man. And try as they might, the Chorus cannot raise the
gloom. Even a song of praise to Zeus the Saviour is sombre,
as the ancient equivalents of the body bags come home:

They knew the men they sent,
but now in place of men
ashes and urns come back
   to every hearth.

[. . .] and they weep,
they praise them, 'He had skill in the swordplay,'
   'He went down so tall in the onslaught,'
'All for another's woman.' So they mutter
in secret and the rancour steals
towards our staunch defenders, Atreus' sons.[17]

Things seem to lighten a little when a Herald enters, delighted
to be safely home from the war. Yet as he delivers the news
of Agamemnon's victory he digresses on the grimness of military life, and although Klytaimnestra keeps affirming her love
for her husband, the audience cannot fail to pick up some
sinister ironies:

Now for the best way to welcome home
My lord, my good lord . . .

No time to lose!
What dawn can feast a woman's eyes like this?[18]

When the queen has left the stage the Herald delivers more
disturbing news: there has been a terrible storm; Menelaos
and his ships are missing.

I see the Aegean heaving into a great bloom
of corpses . . . Greeks, the pick of a generation
scattered through the wrecks and broken spars.[19]

This is important: Agamemnon is isolated, and as the news
sinks in, the Chorus sing a hymn of vitriol directed at Helen,
which concludes with comments on the irrelevance of money
and success if they are not backed up by moral goodness:

But justice shines in sooty hovels,
loves the decent life.
From proud halls crusted with gilt by filthy hands
she turns her eyes to find the pure in spirit –
spurning the wealth stamped counterfeit with praise,
she steers all things towards their destined end.[20]

Things are indeed moving towards their destined end, but
the mood becomes more upbeat with the long-awaited arrival
of Agamemnon. He appears with all the pomp and circum-
stance befitting the winner of the Trojan War. There is not
a shadow of a doubt in his mind that the war was just:

First,
with justice I salute my Argos and my gods,
my accomplices who brought me home and won
my rights from Priam's Troy – the just gods.

[. . .] For their mad outrage
of a queen we raped their city – we were right.[21]

Yet we should be disturbed by what is happening here. There
have been constant reminders that the gods are jealous of
the success that Agamemnon's pageantry seems to personify,
and we know that he has the blood of Iphigeneia's sacrifice
on his hands. Interestingly, when Klytaimnestra comes out
to welcome him, she talks to the Chorus first, and her opening
words are an apology for their son Orestes' absence, which
deprives Agamemnon of another potential ally. Superficially
Klytaimnestra's words are full of love and praise, but the
audience cannot miss the chilling irony of her concluding
words:

We will set things right, with the god's help.
We will do whatever Fate requires.[22]

In one of the finest scenes in Greek tragedy, Klytaimnestra
now lures Agamemnon to his doom. Her maids bring out
splendid tapestries and lay them out from his chariot to the
palace door. There can be no mistaking their sinister symbolism:

Let the red stream flow and bear him home
to the home he never hoped to see – Justice,
lead him in!
Leave all the rest to me.[23]

Agamemnon is uneasy. He knows that to trample on this
finery would be a transgressive act associated with a barbarian, but his wife is extremely persuasive, counters all his
arguments, and manipulates his responses. Despite his

reservations, he steps out of his chariot, still fully aware of
the risks:

> Hurry
> And while I tread his splendours dyed red in the sea,
> May no god watch and strike me down with envy
> From on high. I feel such shame –
> To tread the life of the house, a kingdom's worth
> Of silver in the weaving.[24]

Aiskhylos now brings off a stunning *coup de théâtre*: as
Agamemnon dismounts from his chariot we see a female
prisoner of war. Again the glory is undercut. His final
homecoming as the conqueror of Troy should be Agamemnon's finest moment, but the atmosphere has once again
become one of deep unease. Agamemnon walks along the
tapestries into the palace, followed by Klytaimnestra, after
which the Chorus sing of their fears. They are right to be
afraid.

Klytaimnestra now reappears and addresses the prisoner.
She is Priamos' daughter, the prophetess Kassandra, but she
stays silent until Klytaimnestra gives up on her and goes back
inside. Only then does she speak. In raving prophetic delirium
she predicts the murder of Agamemnon:

> I tell you, someone plots revenge.
> A lion who lacks a lion's heart,
> he sprawled at home in the royal lair
> and set a trap for the lord on his return.
> My lord . . . I must wear his yoke, I am his slave.
> The lord of the men-of-war, he obliterated Troy –
> he is so blind, so lost to that detestable hellhound
> who pricks her ears and fawns and her tongue draws out

her glittering words of welcome –

                        No, he cannot see

the stroke that Fury's hiding, stealth, and murder.
What outrage – the woman kills the man![25]

But the Chorus don't understand her. No one ever does.
Before she leaves the stage, she predicts her own death too.

        I pray to the sun,
The last light I'll see,
That when the avengers cut the assassins down
They will avenge me too, a slave who died,
An easy conquest.[26]

With the Chorus now alone on stage, and Klytaimnestra in
the palace with her victims, the tension is almost too much
to bear. Then it is suddenly released as we hear screams from
the palace:

AGAMEMNON: Aagh!
Struck deep – the death-blow, deep –
CHORUS LEADER: Quiet. Cries,
but who? Someone's stabbed –
AGAMEMNON: Aaagh, again . . .
second blow – struck home.
CHORUS LEADER: The work is done,
you can feel it.[27]

The conventions of Greek drama prohibit us from seeing the
actual murder, but we do see its aftermath when the device
known as the *ekkyklema* rolls out to reveal a macabre view
of the palace interior. Agamemnon and Kassandra lie lifeless;
Klytaimnestra is exultant, and has no qualms about justifying

the murder of her husband, which was itself the product of a complex nexus of cause and effect, transgression and punishment:

> Praise me,
> blame me as you choose. It's all one.
> Here is Agamemnon, my husband made a corpse
> by this right hand – a masterpiece of Justice.
> Done is done. [. . .]
> He thought no more of it than killing a beast,
> and his flocks were rich, teeming in their fleece,
> but he sacrificed his own child, our daughter,
> the agony I laboured into love
> to charm away the savage winds of Thrace.[28]

When the old men of the Chorus ask who will attend Agamemnon's funeral they get a savage response from Klytaimnestra:

> This is no concern of yours [. . .]
> This house will never mourn for him.
> Only our daughter Iphigeneia,
> By all rights, will rush to meet him
> First at the churning straights,
> The ferry over tears –
> She'll fling her arms around her father,
> Pierce him with her love.[29]

At this late stage Klytaimnestra's lover Aigisthos emerges. True to form, this cringing weakling appears when the danger is over, but still claims credit for the murder. He boasts that his part in the killing is vengeance for what Agamemnon's father, Atreus, had done to his own father, Thyestes. He

speaks of how he will rule as king, and leaves the Chorus
in no doubt that it will be a reign of terror; they retort by
questioning his manhood:

> CHORUS LEADER: *You* rule Argos? You who schemed his death
> But cringed to cut him down with your own hand?
> AIGISTHOS: The treachery was the woman's work, clearly
> I was a marked man, his enemy for ages.
> But I will use his riches, stop at nothing
> to civilise his people. All but the rebel:
> > him I'll yoke and break –
> no cornfed colt, running free in the traces.
> Hunger, ruthless mate of the dark torture-chamber,
> trains her eyes upon him till he drops!

The affair threatens to get out of hand: the old men are
prepared to fight with their walking sticks against Aigisthos'
heavy infantry, but Klytaimnestra intervenes: she is sated
with killing.

> Fathers of Argos, turn for home before you act
> and suffer for it. What we did was destiny.
> If we could end the suffering, how we would rejoice.
> The spirit's brutal hoof has struck our heart.
> And that is what a woman has to say.
> Can you accept the truth?[30]

They find it hard to do this. Harsh words are still exchanged,
and before they leave the Chorus express their hope that
Agamemnon's son Orestes will return to avenge him. The
first part of the *Oresteia* trilogy is over.

With the second play in the trilogy, the *Khoephoroi
(Choephori)* or *Libation Bearers*, Aiskhylos moves the drama

into the next generation. In ancient Greece the notion of 'helping friends and harming enemies' was a basic moral tenet, and so looking for revenge was in many ways the norm. Of course, the process of taking revenge automatically makes the avenger the next target, and Aiskhylos makes powerful use of this vicious circle. To put it the Greek way, 'the doer suffers'.

So the cycle continues. Orestes had gone to Delphi and asked whether he should avenge his father. Apollo had approved this course of action, so he headed for Mycenae, accompanied by his great friend Pylades, the son of Strophios. [31] He arrived secretly, met up with his sister Elektra, disguised himself as a foreigner, gained entry to the palace, and killed both Aigisthos and his mother. Sophokles and Euripides each wrote plays on this theme as well, both entitled *Elektra*: in Sophokles' work Orestes does the deed encouraged by his sister from outside the palace, but in Euripides he is far more diffident, and Elektra even has to help him hold the sword as he buries it in Klytaimnestra.

In this mythical world of obligation, violence, justice and punishment, Orestes now had to be punished, and not long after the murder he was afflicted with madness and pursued by the Furies or Eumenides, the divine bringers of retribution. The final play of the *Oresteia* is called the *Eumenides*, and it opens with Orestes seeking sanctuary at Delphi and being purified by Apollo. However, the Furies still pursue him to Athens, where he becomes the defendant in the first murder trial in the Areiopagos court. In the wider tradition he is said to have been brought to trial by Klytaimnestra's father Tyndareus and/or Erigone, her daughter by Aigisthos, but in the *Eumenides* the Furies prosecute and Apollo defends. In a verdict decided by the closest of possible margins, Orestes escapes thanks to Athena's casting vote, and the Furies are persuaded to relinquish their anger against Athens and take up residence there. So there is a sea-change in the justice system: no longer will justice depend on vendetta, but on awe and fear of the Areiopagos and its powers.

The effects of the Curse of the House of Atreus had now been nullified, and in a way that illustrates the links between myth and contemporary politics. In Aiskhylos' lifetime tyranny was replaced by democracy, and he risked his life at the battles of Marathon and Salamis to defend it. It is perhaps no accident that votes and persuasion, the key tools of democracy, finally resolved the Curse of the House of Atreus. A new political order, in which the judges were Athenian citizens rather than gods or heroes, arose: such an outcome could not be more relevant to democratic Athens in the fifth century.

Orestes' madness ceased with the verdict of the Areiopagos, but in other traditions Apollo told him to fetch a wooden image of Artemis from the land of the Taurians (the Crimea) in order to regain his sanity.[32] According to Herodotos, the Taurians made human sacrifices of strangers to a virgin goddess identified with Iphigeneia, either killing them with a club before impaling their heads on stakes and throwing their bodies down a precipice into the sea, or burying them in the ground, or throwing them into the sacred fire which exuded from Hades through a special rock. In Euripides' *Iphigeneia in Tauris*, Orestes and Pylades made their way to the land of the Taurians, but were captured and taken before Thoas the king, who sent them to the temple of Artemis for sacrifice. There was a last-minute recognition between Orestes and his long-lost sister Iphigeneia, who happened to be the priestess there as a result of being spirited away from the sacrifice at Aulis.[33] All three of them managed to get away, taking the wooden image with them. Orestes returned to

Mycenae and took the throne, and is said to have ruled Argos, and Lakedaimon when Menelaos died. Elektra married his best friend Pylades, while he married Hermione. He died as a result of a snake bite and was buried at Tegea.

The poet and artist David Jones (1895–1974) produced a striking image entitled *Aphrodite in Aulis* (1940–41). Its central subject was based on a novel of the same title by the Irish writer George Moore (1930), whose story centres on a sculptor called Rhesos, who falls in love with a callipygian woman called Earine, who has the finest buttocks for his statue of Aphrodite. Jones' Aphrodite, who stands on a column, was originally conceived as Iphigeneia, but was changed

> 'to include all female cult figures, as I have written somewhere the figure is all goddesses rolled into one . . . she's mother figure and *virgo inter virgines* – the pierced woman and mother & all her foretypes.'[34]

With deliberate contrasts between the Doric and Ionic architectural orders, a British soldier on the left and a German on the right, and resonances of a crucifixion scene, the composition seems keen to imply that the goddess belongs to all times and places.

Myth and Tragedy

The fact that the fifth-century tragedians used almost entirely mythical subject-matter means that tragedy confronts humanity's place in the world through mythological stories. Drama could latch on to these stories and invest them with all manner of issues, particularly in relation to morals, and so part of tragedy's cultural relevance concerned the contemporary immediacy of its handling of the myths. The importance of the concept of justice is a good example here. It was a hot topic in fifth-century democratic Athens, and everyone from philosophers to the 'man-in-the-agora' discussed it. In Homer, Nestor has no doubt that Orestes was right to murder Klytaimnestra in order to avenge his father, but in tragedy we find probing questions about how actions like this might be justified. Not all myths make for interesting analysis of morals and values, but the tales about Troy, Argos and Thebes feature very prominently in tragedy: over 25 per cent of the extant titles refer to myths about the Trojan War, while the Argive and Theban royal houses each account for another 10 per cent. The fact that they revolved around war and the family – those classic areas of conflict – made them good material for drama. So tragedy is endlessly questioning whether the Trojan War was just.

In respect of family values, Agamemnon kills his daughter, Klytaimnestra kills her husband, Orestes kills his mother, Oidipous kills his father and marries his mother, Phaidra falls in love with her stepson and when he spurns her she kills herself and leaves a suicide note accusing him of rape. These themes work well on the stage because the issues underlying them are seldom cut and dried; grey is a more interesting colour than black or white. The tragic playwrights might have been seeking to reinforce the core values of society by showing the terrible consequences of transgressing them, or they might just have recognized that dramas built around those themes would be popular, but it is worth noting that many tragic transgressions do not originate from outright human wickedness – the drama is more stimulating when they do not.

Homer predates the invention of democracy, but Aiskhylos was very much a creature of the democratic city-state (*polis*), so he took the old myths of epic poetry, assessed them in

the context of the norms of *polis*, and refashioned them
accordingly. In the *Oresteia*, Aiskhylos' interpretation of the
myth of the Eumenides and Orestes as a confrontation
between the old heroic order and the new *polis* was startlingly
original. It shows once again how these traditional tales could
be reworked in new contexts to bring new issues to the fore:
again we see how 'good to think with' the myths are, and
no one thought better with them than Aiskhylos.

THE *ODYSSEY* AND ITS SEQUELS

Key Characters

Odysseus (Ulysses)	Son of Laertes; wandering home from Troy
Penelope	Odysseus' faithful wife
Telemakhos (Telemachus)	Son of Odysseus and Penelope
Athena (Minerva)	Goddess; helper of Odysseus
Poseidon (Neptune)	God; adversary of Odysseus
Nausikaa (Nausicaa)	Princess who gave Odysseus hospitality on Skherie
Polyphemos	The Cyclops
Kirke (Circe)	Sorceress; detained Odysseus for one year
Kalypso (Calypso)	Nymph; detained Odysseus for seven years
Eumaios (Eumaeus)	Odysseus' faithful swineherd
Eurykleia (Euryclea)	Odysseus' nurse

Like the *Iliad* the *Odyssey* is divided into twenty-four Books. It contains 12,110 lines of poetry, but as Aristotle says:

> The story of the Odyssey is not a long one. A man is kept away from his home for many years; Poseidon is watching him with a jealous eye, and he is alone. The state of affairs at home is

that his wealth is being squandered by his wife's suitors, and plots are being laid against his son's life. After being buffeted by many storms he returns home and reveals his identity; he falls upon his enemies and destroys them, but preserves his own life. There you have the essential story of the Odyssey.[1]

Odysseus was away from his home in Ithaka for twenty years in total:

> [Halitherses] said that after much suffering, with all his
>   companions
> Lost, in the twentieth year, not recognised by any,
> He would come home. And now all this is being accomplished.[2]

Of those twenty years, the Trojan War lasted ten and Odysseus spent seven years with the nymph Kalypso, plus three years undergoing the adventures which he recounts to the Phaiakians in Books 9 –12, one of which was with Kirke:

> But when it was the end of a year . . . [3]

Towards the end of that time a large number of eligible bachelors from Ithaka and the nearby islands started to pay court to Odysseus' wife Penelope:

> And now it is the third year, and will be the fourth year
>   presently,
> since she has been denying the desires of the Akhaians.[4]

Homer does not list all the suitors, although he says that there were 108 of them: 52 from Doulikhion (plus six thralls), 24 from Same, 20 from Zakynthos, and 12 from Ithaka, along with Medon the herald, and 'the divine

singer', and two henchmen.[5] Apollodoros gives the numbers
from these islands as 57, 23, 44 and 12 respectively, a total
of 136, and then itemizes them (though he only names 53
from Doulikhion and 41 from Zakynthos!). Penelope is
worth paying court to, since she is a widow (presumably),
gorgeous, accomplished, intelligent, cunning and the heiress
to a significant kingdom. Still, she is clinging to the hope
that Odysseus will return, and, though she never says that
she will not marry one of them, she keeps the suitors at
arm's length with her stratagem of weaving a shroud for
Odysseus' father Laertes' future funeral. They must wait
until it is finished.

> Thereafter, in the daytime she would weave at her great loom,
> But in the night she would have torches set by, and undo it.[6]

The suitors, uninvited though they are, make themselves very
much at home in Odysseus' palace, at his expense, and ultimately discover Penelope's ruse.

There is less about the wanderings of Odysseus that you
might expect from the title – our hero does not appear until
Book 5: Books 1 to 4 focus on Odysseus' son Telemakhos;
Odysseus' adventures on the way home, which give us our
word 'odyssey', come in Books 5 to 12, with Books 9 to 12
narrated by Odysseus himself in flashback;[7] and Books 13
to 24 are all located on Ithaka.

The *Odyssey* begins with a pretty standard invocation:

> Tell me, Muse, of the man of many ways, who was driven
> far journeys, after he had sacked Troy's sacred citadel.
> Many were they whose cities he saw, whose minds he learned
>   of,[8]
> many the pains he suffered in his spirit on the wide sea,

struggling for his own life and the homecoming of his
  companions.
Even so he could not save his companions, hard though
he strove to; they were destroyed by their own wild recklessness,
fools, who devoured the oxen of Helios, the Sun God,
and he took away the day of their homecoming. From some
  point here,
goddess, daughter of Zeus, speak, and begin our story.[9]

It is important to realize that Odysseus is not a 'drifter, off
to see the world'.[10] Tennyson made Odysseus a vagabond
and a quester,[11] but Homer's Odysseus has a firm focus –
his *nostos*. He frequently has to interrupt his journey, and
for most readers the joy of the *Odyssey* is precisely these
interruptions, but his goalposts never move.

The first lines also give great importance to Odysseus'
comrades. For most of the *Odyssey* they are merely a faceless
crew,[12] but though Odysseus is often at loggerheads with
them, he is still their leader, and desperately wants to bring
them home. He is totally unsuccessful, but the reason for
their destruction is their own 'wild recklessness' – Odysseus
does not fail them. The fact that Odysseus ultimately becomes
the head of a family and the leader of a state is the reason
why his accountability to his followers is heavily stressed at
the outset.

So there are two levels of action in the poem: the personal
story of one man's return to his home and his family; and
the social tale of the king who returns to his native land,
justly eradicates the usurpers, and re-establishes his rule. The
poem is about the function of a society as well as the problems
of an individual.

Odysseus' personal story is preceded by a Council of the
Gods, where the Olympian divinities (minus Poseidon, who

is angry with Odysseus for blinding his son, the Cyclops Polyphemos) convene to hear Athena's complaints about the fate of Odysseus. Zeus lets her have her way, thus allowing Odysseus to start for home, but before we can hear this tale, Homer narrates the 'Telemachy', what some ancient writers called the 'education' of Telemakhos.

Athene disguises herself as a man, visits Telemakhos on Ithaka, and urges him to go in search of his father. Telemakhos is not yet fully grown up, and although he is outraged by the behaviour of the suitors, he cannot handle the situation because of their strength and numbers. His mother Penelope is weeping for Odysseus, and we can sense tensions between her and Telemakhos. He tells her:

> Go therefore back in the house, and take up your own work,
> the loom and the distaff, and see to it that your handmaidens
> ply their work also; but the men must see to discussion,
> all men, and I most of all. For mine is the power in this
> household.[13]

We witness the suitors violating every rule of *xenia* ('hospitality') in an orgy of food, alcohol, song and dance. One of the main motifs in the poem concerns how stranger-guests are received and treated by their hosts, and in the very first encounter in the poem Telemakhos shows the correct way to treat outsiders:

> He caught sight of Athene and set off at once for the porch, thinking it a shame that a stranger should be kept standing at the gates. He went straight up to his visitor, shook hands, relieved him of his bronze spear and gave him cordial greetings.
>
> 'Welcome, sir, to our hospitality!' he said. 'You can tell us what has brought you when you have had some food.'[14]

The suitors, on the other hand, are behaving as though they were (very bad) hosts rather than guests.

There is no one to give Penelope away, even if she were not already married, so, acting on Athene's instructions, Telemakhos summons an assembly on Ithaka and asks the suitors to go home. They refuse, and we see them in their true light: they really will deserve the fate that is coming to them. Telemakhos and Athene (this time in the guise of Mentor)[15] now slip away from Ithaka and make their way to Pylos, where they are generously entertained by the aged, pious and immensely talkative Nestor.

Telemakhos makes a favourable impression on the old man, and, as Athene takes her leave, it becomes apparent that he has divine backing. Nestor's son Peisistratos joins Telemakhos and they leave for Sparta, where they visit Menelaos and Helen. Menelaos is a widely travelled man who has had fabulous encounters of his own, and as he tells stories about Odysseus' prowess in the Trojan War, we receive not only important information about Odysseus' talent for disguise and self-control, but also a report that he is alive:

> That was Odysseus son of Laertes, who makes his home in
> Ithaka, whom I saw on an island, weeping big tears
> in the palace of the nymph Kalypso.[16]

The suitors, meanwhile, discover Telemakhos' absence and prepare to ambush him. We now know exactly what Odysseus is coming back to.

In Book 5 we finally arrive in the fabulous world of Odysseus' travels. Zeus despatches Hermes to tell Kalypso (a daughter of Atlas whose name derives from the Greek *kalypto*, 'I conceal/cover') to let Odysseus go. She has already kept him on her island of Ogygia for seven years,[17] and offers him immortality if he will stay. He appreciates the attractions of her offer, but he rejects it:

> What I want and all my days I pine for
> is to go back to my house and see my day of homecoming.[18]

Odysseus constructs a raft, sets sail, but is wrecked by a mighty storm sent by Poseidon. The goddess 'Ino called Leukothea' (the White Goddess)[19] comes to his rescue in the form of a gannet, and Athena helps too, and after drifting for days, and being battered on rocks, he finally swims ashore on the island of Skherie:

> His very heart was sick with salt water,
> all his flesh was swollen, and the sea water crusted stiffly
> in his mouth and nostrils, and with a terrible weariness fallen
> upon him he lay unable to breathe or speak in his weariness.[20]

But he is still alive, and he makes a hideaway under a shrub and a wild olive, and collapses in 'an exhaustion of sleep and weariness'.

It is on Skherie where the grimy, naked Odysseus encounters the beautiful Nausikaa, princess of the Phaiakians (Phaeacians). He deploys all his tact, sensitivity and courtesy to win her over, and he is accepted as a guest. The Phaiakians respect strangers, live in a divine place far from civilization, are adept sailors, and are not at all warlike; Nausikaa is in the market for a husband, and is not unattracted to Odysseus once he has bathed:

> A while ago he seemed an unpromising man to me. Now
> he even resembles one of the gods, who hold high heaven.
> If only the man to be called my husband could be like this one.[21]

Homer continually teases us with the possibility that Nausikaa might have a relationship with Odysseus, and she takes him home to meet her parents, Alkinoos and Arete. They live in an astonishing palace, perpetually supplied with abundant fruit, vines and vegetables by a miraculous garden. When Nausikaa has to leave, the farewell is extremely touching:

'goodbye, stranger, and think of me sometimes when you are
back at home, how I was the first you owed your life to.'
Then resourceful Odysseus spoke in turn and answered her:
'Nausikaa, daughter of great-hearted Alkinoos,
even so may Zeus, high-thundering husband of Hera,
grant me to reach my house and see my day of homecoming.
So even when I am there I will pray to you, as to a goddess,
all the days of my life. For, maiden, my life was your gift.[22]

Odysseus still does not yet divulge his identity, despite Arete asking him, 'What man are you, and whence?',[23] but using his consummate social skills he wins over the entire court and shows what kind of man he is in Book 8, which features two feasts and some games. Odysseus is reluctant to compete, but when Euryalos tells him 'You do not resemble an athlete',[24] he responds by winning the discus contest by a considerable margin. Three songs from Demodokos, two of which make Odysseus weep, punctuate the entertainment: the first is about a quarrel between Odysseus and Akhilleus (Odysseus is already a celebrity); the last is about the Trojan Horse (again ratifying Odysseus' heroic status). Odysseus' anguish finally prompts Alkinoos to ask him who he is, where he comes from, and what his story is. So we hear of the 'Great Wanderings', told by Odysseus in the first person and in flashback. Some of his adventures must have their origin in the tale of Jason and the Argonauts, but Odysseus gives them a distinctive flavour and offers us interesting insights into his character.

After setting out from Troy, Odysseus touched at Ismaros in Thrace, a city of the Kikones, which he captured in what can only be described as an act of piracy. He pillaged it, sparing only Maro, a priest of Apollo who gave him splendid presents and twelve jars of red honey-sweet wine in return for his and his wife's lives. When other Kikones heard about the assault, they took up arms; having lost six men from each ship, Odysseus put to sea and fled.

From there Odysseus sailed on to the country of the Lotus-eaters on the coast of North Africa. He despatched some of his crew to find out who the local inhabitants were, but they tasted the 'honey-sweet fruit of the lotus', which made anyone who tasted it forget everything and want to stay with the Lotus-eaters. Odysseus had to drag those who had tasted the lotus back to the ships by force, before setting off once again.[25]

Odysseus' travels now brought him to the land of the Cyclopes and his encounter with Polyphemos,[26] which seems to be regarded as Odysseus' finest moment. It also emphasizes Odysseus' key attribute of *metis* ('cunning intelligence'). One of his stock epithets is *polymetis* ('of much cunning intelligence', often rendered 'wily' or 'resourceful'), and as such he is tricky, changeable, adaptable, and a brilliant improviser. When he is faced with overwhelming violence and lawlessness, Odysseus can survive because he can outsmart his adversaries.

The episode begins with Odysseus leaving the rest of his flotilla at a neighbouring island before taking one ship to the land of the Cyclopes, and landing with twelve companions. The adventure is immediately put into a social context:

And we came to the land of the Cyclopes, a fierce, uncivilised people who never lift a hand to plant or plough but put their trust in Providence. All the crops they require spring up unsown and untilled, wheat and barley and the vines whose generous clusters give them wine when ripened for them by the timely rains. The Cyclopes have no assemblies for the making of laws, nor any settled customs, but live in hollow caverns in the mountain heights, where each man is lawgiver to his children and his wives, and nobody cares a jot for his neighbours.[27]

The Cyclops Polyphemos was a son of Poseidon, and while he was out tending his flocks Odysseus and his comrades entered the cavern where he lived, taking with them a skinful of the wine that Odysseus had been given by Maro. Odysseus decided to stay, in the hope of being offered presents, so he and his men made themselves at home, sacrificed some kids, and feasted. The return of the huge, wild cannibal, with one eye in the middle of his forehead, prompted Odysseus to take refuge at the back of the cave, while Polyphemos herded in his flocks and put a massive stone across the entrance. Only then did the Cyclops realize he had visitors, but he immediately violated all the rules for entertaining guests:

'Strangers!' he said. 'And who may you be? Where do you hail from over the highways of the sea? Is yours a trading venture; or are you cruising the main on chance, like roving pirates, who risk their lives to ruin other people?'[28]

This instantly shows that the Cyclops is a bad host: he should not ask Odysseus his name until he has entertained him and seen him all right, but he rejects Odysseus' appeal for hospitality, and claims that the Cyclopes do not concern themselves about Zeus and the Olympians, because they are better than them. And then the true horror of the situation becomes clear:

> [Polyphemos] sprang up and reached for my companions,
> caught up two together and slapped them, like killing puppies,
> against the ground, and the brains ran all over the floor, soaking
> the ground. Then he cut them up limb by limb and got supper
>   ready,
> and like a lion reared in the hills, without leaving anything,
> ate them, entrails, flesh and the marrowy bones alike.[29]

In the morning the Cyclops eats two more men before heading for his pastures, sealing the cave, and consuming two more on his return. Odysseus' *metis* now comes to the fore. His plan is to blind the Cyclops with a huge olive-wood stake, and he succeeds in incapacitating him by means of a generous draught of strong wine. At this point Odysseus tells Polyphemos that his name is 'Nobody', and asks for a guest-gift. The gift consists of a grotesque parody of the rules of hospitality: a promise to eat Odysseus last of all. Homer wants us to admire wily Odysseus' scheme, but he also needs us to understand the extreme brutality of Polyphemos, so that we have no sense of pity for him when the assault takes place:

> He spoke and slumped away and fell on his back, and lay there
> with his thick neck crooked over on one side, and sleep who
>   subdues all
> came on and captured him, and the wine gurgled up from his
>   gullet
> with gobs of human meat. This was his drunken vomiting.[30]

Sleep 'who subdues all' translates the Greek word *pandamator* ('all-subduing'). Its only other use by Homer is when Akhilleus resists 'all-subduing sleep' as he mourns for Patroklos. Sleep usually brings release from tiredness and pain, but not here.

> Then I shoved the beam underneath a deep bed of cinders,
> waiting for it to heat, and I spoke to all my companions
> in words of courage, so none should be in a panic, and back
>   out;
> but when the beam of olive, green as it was, was nearly
> at the point of catching fire and glowed, terribly incandescent,
> then I brought it close up from the fire and my friends about me
> stood fast. Some great divinity breathed courage into us.
> They seized the beam of olive, sharp at the end, and leaned on it
> into the eye, while I from above leaning my weight on it
> twirled it, like a man with a brace-and-bit who bores into
> a ship timber, and his men from underneath, grasping
> the strap on either side whirl it, and it bites resolutely deeper.
> So seizing the fire-point-hardened timber we twirled it
> in his eye, and the blood boiled around the hot point, so that
> the blast and scorch of the burning ball singed all his eyebrows
> and eyelids, and the fire made the roots of his eye crackle [. . .]
> He gave a giant horrible cry and the rocks rattled
> to the sound, and we scuttled away in fear. He pulled the timber
> out of his eye, and it blubbered with plenty of blood.[31]

There are actually some real technical difficulties with all this: olive-wood isn't hardened by burning, and doesn't hold its heat; the Cyclops' eyelid and eyebrow would not spontaneously combust; and the Cyclops would undoubtedly have reacted instantaneously and crushed Odysseus then and there. But Homer's narrative is so brilliantly engaging that we just accept it, and the incident is undoubtedly one of the highlights of the poem. Odysseus' *metis* and courage are at their best when matched against such an awesome opponent, although the blood-and-guts detail of the actual blinding might make a modern reader squirm.

Polyphemos screamed out to the neighbouring Cyclopes for help, and they responded. But when they asked who was hurting him, he answered, 'Nobody'. They took this to be a false alarm, and so retired.

So far so good for Odysseus, but he still had to get out of the cave, whose exit was now guarded by the Cyclops in person. So he tethered rams together in units of three, and lashed his men underneath them, and tied himself underneath the finest ram in the flock. At dawn, when the animals headed for their pastures, the Cyclopes frisked their backs, but missed the men hiding underneath. Once at a safe distance from the cave, Odysseus released his comrades, drove the animals to the ships, and sailed away. He hurled taunts at the Cyclopes; Polyphemos hurled a massive rock at him, which almost wrecked Odysseus' ship, but Odysseus could still not resist divulging his identity:

> You were blinded by Odysseus, sacker of cities,
> Laertes is his father, and he makes his home in Ithaka.[32]

Polyphemos had actually been forewarned by a soothsayer that he would be blinded by Odysseus, but he expresses his surprise at how the prophecy was fulfilled:

> But always I was on the lookout for a man handsome
> and tall, with great endowment of strength on him, to come
>   here;
> but now the end of it is that a little man, niddering, feeble,
> has taken away the sight of my eye, first making me helpless
> with wine.[33]

His words are a great testament to the power of *metis*. He then prays to his father Poseidon to make Odysseus' homecoming impossible, or at least if he does make it,

> Let him come late, in bad case, with the loss of all his
>   companions,
> in someone else's ship, and find troubles in his household.[34]

Polyphemos casts one last mighty missile at Odysseus' ship, narrowly missing the stern and creating a tsunami that washes the vessel on to the safety of the neighbouring island.

Odysseus' next port of call was the island of Aiolia, whose king, Aiolos (Aeolus), had been appointed by Zeus as keeper of the winds 'to hold them still or start them up at his pleasure'.[35] Hospitable, generous and helpful, Aiolos presented Odysseus with an oxhide bag stuffed with all the winds apart from the West Wind, which would blow Odysseus on his way. The voyage went well until Odysseus was close enough to Ithaka to be able to see the men tending the fires, but at that point he fell asleep, whereupon his crew, imagining that the bag contained treasure, undid it. The winds burst free, and the ensuing storm drove them back to Aiolia, where Aiolos refused to provide Odysseus with any further help and expelled him from the island on the grounds that he was hateful to the immortals.

Sailing on, Odysseus came to the land of the Laistrygones. He sent some men to reconnoitre, and they encountered the daughter of King Antiphates of the Laistrygones, who led them to her father's residence. The Laistrygones were cannibalistic giants, and Antiphates grabbed one of the crew members and had him for dinner. The other two were able to flee back to the ship, but the Laistrygones pursued them down to the sea in their tens of thousands, smashing the vessels with man-sized boulders, and slaughtering the sailors before eating them. Odysseus severed the cable of his ship and put out to sea. Whether Odysseus behaved in a cowardly way here, or simply did the sensible thing and cut his losses, is not made clear, but in any case his ship was now the only one left out of the original twelve.

The surviving vessel put in to the Aiaian isle.[36] This was inhabited by the enchantress Kirke (Latinized to Circe), a daughter of Helios who was highly skilled in *pharmaka* ('drugs', 'enchantments' or 'charms'). Odysseus' comrades drew lots as to who should go to investigate the smoke rising from the middle of the island, and Eurylokhos and twenty-two others duly arrived at Kirke's house, a weird place where drugged lions and wolves were behaving like domestic dogs. With the exception of Eurylokhos, the men accepted her hospitality. Having given them a potion of cheese, honey, barley, wine and drugs, Kirke used her wand to change them into swine.[37] Eurylokhos reported back to Odysseus, who set off for Kirke's house. En route he encountered Hermes, who gave him moly, a plant with a black root and a milky white flower,[38] plus some useful instructions, and so Odysseus was able to resist her enchantments, subdue her, and secure the de-metamorphosis of his men. Once she had sworn not to harm him, he accepted her invitation to sleep with her,[39] and a rather sybaritic year-long interlude ensued, before his 'nostalgia' reasserted itself.

Prior to his departure, Kirke tells Odysseus to 'go forward into the moldering home of Hades'[40] and consult the prophet Teiresias. This occupies Book 11 of the *Odyssey*, which is sometimes known as the *nekyia* ('calling-up of ghosts'), and we now get to see both Odysseus' courage and sensitivity, as he is elevated to a level above that of mankind in general. He makes his way north to the land of the Kimmerians, where the sun never breaks through the darkness, digs a pit, and makes blood-sacrifices to Teiresias and to the 'strengthless heads of the perished dead'.[41] This brings the dead up to him. He meets with Elpenor, who had fallen from the roof of Kirke's palace in a drunken stupor; Teiresias, who predicts Odysseus' homecoming (echoing Polyphemos' wish: 'in bad case, with the loss of all your companions, in someone else's ship, and finding troubles in your household'), and also his death; and his mother Antikleia, who had still been alive when he left for Troy. She outlines the situation in Ithaka, and in a desperately emotional moment, three times he attempts to embrace his mother's soul, and three times she flutters out of his hands like a shadow.

Odysseus' narrative is then interrupted by Alkinoos and Arete, who are keen for him to continue his tale. He agrees to stay another day, and tells of three deeply moving encounters with ghosts of his comrades at Troy: Agamemnon, who tells of his death at the hands of Aigisthos 'with the help of my sluttish wife';[42] Akhilleus, who asks for news of Peleus and Neoptolemos; and 'Great' Aias, with whom Odysseus had disputed the arms of Akhilleus, who refuses to speak with him. We are then told about the fates of various individuals in Hades: Minos, sitting in judgement over the dead; Orion[43] in a meadow of asphodel; Tityos, whose liver was constantly devoured by two vultures;[44] Tantalos, hungry and thirsty, but 'tantalized';[45] Sisyphos, rolling his enormous stone up a hill;[46] and Herakles, who empathizes with Odysseus' tribulations. In the end, 'green fear' gets the better of Odysseus, and he returns to his ship and moves on.

After a brief stop at Kirke's island again, they take a route that has already been navigated by the Argonauts, meeting their first severe test at the isle of the Sirens. Homer does not describe the Sirens (presumably they had a normal human form), and he says nothing about their names or parentage, although he does use a special grammatical form of the Greek word 'Sirens', known as the 'dual', which indicates that there were two of them. Odysseus was not the type of hero to pass up the opportunity to hear their song, so as they sailed past, he followed Kirke's advice and stopped up the ears of his comrades with wax, and ordered that he himself should be bound to the mast. The Sirens' song was certainly seductive, and Odysseus begged to be released, but Perimedes and Eurylokhos bound him tighter still, and he was able to sail away.[47]

Further navigational hazards now appear in the shape of a choice between the Wandering Rocks,[48] and Skylla and Kharybdis, which lay on either side of a narrow strait.[49] Skylla was hideous:

> She has twelve feet, and all of them wave in the air. She has six
> necks grown upon her, grown to great length, and upon each
>   neck
> there is a horrible head, with teeth in it, set in three rows
> close together and stiff, full of black death. Her body
> from the waist down is holed up inside the hollow cavern,
> but she holds her heads poked out and away from the terrible
>   hollow.[50]

And in the other cliff was the equally terrifying Kharybdis:

> Who made her terrible ebb and flow of the sea's water.
> When she vomited it up, like a cauldron over a strong fire,
> the whole sea would boil up in turbulence, and the foam flying
> spattered the pinnacles of the rocks in either direction;
> but when in turn again she sucked down the sea's salt water,
> the turbulence showed all the inner sea, and the rock around it

groaned terribly, and the ground showed at the sea's bottom, black with sand.[51]

Following Kirke's advice Odysseus took the channel between Skylla and Kharybdis, keeping much closer to the former. He stood fully armed on the foredeck, but was powerless to prevent Skylla snatching six of his comrades and eating them alive. In what Odysseus describes as the most pitiful scene of any of his sufferings, they suffer an agonizing, long-drawn-out death.

The final destruction of the remainder of Odysseus' crew happened when they arrived at the island of Thrinakia,[52] where the sheep and oxen of Hyperion/Helios, the sun god, were pastured. Odysseus had already been warned about the consequences of harming these animals, and he repeatedly tried to get the message across to his companions, but unfortunately adverse winds kept them on the island for over a month, and having run out of provisions they slaughtered a number of the oxen while Odysseus was asleep. When the winds finally turned and Odysseus put out to sea, Zeus sent a catastrophic storm and blasted the ship with a thunderbolt. All his crew were lost, but when the ship broke up Odysseus lashed the mast and keel together and clung to them while the storms drove him back to Kharybdis. When Kharybdis sucked down the wreckage, he grabbed an overhanging wild fig tree and hung like a bat until the timbers shot back up again. Dropping down into the water, he mounted the wreckage and paddled his way to safety. Ten nights later he was washed ashore on Kalypso's island, and his arrival there concludes his own narrative of his travels.

The tale of the *Odyssey* now resumes back in the land of the Phaiakians. Alkinoos bestows very generous gifts on Odysseus and details a ship to return him to his native land.

The Phaiakians deposit him on Ithaka, still sleeping, in the harbour of Phorkys, the Old Man of the Sea.

After twenty years away, Odysseus is now faced with the problem of the ever increasing disintegration of order in his kingdom and household as the arrogance of the suitors becomes ever more intolerable. The hero we have come to know is unbelievably brave and adaptable, but not without his faults: he was stupid to enter the Cyclops' cavern; he abandoned his men to the Laistrygones; and he failed to control his men on Thrinakia. However, the world of the Great Wanderings is totally different to the real world, and Odysseus will need every ounce of his *metis* if he is to emerge triumphant. Still, we know that he has the mental, verbal, technical and social intelligence to prevail, and he knows it too:

> Dear friends, surely we are not unlearned in evils.
> This is no greater evil now than it was when the Cyclops
> had us cooped in his hollow cave by force and violence,
> but even there, by my courage and counsel and my intelligence,
> we escaped away.[53]

By the time he faces the challenge of confronting the suitors and regaining his wife and kingdom, Odysseus is really well prepared. Like Polyphemos, the suitors ignore *xenia* and consume things they shouldn't, and like the Cyclops, Odysseus will defeat them with disguise and violence.

Once Odysseus is back on Ithaka, Athena advises him to conceal his identity, and disguises him as a dishevelled old beggar. He acts the part well, and arrives first at the shelter of his loyal old servant, the swineherd Eumaios, where he tells a false story of his life. Athena, meanwhile, has gone to Sparta and prompted Telemakhos to come home. He heads straight for Eumaios' hut to gather intelligence about the situation, and sends the swineherd off to announce his return to Penelope. This gives Odysseus the opportunity to reveal himself. His disguise miraculously fades, and father and son are overwhelmed with emotion:

> Telemakhos
> folded his great father in his arms and lamented,
> shedding tears, and desire for mourning rose in both of them;
> and they cried shrill in a pulsing voice . . . [54]

As they plot their revenge, the suitors realize that their plan to ambush Telemakhos on his way home has misfired. Antinoos proposes murdering Telemakhos, but Amphinomos vetoes him.

Athene now renews Odysseus' disguise, and Telemakhos returns to the palace, followed later by Odysseus and Eumaios. Odysseus faces a test of his self-control when the goatherd Melanthios abuses and kicks out at him: 'yet still he stood it, and kept all inside him'.[55] The disguise fails to deceive his old dog Argos, however. The once magnificent animal is now old and neglected, but he recognizes his master, wags his tail, lays his ears back, and dies happy, while Odysseus surreptitiously wipes away a tear.

On arrival at his own palace, Odysseus proceeds to beg food from the suitors, which allows him to see the reality of their behaviour for himself. Again, his self-control is tested when Antinoos hurls a footstool at him. This even offends the other suitors, and Penelope, who shares the outrage, asks Eumaios to summon the stranger to her presence. Odysseus refuses to go immediately, preferring to wait until sunset. 'This way it will be much better,' says Eumaios, 'to talk in private to the stranger and hear his story.'[56]

Playing the role of a down-and-out draws Odysseus into a turf-war with Iros, a rival beggar famed for his ravenous appetite for food and drink. Odysseus is on his patch, so Iros challenges him to box with him;[57] Odysseus must not give himself away, so he decides to hit him lightly . . .

> Odysseus struck the neck underneath the ear, and shattered the bones within, and the red blood came in his mouth, filling it. He dropped, bleating, in the dust, with his face set in a grimace, and kicking at the ground with his feet.[58]

Penelope then makes an appearance in order to open the hearts of the suitors. They are enraptured:

> Their knees gave way, and the hearts in them were bemused with passion,
> And each one prayed for the privilege of lying beside her.[59]

She also drops hints about the possibility of marriage, intimating that some nice presents would assist her decision-making. This type of behaviour makes her incredibly attractive to her husband:

> Great Odysseus was happy
> because she beguiled gifts out of them, and enchanted their spirits
> with blandishing words, while her own mind had other intentions.[60]

Again, Odysseus has to suffer disrespect and conceal his true identity when Melantho, a maid, who is sleeping with the suitor Eurymakhos, scolds him, and he narrowly avoids being hit by another footstool thrown by Eurymakhos. His presence is obviously causing disruption among the suitors, but when Telemakhos attributes this to too much food and alcohol, and suggests that they should all go home to bed, they agree. Odysseus and Telemakhos now take the opportunity to hide all the weapons that are in the house, and Penelope and Odysseus to meet in private. She tells him her story, and he tells her another false one, claiming to have entertained the great hero himself on Crete, and affirming that Odysseus is alive and well and on the point of return. Penelope remains pessimistic, and orders Eurykleia to wash Odysseus' feet. Eurykleia, who had been Odysseus' nurse, notices a scar that Odysseus had incurred years ago on a boar hunt, and recognizes him instantly. He swears her to silence before resuming his conversation with Penelope, during which she comes up with the idea of having a contest with Odysseus' bow:

> Those axes which, in his palace, he used to set up in order
> so that, twelve in all, they stood in a row, like timbers
> to hold a ship. He would stand far off, and send a shaft
> through them.
> Now I will set these up as a contest before my suitors,
> and the one who takes the bow in his hands, strings it with
> the greatest
> ease, and sends an arrow clean through all the twelve axes
> shall be the one I go away with.[61]

That night Penelope has a favourable dream, Odysseus gets good omens from Zeus, Telemakhos' friend Theoklymenos has a prophetic vision of the forthcoming massacre, the oxherd Philoitios arrives to reinforce Odysseus' side, Eumaios confirms his loyalty, and Telemakhos appears ever more proactive. Neither is there any doubt that the suitors' behaviour is so appalling that their ultimate slaughter is morally justified.

Penelope now fetches Odysseus' bow and announces the contest. Telemakhos makes the preparations for the event, and would have strung the bow himself had Odysseus not stopped him. Leiodes makes an unsuccessful attempt, and in the lull that follows Odysseus reveals himself and his plot to Eumaios and Philoitios. Eurymakhos has the next attempt, after which Odysseus himself asks for a turn. The suitors object, but Penelope insists that he is given a go. Telemakhos sends her away, but ensures that Odysseus is allowed to try, and he details Eurykleia and Philoitios to bar the exits from the palace. The suitors now have their last laugh at Odysseus' expense, until he strings the bow without the slightest difficulty:

> Then, plucking it in his right hand he tested the bowstring,
> and it gave him back an excellent sound like the voice of a
>   swallow.
> A great sorrow fell now upon the suitors, and all their colour
> was changed, and Zeus showing forth his portents thundered
>   mightily.[62]

Odysseus' archery is immaculate. The arrow flies straight through the axes and out the other end. This is simply the prelude to carnage: he shoots Antinoos through the throat and finally announces his identity:

> You dogs, you never thought that I would any more come back
> from the land of Troy, and because of that you despoiled my
>   household,
> and forcibly took my serving women to sleep beside you,
> and sought to win my wife while I was still alive, fearing

neither the immortal gods who hold the wide heaven,
nor any resentment sprung from men to be yours in the future.
Now upon all of you the terms of destruction are fastened.[63]

Eurymakhos tries to rally the suitors, but falls to an arrow
though the chest; Amphinomos is struck down by Telemakhos' spear; suitor after suitor succumbs to Odysseus'
arrows until he runs out; the treacherous Melanthios manages
to secure some weaponry for the suitors, but he is captured
and bound to a column by the roof beams; Athene appears
on Odysseus' side in the guise of Mentor; six suitors release
a simultaneous volley of spears at Odysseus, but Athena
makes them all miss; Demoptolemos, Euryades, Elatos and
Peisandros all meet their death; another volley of spears is
deflected by Athene, though Telemakhos and Eumaios suffer
flesh wounds; Eurydamas, Amphimedon, Polybos and Ktesip-
pos are the next suitors to die, followed by Agelaos and
Leokritos; Athene spreads panic with her *aegis*; Leiodes' plea
for mercy only leads to his decapitation by Odysseus; but
the singer Phemios and the herald Medon are spared on Telemakhos' intervention.

Not one suitor survives, but the massacre is not yet
complete. Eurykleia informs Odysseus of the twelve serving
women who have behaved immorally with the suitors. They
are forced to carry off the corpses and clean up the hideous
mess, before Telemakhos supervises their execution.

So he spake, and taking the cable of a dark-prowed ship,
fastened it to the tall pillar, and fetched it about the round-
    house;
and like thrushes, who spread their wings, or pigeons, who have
flown into a snare net set up for them in a thicket, trying
to find a resting place, but the sleep given them was hateful;

> so their heads were all in a line, and each had her neck caught
> fast in a noose, so that their death would be most pitiful.
> They struggled with their feet for a little, not for very long.[64]

The final act of horror is the awful mutilation of Melanthios,
before Odysseus fumigates the palace with sulphur.

We are now left anticipating the climactic reunion of
Odysseus and Penelope. Throughout the *Odyssey* Penelope
has been described by the epithet 'circumspect', and this she
continues to be when Eurykleia delivers the news that the
stranger is Odysseus. Her response lurches from utter disbe-
lief, to semi-belief; Odysseus' filthy appearance gets in the
way of her acknowledging the truth (despite him taking a
bath), and she will only trust a recognition by signs:

> But if he truly is Odysseus,
> and he has come home, then we shall find other ways, and
>   better,
> to recognize each other, for we have signs that we know of
> between the two of us only, but they are secret from others.[65]

This intimate information concerns their marriage bed.
Odysseus built this himself, incorporating a live olive tree
into the structure, and no one else knows this. When Penelope
tells Eurykleia to bring the bed out to Odysseus, he is
outraged: 'What man has put my bed in another place?' This
is the information that Penelope needs. She accepts him, and
he falls weeping into her arms. Her emotions are described
in a brilliantly appropriate simile:

> And as when the land appears welcome to men who are
>   swimming,
> after Poseidon has smashed their strong-built ship on the open

> water, pounding it with the weight of wind and the heavy
> seas, and only a few escape the gray water landward
> by swimming, with a thick scurf of salt coated upon them,
> and gladly they set foot on the shore, escaping the evil;
> so welcome was her husband to her as she looked upon him,
> and she could not let him go from the embrace of her white
>   arms.[66]

The two make love, and then talk, she of her troubles, he of his travels, until sweet sleep overtakes them.

There are those who believe that Homer's *Odyssey* ended here, and that what follows should be attributed to a different author, but the text as we have it deals with two more issues: the response of the relatives of the suitors, who want revenge; and the reunion of Odysseus with his father Laertes.

Hermes, the *psykhopompos* ('escorter of souls'), takes the souls of the suitors down into the Underworld, while Odysseus makes his way to his father's farm, where he decides to put him to the test in a way that will provoke an extreme emotional response. He tells another of his false stories, which does indeed have a devastating effect on Laertes, before he reveals himself. The shell-shocked old man demands a sign, Odysseus reveals his scar, tells of the fifty trees that his father gave him when he was a child, and the two of them embrace. Their joy instantly turns to worry about the aftermath of the massacre, though. Antinoos' father Eupeithes urges revenge, and the suitors' relatives advance on the palace. The three generations of Odysseus' family stand shoulder to shoulder against them, and though fighting starts Athene puts a stop to the conflict. When Odysseus ignores her advice, Zeus throws a thunderbolt at Athene, which terminates the fight. The *Odyssey* then concludes with pledges being given by each side, and ratified by Athene.

The events following the massacre of the suitors come down to us in a number of contradictory traditions. The Epic Cycle is completed by a work known as the *Telegony*, traditionally dated to 568. In *Odyssey* 11, Teiresias had told Odysseus to take up his oar and go to a country where men knew nothing of the sea or ships, where his oar would be mistaken for a winnowing-fan. There Odysseus should sacrifice to Poseidon. We possess a short abstract of the *Telegony*, which speaks of this being accomplished, and Apollodoros gives information of how Kallidike, Queen of the Thesprotians, urged Odysseus to stay, and had a son by him called Polypoites. Odysseus then returned to Ithaka, where he found Poliporthes (or Ptoliporthes), whom Penelope had borne to him. In the meantime Telegonos had learned from Kirke that he was a son of Odysseus,[67] and had as he sailed in search of his father, had landed in Ithaka and ravaged the island. When Odysseus confronted the invaders, Telegonos, unaware of Odysseus' identity, killed him with a spear that was barbed with the spine of a sting-ray. When Telegonos realized what he had done, he transported his father's body, Telemakhos and Penelope to Kirke's island, where she made them immortal.

Apollodoros talks of variants in which Penelope was seduced by Antinoos, banished by Odysseus, and bore Pan to Hermes before she died.[68] Variant versions allege that she was seduced by Amphinomos, and killed by Odysseus on that account.[69] Elsewhere we hear of Odysseus being accused by the bereaved relatives of the suitors, being sentenced to banishment and retiring to Italy.[70] Yet another version, only mentioned by Apollodoros, makes Odysseus go to Thoas in Aitolia, and die there of old age.

The death of Odysseus pretty much marks the end of Greek mythology when looked at from a 'chronological' perspective.

Odysseys Since Odysseus

> Odysseus, as some say, wandered about Libya, or, as some say, about Sicily, or, as others say, about the ocean or about the Tyrrhenian Sea.[71]

Ever since antiquity there has been endless debate concerning the geographical authenticity of Odysseus' travels. However, because of the extent of the oral tradition, which due to its nature is constantly being updated, it is virtually impossible to be sure whether, or in what sense, the *Odyssey* reflects either a historical society or accurate geographical knowledge. We must therefore be deeply circumspect about attempts to identify places and events in the *Odyssey* with historical and geographical 'reality'. The geographer Strabo suggested that Homer only told half the truth, while another geographer Eratosthenes was more sceptical still – he said that he would believe in Odysseus' travels when someone found the leather-worker who made the bag that Aiolos put the winds in. The big problem is that once the North Wind blows him off course and drives him past Kythera in Book 9, we never get clear information. Homer mentions wind directions but these are only approximations, as Peter Jones cogently argues, and when we take into account the close parallels with episodes from the Argonauts tale, and factor in the considerable problems of making sense of those places that do seem to have some historical reality, there is a very strong case for calling off the search for Odysseus' 'real' route.[72] However, that has not stopped the likes of Thor Heyerdahl and Tim Severin making their own personal Odysseys in the hope of finding Homer's. The debate concerning the whereabouts of Homer's Ithaka is also very much alive and well, with the expertise of geologists now being drafted into the search alongside that

of classicists. The most recent theory locates Odysseus' homeland on what is now part of Zakynthos, but could have been
a separate island in the Bronze Age.[73]

This inspirational story has launched many other great
literary journeys. Dante, Goethe and Tennyson all took
Odysseus to their hearts, and James Joyce's *Ulysses* used the
myth 'simply as a way of controlling, of ordering, of giving
shape and significance to the immense panorama of futility and
anarchy which is contemporary history'.[74] Joyce regarded the
story of Odysseus as ' the most beautiful, all-embracing theme
– greater, more human, than that of Hamlet, Don Quixote,
Dante, Faust'.[75] Nikos Kazantzakis (1883–1957) produced an
enormous *Odyssey* (33,333 lines), which took Odysseus on
beyond Ithaka and introduced him to Buddha, Don Quixote
and Christ as he took on all the burdens of Western civilization.
The star-studded, special-effects-filled, critically acclaimed *The
Odyssey* by Hallmark Entertainment (1997) casts Armand
Assante as Odysseus, Isabella Rossellini as Athena and Irene
Papas as Antikleia in a straightforward enough retelling on the
screen, while Arthur C. Clarke's *2001: A Space Odyssey*, and
the fine film by Stanley Kubrick (1968), pick up on the theme
and locate it in outer space. The comedy *O Brother, Where
Art Thou?*, written by Joel and Ethan Cohen (2000), uses the
Odyssey as a springboard for the humorous and touching
adventures of Everett Ulysses McGill, who escapes from a chain
gang in 1930s Mississippi, and features glorious encounters
with the Sirens as close-harmony singing Southern belles, and
the Cyclops as a one-eyed Bible salesman. Derek Walcott's
wonderful poem *Omeros* (1990), set on the Caribbean island
of St Lucia, offers a highly distinctive reworking of Homeric
material where the island itself seems to be the hero of a multi-
layered narrative. Part of the story concerns Achille and Hector
and their love for Helen, with considerable attention paid to

Philoctete, an injured fisherman, and an engaging thread that runs though the tale is that of the poet-narrator, who comments on the action of the poem and undergoes a number of trans-Atlantic wanderings himself.

One of the finest *Odyssey*-inspired works must surely be C.P. Cavafy's wonderful 'Ithaca' (1911), a beautiful application of the *Odyssey* as a lesson for life:

When you set out for Ithaca
ask that your way be long,
full of adventure, full of instruction.
The Laistrygonians and the Cyclops,
angry Poseidon – do not fear them:
such as these you will never find
as long as your thought is lofty, as long as a rare
emotion touch your spirit and your body.
The Laistrygonians and the Cyclops,
angry Poseidon – you will not meet them
unless you carry them in your soul,
unless your soul raise them up before you.
[. . .]
But do not in the least hurry the journey.
Better that it last for years,
so that when you reach the island you are old,
rich with all you have gained on the way,
not expecting Ithaca to give you wealth.
Ithaca gave you the splendid journey.
Without her you would not have set out.
She hasn't anything else to give you.

And if you find her poor, Ithaca has not deceived you.
So wise have you become, of such experience,
that already you will have understood what these Ithacas mean.[76]

18

PLATO AND THE MYTH OF ATLANTIS

Key Characters

Plato	Fourth-century Athenian philosopher: the first to introduce the Atlantis myth
Sokrates (Socrates)	Fifth-century Athenian philosopher; main character in Plato's dialogue
Timaios (Timaeus)	An astronomer from Lokroi in Italy
Hermokrates	A Syracusan general
Kritias (the younger) (Critias)	Plato's great-grandfather; told the Atlantis tale in Plato; heard it from his grandfather Kritias (the elder) when aged ten; now aged ninety
Kritias (the elder)	Reputed to have got the Atlantis tale from Solon
Solon	Sixth-century Athenian political reformer and poet; was allegedly told the Atlantis story in Egypt while visiting the city of Saïs

Who shall say that one hundred years from now the great museums of the world may not be adorned with gems, statues, arms, and implements from Atlantis, while the libraries of the world shall contain translations of its inscriptions, throwing new light upon all the past history of the human race and all the great problems which now perplex the thinkers of our day?[1]

These words, written by Ignatius Donnelly in 1882, have, of course, not yet come true, but the 'Myth of Atlantis' remains one of the tales from antiquity with the greatest impact on the modern consciousness. It has spawned literally thousands of books, and yet it very seldom appears in accounts of Greek mythology. There is a good reason for this. The tale does not concern key writers such as Apollodoros, Pausanias, Ovid and others, and it never makes an appearance in tragedy, comedy, sculpture, vase painting, or any of the other media that expound myths. It first crops up in a late work of the philosopher Plato, where it forms part of an unfinished trilogy of works: *Timaios* (complete), *Kritias* (incomplete) and *Hermokrates* (never started). The trilogy was to present a series of imaginary dialogues held during an Athenian festival in (probably) 425, when Plato himself would have been a small child. That in itself should place a large question mark over the historical veracity of the conversation, which takes place between Sokrates, an astronomer called Timaios, Plato's great-grandfather Kritias (who would have been about ninety years old) and a Syracusan general called Hermokrates.

The characters in the dialogue are discussing the nature of the Ideal State, when something reminds Kritias of a story he heard from his grandfather (also called Kritias) when he was ten years old. Kritias the elder was supposedly told the story by Solon, the Athenian political reformer and poet, who had established the prerequisites for democracy in the 590s.

The story is a strange one, but Solon, the wisest of the seven wise men, once vouched its truth [. . .] It relates the many notable achievements of our city long ago, which have been lost sight of because of the lapse of time and destruction of human life.[2]

Kritias senior says that Solon brought the story back from Egypt:

> 'It was about what may fairly be called the greatest and most noteworthy of all this city's achievements, but because of the lapse of time and the death of those who took part in it the story has not lasted till our day.' 'Tell us from the beginning,' came the reply; 'how and from whom did Solon hear the tale which he told you as true?'[3]

These constant assertions that we are dealing with a true story should not necessarily be taken at face value. Plato frequently deploys mythological material in this way. For instance, in the *Gorgias* Sokrates tells a story about the Isles of the Blessed and Tartaros, introduced like this: 'Give ear then [. . .] to a very fine story, which will, seem fiction to you but is fact to me; what I am going to tell you I tell you as the truth.'[4] In the *Republic* Sokrates comments that, 'We begin by telling children stories. These are, in general, fiction, though they contain some truth.'[5] He talks about how to make the fiction as like the truth as possible, in order to make the lie or untruth useful. Sokrates also poses this question in the *Protagoras*: 'Now shall I, as an old man speaking to his juniors, put my explanation in the form of a story or give it a reasoned argument? [*And he answers his own question*] I think it will be pleasanter to tell you a story.'[6] And perhaps most significantly for our discussion here, the eponymous character in the *Phaidros* listens to Sokrates speak and then exclaims, 'Sokrates, how easily you make up stories, from Egypt or from anywhere else you like.'[7]

We need to be aware from the outset that the Atlantis story is deployed in the same way as the mythical material that appears elsewhere in Plato's writings; in other words, to make his ideas clearer and more accessible.

The historical Solon had left Athens after completing his political reforms, and his travels had taken him to Egypt. Kritias goes on to say how Solon arrived in Saïs,

> and in the course of making inquiries from those priests who were most knowledgeable on the subject found that both he and all his countrymen were almost entirely ignorant about antiquity.[8]

Now, at the start of the sixth century, Egypt was not the great military and cultural powerhouse it once had been, and the historical information that Solon acquires looks full of misunderstandings, distortions and inventions. Kritias tells how Solon narrated the myth of Deukalion's flood, but received a rather dismissive response:

> A very old priest said to him, 'Oh Solon, Solon, you Greeks are all children, and there's no such thing as an old Greek [. . .] You have no belief rooted in old tradition and no knowledge hoary with age. And the reason is this. There have been and will be many different calamities to destroy mankind, the greatest of them by fire and water, lesser ones by countless other means.'[9]

The priest embarks on a rationalizing interpretation of the myth of Phaethon:[10] to him the tale is damaged history, a mythical explanation of how changes in the courses of the celestial bodies cause the fiery destruction of earthly things. Watery destructions also occur, but these damage Egypt less because the Nile mitigates their effects. Consequently, and crucially, he says:

In our temples we have preserved from earliest times a written record of any great [. . .] event which has come to our ears whether it occurred in your part of the world or here or anywhere else [. . .] You remember only one deluge, though there have been many, and you do not know that the finest and best race of men that ever existed lived in your country; you and your fellow citizens are descended from the few survivors that remained, but you know nothing about it because so many succeeding generations left no record in writing. For before the greatest of all destructions by water, Solon, the city that is now Athens was pre-eminent in war and conspicuously the best governed in every way, its achievements and constitution being the finest of any in the world of which we have heard tell.[11]

It should be noted straight away that there are no extant Egyptian documents referring to pre-historic Athens or its destruction, and no references to recurring worldwide cataclysms, be these fiery or aquatic. It should also be stressed that Egyptian records only begin in around 3000, whereas Solon's guide boasts:

The age of our institutions is given in our sacred records as eight thousand years [i.e. c.8600], and the citizens whose laws and whose finest achievement I will now briefly describe to you [. . .] lived nine thousand years ago [i.e. c.9600].[12]

Archaeology makes it quite explicit that, at the time the priest is talking about, there were only Stone Age hunter-gatherers: there were no significant villages, let alone towns, city states like Athens, or empires like that of Atlantis. Something is clearly amiss with the dates here, but still, Solon is suitably impressed, asks for more information, and is treated to a description of an Athenian civilization that strongly resembles

Plato's Ideal State as expounded in his *Republic*. This is perhaps predictable enough, but then the priest introduces an amazing piece of information:

> Our records tell how your city checked a great power which arrogantly advanced from its base in the Atlantic Ocean to attack the cities of Europe and Asia. For in those days the Atlantic was navigable. There was an island opposite the strait which you call [. . .] the Pillars of Herakles,[13] an island larger than Libya and Asia combined.[14]

This, he says, was Atlantis. Its mighty kings ruled an empire that extended to the borders of Egypt and Tyrrhenia (in Italy), but, not satisfied with this, the imperialist Atlanteans set about enslaving Greece and Egypt.

> It was then, Solon, that the power and courage and strength of your city became clear [. . .] She led an alliance of the Greeks, and then when they deserted her and she was forced to fight alone, after running into direst peril, she overcame the invaders and celebrated a victory; she rescued those not yet enslaved from the slavery threatening them, and she generously freed all others living within the Pillars of Herakles.[15]

Two important things emerge here. First, the putative date of the war must be after 8600, when the Egyptian records start; second, the narrative of underdog Athens fighting off marauding outsiders sounds just like the way classical Athenian propaganda interpreted the Persian invasions of Greece which ended in the great Greek victories of Marathon (490), Salamis (480) and Plataia (479). This fact would not be lost on Plato's readership, and we need to remember that Kritias' interjections are entirely concerned with Athens: Atlantis is very much a secondary consideration. He ends by having the priest tell Solon about an awesome natural disaster:

> There were earthquakes and floods of extraordinary violence, and in a single dreadful day and night all your fighting men were swallowed up by the earth, and the island of Atlantis was similarly swallowed up by the sea and vanished; this is why the sea in that area is to this day impassable to navigation, which is hindered by mud just below the surface, the remains of the sunken island.[16]

It says little for the nautical awareness of the fourth-century Greeks if they thought that the Atlantic Ocean was muddy and not navigable. Some commentators have suggested that Plato is reflecting Phoenician knowledge of the Sargasso Sea, where *Sargassum* seaweed floats on the surface and causes difficulties to sailors, while others feel it is more probable that it comes from deliberate Phoenician misinformation about their trading settlement at Tartessos north of Cadiz, which had to be abandoned because of the heavy silting of the Guadalquivir River after 500.

It is important to be clear that the 'Ideal Athens' of Kritias' narrative was engulfed along with arrogant Atlantis, and that the idea of constant cycles of catastrophe is one that Plato is very fond of. Anyone searching for the 'Lost World of Atlantis' should also be aware that Sokrates himself has nothing whatsoever to say about Atlantis anywhere else in Plato's work: he, Timaios and Hermokrates have never heard of it.

The next dialogue in the trilogy, the *Kritias*, contains a rather more detailed description of Atlantis, but also some contradictions relating to the chronology – perhaps not surprising, given that Kritias appeals to the goddess Memory before he starts.

We must first remind ourselves that in all nine thousand years have elapsed since the declaration of war between those who lived outside and all those who lived inside the Pillars of Herakles [*i.e. circa 9425; it was some time after 8600 in the* Kritias]. This is the war whose course I am to trace [*we never hear about it, because the* Kritias *is unfinished*]. The leadership and conduct of the war were on the one side in the hands of our city, on the other in the hands of the kings of Atlantis.[17]

These dating anomalies reinforce the fact that Plato is a philosopher, not a historian, and this becomes obvious when Kritias gives a description of the very ancient Athenians as paragons of virtue, physically beautiful and world-famous because of it. This parallel with the inhabitants of Plato's Ideal State jogged Kritias' memory of the Atlantis story in the first place, and he now presents a detailed description of Atlantis. Starting in the realms of myth, he talks about the division of the world between the gods, in which Athena and Hephaistos get Athens (the likelihood of any Egyptian document stating this is minimal), and Poseidon gets the island of Atlantis (an assertion that does not feature in Hesiod or any other of the seminal texts concerning the origins of the gods and humans). The island is certainly wonderful:

At the centre [. . .] near the sea, was a plain, said to be the most beautiful and fertile of all plains, and near the middle of this plain about 10 km inland a hill of no great size. Here there lived one of the original earth-born inhabitants called Euenor, with his wife Leukippe. They had an only child, a daughter called Kleito. She was just of marriageable age when her father and mother died, and Poseidon was attracted by her and had intercourse with her, and fortified the hill where she lived by enclosing it with concentric rings of sea and land. There were

two rings of land and three of sea, like cartwheels, with the
island at their centre and equidistant from each other, making
the place inaccessible to man (for there were still no ships or
sailing in those days) [. . .] He begot five pairs of male twins,
brought them up, and divided the island of Atlantis into ten
parts which he distributed between them.[18]

We should be aware that no other ancient source endorses
this genealogy.

Atlantis and the surrounding Atlantic Ocean were named
after Atlas, the first king (not to be confused with the Atlas
who held up the world). The wealth of the kings of Atlantis
was staggering; their mineral resources were excellent and
included the mythical metal *orikhalkon* ('orichalc'), whose
value was only exceeded by that of gold; there was a plentiful
supply of timber; every kind of domesticated and wild animal,
including elephants, lived on the island; and the earth
produced foodstuffs in abundance. Atlantis was a veritable
paradise, but its inhabitants still imported goods from their
far-flung empire.

Plato's description of the Atlantean capital city is clear
enough to make reconstruction relatively easy, and its
Pythagorean geometric perfection smacks of the imagination
rather than real architecture. (See map, p. 434.)

The Atlanteans constructed their city by bridging the rings
of water around Kleito's original home, and making a road
to their palace. They excavated a 10-kilometre-long, 100-
metre-wide canal, from the sea to the outermost ring; at the
bridges they constructed tunnels through the rings of land;
the largest of the rings of water was 600 metres wide, as
was the ring of land inside it; the second rings were 400
metres across; and the ring of water around the central island
was 200 metres broad. The island on which the palace was

located was 1 kilometre in diameter, and the entire complex was contained within a stone wall with towers and gates. The whole outer wall was clad in bronze, while tin was applied to the inner wall, and *orikhalkon* faced the wall of the acropolis.

Within the acropolis itself was an amazing palace, and at the very centre was a shrine to Poseidon and Kleito, surrounded by a golden wall. The temple of Poseidon measured 100 by 200 metres (the Parthenon at Athens measures around 30 by 70 metres), decorated with silver, gold, ivory and *orikhalkon*, and vast amounts of statuary; bulls roamed within its precincts; two springs, one cold and one hot, provided unlimited water that was distributed to basins and hot baths; accommodation was provided for royalty, commoners, women, horses and beasts of burden; wonderfully beautiful trees grew in a sacred grove of Poseidon; the ring-islands had temples, gardens, gymnasia and a hippodrome; the barracks for the king's bodyguard were arranged so that the most trustworthy were at the heart of the city; the dockyards were full of state-of-the-art warships; and there was a circular wall 10 kilometres from the largest ring, which sheltered some dense housing settlements.

The region as a whole rose precipitously above the sea, and a flat rectangular plain measuring 600 by 400 kilometres, which was enclosed by mountains, surrounded the city. The whole area was characterized by idyllic scenery, thriving settlements and rich natural resources. The plain was bounded by an immense artificial ditch which channelled the river waters from the mountains to the city and into a chequerboard network of canals that provided transport infrastructure and irrigation which was so effective that Atlantis had two harvests a year. The extent of the mountainous region is not specified, but it would have to cover an absolutely enormous

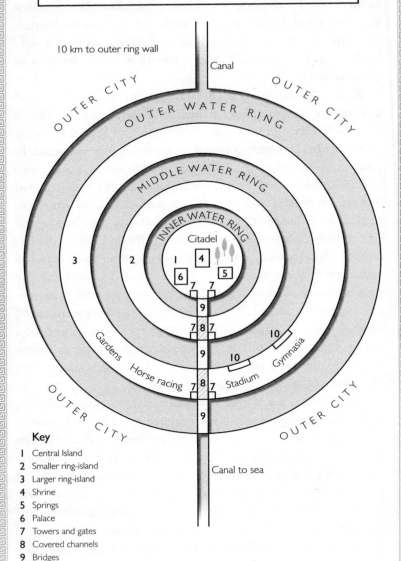

CITY PLAN OF ATLANTIS

10 km to outer ring wall

Canal

OUTER CITY

OUTER CITY

OUTER WATER RING

MIDDLE WATER RING

INNER WATER RING

Citadel

3

2

1

4

6

5

7 7

9

7 8 7

9

10

10

7 8 7

Gardens   Horse racing   Stadium   Gymnasia

9

OUTER CITY

OUTER CITY

Canal to sea

Key
1 Central Island
2 Smaller ring-island
3 Larger ring-island
4 Shrine
5 Springs
6 Palace
7 Towers and gates
8 Covered channels
9 Bridges
10 Docks

area if it were to make up an island bigger than North Africa and Asia put together, which is what Kritias said before: the plain of Atlantis is here only about twice the size of Sicily.

We then hear of the awesome manpower and the despotic powers available to the Atlantean rulers, but Kritias informs us that the kings of Atlantis were just, wise and moral, until, that is, the inevitable moral degeneration set in:

> But when the divine element in them became weakened by frequent admixture with mortal stock, and their human traits became predominant, they ceased to be able to carry their prosperity with moderation. To the perceptive eye the depth of their degeneration was clear enough [. . .] and Zeus [. . .] whose eye can see such things, when he perceived the wretched state of this admirable stock decided to punish them and reduce them to order by discipline.[19]

With Zeus about to make a speech to the gods, the narrative breaks off. The *Kritias* is unfinished and the *Hermokrates* never got written.

Looking for Atlantis

Essentially, Plato is presenting us with a deliberate contrast between the Atlanteans' no-expense-spared barbaric luxury and the understated modesty of his virtuous Athenians. Kritias tells us that the Atlanteans don't speak Greek, which instantly makes them barbarians, and their monarchic government and conspicuous consumption reinforce that prejudice in the Greek mind. So there is no need for Solon to derive the description from Egyptian records, especially since Plato had plenty of authentic and literary barbarian examples to fire his imagination:

- Herodotos had already described the astounding luxuries of Babylon, including the Hanging Gardens with their amazing trees;
- Ekbatana, the capital of the Medes, had seven rings of walls with tunnels cut through them;
- Carthage had a remarkable circular harbour surrounded by dockyards, with the navy's headquarters on a central island;
- Syracuse in Sicily was not barbarian, but it was hostile to Athens, and its tyrant Dionysios I attacked Tyrrhenia. The city was also located on a large island to the west and possessed plentiful agricultural and mineral resources, not to mention hot and cold springs, a citadel on a promontory between two harbours, and a site on the edge of a plain surrounded by mountains. It was also the venue for a failed experiment in establishing an Ideal State on the Platonic model, the whole process stymied by the avaricious ambition of one of Plato's pupils-gone-bad;
- In Homer's *Odyssey,* Skherie, where Odysseus encounters Nausikaa, boasts a settlement surrounded by high fortifications, with marvellous harbours on each side and approached via a narrow causeway; there is an impressive poplar wood where Alkinoos has a royal park and a garden irrigated by two springs; there is a great temple of Poseidon; bronze walls run round the court; and there are golden doors on posts and lintels of silver, furnished with golden door-handles.

These resemblances should provide a warning to those who wish to find a specific location for the 'real' Atlantis. The same caveats should also be applied to thoughts of primeval geological disasters, since plate tectonics conclusively disproves the existence of a sunken continent under the

Atlantic. On the other hand, there were a number of contemporary incidents that could have influenced his narrative. As the historian Thukydides describes, in 426 Greece was hit by earthquakes and tsunamis:

> At Orobiai in Euboia the sea subsided from what was then the shore and afterwards swept up again in a huge wave, which covered part of the city and left some of it still underwater when the wave retreated, so that what was once land is now sea. Those of the inhabitants who were unable to escape in time by running up to the high ground were lost in the flood. An inundation of the same kind took place at Atalanta, the island off the coast of Opuntian Lokris.[20]

Plato would have read his Thukydides, so there seems little need to posit a situation where he can only get his inspiration from Egyptian records. In fact in 373 an earthquake in the Korinthian Gulf did considerable damage. The town of Helike, which had a famous temple of Poseidon, was completely inundated: no bodies were found and shoals made navigation hazardous in the immediate area.

All this has still seemed a little too mundane for some commentators, who see it as feasible that vague echoes of something more elemental reached Plato, potentially through Solon and Egyptian records, combined with a misunderstanding of the chronology and geography. What if Solon mistook the Egyptian numbers, or Kritias or Plato mistakenly multiplied the dates and dimensions by ten – so that 8,000 years before Solon was really 800 (giving a date of c.1400, not 8600), and 9,000 years before the dramatic setting of the dialogue was really 900 (giving dates of c.1325, not 9425)? What if the Atlantis' dimensions as given by Kritias are ten times too big, so that Plato was forced to relocate it in the Atlantic because it could not possibly fit into the Mediterranean (although he must not be made to multiply the dimensions of the capital city by the same factor)? Can we take a Euhemerist approach,[21] get to the 'truth behind the myth of Atlantis', and marry it to hard archaeology? After all, it is argued, Plato makes great play of the fact that he is telling a true story.

One candidate for this 'real Atlantis' was the civilization of Minoan Crete, which flourished from about 2100 to 1450, making it contemporary with Middle and early New Kingdom Egypt. There was a good deal of interaction between the Egyptians and the Minoans (who may be the 'Keftiu' of Egyptian inscriptions), although there is nothing in the surviving records about war between them, or between Crete and Athens. It has also been conjectured that the Egyptians regarded Crete as a big island in the west situated between Libya and Asia, and that Plato misunderstood Solon's information and interpreted the Greek *meson* ('between') as *meisdon* ('bigger than') Libya and Asia. This might be a clever hypothesis, but it is deeply unconvincing.

An anonymous letter to *The Times* in 1909 floated the idea that the end of Minoan culture in about 1450 (pretty securely dated by archaeology) lay behind the story of Atlantis, and in the late 1930s a Greek archaeologist called Spyridon Marinatos saw similarities between Minoan culture and Plato's Atlantis. In fact the Minoan 'palace' at Knossos bears no conceivable resemblance to Atlantis, and although the bull is highly prominent in Minoan art, and the Minoans certainly enjoyed baths, there were definitely no elephants on Crete. In the late 1960s Marinatos excavated the site of Akrotiri on the island of Santorini (Thera), with stunning results, unearthing a significant settlement with a culture very much like that of Minoan Crete, that had been buried in an enormous volcanic event.

Crete is only 100 kilometres to the south of Santorini. The eruption itself could well have been more ferocious than the devastating Krakatoa eruption of 1883, which could be heard 3,000 kilometres away and which claimed 35,000 lives in the tsunamis. Santorini's caldera is four times wider than Krakatoa's, and a lot deeper, so it was a reasonable surmise that earthquakes, air-borne debris, fire, tsunamis and months of darkness might have terminated an entire civilization, and that news of this could have reached Egypt and been documented. Marinatos developed an influential theory that the eruption was both the cause of the demise of the Minoan civilization, and also the historical event behind the Atlantis myth. The eventual occupation of Crete by Mycenaean Greeks in around 1450 might have supplied the idea of the Athenian defeat of the Atlanteans.

At first Marinatos made the eruption coeval with the date for the first wave of destructions on Crete in 1450, but studies of pottery made him revise this theory in favour of making the eruption of Santorini and the destruction on Crete two discrete events separated by one or two generations. However, a revised date of 1500 for the eruption was still close enough for cause and effect to apply, and by the 1970s his theory was widely accepted.

One obvious problem with linking the demise of Minoan Crete and the Santorini eruption with Atlantis is that Plato's island is not destroyed by a volcano: it sinks beneath the sea along with Athens. So if an ancient report of Santorini and Crete had filtered down to him, it is strange that he fails to mention such an important part of it. It is also curious that Herodotos, who went to the temple at Saïs in Egypt between Solon's visit and Plato's telling of the story, has absolutely nothing to say about Cretan catastrophes or Atlantean inundations. Nor does any other Greek writer before Plato. The scholarly Apollonios Rhodios, librarian at Alexandria in Egypt after Plato's death, tells us about the creation of Santorini by the Argonaut Euphemos, but nothing about its destruction.[22]

The Santorini eruption certainly impacted upon the eastern Mediterranean: air-fall debris from the volcano is found in an arc reaching from Turkey to Kos, Rhodes, eastern Crete and Egypt. This caused damage to buildings in places, and also disruption to farming, but the ash falls on Crete only amount to around 1 to 5 centimetres, and the tsunamis that hit the northern coast seem to have been no higher than 8 metres, so it is unlikely that agriculture was devastated by the ash or that ports and fleets were wiped out by the waves. The 'palace' of Knossos is too far inland to have been inundated, and that at Phaistos is on the opposite side of the island.

A major challenge to the linkage with Atlantis came in the 1980s from carbon-14 dating techniques. These suggested that the Santorini eruption could have taken place around 1628–1606, which moves us too far away from the end of Minoan civilization to link it to the volcano. This dating seems to be backed up by dendrochronology, which shows that massive volcanic events can create 'frost events' on the earth's surface which manifest themselves in narrow annual growth rings in trees. Bristle-cone pines in the United States show precisely such characteristics between 1628 and 1626, but no evidence of frost damage from the 1500s or 1400s; and Irish bog oaks also exhibit narrow rings in 1628, as do trees that grew in England and Germany. Santorini could be the cause of this. Interestingly dendrochronological data from Asia Minor records a highly unusual 'growth event' which matches the 1628 data from America and Europe, and it has been mooted that this must be due to unusually cool and wet weather, again caused by the eruption of Santorini.

A volcanic eruption can also emit vast amounts of sulphur dioxide into the atmosphere, which eventually falls back to earth as acid rain and becomes incorporated into the annual layers of ice in the polar icecaps. Danish scientists working in Greenland have suggested that the Santorini eruption took place in around 1645, with an error margin of about 20 years (i.e. 1665 to 1625), which would dovetail with the dendrochronological evidence for a major volcanic eruption affecting the global climate around 1628.

This research has led to the conclusion that the Bronze Age eruption happened in the seventeenth century, and that it did not cause the demise of Minoan Crete. The theory is not unchallenged, since recent finds of pumice at Tell el Dab'a in Egypt in contexts dating to around 1540 have been shown to be from Santorini, but the final analysis does not change: we cannot link the destruction of Minoan Crete with the destruction of Atlantis.

Eberhard Zangger, in a work entitled *The Flood From Heaven* (1984), wishes to locate the Atlantis myth in the Late Bronze Age, but not at Santorini. His hypothesis is that the Atlantis story originates at Troy. His theory is built on two main premises:

1. The story of the Trojan War was altered in transmission over the generations by the Egyptian priests, who told it to Solon as the story of Atlantis. He simply failed to recognize the tale for what it was;

2. The archaeology of Troy meshes beautifully with Plato's description of the Atlantean capital. The citadel of Troy is not large, but he argues that it was just part of a much bigger city that featured impressive engineering projects in the shape of artificial harbours and canals.

Recent work at Troy has certainly raised the possibility that Troy could have been a significant power in the eastern Mediterranean during the Late Bronze Age, but it takes a significant leap of faith to become a disciple of the Zangger theory: the situation of Troy on a plain near the sea, and the existence of hot and cold springs in Homer's description may resonate slightly, as may the idea of a conflict between Greece and a foreign enemy (although in Homer the Greeks are the invaders), but the mound of Hisarlik bears little resemblance to Plato's Atlantic island, and although earthquake damage may be detected at certain levels, none of the cities was swallowed beneath the waves. It is a long way from 'an outpost vassal state of the Hittite empire'[23] to the east of Greece, to a decadent imperial power to the west.

In the 1920s a journalist by the name of Lewis Spence suggested that a trace of Atlantis still persists fragmentally in the Antillean group, or West Indian Islands. With cavalier abandon he equates the Aztec Atzlan with Atlantis (overlooking some staggering chronological discrepancies – the Aztecs thought they had left Atzlan in 1168 CE); equates the nymph Kleito with the Mexican Coatlicue, and Atlas with the first part of the name of Uitzilopotchi; and he introduces a hideously distorted comparatist methodology in support of his theory, as he shoehorns Plato's Atlantis into American mythology:

> The Peruvian god arrived, as Poseidon had done, in a hilly country. But the people reviled him, and he sent a great flood upon them, so that their village was destroyed. [*In Plato Poseidon came to an island; the Atlanteans worshipped him, and did not revile him; there was no flood in that sense.*]
>
> He met a beautiful maiden, Choque Suso, who was weeping bitterly. [*Spence equates her with the Kleito of Plato, although*

he argues for Kleito's similarity with Coatlicue elsewhere, on the grounds that the two names sound alike.]

He enquired the cause of her grief, and she informed him that the maize crop was dying for lack of water. He assured her that he would revive the maize if she would bestow her affections on him. [*None of these motifs occur in Plato.*]

When she consented to his suit he irrigated the land by canals. Eventually he turned his wife into a statue. [*Poseidon did not turn Kleito into a statue.*][24]

This theorizing appeals to Spence's imagination, but when he triumphantly concludes, 'Is it possible for [these] circumstances to be more positively paralleled?' the only possible response is, 'Yes'. This is a very typical piece of what might be called 'Atlantological' speculation. All such theories have a strong vested interest: the speculation is only valid if it can come up with something to justify itself, usually in the form of 'new evidence' for 'historical truth' underlying the myth. The 'Atlantis industry' is alive and kicking, and these days Atlantis can be found anywhere from America to Santorini, Crete, Cyprus, Sweden, England, the Sahara Desert, the Azores, the Canary Islands, the North Pole, Antarctica, Bolivia, the Bahamas, Utah, Pennsylvania and Alabama, not to mention outer space.

'Many things are conceivable without being demonstrable.'[25] Such is the beauty of conspiracy theories, but all the various hypotheses mentioned above suffer from the fact that key (inconvenient) elements in Plato have to be disregarded – date, location, whatever. The problem is this:

You cannot change all the details of Plato's story and still claim to have Plato's story. That is like saying the legendary King Arthur is 'really' Queen Cleopatra. All you have to do is to change Cleopatra's sex, nationality, period, temperament, moral character, and other details and the resemblance becomes obvious.[26]

Too many difficulties get in the way of accepting Plato's story at face value: the chronology of putting a developed civilization in the Mesolithic period; the geological impossibility of there being a sunken continent beneath the Atlantic; the total absence of any finds from the ancient world carrying the name Atlantis; and the fact that there is no mention anywhere of Atlantis in any ancient text prior to Plato's – not even in Herodotos or Solon. Put bluntly, there is no source of the Atlantis story other than Plato. Atlantis is just a tale from Egypt, 'the most brilliant and enduring of all hoaxes'.[27]

What the Atlantean theorizing singularly fails to do is to consider why Plato told the tale.[28] A number of ancient writers including Theophrastos, a student of Aristotle's, did regard Atlantis as history,[29] but Aristotle himself, Plato's greatest pupil, did not. He regarded it as a literary creation for philosophical ends, and we have a quotation in Strabo's *Geography* which shows that he saw it as being like the fictional devices in Homer: as far as Aristotle was concerned, says Strabo: 'He who created it also destroyed it.' Atlantis only existed in Plato's imagination.

SECTION 3

SOME APPROACHES TO GREEK MYTHOLOGY

Ever since antiquity people have tried to interpret the myths; questions of where they come from and what they mean is part of their ongoing fascination, and there is a modern predilection for trying to get to the 'truth' behind the myths, or to prove that they are historically factual. Book titles like *The Ulysses Voyage: Sea Search for the Odyssey*; *In Search of the Trojan War*; *Odysseus Unbound: The Search for Homer's Ithaca*, and even *Odyssey of the Gods, an Alien History of Ancient Greece*, generally accompanied by television programmes, make for entertaining and often thought-provoking reading and watching, but Greek myths do not tell history (even if they pretend to), do not merely entertain (because they have too much social significance), are not scriptures in any biblical sense (although they are closely connected with religion), and do not provide explicit guidance pertaining to beliefs and lifestyles. This raises a big issue: if they are not history, entertainment, or religious dogma, what are they for? A large number of systems of interpretation have been proposed over the centuries, of which a selection (by no means comprehensive) is outlined here, but it should be stressed that a one-size-fits-all solution does not seem a realistic goal; in fact, one major scholar goes as far as to say that all universal theories of myth are automatically wrong.[1]

There are those who see myths simply as damaged history, real events that have become distorted with the passage of time. This approach motivated Schliemann famously to boast that he had 'gazed upon the face of Agamemnon' when he unearthed a gold death mask at Mycenae, and to dress his wife in the 'Jewels of Helen' which he found at Troy. It also motivates modern TV explorers to go seeking Odysseus' 'real' itinerary and the whereabouts of Atlantis. It is an approach at least as old as Euhemeros, who, around 300, wrote an interesting text called the *Hiera Anagraphe*, 'the Sacred Record', which described a column on which the achievements of ancient kings were recorded. These kings, Ouranos, Kronos, Zeus and so on, came to be thought of as gods as time occluded people's memories. So, essentially, Euhemerism, as the method is called, reduces all mythology to history: Zeus is just another man.

Another view that had credence among ancient thinkers was that myth was allegorical (Greek *allegoria*, 'saying something else'): it was disguised philosophy or theology, whose secrets could be unlocked by deciphering its allegories. This also allowed scholars to defend Homer from unfair criticism in the way that Pseudo-Herakleitos does in his *Homeric Problems*, written in the first century CE:

> Homer has taken Odysseus as a sort of tool for every virtue and used it to philosophise, since he detested the vices that feed on human life. Take for instance pleasure, the country of the Lotus-Eaters, which cultivates a strange enjoyment: Odysseus exercises his restraint and sails past. Or the savage spirit in each of us: he incapacitated it with the branding instrument of his verbal advice. This is called the 'Cyclops', that which 'steals away' our rationality. Wisdom goes down as far as Hades so that no part even of the world below should be uninvestigated. Who, again, listens to the Sirens, if he has learnt the breadth of experience contained in the accounts of every age? And 'Kharybdis' is a good name for lavish wastefulness, insatiable in its desire for drink. Skylla is his allegory for the shamelessness that comes in

many shapes: hence she is not without good reason equipped with the dogs' heads that comprise rapacity, outrage, and greed. And the cattle of the sun are restraint of the stomach (sic) – he counts not even starvation as a compulsion to wrongdoing.[2]

The allegorical approach, though with a different slant, was picked up by F. Max Müller (1823–1900), who wrote a major essay entitled 'Comparative Mythology'. Rather typically for a nineteenth-century thinker, Müller was unsettled by the similarity between the mythologies of 'savages' and those of the early Europeans, particularly the Greeks:

> But the more we admire the native genius of Hellas, the more we feel surprised at the crudities and absurdities of what is handed down to us as their religion [. . .] they believed in many gods, and ascribed to all of them, and more particularly to [Zeus], almost every vice and weakness that disgraces human nature. Their poets [. . .] would relate of their gods what would make the most savage of the Red Indians creep and shudder.[3]

In seeking to show that the Greeks (and hence their nineteenth-century European ancestors) were not savages, and that studying mythology was not the same as being obsessed with disgusting, perverted nonsense, Müller formulated the theory that primitive man created myths in order to express the religious awe inspired by natural phenomena like the dawn and the sun. Müller's 'primitives' attributed personalized qualities to the sun, but as language developed people lost their understanding of the original myths so that their meaning could only be retrieved by pinpointing the original meanings of the myths and of the names of their characters. For instance, he explains Endymion as coming from the Greek word *dyo*, 'I dive into', which can be used of the sun going down. He then argues that the word *endyo* was used in the same sense, and that gave rise to the noun *endyma*, 'the sunset'. And so we get Endymion, 'the setting sun'. Then, he says, the original meaning of Endymion was forgotten, and tales once told of the setting sun were now told of a name, which had to be changed into a god, and rather than saying, 'It is night,' people said, 'Selene [the Moon] kisses Endymion [the sunset] into sleep.'

This approach, often described as 'Solar Mythology', was incredibly popular in Victorian England. Müller was a huge celebrity, even though his approach is no longer regarded as valid.

Müller's theorizing was succeeded by the method known as Comparative Mythology, epitomized by the work of J.G. Frazer (1854–1941). Frazer's great work was the staggeringly erudite *The Golden Bough*, and his great fascination was with comparing the myths of different peoples and finding interesting correlations between them. His approach works rather like this:

1. Find a weird myth. If it seems odd, self-contradictory or irrational, it is probably because it goes back to an earlier stage of cultural development;
2. Track down as many examples of this myth from as many different cultures as possible;
3. Find a general explanation for it which accounts for all the examples;
4. Reapply the general explanation to the original problem.

For instance, Frazer collects thirty-six tales dating from the twelfth to the nineteenth centuries CE, which all have strong similarities to Odysseus's encounter with Polyphemos in the *Odyssey*. These range from a story told by a blind fiddler from Islay to episodes from *The Arabian Nights* and the Mongolian tale of Depé Ghoz ('Eye-Head'). This invites analysis of the Polyphemos episode on the comparatist model, along with a search for an 'Urmyth' – the story underlying all the later variants:

> The resemblance between the various versions of the tale [is so close] that they must all apparently be derived from a common original, whether that original was the narrative in the Odyssey, or, more probably, a still older folktale which Homer incorporated in his epic.[4]

Frazer is essentially making two key assumptions:

1. All these stories are the same; they are versions or variants of one another;
2. There is an original version of the myth, and later tellings are distorted versions of it.

The comparatist's assignment is to reassemble the original tale using the surviving corrupted versions. Just as comparative linguistics can reconstruct the Indo-European word for 'brother' as *bhrater* by analysing its variants *brodthor* (Old English), *bruodar* (Old High German), *frater* (Latin), *bhratr* (Sanskrit), and so on, so the comparative mythologist attempts to reconstruct myths. So, as far as the Cyclops tale goes, the most common version of the tales that Frazer analyses goes like this:

1. The hero and companions are imprisoned in the cave of a one-eyed giant shepherd;
2. Some or all of the companions are cooked by the giant on a metal spit over a fire;

3. The giant falls asleep after his meal;
4. The hero takes the spit, heats it in the fire and drives it into the giant's eye;
5. In the morning the giant opens the cave to let out the sheep and the hero escapes by walking out on all fours under a sheepskin, or by clinging to the underside of a sheep;
6. The hero is located when he puts on a magic ring which shouts 'Here I am';
7. The hero only escapes by cutting off his finger.[5]

In Homer, Odysseus' decision to stay in Polyphemos' cave to see if he can get gifts from him seems odd, given that the Cyclops only owns goats and cheese, but comparison with Frazer's other tales shows that some heroes are caught while raiding the giant's home, or while looking for a handout. The comparatist believes that in the Urmyth the hero went to the giant's cave looking for food and shelter but was caught there when the giant came home. However, the problem with this approach is that it ignores aspects of the tale that are unique to the *Odyssey*, like Odysseus' obsession with glory, the theme of *xenia* (hospitality), and Polyphemos' disrespect for the gods. It also misses some important dissimilarities:

1. Polyphemos eats the men raw – he doesn't cook them;
2. Odysseus puts the giant to sleep by getting him drunk;
3. The stake used to blind the Cyclops is wooden, not metal;
4. Odysseus tricks the giant by calling himself 'Nobody';
5. Odysseus is not located by a magic ring – he does the shouting himself;
6. Odysseus doesn't cut off his own finger.

These changes are essential, particularly the eating of raw human flesh, which emphasizes Polyphemos' total barbarity,

Odysseus' *metis*, which gives him the ability to emerge victorious, and the motif of identity and revelation, which is fundamental to the entire story of the *Odyssey*.

The fact that the ring motif occurs in the majority of variants but not in the *Odyssey* leads Frazer to argue that (a) the ring motif was part of the Urmyth, and (b) therefore the Cyclops episode is a variant of a much older tale. The problem with this, though, is that there is no way of knowing whether the ring is a later addition to the hypothetical original tale. It could be that the comparatist is interpreting tales as the same, when in fact they are different, albeit superficially similar. The approach is interesting, but this search for the origins of myths is almost as perilous as Odysseus' journey home.

Frazer's work was developed by Jane Harrison, most especially in a work entitled *Themis* (1912). She was particularly interested in the links between myth and ritual, and argued that it would be helpful if the use of the word 'myth' were limited to stories that dealt with rites. She developed the idea that all myths were, or had once been, the words (*legomena*, 'things spoken') that relate to the ritual (*dromena*, 'things performed'): in other words, myth was a representation of the same concerns as the ritual. This type of approach filters through into the theories of other members of the so-called 'Cambridge School', with, for instance, F.M. Cornford's theory that Greek comedy originated in a New Year ritual, and Gilbert Murray's musings on the ritual origins and structure of Greek tragedy. Interesting pieces of the mythological jigsaw were put into place, but no sooner had they been formulated than the scholarship moved on.

In the 1920s the comparative method resurfaced in the work of Georges Dumézil, although he gave it a new slant.

Dumézil explored the structure of the myths, and developed a thesis that Indo-European society had been divided into three hierarchical ideological areas, or 'functions':

1. The priest/ruler;
2. The warrior;
3. The 'productive' (fertility and farmers belong here).

He suggested that Indo-European mythologies express these divisions of society, and so, for instance, in the Judgement of Paris, the Trojan prince has to choose between the three 'functions' of ruler (Hera, Queen of the Gods), warrior (Athene, warrior goddess) and productive (Aphrodite, love goddess). It also explains the fall of Troy, because Paris upsets the hierarchy by choosing Aphrodite and so putting the productive to the top.

Sigmund Freud (1856–1939) is perhaps best known for the 'Oedipus complex', but his ideas have had much wider ramifications for the study of myth. In *The Interpretation of Dreams* (1900), he asserted that the Oedipus complex stems from the child's repression of erotic feelings for the parent of the opposite sex, alongside the desire to suppress the parent of the same sex. This makes the myth of Oidipous, who kills his father and marries his mother, highly relevant.[6] *The Interpretation of Dreams* also suggests that folk-tales, myths, sagas, jokes, etc. are related to dreams in form and content.

Freud tells us that there are two parts of the mind, the conscious and the unconscious, whose desires are often opposed, and as unconscious desires clash with conscious ones, dreams become the disguised fulfilment of suppressed or repressed wishes. And myths, he says, are similar and important, because they permit unconscious, usually repressed, ideas to be expressed in a conventional and socially admissible form. For Freud, dreams exist on two levels. They have 'manifest content' (the dream as you remember it), and the 'latent content' (the ideas that go together to create the manifest content). The process of turning latent content into manifest content is called the 'dreamwork', which operates a bit like someone translating one language into another. The images produced by the dreamwork are called symbols, and may be private (only the dreamer can account for them) or universal (a total mystery to the dreamer, but obvious to the psychoanalyst).

Allied to these ideas is Freud's theory that sexuality exists from infancy, and that boys mature in four stages:

1. Autoeroticism: the infant is governed by the 'pleasure prin-ciple'; finds pleasure in its his own body; knows no repression; and is dominated by the part of the mind called the *id*, which seeks the immediate gratification of his desires.
2. Oedipal stage: between the ages of three and seven the child selects his mother as an erotic object; he wants her exclusively to himself, and this creates conflict with his father, and a sense that he is threatened by the father, which brings a fear of castration; but because the child loves his father and is afraid for him because of his own hostility, he feels fear and guilt.
3. Latency: because of these feelings, the child now suppresses his sexuality altogether through the formation of the *super-ego*, which keeps the impulses of the *id* under control.
4. Maturity: the child reaches puberty; detaches himself from his mother; reconciles himself with his father; and tries to find an erotic object resembling, but not the same as, his mother.

If societies are like individuals (a big 'if'), then psychoanalysis can be used to explain myths, which are 'the distorted vestiges of the wish fantasies of whole nations – the age-long dreams of young humanity'.[7] For Freud the content of myths is symbolic but not overly distorted by the dreamwork, so he finds it quite easy to apply dream-analysis and unravel the latent thoughts behind them. Using folk-tales, myths, jokes and the like, Freud composed a list of universal 'Freudian' symbols. (See the table on p. 457.)

Given that Greek myths are full of the motifs in the left-hand column, it is not surprising that they lend themselves to Freudian analysis so readily. A good example for Freud was the tale of Medousa[8]:

- cutting off her head = castration;
- the terror she inspired = terror of castration.

This is then linked to the moment when a boy, who used not to believe in the threat, sees female genitals surrounded by pubic hair, in principle the mother's. The analysis continues:

- the snaky hair of Medousa serves to mitigate the horror, because the phallic snakes replace the penis;
- Freud's technical rule called 'compensation' is applied here, because a multiplicity of penis symbols means castration;
- the sight of the Medousa's head turns the viewer into stone, which is the same emotional reaction to the castration complex;
- being turned to stone means erection: this is comforting, because the viewer still has a penis, and confirms it by getting an erection;

Symbol	Meaning
Kings and queens	Father and mother
Little animals	Children
Enclosed spaces (houses, towns, citadels, castles and fortresses)	Female body
Gates, doors, windows, and other openings. Ovens, hearths, vessels, containers. Earth, landscapes, horseshoes, diamond-shaped objects, linen	Female genitals
Anything longer than it is wide (tools and implements, ploughs, fire, heads, feet, hands, fingers, tongues, trees, snakes, birds, swords, knives); the number 3; eyes	Male genitals
Falling into, or coming out of water	Birth
A journey	Death
Clothes	Nakedness (here he applies the logic of inversion)
Climbing stairs or ladders; steep places; flying; riding horses	Sexual intercourse
Wild animals and monsters	Evil impulses or passions
Playing games, or musical instruments, sliding, gliding, or pulling off a branch	Masturbation
The knocking out of a tooth	Castration as an imagined punishment for masturbation

- Athena, a virgin goddess, carries Medousa's head, this 'symbol of horror' on her clothes, displaying the 'fearful genitals' of the mother to ward off sexual advances;
- this depiction of woman threatening man with his own castration is only to be expected of the 'thoroughly homosexual' Greeks . . .[9]

Freud's idea that there is a concealed or latent meaning behind the apparent or manifest content of a myth was highly influential. Most theories now take it for granted that myth has hidden meanings which are picked up by the societies in which the myths are told, though this is not necessarily a conscious process – indeed, it is usually not.

Carl Jung (1875–1961) was a student of Freud's who seceded in 1912 and developed the idea of the 'collective unconscious'. As far as he was concerned, fundamentally similar symbols recur in myths and dreams. He calls them 'archetypes', traditional expressions of collective dreams, developed over millennia, which we all inherit collectively, just as we all collectively inherit the shape of our bodies. Myths come out of a great store of archetypes, and so become expressions of the human spirit. Jung proposed an entire series of archetypal images (divine child, wise old man, mother and daughter, etc.) that come out of the preconscious psyche and find expression in myth. However, he says, when the collective psyche becomes conscious, it needs to be repressed in order for personality to develop, and that victory is symbolized by myths telling of successful quests, winning treasures and such like. In fact, Jung believed that no expressions of the collective unconscious were more important than those found in the familiar myths.

Jung's work demands a leap of faith to accept, but it does illustrate how fundamental and deep-seated the images of myth can be.

Another important work for the study of myths was Vladimir Propp's *Morfologiya Skazki* (*Morphology of the Folktale*), published in Russian in 1928. This analyses the structure underlying a particular kind of Russian folk-tale known as the 'wondertale'. He noticed that although the characters in these tales altered, the plots did not, so he analysed the wondertales on the basis of the characters' actions, which he designated 'functions'. He discovered lots of examples where the characters and actions were different, but the functions were the same: a tsar gives an eagle to a hero, and the eagle takes the hero to another kingdom; an old man gives Sucenko a horse, which takes Sucenko to another kingdom; a princess gives Ivan a ring, and then young men appear from the ring and take Ivan to another kingdom. These incidents are all 'functionally' the same: someone gives the hero something and it takes him to another place. The important thing here is not the characters or the actions *per se*, but the actions in the context of their relation to the tale's overall structure.

Propp analysed the functions of a hundred wondertales and found two remarkable things (see table overleaf):

1. The total number of functions is exactly thirty-one (although they don't appear in every story);
2. The functions always occur in exactly the same sequence.

It is interesting that Propp also claimed that the myths of Perseus, Theseus and the Argonauts were based on this system, and it is possible to construct an analysis on that basis, but only by a rather liberal interpretation of the rules and a certain amount of goodwill towards the theory.

The French scholar Claude Lévi-Strauss (b. 1908) is

Number	Function
1.	One of the members of a family absents himself from home
2.	An interdiction is addressed to the hero
3.	The interdiction is violated
4.	The villain makes an attempt at reconnaissance
5.	The villain receives information about his victim
6.	The villain attempts to deceive his victim in order to take possession of him or of his belongings
7.	The victim submits to deception and thereby unwittingly helps his enemy
8.	The villain causes harm or injury to a member of a family
8a.	One member of a family either lacks something or desires to have something
9.	Misfortune or lack is made known; the hero is approached with a request or command; he is allowed to go or he is despatched
10.	The seeker agrees to or decides upon counteraction
11.	The hero leaves home
12.	The hero is tested, interrogated, attacked, etc., which prepares the way for his receiving either a magical agent or helper
13.	The hero reacts to the actions of the future donor
14.	The hero acquires the use of a magical agent
15.	The hero is transferred, delivered, or led to the whereabouts of an object of search
16.	The hero and the villain are joined in direct combat
17.	The hero is branded
18.	The villain is defeated
19.	The initial misfortune or lack is liquidated
20.	The hero returns
21.	The hero is pursued
22.	Rescue of the hero from pursuit
23.	The hero, unrecognized, arrives home or in another country
24.	A false hero presents unfounded claims
25.	A difficult task is proposed to the hero
26.	The task is resolved
27.	The hero is recognized
28.	The false hero or villain is exposed
29.	The hero is given a new appearance
30.	The villain is punished
31.	The hero is married and takes the throne

strongly associated with an approach that has been deeply influential in the study of myth. In 1955 he published an essay entitled 'The Structural Study of Myth',[10] and 'structuralism' became the centre of frenzied academic activity in the 1960s and 1970s. It is, however, extremely hard to pin down precisely what the term means when it is applied to the analysis of Greek myths. Lévi-Strauss regarded myth as a mode of communication analogous to language or music: in language and music it is not the sounds that matter, but how they relate to one another, how they are structured. And so with myth. His methodology was to collect all possible versions of a myth, no matter where, when or by whom they were told, and then break them down into their constituent motifs ('mythemes', he called them). These mythemes all relate to one another, and the structure of that relationship suggests issues: the challenge for the structuralist is to discover what the issues are. So, for instance, an analysis of the myths of Kadmos, Oidipous and the Seven Against Thebes might look like that shown in the table on p. 462.

The myth can be read diachronically (in the logical sequence of events) from top to bottom on the table. That is how it is *told* (rather like following the melody of a piece of music). Or it can be read synchronically from right to left, column by column. That is how it is *understood* (like following the harmony of a piece of music). What the structuralist needs to do is to discover what the issues are (the bold headings on the table), and then how they relate to each other. The problem here is ascertaining what the third and fourth columns have to do with each other. Lévi-Strauss suggests that the monster-slaying is related to the 'denial of the autochthonous (earth-born nature) origin of man' (the dragon is earth-born and has to be killed so that the Spartoi can be born; the Sphinx is a

The over-rating of blood relationships	The under-rating of blood relationships	Monsters being slain, or 'denial of the autochthonous origin of man'	Difficulties in walking straight and standing upright, or 'the persistence of the auto-chthonous origin of man'
Kadmos seeks his sister Europa, who has been ravished by Zeus			
		Kadmos kills the dragon	
	The Spartoi kill each other		
			Labdakos (Laios' father) = 'the Limper'? Laios (Oidipous' father) = 'Left-sided'?
	Oidipous kills his father, Laios		
		Oidipous kills the Sphinx	
			Oidipous = 'Swollen-foot'?
Oidipous marries his mother Iokaste			
	Eteokles kills his brother Polyneikes		
Antigone defies Kreon's edict and buries her brother Polyneikes			

monster unwilling to let men live), and that the common feature of column four is 'the persistence of the autochthonous origin of man' (earth-born men are clumsy). Therefore column three is to column four as column one is to column two, and Lévi-Strauss can conclude: 'the inability to connect two kinds of relationships is overcome (or rather replaced) by the assertion that contradictory relationships are identical inasmuch as they are both self-contradictory in a similar way'.[11]

For Lévi-Strauss the basic structure of the mind is binary; it constantly deals with pairs of opposites, and what myths do is mediate between those opposites: raw/cooked; life/death; hunter/hunted; nature/culture; and so on. So in his analysis myths operate by binary opposition, antithesis, or the presentation of opposite poles, but this ultimately leads to some kind of resolution. It is striking that in his analysis Oidipous' incest and parricide have no meaning in themselves, but are part of a code: they have none of the associations that Freud would give them.

More modern approaches often mix structural approaches with more traditional ones. Jane Harrison had concluded that some myths are linked to local rituals, especially initiation-rituals, but the German luminary Walter Burkert has moved things on with his ideas that traditional tales cannot be interpreted unless we factor in the cultural and historical context (which Lévi-Strauss did not do); the myth satisfies the needs of both its teller and its audience, and it is useful. It is a 'traditional tale applied'. For instance, in relation to the visit of the Argonauts to Lemnos,[12] Burkert argues that the Lemnian women's massacre of their husbands corresponds to a ritual separation of the sexes in a New Year festival held on Lemnos; and the arrival of the Argonauts corresponds to the ritual arrival of a ship bringing new fire, and denotes the restoration of the state of marriage.

Again, examining the myths of Kallisto, Danae, Auge, Io, Antiope and others,[13] Burkert observes that these stories have the same structure, and their sequence of action can be boiled down to a pattern of five *motifemes* ('mythemes' to Lévi-Strauss; 'functions' to Propp).

Event	Motifeme
The girl is separated from childhood and family life	Leaving home
Kallisto joins Artemis; Auge and Io become priestesses; Danae is locked in an underground chamber; Antiope becomes a maenad	The idyll of seclusion
The girl is surprised, violated and impregnated by a god	Rape
The girl is severely punished and threatened with death	Tribulation
The mother, having given birth to a boy, is saved from death and grief as the boy is about to take over the powers to which he is destined	Rescue

He also points out that these myths concern the mothers of either city-founders or tribal ancestors:

• Kallisto is mother of Arkas, ancestor of the Arkadians;
• Danae is mother of Perseus, the founder of Mycenae;
• Auge is mother of Telephos, the founder of Pergamon;
• Io is mother of Epaphos, ancestor of the Danaoi;
• Antiope is mother of Amphion and Zethos, the founders of Thebes.

His conclusion to this is that the 'Girl's Tragedy', as he calls it, reflects initiation rituals, which are in turn determined by natural sequences of puberty, loss of virginity, pregnancy and childbirth. If, as does happen in some tribes, girls are made to leave home at their first menstruation, and only attain full adult status on the birth of a son, the correspondence to the tale structure is very strong.[14]

There is often an expectation outside academic circles that the study of a topic several thousands of years old would be either complete or at least static, but in fact academic interest in myths and their interpretation is incredibly dynamic, with interesting and illuminating work going on all over the world. The contemporary approach is often quite eclectic, as scholars combine the strong features of the interpretations mentioned above to create new angles of attack. There is also a good deal of inter-disciplinary activity, as scholars interested in mythology draw on the ideas of other subject areas. The so-called 'Rome school' makes great play of comparing data from different fields, in particular information from traditional cultures around the world, and stresses the need to set this in a historical context. The French scholars J-P. Vernant, P. Vidal-Naquet and M. Detienne have proved highly influential, and though they are often labelled 'structuralists' (which seems to irritate them) they also make use of historical data and anthropological approaches.

Other, more ideological approaches are taken too: feminist interpretations of the tales often challenge conventional assumptions and methodologies with compelling results, especially pertaining to myths centred on female characters; Marxist interpretations have their part to play, for example in analysing the myth of Herakles on the basis of slavery, wage-labour and aristocratic spin; the myths are even used to express theories of economics, as in the case of Jim Willie's article 'Modern American Economic Mythology',[15] where the Delphic Oracle is the Federal Reserve, whose spokesman is Alan Greenspan; Zeus is Robert Rubin, architect of the Strong Dollar; his wife Hera might be the Japanese central bank, which lifts him whenever he falls on his face; Akhilleus, the great warrior, is the US military ready to do battle to defend Greece, the US-centric world of commerce; the many nymphs prancing about, exploiting their sexuality, are the money-lenders, whether bank leaders or car dealers or electronics merchants with their sexual front; the satyrs chasing the nymphs are household consumers, who find themselves thoroughly spent after satisfying the loan terms; and so on. His conclusion: 'the modern American economic mythology is soon to turn into a Greek tragedy.'

The fact that the Greek myths remain at the centre of so much cutting-edge thought is an extraordinary testament to their power, as is the way that they influence those whose thought is rather more left-field. In his *Odyssey of the Gods, an Alien History of Ancient Greece,* Erich von Däniken cannot see how Talos, the bronze guardian of Crete,[16] cannot have been anything but a robot: 'where does the metal monster come from [. . .] and, where did they get the idea of the firespitting dragon? Such creatures never existed in the whole evolution of this planet. No one could have just dreamed it up.' He also thinks the Golden Fleece was some sort of flying machine. The study of Greek mythology is a very broad church.

The dangers inherent in all these approaches to mythology seem to lie in pushing them to extremes; historicism, allegory, comparative mythology, psychoanalysis, myth-ritual, structuralism and so on all have things to offer, despite their weaknesses, and between them they have shed a great deal of light on both the myths and those who interpret them. Ever since their inception Greek myths have combined entertainment with insights into 'things as they are', and there seems little sign that they are fading. Roberto Calasso pertinently wrote in his brilliant *The Marriage of Cadmus and*

Harmony: 'For centuries people have spoken of the Greek myths as of something to be rediscovered, reawoken. The truth is, it is the myths that are still out there waiting to wake us and be seen by us, like a tree waiting to greet our newly opened eyes,'[17] and the book is prefaced by a highly apt quotation from Sallustius, the fourth-century author of a manual of Neoplatonic piety:

These things never happened, but are always.[18]

He is quite right. The Greek myths may go back to time immemorial, but they have a glorious and vibrant future ahead of them.

Section 2 The Main Greek Myths
Chapter 1: From Chaos and Castration to Order

1. Hesiod, *Theogony* 121 f. The translations from Hesiod are from *Theogany: Works and Days, Elegies* by Hesied and Theognis, translated with an Introduction by Dorothea Wender, Penguin Classics, 1973. Copyright © Dorothea Wender, 1973. Reproduced by permission of Penguin Books Ltd.

2. Ibid. *Theogony* 127 ff.

3. Ibid. 207 ff.

4. Ibid. 178 ff.

5. In a different variant Apollodoros describes how Gaia, devastated that her children had been cast into Tartaros, persuaded the Titans to attack their father and gave Kronos a sickle of adamant. All of them except Okeanos took part in the attack, and Kronos cut off his father's genitals and threw them into the sea. The Erinyes were born from the drops of blood. Kronos was said to have hurled the sickle into the sea at Cape Drepanon in Akhaia (Greek *drepanon*, 'sickle').

6. Lucretius, *De Rerum Natura* 1.10ff., tr. R. Latham, *Lucretius, On the Nature of the Universe*, Penguin Classics, 1951.

7. Euripides, *Hippolytos* 557 ff., tr. P. Vellacott in *Euripides, Three Plays: Alcestis, Hippolytus, Iphigenia in Tauris*, Penguin Classics, 2nd edn, 1974. Greek spellings adapted.

8. Himeros in Greek.

9. Hesiod, *Theogony* 201 ff.

10. Traditions about the origins of the Kouretes (Curetes) vary. Most often they are the sons of Kombe and Sokos: Prymneus, Mimas, Akmon, Damneus, Okythoos, Idaios and Melisseus.

11. There is also a tale that Zeus took one of the goat's horns (the goat here is called Aix) and gave it to Amaltheia with the promise that it would be full of any type of fruit she wanted; this is the Horn of Amaltheia, or Cornucopia.

12. Plutarch, *On the Obsolescence of Oracles* 420a.

13. I.e. their battle cry.

14. Hesiod, *Theogony* 678 ff.

15. It is interesting, given the Cyclopes' inclusion among the Titans above, that they fight against them now. The same applies to the Hundred-handers.

16. Homer, *Iliad* 15.185 ff.

17. Aiskhylos, *Heliades,* fr. 73 Nauck, tr. C.M. Bowra.

18. Hesiod, *Works and Days* 3 ff.

19. In Euripides' tragedy, *Ion*, Prometheus initiates the delivery; other sources make Palaimon or Hermes split Zeus' head.

20. Phlegrai is said to have been the old name of Pallene.

21. Other accounts have Mimas killed either by Zeus with a thunderbolt or by Ares.

22. Hesiod, *Theogony* 824 ff.

23. In a variant tradition, Kadmos disguises himself as a shepherd and gets hold of the sinews by pretending he wants them for the strings of a lyre, with which to serenade the creature.

24. There could be an eastern influence here. In *Enuma Elish*, the Babylonian creation poem, Marduk the supreme god is also called Sirsir, which means 'he who heaped up a mountain over Tiamat', his serpent-like adversary. The battle between Marduk and Tiamat invites comparison with the battle between Zeus and Typhoeus in that both accounts explain the origin of the evil winds, although they do not correspond in every detail. Hesiod says that the moist, unpleasant winds were formed from Typhoeus after he was overcome by Zeus' thunderbolts (the good winds had been created by Eos long before then); in *Enuma Elish*, on the other hand, Marduk creates the winds to help him in his struggle against Tiamat (Marduk had received the four good winds from his grandfather Anu).

25. Hesiod says that Hera was Zeus' third consort, after Metis and Themis.

26. Homer, *Iliad* 14.315 ff.

27. Depending on how you read Homer, it could be inferred that Hephaistos was one of Hera's children by Zeus. Hephaistos unquestionably recognizes Hera as his mother, and he uses the epithet 'father' in relation to Zeus, but this was a common description of Zeus used by people who were not his children.

28. Plato, *Republic* 2.377e ff.

29. The table here follows the analysis given in E. Csapo, *Theories of Mythology*, Blackwell, 2005, pp. 74–5.

30. See p. 196 ff.

Chapter 2: Apollo and Artemis

1. Kallimakhos, *Hymn IV Delos*, 36 ff., tr. A.W. Mair, Loeb Classical Library, rev. edn, 1955.

2. Ibid. 114–15.

3. Ibid. 191 ff.

4. Ibid. 212 ff.

5. Ibid. 249 ff.

6. According to Ovid, it was Themis, rather than Apollo, that Deukalion consulted at Delphi about the best way to re-people the earth after the Great Flood.

7. There are many discrepancies concerning the parentage of Linos: the Muse Ourania; Psamathe, daughter of Krotopos; and Aithousa, daughter of Poseidon, are all mentioned in connection with Apollo, and elsewhere he is a son of Magnes by the Muse Klio.

8. Orpheus is also commonly said to be a son of Oiagros and Kalliope although the Muse Polymnia is also mentioned.

9. Ovid, *Metamorphoses* 10.53 ff. The translations from the *Metamorphoses* are from *Metamorphoses* by Ovid, translated by David Raeburn, Penguin Books, 2004. Translation copyright © david Raeburn, 2004. Reproduced by permission of Penguin Books Ltd.

10. See p. 264 ff. with n. 10.

11. Sometimes it is the North Wind who loves Hyakinthos.
12. *Two Gentlemen of Verona*. III. ii. 78–81.
13. Tr. D. Patterson in *Orpheus: A version of Rilke's Die Sonette an Orpheus*, Faber & Faber, 2006.

Chapter 3: The Creation of Man and Woman

1. Hesiod, *Works and Days* 174–5.
2. Hesiod, *Theogony* 565 ff.
3. Hesiod, *Works and Days* 57 f.
4. Hesiod, *Theogony* 588 ff.
5. Hesiod, *Works and Days* 94 ff.
6. Pausanias 8.1.4. The translations from Pausanias are by P. Levi, *Pausanias, Guide to Greece, Volume I: Central Greece*, and *Volume II: Southern Greece*, rev. edn, Penguin Classics, 1979.
7. Hesiod says she was a nymph, others that she was a daughter of Nykteus, or Keteus, granddaughter of Lykaon, and she is sometimes called Megisto.
8. Ovid, *Metamorphoses* 2.423–4.
9. He is said to have assumed the likeness of Artemis or Apollo; she was unwilling. The transformation of Kallisto is also ascribed to Hera (jealous) and to Artemis (indignant).
10. The accounts of his parentage vary: he can be a son of Eleusis, or a son of Ocean and Earth, and sometimes he is identified with the child Demophon.
11. Their second child was Amphiktyon, who reigned over Attica after Kranaos; the third was a daughter Protogeneia, who became the mother of Aithlios by Zeus.
12. Sometimes Xouthos was a son of Aiolos.
13. Being immortal, the gods frequently appear interspersed among the various generations of the mythical families.
14. The identification of the seabird *keyx* is actually doubtful.
15. Other traditions make him a son of Zeus.
16. Marpessa had been courted by Apollo, but he was initially

thwarted when Idas carried her off in a winged chariot he had acquired from Poseidon. Her father Euenos used to challenge Marpessa's suitors to a chariot race: if the suitor won, he would get the girl, but if not Euenos would decapitate him and nail his head to the walls of his house. Euenos failed in his pursuit of Idas, although he did slaughter his horses. He then threw himself into the River Lykormas, which became known as the Euenos after him. Having escaped the dangerous father, Idas still had to contend with Apollo, and they fought until Zeus intervened and gave Marpessa the choice between them. She was uneasy about the prospects of Apollo's commitment to her in her old age, and so opted for Idas.

17. Iasos, Iasios, Iasion, Skhoineus, or Mainalos. Her mother was Klymene.

18. Ovid, *Metamorphoses* 10.564–6.

19. Melanion or Milanion is also named as her suitor in this context.

20. Ovid, *Metamorphoses* 10.591–6.

21. Theokritos, *Idyll* 3.40—3. The translations from Theokritos are by A. Rist, *The Poems of Theokritos*, University of North Carolina Press, 1978.

22. Sophokles wrote a tragedy called *Athamas*, in which Athamas himself was led to the altar to be sacrificed, but was rescued by Herakles.

23. See p. 197.

24. Homer, *Odyssey* 11.593 ff. Translations from the *Odyssey* are from R. Lattimore, *The Odyssey of Homer*, Harper Perennial, New York, 1999.

25. Ibid. 11.239 ff.

26. Or of his son Iphikles/Iphiklos. Even within Homer's *Odyssey* there are contradictions: in Book 11 the cattle belong to Iphikles; in Book 15 they belong to Phylakos.

27. See p. 232.

28. Euripides, *Alkestis* 642 ff., tr. J. Davie, *Euripides, Medea and Other Plays*, Penguin Classics, 2003.
29. Ibid. 682 ff.
30. Ibid. 935 ff.
31. For the psychoanalytical approach to myth, see pp. 454 ff.
32. Like Gulliver in Lilliput, Jonathan Swift, *Gulliver's Travels*, 1726.
33. E. Burnouf, *The Science of Religions*, S. Sonnenschein, 1888, p. 187 f.

Chapter 4: Jason and the Argonauts

1. She is also called Alkimede, Perimede, or Amphinome.
2. Pindar, *Pythian* 4.75 ff. The translations from Pindar are by R. Lattimore, *The Odes of Pindar*, 2nd edn, University of Chicago Press, 1976.
3. The Hellenistic Age is normally said to run from the death of Alexander the Great to the death of Kleopatra VII of Egypt, i.e. 323–30.
4. Apollonios Rhodios, *Argonautika* 1.307 ff. The translations from the *Argonautika* are by R.C. Seaton, *Apollonius Rhodius, the Argonautica*, Loeb Classical Library, 1912.
5. Ibid. 1.311 ff.
6. Ibid.1.318 f.
7. Ibid. 1.321 ff.
8. Ibid. 1.334 ff.
9. Ibid. 1.341 ff.
10. Ibid. 1.343 ff.
11. This could possibly derive from Pindar, *Pythian* 4, where Jason's striking looks are also stressed.
12. Apollonios Rhodios, *Argonautika* 3.919 ff.
13. In some versions, Aphrodite makes the women incredibly smelly.
14. Apollonios Rhodios, *Argonautika* 1.609ff.
15. See p. 327 with n. 9..
16 See p. 299 ff.

17. Hypsipyle is said to have borne two sons, Euneus and Nebrophonos, to Jason.

18. Kleite means 'illustrious' in Greek.

19. Apollonios Rhodios, *Argonautika* 1.1063 ff.

20. Ibid. 1.1163 ff.

21. Ibid. 1.1190 ff.

22. The Hylas and Herakles episode is also beautifully narrated by another Hellenistic poet, Theokritos, in his *Idyll* 13.

23. Polyphemos subsequently founded a city, Kios, in Mysia and reigned as king; Herakles returned to Argos, although in Theokritos' version he made his way on foot to Kolkhis. Herodotos locates the incident at Aphetai in Thessaly, and Pherekydes says that he was left there because the *Argo* declared that she could not bear his weight.

24. Theokritos also tells the tale of the boxing match in his *Idyll* 22.

25. Apollonios says he was a son of Agenor, but others make him a son of Poseidon. His blindness came either from Zeus for foretelling the future to mankind; or from Boreas and the Argonauts because he blinded his own sons at the instigation of their stepmother; or from Poseidon, because he told the children of Phrixos how they could sail from Kolkhis to Greece.

26. Virgil, *Aeneid* 3.214 ff. The translations from Virgil are by C. Day Lewis, in *The Eclogues, Georgics and Aeneid of Virgil*, Oxford University Press, 1966.

27. Hesiod says there were two Harpies, Aello and Okypete, *Theogony*, 265–9.

28. According to the author of the Orphic *Argonautika*, the bird that the Argonauts, or rather Athena, let fly between the Clashing Rocks was a heron (*erodios*), a bird specially associated with Athena.

29. Apollonios Rhodios, *Argonautika* 3.284.

30. Ibid. 3.409 ff.

31. Ibid. 3.755 ff.
32. Ibid. 3.966 ff.
33. Ibid. 3.1069 f.
34. Ibid. 3.1204 ff.
35. In Pindar, *Pythian* 4, Jason slays the serpent himself (though Pindar does not say how).
36. The route is unique to Apollonios, since other versions have them sail down the Phasis to the great River Okeanos, and into the Mediterranean from there; or via various rivers across continental Europe, into the Baltic, and down through the Strait of Gibraltar; or simply return the same way that they had come.
37. Apollodoros gives a different variant, in which Apsyrtos had accompanied Medeia when she first went over to Jason. Early in the pursuit, as the Kolkhians were getting too close for comfort, she murdered him, dismembered the body, and threw the pieces into the sea. Gathering his son's limbs, Aietes fell behind in the pursuit, turned back, and buried the pieces of his child he had rescued. According to Sophokles, in his play *The Kolkhian Women*, Apsyrtos was murdered in the palace of Aietes, a version accepted by Euripides in his tragedy *Medeia*.
38. See p. 263 f.
39. Homer, *Odyssey* 12.67–72.
40. However, a different source gives the names as Thelxiope, or Thelxione, Molpe and Aglaophonos.
41. Sterope, daughter of Porthaon, is also mentioned as their mother, however.
42. There were better performers around, however. Pausanias related a tradition that at Hera's instigation they once vied unsuccessfully with the Muses in singing, and that the Muses plucked off the Sirens' feathers to make crowns for themselves.
43. The Wandering Rocks are sometimes said to be the Lipari Islands, two of which are still active volcanoes.
44. 'Sickle', so called either because the sickle used by Kronos to

castrate Ouranos lies buried there, or because Demeter once lived there, and taught the Titans how to reap corn.

45. Apollonios Rhodios, *Argonautika* 4.1318 ff.

46. See p. 167 ff.

47. Other authors say that he was given to Minos by Hephaistos; some say that he was a bull.

48. In other versions Talos had a single vein extending from his neck to his ankles, with a bronze nail rammed home at the end of the vein. Some sources (including vase paintings) make Medeia drive him mad with drugs, or promise to make him immortal and then pull out the nail, so that all the *ikhor* poured out. Others say that Poias shot him in the ankle.

49. 'Aetiology' is the word used for 'the assignment of causes and origins'.

50. Apollonios Rhodios, *Argonautika* 4.1773 ff.

51. The ancients believed that bull's blood was poisonous. Ovid has a different version, in which Aison did see Jason again and was magically restored to youth by Medeia.

52. Diodorus Siculus says that she stabbed herself after cursing Pelias.

53. Ovid, *Metamorphoses* 7.312 ff.

54. Euripides, *Medeia* 20 ff. The translations are by P. Vellacott in *Medea and Other Plays* by Euripides, translated with an Introduction by Philip Vellacott, Penguin Classics, 1963. Copyright © Philip Vellacott, 1963. Reproduced by permission of Penguin Books Ltd.

55. Ibid. 96 ff.

56. Ibid. 146 ff.

57. Ibid. 230 ff.

58. Ibid. 282 ff.

59. Ibid. 402 ff.

60. Ibid. 415 ff.

61. Ibid. 476 ff.

62. Ibid. 536 ff.

63. Ibid. 567 ff.

64. Aphrodite, goddess of love.
65. Euripides, *Medeia* 639 ff.
66. Ibid. 727 ff.
67. Ibid. 792 ff.
68. Ibid. 882 ff.
69. Ibid. 964 f.
70. Ibid. 1029 ff.
71. Other traditions say that in her agony Glauke threw herself into a fountain, which was later named after her.
72. According to Apuleius, Medeia burned the king's palace and the king himself in it, as well as his daughter. Yet another tradition says that she left her infant children behind as suppliants at the altar of Hera of the Height, but the Korinthians killed them anyway.
73. Pausanias relates that the Korinthians did in fact stone the boys to death. This meant that their spirits haunted Korinth and destroyed newborn babies. Having consulted an oracle the Korinthians set up a statue of Terror and made annual sacrifices to Medeia's children. He also tells of a story in which Mermeros was killed by a lioness.
74. Euripides, *Medeia* 1415 ff.
75. Hesiod, *Theogony* 992—1002.
76. See p. 459 ff.
77. Edmund Spenser, *The Faerie Queene* (1590) 2.12.41, ed. T.P. Roche jr, and C.P. O'Donnell jr, Penguin Classics, 1978.
78. N. Hawthorne, introduction to *A Wonder-Book for Girls and Boys*, Ticknor, Reed and Fields, 1852.
79. C. Kingsley, preface to *The Heroes*, Macmillan, 1856.
80. W. Morris, *The Life and Death of Jason*, Bell and Daldy, 1867, Book XVII, p. 325.

Chapter 5: Argos and the Monster-slayers

1. Hesiod, on the other hand, says that Pelasgos was a son of Gaia.
2. Argos' genealogy is greatly disputed. He also appears as: a son

of Arestor; a son of Inakhos; a son of Argos and Ismene, daughter of Asopos; or earth-born.

3. He and Ismene, the daughter of Asopos, had a son called Iasos, who is said in one tradition to have been the father of Io, although another tradition makes Io a daughter of Inakhos and Melia, and yet another a daughter of Peiren (or Peiras).

4. Ovid, *Metamorphoses* 1.608.

5. In Apollodoros' version Argos tethered her to an olive tree that was in the grove of the Mycenaeans. Zeus ordered Hermes to steal her. Hermes could not do this secretly because Hierax had revealed the scheme, so he killed Argos by throwing a stone at him.

6. Herodotos observed that Isis was represented in art, like Io, as a woman with cow's horns.

7. A.E. Housman, 'Fragment of a Greek Tragedy', 1883.

8. According to Euripides they also had Kepheus and Phineus.

9. Pausanias records that the heads were buried on the acropolis of Argos, and the headless trunks at Lerna.

10. There is also, though, a variant tradition in which Lynkeus killed Danaos and the forty-nine murderesses.

11. Other victims mentioned include his brother Deliades, Piren and Alkimenes.

12. Euripides wrote a tragedy called *Stheneboia*. In Aristophanes' comedy *The Frogs*, Aeschylus accuses Euripides of turning her into a whore.

13. This is the only reference to writing in Homer.

14. Hesiod, *Theogony* 319 ff. cf. the Beast of Revelations.

15. See below, p. 299 ff.

16. Ovid, *Metamorphoses* 4.654—60.

17. The scene of the tale was located at Joppa in the eastern Mediterranean, where traces of Andromeda's fetters and the monster's skeleton were still pointed out in the first century CE. Compare the tale of Herakles and Hesione, p. 164.

18. Alkaios, Sthenelos, Heleios, Mestor and Elektryon.

19. R. Caldwell, 'The Psychoanalytical Interpretation of Greek Myth', in L. Edmunds (ed.), *Approaches to Greek Myth*, John Hopkins University Press, 1990, points out these patterns and produces an interesting psychoanalytical interpretation as Freud might have done.

20. M.P. Nilsson, *The Mycenaean Origin of Greek Mythology*, Cambridge University Press, 1932, p. 130.

21. Pausanias 9.1.2.

22. PYLOS En 74.

23. K. Dowden, *The Uses of Greek Mythology*, Routledge, 1992, p. 62. This discussion draws very heavily on Dowden's ideas.

24. Homer, *Iliad* 2.662.

25. Strabo 14.2.6, tr. H.L. Jones, Loeb Classical Library, 1929. The quotation is from Homer, *Iliad* 2.656.

26. See p. 456 ff.

27. W. Sutcliffe, 'William Sutcliffe's favourite relationship novels' at http://books.guardian.co.uk/top10s/top10/0,395104,00. html.

Chapter 6: Herakles

1. Apollonios Rhodios, *Argonautika* 1.747–51, tr. E.V. Rieu, Penguin Classics, 2nd edn, 1971.

2. Again Hesiod tells a variant tale in which Amphitryon and Elektryon quarrelled over the cattle and Elektryon was killed in the fight.

3. The animal's lair was at Teumessos, hence it is often referred to as the Teumessian fox.

4. Ovid, *Metamorphoses* 7.774 ff.

5. The story forms the basis of a Roman comedy by Plautus called the *Amphitryo*.

6. In Hesiod, Eileithyia (in the singular) is a daughter of Zeus and Hera. Other sources make her and the Fates delay the birth of Herakles.

7. Pindar, Theokritos, Plautus and Virgil all tell the tale. Usually the boys are eight months old, but they are ten in Theokritos.

8. Pausanias gives another account, in which this lion is slain by Alkathoos.

9. Other sources say he achieved the procreative feat in either just seven nights, or even in one.

10. Xenophon, who records the incident, says the story came from the sophist Prodikos.

11. Another tradition makes Erginos survive, but in childless, lonely poverty, until the Delphic Oracle told him to fit a new tip to his ploughshare. He married a young woman and had two sons, Trophonios and Agamedes, who were brilliant builders.

12. They had between three and eight sons, whose names and numbers differ considerably from author to author.

13. There is another account in which Herakles is known as Alkaios before he gets his better-known name from Apollo.

14. Pausanias 5.10.2.

15. Hesiod says it was the offspring of Orthos, the hound of Geryon, and Ekhidna or the Khimaira. Apollodoros makes it a child of Typhoeus.

16. Kopreus, son of Pelops, had killed Iphitos and fled to Mycenae, where Eurystheus purified him.

17. See p. 286 ff.

18. Apollodoros says that others (unspecified) say that it was the bull that carried Europa to Crete for Zeus, but in most traditions Zeus takes the form of a bull to do this. For the Minotaur tale see p. 183 ff.

19. See p. 281 ff.

20. Their names are given as Podargos, Lampon, Xanthos and Deinos.

21. Apollodoros says that Eurystheus let them go, and that they went to Mount Olympos, where they were destroyed by wild beasts.

22. See p. 142.
23. Ganymedes was an especially good-looking boy who had been raped by Zeus and whose duty was to pour nectar from a golden bowl on Olympos. In a different account the compensation given to Tros was a golden vine made by Hephaistos.
24. Stesikhoros, *Geryoneis*, tr. J. March, in *The Cassell Dictionary of Classical Mythology*, Cassell, 2001, s.v. 'Geryon'.
25. The aggressors are sometimes called Ialebion (or Alebion) and Derkynos, sons of Poseidon, or Ligys, Alebion's brother.
26. Or from the Latin *vitulus*, 'a calf'.
27. There are differences of opinion over the location of the story: Apollodoros asserts that Herakles found Atlas among the Hyperboreans in the north, and Apollonios places the apples near Mount Atlas in Libya. Hesiod says they were the daughters of Nyx (Night).
28. Herodotos 2.45, tr. A. de Sélincourt, *Herodotos, the Histories*, Penguin Classics, rev. edn, 1972.
29. Hesiod, *Theogony* 770 ff.
30. Ibid. 310 ff.
31. Diodoros says that the initiation was performed by Orpheus' son Mousaios.
32. The location of Oikhalia varies from Thessaly to Euboia, Arkadia, or Messenia.
33. One year, according to Herodotos and Sophokles.
34. Pherekydes says the Kerkopes were turned into stone; Herodotos says they were captured near Thermopylai in Greece; and Ovid's version is that they were tricksters punished by Zeus, who turned them into monkeys and sent them to live on Pithecusae ('Monkey Island'), now Ischia, near the Bay of Naples. We also hear of an entire tribe of Kerkopes; Herakles killed some and took others back to Omphale.
35. See p. 164.
36. Or *Alexikakos*, 'the Averter of Evil'.

37. See p. 37 f

38. See p. 160 f.

39. Or Aktoriones after their stepfather Aktor (Augeias' brother).

40. A different version, dramatized by Euripides in his lost play *Auge*, sees Auge and Telephos put in a chest and thrown into the sea, where they end up in Mysia with Teuthras. The Hesiodic *Catalogue of Women* gives a unique account, in which Auge fell pregnant by Herakles as he was on his way to perform the Labour of the Mares of Diomedes, and was taken in by Teuthras as his daughter.

41. Telephos' silence appears to have been proverbial.

42. Sophokles, *Trakhiniai* 10 ff., tr. E.F. Watling, *Sophocles, Electra and Other Plays*, Penguin Classics, 1953.

43. Ovid, *Metamorphoses* 9.66–76.

44. Ibid. 9.101–2. On vases Nessos is sometimes killed with a sword.

45. Ibid. 9.131—3.

46. Apollodoros says that no one would take responsibility, at least until Poias, a passing shepherd, was persuaded to. According to a different and less famous version of the legend, Herakles was not burned to death on a pyre, but, tortured by the agony of the poisoned robe, which caught fire in the sun, he flung himself into a neighbouring stream to ease his pain and was drowned. The waters of the stream have been hot ever since, and are called Thermopylai, 'The Hot Gates'.

47. Ovid, *Metamorphoses* 9.232–8.

48. Strabo, however, records that Eurystheus died fighting against the Heraklids and Iolaos at Marathon.

49. Different versions say he was shot by Apollo at Delphi for not consulting the oracle, or murdered by the children of Pylades and Elektra.

50. The painter Polygnotos is said to have depicted Menelaos, King of Lakedaimon, bearing the device of a snake on his shield.

51. See p. 100 ff.
52. See chapter 10 below.

Chapter 7: Thebes and Oidipous

1. Ovid, *Metamorphoses* 2.853–7.
2. Ibid. 2.862–3.
3. Homer makes Sarpedon the offspring of Zeus and Bellerophontes' daughter Laodameia, however.
4. Sometimes he marries her in the Underworld.
5. Herodotos, *Histories* 1.5.
6. The Roman writer Varro says that Thebes was built by King Ogyges before the Great Flood, making it the oldest city in the world.
7. Ovid, *Metamorphoses* 3.32–4.
8. Some say Hephaistos gave the necklace to Kadmos, others that it was given to him by Europa, who had got it from Zeus, others that Aphrodite was the donor, others that Athena gave both the necklace and the robe.
9. Ovid, *Metamorphoses* 3.229–33.
10. In one source Dionysos was reared by Rhea.
11. According to Sophokles, Lykourgos was merely imprisoned in a cave by his subjects, where his madness gradually abated. According to Hyginus, Lykourgos got drunk and tried to rape his own mother, killed his wife and son, and then hacked off one of his own feet, thinking it was a vine, before being eaten alive by panthers.
12. Euripides, *Bakkhai* 39 ff., tr. P. Vellacott, *Euripides: The Bacchae and Other Plays*, Penguin Classics, rev. edn, 1973.
13. In some sources he kills the female snake to become a woman, and kills the male snake to change back into a man. According to Ovid he remained a woman for seven years, and recovered his male sex in the eighth.
14. Other deaths in tragedy are welcomed (Lykos in *Herakles*, the

Egyptian sailors in *Helen*), but there the victims are unknown or unsympathetic characters. The nearest parallel to this is perhaps in *Medeia*, when Medeia rejoices at the deaths of Glauke and Kreon.

15. Euripides only mentions the transformation into snakes, and says nothing about Illyria, but there is a large lacuna in the text here. According to Hyginus, the metamorphosis into serpents was inflicted by Ares, because Kadmos had killed the serpent that guarded the spring at Thebes.

16. In other traditions, their madness is inflicted by Hera.

17. Zethos eventually talked Amphion out of playing the lyre.

18. The myth forms the subject of the famous group of statuary called the Farnese bull, which is now in the National Archaeological Museum at Naples.

19. Sometimes there are one or two survivors: Apollodoros names the male Amphion and the eldest female Khloris. Another source gives the survivors as Amyklas and Meliboia, and Pausanias says that Meliboia was the original name of Khloris ('Pale Woman'), who turned pale with fear at the slaughter of her siblings.

20. In Homer she is called Epikasta. Sometimes there is a Eurykleia as the first wife before Iokaste.

21. She is sometimes called either Periboia or Medousa.

22. According to Seneca (*Oidipous* 1034 ff.), Jocasta stabbed herself. In another version Euripides makes Iokaste survive, and stab herself after her sons die.

23. Either because they had acquiesced in his exile, or because although they always sent him the shoulder of every sacrificial victim, one day they sent him the haunch instead by mistake. He was so enraged him that he prayed that they would die by each other's hands.

24. Some sources say his children were borne to him by Eurygania, daughter of Hyperphas, and in another version, Oidipous

married Astymedusa after Iokaste's death. Astymedusa then falsely accused her stepsons of rape.

25. Euripides even gives different lists in different plays: Adrastos is named in *The Phoenician Women*, but Eteokles appears in his *The Suppliant Women*. Adrastos' brother Mekisteus also appears in other sources.

26. Homer, *Iliad* 4.389–97. The survivor was Maion.

27. The names of the gates can vary, as can who attacks which.

28. Euripides, *Phoenician Women* 931 ff., tr P. Vellacott, *Euripides: Orestes and Other Plays*, Penguin Classics, 1972.

29. Ibid. 1090 ff.

30. Ibid. 1172 ff.

31. Slain either by Tydeus, Amphiaraos or Kapaneus.

32. Euripides, *Phoenician Women* 1423 f.

33. Pindar, *Nemean* 9.24–7.

34. Diodoros says that Adrastos escaped back to Argos, but according to Pausanias he died at Megara, consumed by anguish at his son's death, as he was leading the defeated army away from Thebes.

35. Sophokles, *Antigone* 441–55, tr. E.F. Watling, *Sophocles: The Theban Plays*, Penguin Classics, 1947.

36. Ibid. 1064 ff.

37. A different version is told by Hyginus, in which, when Antigone is caught performing funeral rites for Polyneikes, Kreon hands her over to Haimon for execution. Haimon pretends to kill her, but actually smuggles her away and marries her. They have a son who grows up and returns to Thebes, but Kreon recognizes him by the mark that all descendants of the Spartoi had on their bodies. Herakles tried to intercede for Haimon, but Kreon was implacable, so Haimon killed both himself and Antigone.

38. See p. 389 ff.

39. Some sources say that he killed her with his brother Amphilokhos, others that he did it on his own.

40. Apollodoros calls her Arsinoe. Euripides also made use of a tradition in which, while pursued by the Erinyes, he had two children, Amphilokhos and Tisiphone, by Manto, daughter of Teiresias. He took them to Korinth and gave them to Kreon to rear. Tisiphone, who grew up to be incredibly beautiful, was sold as a slave by Kreon's wife, who was afraid that Kreon would fall for her and marry her. By chance it was Alkmaion who bought her. Then when he went to Korinth to demand his children back, Kreon could only return Amphilokhos, but it was eventually realized that the slave that Alkmaion had bought was Tisiphone.

41. Pausanias says it was the sons of Phegeus that dedicated the necklace at Delphi.

42. There is a good survey in L. Edmunds, *Oedipus*, Routledge, 2006.

Chapter 8: From Atlas to Hektor

1. A fragment of a poem by Kallimakhos makes them the daughters of the Queen of the Amazons.

2. Other traditions make them turn into stars out of grief for their father Atlas when Zeus condemned him to hold up the sky, or say that they and their five sisters, the Hyades, were all made into stars after the death of their brother Hyas, who died from a snake bite.

3. *Homeric Hymn to Hermes* 3 f., tr. J. Cashford, *The Homeric Hymns*, Penguin Classics, 2003.

4. Ibid. 12 ff.

5. Ibid. 76 ff.

6. The precise sequence of events varies in different versions, e.g. in the *Homeric Hymn to Hermes* he invents the lyre before he steals the cattle. The *Homeric Hymn to Hermes* also adds the invention of fire and fire sticks to his achievements.

7. *Homeric Hymn to Hermes* 529 ff.

8. Pausanias 2.26.7.

9. Pindar, *Pythian* 3.8–46

10. These include Kapaneus, Lykourgos (we have no idea which Lykourgos – there are many), Hippolytos, Tyndareus, Hymenaios, Glaukos, son of Minos, Androgeos, son of Minos, and the people who died at Delphi.

11. According to Kallimakhos' *Hymn II to Apollo*, the motive for Apollo's servitude was that he was fired with love for Admetos. Apollo is also said to have served Brankhos and Laomedon.

12. Euripides, *Helen* 16 ff., tr. P. Vellacott, *Euripides, Bacchae and Other Plays*, Penguin Classics, rev. edn, 1973.

13. Nemesis had an important sanctuary there.

14. The disparity of their ages led some mythographers to say that Theseus did not carry her off himself: either Idas and Lynkeus did it, or Tyndareus handed her over to Theseus for protection from one of Hippokoon's sons.

15. Homer, *Iliad* 3.156–8.

16. Homer, *Iliad* 3.237; *Odyssey* 11.300.

17. See p. 102 f.

18. Theokritos, *Idyll* 22.182–9.

19. Ibid. 22.196 f.

20. Pindar, *Nemean* 10.83 ff.

21. Homer, *Odyssey* 5.125–8.

22. Ibid. 20.232–5.

23. Other abductors of Ganymedes are also mentioned: Minos, Tantalos and Eos (Dawn). The incident is usually located on Mount Ida in the Troad, but Crete, Euboia and Mysia occur in other traditions. The eagle, which figures conspicuously in later versions of the myth and its representation in art, was said to have become a constellation.

24. Hesiod, *Theogony* 1008–10. Aineias is Latinized to Aeneas – the great hero of the Romans.

25. Homer tells how, after Hera had deceived him about the timing

of the births of Eurystheus and Herakles, Zeus banned Ate, the goddess of delusion, from Olympos, grabbed her by the hair and flung her down to earth. The Hill of Ate was where she landed.

26. In the Roman tradition the Palladium was rescued by Aeneas after the sack of Troy and conveyed to Italy, where it was placed in the temple of Vesta at Rome.

27. These also involved Orion, Kephalos and Phaethon.

28. Homer, *Iliad* 11.1–2.

29. In some versions Tithonos himself asked for immortality.

30. *Homeric Hymn to Aphrodite* 222–38, tr. J. Cashford, *The Homeric Hymns*, Penguin Classics, 2003.

31. See p. 164.

32. Apollodoros says he married Asterope, like Hesperia a daughter of Kebren, and was metamorphosed through grief after she died.

33. Ovid, *Metamorphoses* 11.783–95.

34. Suetonius, *Tiberius* 70.

35. Spoken by the Chorus in Euripides' *Andromakhe* 296 ff.

36. Derived from *alexo*, 'I defend', and *andros*, 'a man' (in the genitive case).

37. Aeschylus, *Agamemnon* 1203 ff. The translations from *Agamemnon* are in *The Oresteia*, by Aeschylus, translated by Robert Fagles, Penguin Ancient Classics, copyright © 1966, 1967, 1975, 1977 by Robert Fagles. Used by permission of Viking Penguin, a division of Penguin Group (USA) Inc., and reproduced by permission of Penguin Books, Ltd.

38. T. Harrison, *The Trackers of Oxyrhynchus, The Delphi text, 1988*, Faber and Faber, 1990, pp. 31–3.

39. Ibid. p. 55.

40. Ibid. p. 59.

41. Ibid. p. 68.

42. C. Marlowe, *Doctor Faustus* 1328 ff.

Chapter 9: From Asopos to Akhilleus

1. See above, p. 80 f.
2. Another old name for the island of Aigina was Oinopia.
3. Pherekydes argues that Telamon was from Salamis and a son of Aktaios and Glauke, daughter of Kykhreus, King of Salamis. Telamon was certainly associated with Salamis. Diodoros recounts that he married Glauke, daughter of Kykhreus of Salamis.
4. Nereus.
5. Hesiod, *Theogony* 1003 ff.
6. Diodoros attributes the calamity to another murder, namely the assassination of Minos' son Androgeos. The Cretan king prayed to Zeus for Athens to be afflicted with drought and famine, and these soon spread all over Greece.
7. Clement of Alexandria, *Strom.* vi.3.28, p. 753, tr. J.G. Frazer.
8. Aristophanes, *The Frogs* 464 ff., tr. D. Barrett, *Aristophanes, The Wasps, the Poet and the Women, the Frogs*, Penguin Classics, 1964.
9. Pausanias records that at the Battle of Salamis in 479 a snake appeared among the Greek ships, and was identified as Kykhreus.
10. See p. 164. Some authors say it was Peleus who went with Herakles to Troy – indeed some writers (Pindar, Euripides) say one hero in one work and the other in another.
11. Pindar, *Isthmian* 6.49 ff.
12. See p. 75 f.
13. See p. 306.
14. Apollonios Rhodios, *Argonautika* 4.875 ff.
15. Apollodoros gives a rather fanciful derivation of the name Akhilleus from the Greek *a-* (the so-called 'alpha privative', meaning 'not') and *kheile* ('lips'), suggesting that he was called 'Not-lips' because he had not been breast-fed; prior to that he was apparently called Ligyron.

16. Homer, *Iliad* 11.785 ff.
17. Ibid. 18.324ff.

Chapter 10: Athens: The Early Kings

1. The mark of Poseidon's trident on the acropolis at Athens was a tourist attraction in antiquity. It and the sea-water well, 'the Sea of Erekhtheus', were incorporated in the design of the Erekhtheion on the acropolis; Pausanias says that when the south wind blew the well gave forth a sound of waves.

2. It stood in the Pandroseion, an enclosure to the west of the Erekhtheion. The olive tree was (and still is!) another tourist attraction, and seems to have survived down to the second century CE; some guides will still show it to you.

3. Kephalos is also said to have been a son of Deion or Deioneus by Diomede, or of Hermes by Kreousa, daughter of Erekhtheus.

4. He can also be the son of Hemera (the Day), or of Helios (the Sun) and Klymene (or Rhode).

5. Hesiod, *Theogony* 986 ff.

6. Ovid, *Metamorphoses* 2.47 f.

7. Another tradition makes Adonis the daughter of Kinyras and Metharme, daughter of King Pygmalion of Cyprus. Hesiod says Adonis was the son of Phoinix and Alphesiboia; Panyasis says he was a son of Thias, King of Assyria, and his daughter Smyrna; elsewhere Smyrna is a daughter of Belos.

8. Ovid, *Metamorphoses* 10.300 ff.

9. Ibid. 10.465 ff.

10. A different version of the story made Zeus delegate the decision-making to the Muse Kalliope, who opted for a 50/50 split. This enraged Aphrodite so much that she induced the Thracian women to tear Kalliope's son Orpheus limb from limb.

11. Ovid, *Metamorphoses* 10.736 ff. Greek *anemos* = wind.

12. The institution of the Panathenaia is also attributed to Theseus.

13. The fact that there are two kings called Pandion and Kekrops leads some scholars to feel that they are simply a chronological device inserted into the broken framework of tradition by a later historian.

14. Ovid, *Metamorphoses* 6.428 ff.

15. Ibid. 6.650 ff.

16. Aeschylus and Hyginus say Tereus was transformed into a hawk.

17. Ovid says Erekhtheus had four sons and four daughters.

18. These events are also ascribed to the reign of Pandion I.

19. See p. 198 f.

20. In other versions she gets these from Minos, as a reward for sleeping with him.

21. Ovid, *Metamorphoses* 7.837 ff.

22. For events there, see p. 276.

23. The tradition surrounding Eumolpos' parentage is highly complex. The *Parian Chronicle* says that he was a son of Mousaios, and that he founded the Eleusinian Mysteries. But other sources differentiate the Eumolpos who founded the Mysteries from the Eumolpos who invaded Attika and say that the mother of the Eleusinian founder was Deiope, daughter of Triptolemos. Indeed, some writers speak of as many as three different people called Eumolpos, with the one who instituted the Eleusinian Mysteries coming in the fifth generation after the first.

24. Sometimes it is the youngest daughter that is sacrificed; sometimes the two eldest (Protogoneia and Pandora) offer themselves; and sometimes the youngest (Kreousa) is spared because she is a babe in arms.

25. Pylas is also named Pylos or Pylon.

26. Some claimed that Aigeus was actually the son of Skyrios, ruler of Skyros, and was merely adopted by Pandion II.

27. Quote by Apollodoros, *Library* 3.15.6, tr. J.G. Frazer, *Apollodorus, the Library, Volume II*, Loeb Classical Library, p. 115.

28. W. Shakespeare, *Venus and Adonis*, 1183 ff.

Chapter 11: Theseus and the Minotaur

1. For the myth of Europa, see pp. 191 ff.

2. Asklepiades says that Minos' wife was Krete, daughter of Asterios.

3. There is a tradition that the bull was sent by Zeus rather than by Poseidon.

4. See p. 162.

5. Compare the tale of Pterelaos and his daughter Komaitho, p. 152.

6. See p. 271.

7. According to the *Parian Chronicle*, Theseus killed Sinis, after he had become King of Athens. He returned to the Isthmus of Korinth, killed Sinis, and celebrated the Isthmian Games.

8. Hyginus calls the animal 'the boar from Kremyon'. There was a rationalistic version which said that the sow was actually a female robber called Phaia.

9. Diodorus Siculus says he just had one bed, and modified his visitors with the hammer or the saw according to their size.

10. See p. 127 f.

11. Bakkhylides, *Dithyramb* 17.92 ff., tr. A. Miller in S.M. Trzaskoma, R. Scott Smith and S. Brunet, *Anthology of Classical Myth*, Hackett, 2004, p. 72.

12. There is another tradition in which he wears a wreath, which lights up the darkness in the Labyrinth. Ariadne wore it until she was deserted by Theseus and rescued by Dionysos, when it became the constellation Corona.

13. Catullus 64.52–59, tr. P. Whigham, *The Poems of Catullus*, Penguin Classics, 1966.

14. They are called Thoas, Staphylos, Oinopion and Peparethos.

Homer's account in the *Odyssey* is very different: Ariadne is killed by Artemis on Dia at Dionysos' instigation. Some said that Staphylos and Oinopion were her children by Theseus.

15. Ovid, *Metamorphoses* 8.203 ff.

16. According to one account, Daidalos landed at Cumae in Italy, where he dedicated his wings to Apollo.

17. So was Erikhthonios, though. See p. 267.

18. For the Kalydonian Boar hunt, see pp. 75 ff.

19. His wife is named Hippodameia or Deidameia.

20. The others were Sisyphos, Tantalos and Tityos.

21. Apollonios Rhodios, *Argonautika* 1.59 ff. After his death, Kaineus was changed back into a woman, and according to Ovid an otherwise unidentified 'rust-winged' bird rose from the pile of logs, which the seer Mopsos explained was Kaineus metamorphosed. Another tradition was that Kaineus rejected all the gods, and erected his spear in the marketplace and ordered people to worship it, like he did. This impiety incurred the wrath of Zeus, who mobilized the Centaurs to overwhelm him.

22. See p. 233.

23. See p. 170 ff.

24. Euripides, *Hippolytos* 616 ff., tr. P. Vellacott, *Euripides, Three Plays: Alcestis; Hippolytus; Iphigeneia in Tauris*, Penguin Classics, rev. edn, 1974.

25. Ibid 885 f.

26. Ibid. 1004 f.

27. Euripides, *The Suppliant Women* 339 ff.

Chapter 12: Curses and Cannibalism

1. Pindar, *Olympian* 1.47 ff.

2. Sometimes Thetis eats some of Pelops.

3. Homer, *Odyssey* 11.582 ff.

4. Hippodameia makes the sexual offer herself in some accounts.

5. Apollonios Rhodios, *Argonautika* 1.752 ff.

6. Pelops is also said to have had a bastard son called Khrysippos, who predated his marriage to Hippodameia. She became jealous of his affection for the boy, and got Atreus and Thyestes to murder him by throwing him down a well. Pelops cursed and banished them, and Hippodameia fled to the Argolid.

7. Another tradition makes Aerope marry a son of Atreus called Pleisthenes, and have Agamemnon and Menelaos by him, although after he died young Atreus married Aerope and brought the boys up.

8. A different version makes Myrtilos' father Hermes provide it, in order to cause trouble in revenge for the death of his son.

9. Latin poets often made the reversal of the sun's course a sign of disgust at Atreus' later murder and cuisine of his nephews.

10. In some versions they are called Aglaos, Kallileon (or Kallaos) and Orkhomenos; other sources name just two sons, Tantalos and Pleisthenes.

11. Hyginus, *Fabulae* 88.

Chapter 13: The Trojan War

1. See p. 252.

2. Euripides, *The Trojan Women* 932 ff., tr. P. Vellacott, *Euripides, The Bacchae and Other Plays*, Penguin Classics, rev. edn, 1973.

3. See p. 234.

4. A different source says Odysseus bribed one of Palamedes' servants to conceal the letter and the gold under his master's bed.

5. See p. 376 f.

6. See p. 254.

7. Apollodoros says that the fifteen-year-old Akhilleus was admiral of the fleet, though no other source agrees with him.

8. Homer, *Iliad* 19.388 ff.

9. The Scholiast says Dionysos made Telephos trip over the vine branch for depriving him of the honours that were his due.

10. The Telephos episode was dramatized by Euripides in a play called *Telephos*, which in its turn became a target for Aristophanes' parody. In his *Akharnians*, the comic poet ridiculed the tattered rags in which Telephos appeared to make his appeal to the Greeks in Euripides' play.

11. Iphiklos was cured of his impotence by the rust of the same knife that had caused it – see p. 84. Both remedies are classic instances of the proverbial cure by 'the hair of the dog'.

12. See p. 302.

13. Aiskhylos, *Agamemnon* 206 ff.

14. Ibid. 212 f.

15. Lucretius, *On the Nature of the Universe*, 1.96 ff., tr. R. Latham, *Lucretius: On the Nature of the Universe*, Penguin Classics, 1951.

16. Aiskhylos, *Agamemnon* 224 ff.

17. In Apollodoros' version Tenes tried to repel the Greeks as they landed by throwing stones at them, but Akhilleus hacked him down with his sword.

18. In Sophokles' tragedy *Philoktetes* the incident is located on the island of Khryse, where Philoktetes is bitten by a snake that was the guardian of the shrine of the goddess Khryse.

19. See 180.

20. Its timing varies: before the Greek army assembled at Aulis; from Tenedos; before the first battle, in which Protesilaos fell; and after the landing of the army in the Troad are all given as possibilities.

21. Other writers make his killer Aineias, Akhates, or Euphorbos. Homer just refers to 'a Dardanian man', i.e. a Trojan.

22. According to the author of the *Kypria* her name was Polydora, daughter of Meleagros. In one tradition she stabbed herself to death.

23. Hyginus, *Fabulae* 104, tr. S.M. Trzaskoma, R. Scott Smith, and S. Brunet, in *Anthology of Classical Myth: Primary Sources in Translation*, Hackett, 2004.

24. That has not prevented enthusiasts from doing so. R. Castleden's *The Attack on Troy* (Pen & Sword Military Classics, 2006) features both a 'minimal reconstruction' and a 'maximal reconstruction' of Mycenaeans v. Trojans, complete with maps of the dispositions and a battle-by-battle synopsis, which he feels presents 'a more exciting possibility' that 'the Epic Cycle version of Trojan War was closer to the historical reality'. The key words here are 'exciting' (of course) and 'possibility' (of course not).

25. Homer, *Iliad* 21.36 ff. Lykaon was subsequently ransomed and returned to Troy, but had the misfortune to encounter Akhilleus again. This time he was slain.

26. Ibid. 20.187 ff.

27. J.G. Frazer, *Apollodoros, the Library*, Loeb Classical Library, 1921, Vol. II, p. 183, n. 2.

28. Aeschylus, *Agamemnon*, 919 ff.

Chapter 14: Homer's *Iliad*

1. Homer uses three names for the Greeks: Akhaians (Achaeans, men of Akhaia), Argives (men of Argos) and Danaans (descendants of Danaos).

2. Homer, *Iliad* 1.152 ff.

3. Ibid. 1.505 ff.

4. Ibid. 6.454 ff.

5. Ibid. 9.530–625. See p. 76.

6. Ibid. 9.378 ff.

7. Scholars generally agree that Book 10 is not by Homer. It is entirely self-contained, never referred to again, has no effect on anything else in the story, narrates the entirely unheroic slaughter of sleeping men, and contains quite a lot of oddities of language.

8. Homer, *Iliad* 16.83–90.

9. Constellations; marriage; a court case; siege and ambush; ploughing; reaping; grape harvest; cattle-herding; sheep flocks; the mighty stream of Ocean.

10. Homer, *Iliad*. 19.73 ff.

11. Ibid. 19.418 ff.

12. Ibid. 20.490 ff.

13. Ibid. 22.104 ff.

14. Ibid. 22.317.

15. We are at the end of Book 22.

16. Homer, *Iliad* 24.503 ff.

17. Ibid. 24.762 ff.

18. Ibid. 6.466 ff.

19. Ibid. 18.80 ff.

20. Ibid. 3.38 ff.

21. Ibid. 16.97 ff.

22. Ibid. 12.310 ff.

23. Ibid. 9.602 ff.

24. Ibid. 1.275 ff.

25. Ibid. 6.441 ff.

26. Ibid. 18.329 ff.

27. Euripides, *Trojan Women* 1319 ff.

28. Flaxman's design of *The Apotheosis of Homer* on a Wedgwood urn.

29. Privately – first public edition 1775, posthumous.

30. Rupert Brooke, *Fragment* 2, 1915, published in *Collected Poems of Rupert Brooke with a Memoir*, Sidgwick and Jackson, 1918.

31. P. Shaw-Stewart, 'Achilles in the Trench', 1916.

32. J. Buchan, *Memory Hold-the-door*, Hodder and Stoughton, 1940.

33. G. Steiner, interviewed for Channel 4's series *Greek Fire*, Episode 7, 'War Music', Transatlantic Films, 1989.

34. *L'Iliade ou la Poème de la Force*, tr. M. McCarthy in S. Weil and R. Bespaloff, *War and the Iliad*, New York Review Books, 2005, p. 37.

35. G. Steiner, loc cit.

36. See pp. 380 ff.

37. Patroklos' father Menoitios is normally the half-brother of Akhilleus' grandfather Aiakos, but in Pseudo-Hesiod, *Catalogue of Women* 212a M–W, he is the son of Aiakos, and so the brother of Peleus. Therefore Akhilleus and Patroklos are cousins. This is a classic living example of the way mythological material is open to manipulation for reasons outside the tales themselves.

38. F. Ahl, 'Troy and Memorials of War', in M.M. Winkler (ed.), *Troy From Homer's Iliad to Hollywood Epic*, Blackwell, 2007, p. 180.

Chapter 15: The Wooden Horse and the Sack of Troy

1. Other sources make him noble, a son of Agrios and cousin of Diomedes.

2. See p. 252 f.

3. See p. 315.

4. Homer, *Odyssey* 24.61 ff.

5. Ibid. 11.487 ff.

6. The winners were Eumelos, Diomedes, Aias and Teukros respectively.

7. Sophokles, *Aias* 479 f., tr. E.F. Watling, in *Sophocles, Electra and Other Plays*, Penguin Classics, 1953.

8. See p. 251 for the birth of Aias.

9. Sophokles, *Aias* 1339 ff.

10. Ibid. 121 ff.

11. The flower also commemorates the death of Hyakinthos. See p. 56.

12. The capture of Helenos usually comes after the death of Paris.

13. See p. 241.

14. See p. 238.

15. Homer, *Odyssey* 526 ff.

16. Earlier versions of this tale, going back to the *Iliou Persis* (Sack of Troy) of Arktinos, say that only one son was strangled by the serpents, as opposed to Virgil's two.

17. Virgil, *Aeneid* 1.201 ff., tr. C. Day Lewis, *The Eclogues, Georgics and Aeneid of Virgil*, Oxford University Press, 1966.

18. Euripides makes the murder of the child a cold-blooded execution after the capture of the city.

19. Euripides, *Hekabe* 543 ff., tr. P. Vellacott, *Euripides, Medea and other Plays*, Penguin Classics, 1963.

20. W. Shakespeare, *Hamlet*, Act II, scene II, ll. 544 ff.

21. Ibid. 593 f.

22. For the images, see S. Woodford, *The Trojan War in Ancient Art*, Duckworth, 1993.

23. The inscription dates from 264/3.

24. Report of 4 August 1872 in *Troy and Its Remains*, John Murray, 1875, p. 211.

25. Precise dates vary according to which archaeologist one consults.

26. Or: [they] set out to the country of Wilusa in order to attack [it] again. Restored and translated by P.H.J. Houwink ten Cate in 'Sidelights on the Ahhiyawa Question from Hittite Vassal and Royal Correspondance', *Jahrbericht Ex Oriente Lux* 28, 1983–4, p. 40. The words in square brackets are restored.

27. Purists like to call it 'Proto-Indo-European'.

28. See pp. 450 ff.

29. See p. 235.

30. C. Wolf, *Conditions of a Narrative: Cassandra*, tr. J. van Heurk, in *Cassandra: a novel and four essays*, Farrar, Straus and Giroux, Inc., 1984, p. 262.

31. Herodotos 2.120.

32. M. Korfmann, 'Was There a Trojan War?', in M.M. Winkler (ed.), *Troy From Homer's Iliad to Hollywood Epic*, Blackwell, 2007, p. 23.

33. M.I. Finlay, J.L. Caskey, G.S. Kirk and D.L. Page, 'The Trojan War', *Journal of Hellenic Studies* 84, 1964, 1–20.

34. Iman J. Wilkens, 'The Trojan Kings of England', Lecture to the Classical Society of the University of Cambridge, 26 May 1992.

35. 'Peter Jones reviews *The Trojan War: A New History* by Barry Strauss (Hutchinson)', *Sunday Telegraph*, 25 Feb. 2007.

Chapter 16: The Returns of the Heroes

1. Sources do differ over the riddle of the pregnant sow: 'Three piglets, one of them female', or 'Ten piglets, one of them male' are also mentioned.
2. Some myth-tellers make him delay on the advice of the Trojan seer Helenos, who had foreseen the problems.
3. Homer, *Iliad* 4.505 ff.
4. *Argonautika* 1.134 ff.
5. See p. 309.
6. Euripides, *Helen* 1126 ff., tr. P. Vellacott, *Euripides: The Bacchae and Other Plays*, Penguin Classics, rev. edn, 1973.
7. Aphrodite helped out here, since Diomedes had wounded her on the Trojan battlefield.
8. Euripides, *Andromakhe* 967 ff., tr. P. Vellacott, *Euripides: Orestes and Other Plays*, Penguin Classics, 1972.
9. Ibid. 1151.
10. Pausanias 1.13.9.
11. Pindar, *Nemean* 7.40 ff.
12. See p. 302.
13. Aiskhylos, *Agamemnon* 29 ff.
14. Ibid. 60 ff.
15. Ibid. 326 ff.
16. Ibid. 351 ff.
17. Ibid. 433 ff.
18. Ibid. 600 ff.
19. Ibid. 659 ff.
20. Ibid. 772 ff.
21. Ibid. 810 ff.
22. Ibid. 912 ff.
23. Ibid. 910 ff.

24. Ibid. 946 ff.
25. Ibid. 1223 ff.
26. Ibid. 1323 ff.
27. Ibid. 1343 ff.
28. Ibid. 1403 ff.
29. Ibid. 1551 ff.
30. Ibid. 1657 ff.
31. In the *Agamemnon* Klytaimnestra had sent Orestes away. Else-where Pindar says that, after the murder of Agamemnon, the young Orestes was taken to Strophios at the foot of Mount Parnassos. Pindar does not say who did this, but Sophokles and Euripides both say it was an old family retainer. Sophokles says that Elektra gave him to the old man.
32. Pausanias records another version: the Furies were about to drive him mad and appeared to him coloured black, but he bit off one of his own fingers, after which they looked white, and he recovered his sanity.
33. See pp. 310 ff.
34. David Jones to René Hague, quoted in P. Hills, *David Jones*, exhibition catalogue, Tate Gallery, 1981, p. 109.

Chapter 17: The *Odyssey* and its Sequels

1. Aristotle, *Poetics* 17, tr. T.S. Dorsch, *Aristotle, Horace, Longinus: Classical Literary Criticism*, Penguin Classics, 1965.
2. Homer, *Odyssey* 2.174 ff.
3. Ibid. 10.469.
4. Ibid. 2.89 f.
5. Ibid. 16.245–53.
6. Ibid. 2.104 f.
7. Tales like this are often called *apologoi* stories in Greek, and 20 per cent of the *Odyssey* consists of tales told in flashback.
8. Not strictly accurate: pretty much the only city he sees is that of the Phaiakians, who seem like fairly typical Bronze Age Greeks.

9. Homer, *Odyssey* 1.1 ff.

10. Lyrics from 'Moon River', by Henry Mancini.

11. 'I cannot rest from travel; I will drink/Life to the lees'.

12. Apart perhaps from Eurylokhos, who leads the first reconnaissance party to Kirke's house in Book 10, escapes back to Odysseus and then refuses to guide him back, and the daft young Elpenor who gets drunk at the end of Book 10 and falls off Kirke's roof.

13. Homer, *Odyssey* 1.356 ff.

14. Ibid. 1.119 ff.

15. Mentor was a friend of Odysseus who looked after his household while he was away at Troy. Athene used his likeness when supporting both Telemakhos and Odysseus, hence the modern usage of 'mentor' as one who is wise and supportive.

16. Homer, *Odyssey* 4.555 ff.

17. Apollodoros says five years; Hyginus one year. Apollodoros also mentions a son Latinus; Homer mentions no such thing. In Hesiod's *Theogony* it is said that Kirke (not Kalypso), bore two sons, Agrios and Latinos, to Odysseus, but the lines could well be a later interpolation by a Roman poet to provide the Latins with some heavyweight Greek ancestry. Eustathius says that, according to Hesiod, Odysseus had two sons, Agrios and Latinus, by Kirke, and two sons, Nausithoos and Nausinoos, by Kalypso.

18. Homer, *Odyssey* 5.219 f.

19. See p. 197.

20. Homer, *Odyssey* 5.454 ff.

21. Ibid. 6.242 ff.

22. Ibid. 9.461 ff.

23. Ibid. 7.238.

24. Ibid. 8.164.

25. The motif of having to avoid tasting certain food in order to be able to return home is very widespread. The tale of Persephone eating pomegranate seeds in Hades is another example.

26. Homer, *Odyssey* 9.105—542.

27. Ibid. 9.105 ff., tr. E.V. Rieu, *Homer: The Odyssey*, Penguin Classics, 1946.

28. Ibid. 9.252 ff.

29. Ibid. 9.288 ff., tr. R. Lattimore, op. cit.

30. Ibid. 9.371 ff.

31. Ibid. 9.375 ff.

32. Ibid. 9.504 f.

33. Ibid. 9.513 ff.

34. Ibid. 9.534 f.

35. Ibid. 10.22.

36. Aia is Kolkhis, home of Aietes, father of Medeia, where Jason went to get the Golden Fleece. The influence of the *Argonautika* is strongly felt here: Strabo says that Homer invented the link between Kirke and Medeia, and invented Aiaia by analogy with Aia.

37. Apollodoros says they became wolves, swine, asses and lions.

38. The ancient botanist Theophrastos says that moly resembled *Allium nigrum*, which was found in the valley of Pheneus and on Mount Kyllene in northern Arcadia; he says it had a round root, like an onion, and a leaf like a squill, and that it was used as an antidote to spells and enchantments. But Homer's moly can only belong to the realm of the gods.

39. Some traditions mention a son, Telegonos, who is born to Kirke and Odysseus. See p. 420 and n. 17 above.

40. Homer, *Odyssey* 10.512.

41. Ibid. 11.29–30.

42. Ibid. 11.410 f. In Aiskhylos' *Agamemnon* it is Klytaimnestra who takes the lead role in the murder, with Aigisthos a rather cringing weakling.

43. See p. 58 f.

44. See p. 54.

45. See p. 298 f.

46. See p. 80 f.

47. The Sirens are already established in the mythological tradition via the Argonauts tale. Although the tradition is not mentioned by Homer, some sources say that it was predicted that Sirens would die when a ship managed to sail past them, and that out of pure vexation they now threw themselves into the sea and were drowned. This creates problems with the mythical chronology, though, since the *Argo* has already successfully done this. See p. 111 f.

48. Homer acknowledges that this hazard has already been successfully faced by the Argonauts. See p. 112.

49. Homer makes Skylla a daughter of Krataeis but says nothing about her father. Apollonios Rhodios makes her a daughter of Phorkos by Hekate, though others call her father Phorkys, not Phorkos. Hyginus says she was a daughter of Typhoeus and Ekhidna, though here her father also becomes Tyrrhenos, Triton or Trienos. According to Stesikhoros, her mother was Lamia.

50. Homer, *Odyssey* 12.89 ff.

51. Ibid. 12.237 ff.

52. *Thrinax* in Greek means 'trident', reminding us of Odysseus' great adversary Poseidon.

53. Homer, *Odyssey* 12.209 ff.

54. Ibid. 16.213 ff.

55. Ibid. 17.237 f.

56. Ibid. 17.583 f.

57. See Homer, *Odyssey* 18.1–107; Hyginus and Apollodoros both substitute wrestling for boxing.

58. Homer, *Odyssey* 18.96 ff.

59. Ibid. 18.212 f.

60. Ibid. 18.281 ff.

61. Ibid. 19.573 ff.

62. Ibid. 21.410 ff.

63. Ibid. 22.35 ff.

64. Homer, *Odyssey* 22.465 ff. An engaging modern exploration of 'What led to the hanging of the maids, and what Penelope *really*

got up to' appears in Margaret Atwood's *The Penelopiad*, Canongate, 2005. Penelope and her chorus of wronged maids get the chance to tell their side of the story, through song, dance and story-telling in a stage version by Margaret Atwood (RSC, 2007).

65. Ibid. 23.107 ff.

66. Ibid. 23.233 ff.

67. The whole Telegonos episode is unknown to Homer, where there is no mention of children to Odysseus and Kirke. Telegonos is named as a son of Odysseus and Kirke by Hesiod (the line is suspected of being spurious, however). In the *Telegony*, Telegonos was a son of Kalypso, not Kirke. According to Hyginus Odysseus had two sons by Kirke: Nausithoos and Telegonos. There is an extraordinary tradition in which Telegonos married his father's widow Penelope, and Telemakhos married his father's concubine Kirke.

68. This tradition is mentioned by the Roman author Cicero (Hermes = Mercury in Latin). One tradition makes Penelope the mother of Pan by all the suitors. When Odysseus came home and found the beastly child in the house, he promptly set off on his wanderings again.

69. In Homer Penelope liked to talk to Amphinomos more than to the other suitors because of his good sense and discretion, but he was still killed by Telemakhos. These allegations of Penelope's unfaithfulness never surface in Homer.

70. Apollodoros says Neoptolemos condemned him to exile in the hope of getting possession of Kephallenia.

71. Apollodoros, *Epitome* 7.1.

72. P. Jones, *Homer's Odyssey: A Commentary*, Bristol Classical Press, 1998, p. 80.

73. R. Brittlestone, with J. Diggle and J. Underhill, *Odysseus Unbound: the Search for Homer's Ithaka*, Cambridge, 2005.

74. T.S. Eliot, 'Ulysses, Order, and Myth', *Dial* 75.5, Nov. 1923, p. 480.

75. Recorded by Joyce's pupil Georges Borach in his journal on 1 August 1917. See R. Ellman, *James Joyce*, Oxford University Press, rev. edn 1983, pp. 429–30.

76. Tr. E. Keeley and P. Sherrard, C. P. Cavafy, *Collected Poems*, The Hogarth Press, 1984.

Chapter 18: Plato and the Myth of Atlantis

1. I. Donelly, *The Antediluvian World*, Harper and Brothers, 1882, p. 479.

2. Plato, *Timaios* 20, tr. D. Lee, *Plato: Timaeus and Critias*, Penguin Classics, rev. edn, 1977.

3. Ibid. 21.

4. Plato, *Gorgias* 523, tr. W. Hamilton, *Plato: Gorgias*, Penguin Classics, rev. edn, 1971.

5. Plato, *Republic* 377, tr. D. Lee, *Plato: The Republic*, Penguin Classics, 2nd edn (rev.), 1987.

6. Plato, *Protagoras* 320, tr. W.C.K. Guthrie, *Plato: Protagoras and Meno*, Penguin Classics, 1956.

7. Plato, *Phaidros* 275, tr. C. Rowe, *Plato: Phaedrus*, Penguin Classics, 2005.

8. Plato, *Timaios* 21–2.

9. Ibid. 22.

10. See p. 263 f.

11. Plato, *Timaios* 23.

12. Ibid. 23.

13. I.e. the Strait of Gibraltar.

14. Plato, *Timaios* 24.

15. Ibid.

16. Ibid. 25

17. Plato, *Kritias* 108, tr. D. Lee, *Plato: Timaeus and Critias*, Penguin Classics, rev. edn., 1977.

18. Ibid. 113.

19. Ibid. 121.

20. Thukydides 3.89, tr. R. Warner, *Thucydides: The Peloponnesian War*, rev. edn, Penguin Classics, 1972.

21. See p. 448.

22. See p. 114.

23. T. Bryce, *The Trojans and Their Neighbours*, Routledge, 2006, p. 193.

24. L. Spence, *Atlantis in America*, Ernest Benn, 1925, p. 66. He repeats this verbatim in *The History of Atlantis*, Rider & Co., 1926, p. 151.

25. P. Jordan, *The Atlantis Syndrome*, Sutton Publishing, 2003, p.80.

26. L. Sprague de Camp, *Lost Continents: The Atlantis Theme in History, Science and Literature*, Gnome Press, 1954, 80.

27. T. Bryce, *The Trojans and Their Neighbours*, p. 193.

28. See Pierre Vidal-Naquet, 'Athènes et l'Atlantide', *Revue des études grecques* 77 (1964), pp. 420–44, reprinted in *Le Chasseur noir*, Maspero, 1981, pp. 335–60; idem, 'Hérodote et l'Atlantide: entre les Grecs et les Juifs. Réflexions sur l'historiographie du siècle des Lumieres', *Quaderni di Storia* 16 (July–December 1982), pp. 3–76; Christopher Gill, 'The Genre of the Atlantis Story', *Classical Philology* 72 (1977), pp. 287–304; Luc Brisson, Platon, *Timée/Critias*, Flammarion, 1992; Gerard Naddaf, 'The Atlantis Myth: An Introduction to Plato's Later Philosophy of History', *Phoenix* 48 (1994). pp 189–209.

29. It is said that a pupil of Plato's called Krantor accepted the Atlantis tale as history and believed that the tale was recorded on pillars in Egypt, but our only evidence for this comes from Proclus, writing about 700 years later, who was himself ambivalent about the historical validity of the story.

Section 3: Some Approaches to Greek Mythology

1. G.S. Kirk, 'Methodological reflexions on the myths of Heracles', in B. Gentili and G. Paioni (eds.), *Il Mito Greco: Atti del convegno internazionale (Urbino 7–12 maggio 1973)*, Rome, 1977, p. 293.

2. 'Pseudo-Herakleitos', *Homeric Problems* 70, tr. K. Dowden, in *The Uses of Greek Mythology*, Routledge, 1992, p. 24 f.

3. F. Max Müller, *Lectures on the Science of Language, delivered at the Royal Institution of Great Britain, March, April and May 1863*, second series, New York, pp. 384-5.

4. J.G. Frazer, *Apollodorus: The Library* II, Loeb Classical Library, 1921, p. 404.

5. This and the following list are derived from P. Jones, *Homer's Odyssey: A Commentary*, Bristol Classical Press, 1998, p. 78f.

6. See pp. 207 ff.

7. S. Freud, *The Relation of the Poet to Day Dreaming* (1908), (A. Freud et al. (eds.), *Gesammelte Werke, chronologisch geordnet*, 1940–68, 7: 222).

8. See pp. 140 ff.

9. S. Freud, *Gesammelte Werke, chronologisch geordnet*, ed. A. Freud et al., 1940–68, 17: 47–8.

10. English version available in C. Lévi-Strauss, *Structural Anthropology*, Penguin, 1972, pp. 206–31.

11. Ibid. 216.

12. See pp. 98 ff.

13. See p. 70 (Kallisto); 140 ff. (Danae); 176 (Auge); 134 ff. (Io); and 205 f. (Antiope).

14. W. Burkert, *Structure and History in Greek Mythology and Ritual*, University of California Press, 1979, p. 6 f.

15. http://www.gold-eagle.com/editorials_04/ willie092704.html. (28 September 2004).

16. See p. 114.

17. R. Calasso, *The Marriage of Cadmus and Harmony*, tr. T. Parks, Vintage, 1994, p. 280.

18. Sallustius, *On the Gods and the World*, 4.

FURTHER READING

Translations

These days there is a wide range of high quality translations of most of the crucial texts relevant to Greek mythology. A selection of good, readable and relatively accessible works is included here in chronological order of author:

Homer, *Iliad*: R. Lattimore, *The Iliad of Homer*, University of Chicago Press, 1951

Homer, *Odyssey*: R. Lattimore, *The Odyssey of Homer*, Harper Perennial, New York, 1999

Hesiod: Dorothea Wender, *Hesiod and Theognis*, Penguin Classics, 1973

The Homeric Hymns: J. Cashford, *The Homeric Hymns*, Penguin Classics, 2003

Aesop: O. and R. Temple, *Aesop: The Complete Fables*, Penguin Classics, 1998

Pindar: R. Lattimore, *The Odes of Pindar*, 2nd edn, University of Chicago Press, 1976

Herodotos: A. de Sélincourt, *Herodotus: The Histories*, Penguin Classics, rev. edn, 1972

Aiskhylos: R. Fagles, *Aeschylus, the Oresteia*, Penguin Classics, rev. edn, 1979; P. Vellacott, *Aeschylus: Prometheus Bound, the Suppliants, Seven Against Thebes, the Persians*, Penguin Classics, 1961

Sophokles: E.F. Watling, *Sophocles: The Theban Plays*, Penguin, 1947; *Sophocles: Electra and Other Plays*, Penguin, 1953

Euripides: J. Davie, *Euripides, Medea and Other Plays*, Penguin Classics, rev. edn 2003; P. Vellacott, *Euripides, The Bacchae and Other Plays*, Penguin Classics, rev. edn, 1973; *Euripides, Orestes and Other Plays*, Penguin Classics, 1972; *Euripides, Three Plays: Alcestis; Hippolytus; Iphigeneia in Tauris*, Penguin Classics, rev. edn, 1974; *Euripides: Medea and Other Plays*, Penguin Classics, 1963

Aristophanes: D. Barrett, *Aristophanes: The Wasps/The Poet and the Women/The Frogs*, Penguin Classics, 1964; A.H. Sommerstein, *Aristophanes: Lysistrata/The Acharnians/The Clouds*, Penguin Classics, 1973

Plato: D. Lee, *Plato: The Republic*, Penguin Classics, 2nd edn (rev.), 1987; *Plato: Timaeus and Critias*, Penguin Classics, rev. edn, 1977

Kallimakhos: A.W. Mair, *Callimachus; Hymns and Epigrams; Lycophron; Aratus*, Loeb Classical Library, rev. edn, 1955

Apollonios Rhodios: R.C. Seaton, *Apollonius Rhodius, the Argonautica*, Loeb Classical Library, 1912

Theokritos: A. Rist, *The Poems of Theocritus*, University of North Carolina Press, 1978

Virgil: C. Day Lewis, *The Eclogues, Georgics and Aeneid of Virgil*, Oxford University Press, 1966

Ovid: D. Raeburn, *Ovid: Metamorphoses*, Penguin Classics, 2004

Plutarch: I. Scott-Kilvert, *The Rise and Fall of Athens, Nine Greek Lives by Plutarch*, Penguin Classics, 1960

Pausanias: P. Levi, *Pausanias. Guide To Greece. Volume 1: Central Greece*, Penguin Classics, rev. edn, 1979; *Pausanias. Guide To Greece. Volume 2: Southern Greece*, Penguin Classics, rev. edn, 1979

Apollodoros: J.G. Frazer, *Apollodorus: The Library*, Loeb Classical Library, 1921

Quintus of Smyrna: A. James, *Quintus of Smyrna: The Trojan Epic: Posthomerica*, Johns Hopkins University Press, 2004

Various authors: S.M. Trazaskoma, R. Scott Smith and S. Brunet (eds. and tr.), *Anthology of Classical Myth: Primary Sources in Translation*, Hackett, 2004

Dictionaries of Mythology

There are many dictionaries of mythology available, which provide useful 'Who's Who' listings, as these do:

Grimal, P., *The Penguin Dictionary of Classical Mythology*, edited by Stephen Kershaw from the translation by A.R. Maxwell-Hyslop, Penguin, 1991

March, J., *Cassell's Dictionary of Classical Mythology*, Cassell, 2001

Price, S. and Kearns, E., *The Oxford Dictionary of Classical Myth and Religion*, Oxford University Press, 2003

General Reading

References have been made to interesting and helpful books throughout the text, but anyone wishing to explore scholarly discussions about the subject might be interested in the following volumes:

Anderson, M.J., *The Fall of Troy in Early Greek Poetry and Art*, Oxford University Press, 1997

Arafat, K.W., *Classical Zeus: A Study in Art and Literature*, Oxford University Press, 1990

Armstrong, K., *A Short History of Myth*, Canongate, 2005

Bernal, M., *Black Athena: The Afroasiatic Roots of Classical Civilisation*, 2 vols., Rutgers University Press, 1987–91

Bremmer, J. (ed.), *Interpretations of Greek Mythology*, Routledge, 1988

Brisson, L., *Plato the Myth Maker*, tr. G. Nadaff, University of Chicago Press, 1998

Brisson, L., *How Philosophers Saved Myths: Allegorical Interpretation and Classical Mythology*, University of Chicago Press, 2004

Brittlestone, R., with Diggle, J. and Underhill, J., *Odysseus Unbound: The Search for Homer's Ithaca*, Cambridge University Press, 2005

Bull, M., *The Mirror of the Gods: Classical Mythology in Renaissance Art*, Penguin, 2006

Burkert, W., *Structure and History in Greek Mythology and Ritual*, University of California Press, 1979

Burkert, W., *Greek Religion: Archaic and Classical*, tr. J. Raffan, Basil Blackwell, 1985

Buxton, R. G. A. B., *The Complete World of Greek Mythology*, Thames & Hudson, 2004

Caldwell, R., *The Origin of the Gods: A Psychoanalytic Study of Greek Theogonic Myth*, Oxford University Press, 1989

Carpenter, T.H., *Art and Myth in Ancient Greece: A Handbook*, Thames & Hudson, 1991

Castleden, R., *The Attack on Troy*, Pen & Sword Military, 2006

Davies, J.K. and Foxhall, L. (eds.), *The Trojan War: Its Historicity and Context*, Bristol Classical Press, 1984

Doty, W.G., *Mythography: The Study of Myths and Rituals*, 2nd edn, University of Alabama Press, 2000

DuBois, P., *Centaurs and Amazons: Women and the Pre-History of the Chain of Being*, University of Michigan Press, 1982

Easterling, P.E. and Muir, J.V. (eds.), *Greek Religion and Society*, Cambridge University Press, 1985

Erskine, A., *Troy Between Greece and Rome: Local Tradition and Imperial Power*, Oxford University Press, 2001

Forsyth, P.Y., *Thera in the Bronze Age*, Peter Lang, 1997

Galinsky, G.K., *The Herakles Theme: The Adaptations of the Hero in Literature from Homer to the Twentieth Century*, Rowman & Littlefield, 1972

Graf, F., *Greek Mythology: An Introduction*, tr. T. Marier, Johns Hopkins University Press, 1993

Hughes, B., *Helen of Troy: Goddess, Princess, Whore*, Pimlico, 2006

Jenkyns, R., *The Victorians and Ancient Greece*, Blackwell, 1980

Kirk, G.S., *Myth: Its Meaning and Functions in Ancient and Other Cultures*, Cambridge University Press, 1970

Kirk, G.S., *The Nature of Greek Myths*, Penguin, 1974

Lefkowitz, M.R., *Heroines and Hysterics*, Duckworth, 1981

Lefkowitz, M.R. and Rogers, G.M., *Black Athena Revisited*, University of North Carolina Press, 1996

Lévi-Strauss, C., *Structural Anthropology*, tr. C. Jacobson and B. Grundfest Schoepf, Penguin, 1968

Logue, C., *War Music: An account of Books 1–4 and 16–19 of Homer's Iliad*, Faber & Faber, 2001

Luce, J.V., *Celebrating Homer's Landscapes: Troy and Ithaca Revisited*, Yale University Press, 1998

Reid, J.D., *The Oxford Guide to Classical Mythology in the Arts, 1300–1990s*, Oxford University Press, 1993

Seznec, J., *The Survival of the Pagan Gods: The Mythological Tradition and Its Place in Renaissance Humanism and Art*, tr. B.F. Sessions, Princeton University Press, 1972

Strauss, B., *The Trojan War: A New History*, Hutchinson, 2007

Veyne, P., *Did the Greeks Believe in Their Myths? An Essay on the Constitutive Imagination*, tr. P. Wissing, University of Chicago Press, 1988

Winkler, M.M., *Troy: From Homer's Iliad to Hollywood Epic*, Blackwell, 2007

Wood, M., *In Search of the Trojan War*, BBC Books, 1985

Woodford, S., *The Trojan War in Ancient Art*, Duckworth, 1993

Woodford, S., *Images of Myths in Classical Antiquity*, Cambridge University Press, 2003

INDEX

Page numbers in italic indicate illustrations

To order further *Brief History* titles just fill in this form (*cont. over page*)

No. of copies	Title	Price	Total
	A Brief Guide to Islam Paul Grieve	£9.99	
	A Brief History of 1917: Russia's Year of Revolution Roy Bainton	£8.99	
	A Brief History of the Birth of the Nazis Nigel Jones	£7.99	
	A Brief History of British Sea Power David Howarth	£9.99	
	A Brief History of the Circumnavigators Derek Wilson	£7.99	
	A Brief History of the Cold War John Hughes-Wilson	£8.99	
	A Brief History of the Crimean War Alex Troubetzkoy	£8.99	
	A Brief History of the Crusades Geoffrey Hindley	£7.99	
	A Brief History of the Druids Peter Berresford Ellis	£7.99	
	A Brief History of the Dynasties of China Bamber Gascoigne	£7.99	
	A Brief History of the End of the World Simon Pearson	£8.99	
	A Brief History of the Future Oona Strathern	£8.99	
	A Brief History of Globalization Alex MacGillivray	£8.99	
	A Brief History of the Great Moghuls Bamber Gascoigne	£7.99	
	A Brief History of the Hundred Years War Desmond Seward	£7.99	
	A Brief History of the Middle East Christopher Catherwood	£8.99	
	A Brief History of Misogyny Jack Holland	£8.99	

	A Brief History of Medicine Paul Strathern	£9.99	
	A Brief History of Mutiny Richard Woodman	£8.99	
	A Brief History of Painting Roy Bolton	£9.99	
	A Brief History of Science Thomas Crump	£8.99	
	A Brief History of Secret Societies David V. Barrett	£8.99	
	A Brief History of Stonehenge Aubrey Burl	£8.99	
	A Brief History of the Vikings Jonathan Clements	£7.99	
	P&P & Insurance		£2.50
	Grand Total		£

Name: _____

Address: _____

_____ Postcode: _____

Daytime Tel. No. / Email:_____
(in case of query)

Three ways to pay:

1. **For express service telephone the TBS order line on 01206 255 800 and quote 'BGT'. Order lines are open Monday – Friday 8:30a.m. – 5:30p.m.**
2. I enclose a cheque made payable to TBS Ltd for £ _____
3. Please charge my ☐ Visa ☐ Mastercard ☐ Amex
   ☐ Switch (switch issue no. . . .) £ _____

   Card number: _____

   Expiry date:_____ Signature_____

Please return forms (*no stamp required*) to,
FREEPOST RLUL-SJGC-SGKJ, Cash Sales/Direct Mail Dept., The Book Service,
Colchester Road, Colchester, Frating CO7 7DW . All books subject to availability.

Enquiries to readers@constablerobinson.com
www.constablerobinson.com